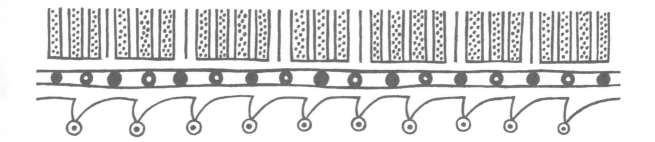

CUISINE OF
THE WATER GODS

THE AUTHENTIC SEAFOOD
AND VEGETABLE COOKERY
OF MEXICO

PATRICIA QUINTANA

WITH JACK BISHOP

SIMON & SCHUSTER

NEW YORK · LONDON · TORONTO · SYDNEY · TOKYO · SINGAPORE

FOR MEXICO, MY COUNTRY

SIMON & SCHUSTER
Rockefeller Center
1230 Avenue of the Americas
New York, New York 10020

Designed by Levavi & Levavi, Inc.

Manufactured in the United States of America

1   3   5   7   9   10   8   6   4   2

Library of Congress Cataloging-in-Publication Data

Quintana, Patricia.
Cuisine of the water gods: the authentic seafood and vegetable
cookery of Mexico / Patricia Quintana, with Jack Bishop.
p.   cm.
Includes index.
1. Cookery, Mexican.   2. Cookery (Seafood)   3. Cookery
(Vegetables)   4. Menus.   I. Bishop, Jack.   II. Title.
TX716.M4C86   1994
6941.6'92'0972—dc20   94-30886
CIP

ISBN: 0-671-74898-X

ACKNOWLEDGMENTS

Many thanks to Maria Losón de Fabregas and Diana Penagos for their help with research, and to Agustín Monsreal and Maria Losón de Fabregas for their assistance in preparing the recipes. Special thanks to Tlatoani Compadre Miguel Contreras, who contributed the original drawings for the book, based on "Borbónica," "Borgia," "Columbino," "de Azoyu," "Florentino," "Magliabecchi," "Mendocino," "Nuttall," "Selden," and "Vaticano," anonymous manuscripts held in the Anthropological Library of Mexico. And my deepest thanks to Barbara Kafka, whose words in a conversation of many years ago inspired the theme of the book.

CONTENTS

This book is somewhat different from the works we traditionally call "cookbooks" and therefore needs some words of explanation to readers.

Five years ago, I set out to write about the regional cuisines of coastal Mexico that rely on seafood, vegetables, and grains. As I explored the coasts, rivers, and lagoons of my country, learning about the ways of Mexico's first inhabitants, I felt an irrepressible connection with the past.

Although I make my home in Mexico City, the inland capital of my country, I found myself being drawn back to the sea for sustenance. It became the source of my spiritual and intellectual inspiration.

When it was time to write, I could not decide where to begin. How should I capture my feelings and thoughts in words? The scope of the project—to catalog the indigenous coastal cuisines and the changes that have occurred as a result of the introduction of new peoples and ingredients over the past five centuries—was massive. No easy formula or structure could do it justice.

As I tried to develop a logical organization for the book, it dawned on me that the shape of Mexico's coastline, which swings south from the California border along the Pacific, then curves east to the Yucatán, and eventually rides back north along the Gulf coast to Texas, matches the mythical icon of Mexican culture, the snail. Water quite literally surrounds and encircles Mexico, with the Aztec capital—the sacred kingdom upon which Mexico City was built—at the center of this spiral.

The silhouette of the snail has inspired me to organize this book along somewhat unusual lines. The book is divided into sixteen chapters, each devoted to one coastal state. (I have added the central region, which includes Mexico City, because of its role as disseminator of Mexican gastronomy and culture.) I also wanted to write about the customs, traditions, and culinary specialties of each coastal state, but found that a standard descriptive approach did not suffice. Instead, I have created a number of characters—local individuals who relate their personal and cultural histories—at the beginning of each chapter. They speak in their own language about their own experiences and describe how the waters of their lands have shaped their lives. I invoke, among others, the spirits of a Seri grandmother from Sonora, a young Mayan from the Yucatán, a knowledgeable cook from Tamaulipas, and the learned Spanish friar Bernardino de Sahagún (who witnessed the Conquest firsthand) to tell their stories.

These stories intertwine along with a brief overview of the state and selected local recipes to produce a powerful impression of the particular region and its cuisine. While not necessarily the most straightforward approach, this circuitous route—its twists and turns harking back to the shape of the snail—reflects the complexity and diversity of Mexican culture.

The journey I have taken in these pages begins and ends with water. While providing a constant reference point, water has worked its magic differently at each spot. The history of pre-Hispanic Mexico is one of movement, contact, and change. Each indigenous people has celebrated—and continues to honor—the water gods for the foods they have provided. Whether along the coast or on farms where water filters and nourishes the soil, the presence of these gods is felt and respected.

The same waters that are tame and gentle at mountain springs become fierce and wild ocean swells. The same waters that provide fishermen with seafood also sustain the vegetables, grains, and fruits tended by farmers. Throughout this book, I have tried to convey this respect for water as well as the close relationship to both earth and sea that marks Mexican culture. In the process, I have written about the gastronomic heritage of each region as practiced by its inhabitants and their ancestors. Some dishes are preserved and presented with no modern adjustments or improvements needed. Others have been modified—the products transported over water from Europe and Asia have had a profound effect on the cuisine of Mexico—and I try to express these changes in many recipes. Whether talking about rice and cilantro or black peppercorns and cinnamon, "new" ingredients have been adapted and "naturalized," each with its own story to tell.

While European traditions, including culinary ones, were adopted wholesale in North America, Mexico's strong indigenous culture acted as an aquifer, filtering out certain elements and blending others with elements of pre-Hispanic gastronomy. Of course, many ingredients—corn, beans, potatoes, tomatoes, chocolate, and countless more—are native to Mexico and have deep roots in this land. In many respects, then, this book is about the mixing and stirring that have taken place over many centuries and have produced what we call today Mexican cuisine or, more accurately, Mexican cuisines.

My goal is to awaken in each reader a sense of this history as well as an understanding of the unique gastronomy of each coastal region. The men and women of the sea who introduce each chapter in this book weave together the stories of my land. They live with our legends and traditions and still travel the ancestral paths laid out by the gods in this land of the snail. Let them take us by the hand to join them on their journey.

Distance Scale
in miles

0 100 200 300 400

Gulf of California

Sonora

Baja California

Sinaloa

Nayarit

Jalisco

Colima

Michoacán

Guerrero

Oaxaca

Mexico

Centro (Mexico City)

Veracruz

Tamaulipas

Tabasco

Chiapas

Campeche

Yucatán

Quintana Roo

Gulf of Mexico

Pacific Ocean

N
W E
S

TODOS SANTOS OASIS SALAD

SANTA ROSALÍA SALAD

ISLA DEL ESPÍRITU SANTO FISH BROTH

SHREDDED FISH

MEXICALI RICE

POBLANO CHILES STUFFED WITH SEAFOOD AND
CLAM SAUCE, LORETO STYLE

PUERTO NUEVO LOBSTER

FRIED FISH GUAYCURA STYLE

ENSENADA EMPANADAS

FIG COMPOTE

DAMIANA TEA

BAJA CALIFORNIA

The Baja Peninsula, which is located in the northwestern corner of Mexico, is divided into two territories—North and South Baja. The name Baja comes from a local Indian dialect and translates loosely as "hot oven," no doubt a reference to the searing desert climate.

Before the Conquest, the Peninsula was inhabited by the Guaycuras, Pericúes, and Cochimíes tribes. These first residents lived by hunting, fishing, and collecting desert fruits and roots. During the colonial period, Jesuit missionaries, such as Eusebio Kino, forever changed the character of this land by introducing formal agriculture. Wheat, olives, grapes, cotton, potatoes, tomatoes, lettuce, and chiles are now the state's leading crops. Kino is directly responsible for bringing the first three of these crops to Baja.

The northern area is bordered by the United States and has a semidesert climate. Most of the state's farms and wineries are located here. The capital of this region, bounded by the Gulf of California (also known as the Sea of Cortés) to the east and the Pacific Ocean to the west, is Mexicali. Of course, the best-known city in all of Baja is Tijuana, the number-one destination for American visitors to Mexico. The Sea of Cortés is home to thousands of birds, fish, and mammals. The principal fishing center is at Ensenada.

Southern Baja has a dry desert climate with very little rain.

The capital, La Paz, is known for its alluring beaches, which attract thousands of tourists every year. The local economy depends on tourism—national parks along the coast are a big draw for water sports enthusiasts. In addition to seafood, the cuisine depends on tropical fruits such as mangoes, figs, and dates, which are cultivated in desert oases.

I am Guayperí, the natural son of this mother earth, known since ancient times as the land of the two hearts of the sea. I am the natural son of the three tribes that forged life here and spread across waters and deserts and amid the wild birds and plants during countless suns and moons. I am the son of the Pericúes, the Guaycuras, and the Cochimíes. I am the son of the sand, the water, and the coast. ¶ I am Guayperí, and my ancestors were guided by the four divine winds that stood guard over this rugged arm of land. They traveled the long path from north to south and the shorter route from east to west. They knew Mother Nature's secrets and created all that lives here, blowing from the shoreline to the heights of the serpentine mountains that rise up from the desert. Here, in the mountains far above the sea, lies Mother Nature's secret source of crystal-clear spring water. Buried deep beneath the desert floor, these waters nurture the plants that conserve moisture in their bosom—*cardón*, teasel (giant cactus), *nopal* (cactus), *biznaga (Ferocactus wislizeni)* and the venerable *pitahaya*, both sweet and sour. There are other vigorous plants—gakil, jojoba, medesá, mangle (mangrove tree), agave, sweet yuca, jícama, copal (resin), *la higuera (Ficus radulina), el añil* (which produces indigo plant dye), and *el saguaro (Carnegiea gigantea)*, another of the enormous cactuses on which insects and wild birds reproduce. These majestic plants preserve my virgin earth in this region where the sounds of the desert magically converge with the voices of the waves. ¶ I am Guayperí, and I keep in my memory the old stories and tales that my Pericúes brothers once told. Niparajá, the great Lord who created the sky, earth, and sea, was a benevolent and peaceful god. One day, the happiness of Niparajá gave rise to envy within Tuparán, an inhabitant of the divine territory who possessed a bellicose and rebellious character. After a bloody quarrel, Niparajá defeated Tuparán and took away his *pitahaya* plantations and his other blessed lands covered with bountiful fruit trees. Niparajá imprisoned him in a cave on the cliffs rising from the Sea of the East. Niparajá gave life to the whales, who serve as wardens to Tuparán. The whales still return to breed in these waters, ever vigilant to keep their evil prisoner. ¶ I am Guayperí, inheritor of our ancestors' spirit that illuminates the heavens and reflects down on the seas. In these deep waters divers search for shells that hide brilliant pearls. The quest for pearls starts two hours before noon and ends two hours after midday, when the sun's rays make clear the mysteries of the rocky sea bottom. Divers swim past baby sharks, sardines, dogfish, cabrilla, grouper, red snapper, manta ray, salmon, tuna, bonito, California halibut, sharks, *chernas*, California corvina, spider crab, oysters, sea bass, tarpon shad, dorado, ailhead bream, and more. ¶ Back at the coast, the waters are rough, and sunlight cannot penetrate the dark churning. Here, the waves thrash against the sand, leaving fishermen no option but to throw their nets into inlets and bays and wait until the tide recedes and the violent clamor of the waves subsides. While divers must show daring and fortitude to pluck pearl oysters from the calm midday seas, patience and ingenuity yield abundant riches on shore. ¶ I am Guayperí, and for many centuries I have known through the voices of my brethren Guaycuras of the cosmic renewal that occurs when stars in the celestial firmament fall into the sea at twilight, only to become swimming men and women the next day. I also know that the stars that ignite in a flash of fire at dawn are really being thrown by minor gods into brackish waters. Even though some say that the light is rekindled in the heavens, I know these stars are transformed into the fish that inhabit the waters and guard against evil spirits. ¶ I am

Guayperí, and when the invaders came to my land it was baptized with the name California and life changed. Other men arrived, ones who didn't understand the soul of my territory, my desert, and my waters. They had other beliefs. First came the Jesuits, then the Franciscans, and later on, the Dominicans. They tried to comprehend the cosmic course that had guided the civilization of this region for centuries. They were astonished by the half-fish, half-woman creature, a woman above the waist and a marine animal below. They were horrified by the fish with large eyes on top of its head that looks toward the heavens, and the fish with just one eye in the center of its head, and the dangerous-looking swordfish.

¶ I am Guayperí, and this is my vision of my existence. I am the son of the two hearts of this land. I live in intimacy with Father Heaven and with the eternity of the waters from the sea. I live with the door open to the four infinite horizons.

TODOS SANTOS OASIS SALAD
ENSALADA DEL OASIS DE TODOS SANTOS

Serves 8

Since the time of the Pericúes Indians, who first inhabited southern Baja, the people of this region have been seed collectors, hunters, and fishing experts. The ability to wisely use nature's limited resources has been part of survival and daily life on this narrow peninsula for centuries. The Pericúes understood the medicinal powers of aloe, jojoba, and a number of cactus plants. In this way, they were able to live off the barren desert land. Near this particular oasis we can see the contrast between bleak sand and lush vegetation—including tall palms laden with hanging bunches of dates as well as fruit trees bearing oranges and mangoes—that makes this land so magical.

PREPARE THE FRUIT: Place the sliced mangoes on one side of each serving plate and a papaya half on the other side. Sprinkle with sugar or honey. Use 8 orange sections to form a "flower" in the center of each plate, and place a lime half, 2 dates, and some spearmint leaves in the center of each flower.

PREPARE THE SAUCE: Puree the orange juice with the papayas and the mangoes. Add the sherry and sugar to taste. Blend until smooth. Spoon the sauce over the prepared fruit and refrigerate the salads for at least 30 minutes. Serve chilled.

VARIATION: Serve the sauce on one side of the plate and place the fruit on top. Sprinkle cocoa powder or confectioners' sugar over the other side of the plate.

FOR THE FRUIT

- 4 large ripe mangoes, sliced but not peeled
- 4 small ripe papayas, halved and seeded
- Sugar or honey to taste
- 64 orange sections
- 4 limes, halved
- 16 large dates, pitted
- 1 bunch spearmint

FOR THE SAUCE

- Juice of 8 oranges
- 2 cups sliced papaya
- 2 large ripe mangoes, peeled and sliced
- 1/2 cup sweet sherry or damiana liqueur
- Sugar to taste

SANTA ROSALÍA SALAD
ENSALADA SANTA ROSALÍA

Serves 8

FOR THE VEGETABLES

16 fresh poblano, California green, or Anaheim chiles, roasted, peeled, seeded, and deveined (see page 296)

4 cups warm water

¾ cup cider vinegar or white wine vinegar

¾ cup tarragon vinegar

Salt to taste

1 tablespoon freshly ground black pepper

¾ cup extra-virgin olive oil

6 medium white or red potatoes, cooked, peeled, and sliced

2 medium red onions, peeled and sliced into thin wedges

2 medium white onions, peeled and sliced into thin wedges

FOR THE VINAIGRETTE

1 cup white wine vinegar, champagne vinegar, or tarragon vinegar

Salt to taste

1 tablespoon freshly ground black pepper

1½ tablespoons sugar

½ teaspoon Tabasco sauce

4 medium cloves garlic, peeled and minced

3 tablespoons Dijon or tarragon mustard

¾ cup extra-virgin olive oil

1½ cups vegetable oil

FOR THE GARNISH

48 steamed clams

8 medium scallions, cut into

Santa Rosalía lies along the northern part of the Sea of Cortés, as the Gulf of California is called in this region. Once a small mining town, Santa Rosalía is home to an interesting collection of old train cars that helped move copper to the port, where it was loaded onto ships bound for Belgium and France. Today, mining has been replaced by fishing, especially for clams, oysters, and pearls. However, the Europeans who came because of the copper mines left their mark on the region. One of the more unusual pieces of architecture in this lovely seaside community is a prefabricated church designed by Alexandre-Gustave Eiffel, the French engineer who lent his name to the Paris monument he built. Ingredients like the tarragon vinegar and Dijon mustard in this salad reflect the European influence that once was so strong in this former mining town. Because the vinaigrette must be refrigerated for 12 hours, begin this recipe well ahead of serving.

PREPARE THE VEGETABLES: Soak the chiles for 20 minutes in the warm water mixed with the cider vinegar. Drain and dry the chiles on paper towels, then put the chiles in a glass bowl. In a separate bowl, mix the tarragon vinegar, salt, and pepper. Slowly whisk in the olive oil until the mixture forms a vinaigrette. Pour this dressing over the chiles and refrigerate for 2 hours. Prepare the potatoes and the onions and refrigerate them separately.

PREPARE THE VINAIGRETTE: Put the vinegar in a medium bowl, add the salt, pepper, sugar, Tabasco sauce, garlic, and mustard and blend until smooth. Slowly whisk in the oils and blend until the sauce has a creamy consistency. Taste and correct the seasoning. Pour the vinaigrette into a glass bottle and refrigerate for 12 hours.

TO SERVE: Place 2 marinated chiles and 6 clams on one side of each plate. On the other side, place the potatoes, the sliced onions, a scallion flower, and a radish flower. Drizzle with the vinaigrette. Serve immediately.

VARIATIONS: Serve with tomato and avocado slices, if desired. Serve with boiled shrimp.

flowers and chilled in ice water for 2 hours (see page 298)

8 small radishes, cut into flowers and chilled in ice water for 2 hours (see page 298)

ISLA DEL ESPÍRITU SANTO FISH BROTH
CALDO DE PESCADO ESTILO ISLA DEL ESPÍRITU SANTO

Serves 8 to 12

Isla del Espíritu Santo is located at the same latitude as the city of La Paz, about 120 miles off the coast of southern Baja. This beautiful island is known for its abundance of local seafood and fish, including *abulón* (abalone), jurel, sierra (or mackerel), cabrilla (rockfish), sardines, *pargo* (porgy), and *cherna* (a type of sea bass). In the authentic version of this recipe, these fish are cooked in seawater to make a heady fish broth. In this adaptation, plain water can be used with a touch of seawater. As for the fish, try mackerel, sea bass, red snapper, flounder, or barracuda.

PREPARE THE STOCK: Bring the water to boil in a large pot; simmer uncovered for 15 minutes. Add the fish heads and tails, wine, celery, tomatoes, onions, garlic, marjoram, peppercorns, and oregano. Season with salt. (Season sparingly if using seawater.) Cook for 2 hours uncovered or until the stock is reduced by half. Remove the bones. Strain, mashing the vegetables to extract their liquid. Keep the stock warm.

PREPARE THE SOUP: Heat the butter and the oil in a deep pot. Sauté the garlic and the onions until light brown. Add the chile strips and stir-fry for 2 minutes. Season with salt and the marjoram, thyme, and oregano. Pour the hot stock into the pot and simmer uncovered for 20 minutes over low heat. Add the fish and cook until it just flakes, 3 to 5 minutes. Taste and correct the seasoning.

FOR THE FISH STOCK

4 quarts plain water (add a small amount of seawater, if desired)
2 medium fish heads
2 pounds fish tails
2 cups dry white wine
1/2 rib celery, chopped
6 medium ripe tomatoes, halved
2 medium white onions, peeled and quartered
1 head garlic, halved but not peeled
10 sprigs marjoram
1/2 teaspoon black peppercorns
1 1/2 teaspoons dried oregano leaves
Salt to taste

FOR THE FISH SOUP

1/3 cup butter, cut into pieces
1/4 cup olive oil
1/3 cup finely chopped garlic
2 cups finely chopped white onions

CONTINUED

16 fresh Anaheim chiles, lightly
    roasted, peeled, seeded, and
    deveined (see page 296), and
    cut into thin strips
Salt to taste
12 sprigs marjoram
 8 sprigs thyme
1½ teaspoons dried oregano
    leaves
 3 pounds fish fillets, cut into
    ½-inch pieces

FOR THE GARNISH
16 sprigs marjoram
16 lime slices

TO SERVE: Pour the piping hot soup into a tureen or individual soup bowls. Garnish with the fresh marjoram and the lime slices. Serve immediately.

SHREDDED FISH
MACHACA DE CABRILLA
Serves 8

Cabrilla *(Epinephelus adscensionis)* lives underneath the rocks near coral reefs in shallow waters and feeds on crab and shrimp. The cabrilla, also called rockfish, has a colorful skin with reddish shading and brownish or even darker spots. In some species, cabrillas have stripes on the side of the body. The flesh can be eaten raw or in fillets in soups or shredded *(machaca)* and served for breakfast.

FOR THE FISH
½ cup olive oil
½ cup butter
1½ medium white onions, peeled
    and finely chopped
 4 large ripe tomatoes, chopped
 4 fresh serrano chiles, chopped
 6 cups (1½ pounds) cabrilla, red
    snapper, grouper, perch, or sea
    bass, steamed, shredded, and
    liquid pressed out
Salt to taste
 1 teaspoon freshly ground black
    pepper

FOR THE GARNISH
 3 tablespoons chopped cilantro

Heat the oil and the butter in a pan or a wok. Add the onions, tomatoes, and chiles and sauté until the chile oil is released or comes to the surface. Add the shredded fish and season with salt and the pepper. Continue cooking until the fish absorbs the sauce.

TO SERVE: Place the hot shredded fish on a platter and sprinkle with the chopped cilantro. Serve with hot flour tortillas.

VARIATIONS: You can also prepare this dish with dried or fresh *mantarraya* (manta ray) after soaking and shredding it. Or, add 6 to 8 eggs and stuff the mixture into hot flour tortillas.

CUISINE OF THE WATER GODS

MEXICALI RICE
ARROZ ESTILO MEXICALI

Serves 8

Mexicali is blessed with several water sources. The Colorado River runs through the city and both fresh- and saltwater lakes dot the outlying countryside. Tucked into the northwestern corner of the country, Mexicali has a long history as the first stopover for immigrants arriving from Asia. In the seventeenth century, Mexicali's Chinese community popularized the use of rice, which soon became an essential staple throughout Baja. Today, rice is usually steamed or sautéed with tomatoes. This recipe is often served with grilled lobsters, flour tortillas, and salsa for a true California meal.

Heat the oil in a deep casserole. Sauté the 6 large garlic cloves and the quartered onion until light brown. Add the drained rice and cook over medium heat, stirring occasionally with a wooden spoon, until the rice is evenly light brown. Do not overstir or the rice will become mushy. Pour the rice through a strainer to drain off the oil. Return the rice to the casserole and cook for 3 minutes. Puree the tomatoes with the 3 medium garlic cloves and the chopped onion. Add the mixture to the rice and cook until the liquid is absorbed and the rice turns red. Add the hot water and cook over high heat, letting the water boil for 3 minutes. Add the salt and season to taste; reduce the heat, and add the tied parsley and the chiles. Cover and cook over very low heat for 40 to 45 minutes. Do not uncover. Let the rice rest until it has doubled in volume.

TO SERVE: Serve the rice in small clay pots with a parsley sprig and a whole or slices of jalapeño chile.

VARIATIONS: Add 1½ cups boiled potatoes that have been cut into small pieces along with 1½ cups cooked peas or carrots. Serve with scrambled eggs, sautéed shrimp with scallions, or grilled lobster.

FOR THE RICE

1½ cups safflower oil

6 large plus 3 medium cloves garlic, peeled

1 medium white onion, peeled and quartered

2 cups long-grain rice, washed, soaked in hot water for 15 minutes, rinsed until the water runs clear, and drained

2 medium ripe tomatoes, quartered

½ medium white onion, peeled and chopped

3¼ cups hot water (amount depends on the variety of rice)

1 tablespoon salt, or to taste

50 sprigs Italian parsley, tied

4 whole fresh jalapeño chiles

FOR THE GARNISH

Whole or sliced cooked jalapeño chiles

Sprigs of Italian parsley

POBLANO CHILES STUFFED WITH SEAFOOD AND CLAM SAUCE, LORETO STYLE
CHILES POBLANOS RELLENOS CON MARISCOS Y SALSA DE ALMEJAS, COCINA LORETANA

Serves 8

FOR THE CHILES

16 medium fresh poblano or Anaheim chiles, roasted, peeled, seeded, and deveined (see page 296)
4 cups warm water
3/4 cup cider vinegar or white wine vinegar
Salt to taste

FOR THE STUFFING

3/4 cup olive oil
3 tablespoons butter
1 1/2 cups finely chopped white onions
1 1/2 pounds ripe tomatoes, finely chopped
Salt and freshly ground black pepper to taste
4 cooked lobster tails, shredded
3 cups shredded cooked shrimp
2 cups finely chopped cooked clams

FOR THE SAUCE

4 cups fish stock, reduced to 1 1/2 cups
2 cups crème fraîche, reduced to 1 1/3 cups
2 cups heavy cream, reduced to 1 1/3 cups
1 1/2 cups minced steamed clams
4 tablespoons butter, cut into pieces
Salt and freshly ground black pepper to taste

FOR THE GARNISH

16 large steamed clams
8 small plum tomatoes, sliced but attached at one end to resemble fans
3 tablespoons minced parsley

Colored by the nearby desert, Loreto is a small town with a distinct flavor. The surrounding mountains lend their own majestic air. In the higher elevations of the Sierras, *ojos de agua* (freshwater springs) can be found in inhospitable woods where few humans venture. However, outstanding cave drawings in the San Javier area serve as testimony to the long-ago presence of ancient peoples in the region. Today, only hunters looking for white-tailed deer and Simarrón lambs traverse these sylvan heights marked by waterfalls and vegetation that changes with the elevation. Closer to town, the undulating crystal-blue waters of Loreto Bay contrast with the arid and barren desert. Before dawn, fishermen stroll the beach carrying woven baskets and canelike magic wands to harvest clams that the sea has left buried in the sand.

PREPARE THE CHILES: Soak the chiles for 20 minutes in the warm water mixed with the vinegar and the salt. Drain and dry the chiles on paper towels.

PREPARE THE STUFFING: Heat the oil and the butter in a large casserole. Add the onions and fry until light brown. Add the tomatoes and simmer uncovered for 20 minutes. Season with salt and pepper. Add the lobster, shrimp, and clams and continue cooking uncovered for 30 minutes, or until the mixture is thick enough to use as stuffing. Fill the chiles with the mixture and set aside.

PREPARE THE SAUCE: Heat the reduced fish stock and creams and the clams in a saucepan and simmer uncovered for 20 minutes or until the sauce is thick. Swirl the pieces of butter into the sauce and immediately remove the pan from the heat. Season with salt and pepper. Put the pan in a water bath and let sauce cool to room temperature.

TO SERVE: Spoon some of the cooled sauce onto each plate and top with 2 stuffed peppers. Garnish each plate with 2 clams and 1 tomato "fan." Spoon more sauce over the chiles and sprinkle with the parsley. Serve at room temperature.

PUERTO NUEVO LOBSTER
LANGOSTA ESTILO PUERTO NUEVO
Serves 6

Lobster has been pulled from the waters off this small fishing village since the Guaycuras, Pericúes, and Cochimíes inhabited Baja. These tribes caught lobster in straw baskets or with their hands. Modern-day fishermen still use these techniques as their boats cruise the deep waters beneath the town's rocky cliffs. Rays of sunshine reflect off the brown-and-orange-speckled shells of the lobsters, helping to spot the day's catch. Once sighted, lobsters must be caught with care so as to avoid the dangerous claws. Back on land, fishermen once grilled lobster over open wood fires set up near beachside huts. Today, these huts house tiny restaurants that carry on the tradition. Tomato rice, pinto beans, and a sauce made with tomatoes, onions, chiles, and cilantro were and still are the usual accompaniments. When served with Baja's flour tortillas (which are larger and softer than regular tortillas), lobster lends a distinctive flavor to the *ranchero* tacos of Puerto Nuevo.

6 Pacific or Maine lobsters
   (about 2½ to 3 pounds each)
1¼ cups clarified butter
Salt and freshly ground black
   pepper to taste
   Sprigs of parsley
   Sliced tomatoes
   Grilled flour tortillas

Preheat the oven to 400°F for 40 minutes and light a grill fire if using. Halve the lobsters lengthwise. Clean the halved lobsters and brush with some of the butter. Sprinkle with salt and pepper. Put the lobsters on baking sheets and cook for 8 minutes in the hot oven. Remove from the oven, baste with butter, and cook either in a preheated heavy skillet on top of the stove or directly on the hot grill, cut side down, for 3 to 5 minutes or until the lobster meat is lightly browned. Do not overcook; the lobster should still be juicy.

TO SERVE: Place 2 lobster halves on each of 6 oval plates. Brush with warm butter and garnish with parsley sprigs and tomato slices and grilled flour tortillas.

Note: Serve the lobster with Mexicali Rice (page 23), *Pico de Gallo* (page 74), and Playa la Ropa Beans (page 121).

FRIED FISH GUAYCURA STYLE
PESCADO FRITO A LA GUAYCURA

Serves 8

FOR THE FISH

- 8 thick mahimahi, sea bass, or red snapper fillets (about 4 ounces each)
- 1/3 cup fresh lime juice
- Garlic salt to taste
- Freshly ground black pepper to taste
- 4 eggs
- 2 tablespoons sour cream
- 2 cups bread crumbs
- 1 tablespoon dried oregano
- 1 1/2 teaspoons black peppercorns, ground
- 3 cups vegetable or extra-virgin olive oil
- 1 cup clarified butter

FOR THE GARNISH

- 6 medium cucumbers, unpeeled and thinly sliced
- 1/2 cup fresh lime juice
- Salt to taste
- 1 tablespoon freshly ground black pepper
- 3/4 cup olive oil
- 16 tomato slices
- 32 lime slices
- 2 tablespoons minced parsley
- Coarsely ground black pepper to taste

The ancient Guaycura Indians used several specialized tools to help them harvest food from the sea. Nets were made from the fibers of the agave plant as were the deep baskets used to "scoop" fish from sea beds. Harpoons also were made from fibrous plants as well as from animal bones and seashells. This dish comes from the seaside village of Bahía Concepción. Here the silent desert meets calm, turquoise waters. Waves gently wash against the powdery white sand and rocks that line the coast. As in Indian times, Bahía Concepción is a true paradise.

PREPARE THE FISH: Place the fish in a shallow glass dish and sprinkle with the lime juice, garlic salt, and pepper. Marinate for 10 minutes at room temperature. Beat the eggs with the sour cream. Combine the bread crumbs with the oregano and the pepper. Dip the fish fillets into the egg mixture, then coat completely with the prepared bread crumbs. Refrigerate the fish for 2 hours. Preheat the oven to 350°F. Heat the oil and the clarified butter in a large skillet. Fry the fish until it is light brown and flakes easily. Do not overcook. Drain on paper towels and keep warm in the hot oven.

PREPARE THE GARNISH: Meanwhile, place the cucumbers in a glass bowl and mix with the lime juice, salt, pepper, and olive oil. Marinate for 25 minutes.

TO SERVE: Place the fried fish on 8 large plates. Garnish with the marinated cucumbers and the tomato and lime slices. Sprinkle the plates with the parsley and coarsely ground black pepper. Serve immediately.

ENSENADA EMPANADAS
EMPANADAS ESTILO ENSENADA

Makes about 40 empanadas

Ensenada is a small port on the Pacific coast surrounded by white sand, rocky cliffs, and, of course, blue-green waters. From the town's cliffs, visitors watch whales heading to Guerrero Negro and to the national park of gray whales and to Bahía Ojo de Liebre, where thousands of whales meet after a 4,000-mile trip from the Bering Sea. These flour turnovers are a local delicacy. The sweet filling is made from an exotic combination of pinto beans and sugar that is used in many Baja recipes.

PREPARE THE DOUGH: Place the yeast in ⅓ cup of warm water and let sit for 10 minutes. Spread the flour over a work surface. Add the yeast mixture, lard, and salt. Work the dough with your hands until it has the consistency of sand. Add the remaining warm water in small amounts and work the dough until it is smooth and elastic like a bread dough. Cover and let rest for 1 hour. With your hands, form small dough balls. On a floured surface, use a rolling pin to work the balls into 3-inch circles. Cut the circles with a large round cookie cutter to ensure that they are of equal size.

PREPARE THE FILLING: Heat the water in a large pot. Add the beans and ⅓ cup of the lard and cook until the beans are soft, adding more warm water if necessary. Drain. Season the beans with the salt and puree. Heat the remaining lard in a casserole. Add the beans, little by little, simmering the mixture uncovered over low heat until the beans begin to dry out. Add the sugar to taste; continue cooking until the mixture thickens. Allow the mixture to cool.

PREPARE THE EMPANADAS: Heat the oil in large frying pan. Meanwhile, place 1 tablespoon of the bean mixture in the center of each dough circle. Fold the dough over the filling and seal the edges with the beaten egg. Use a fork to mark the edges and check that the seal is tight by pressing the edges with your fingers. Reshape the empanadas on a floured surface, if necessary. Fry the empanadas until light brown. Remove with a slotted spoon and drain on paper towels and sprinkle with sugar. Serve hot.

FOR THE DOUGH

- 1¾ to 2¼ cups warm water or enough to form a smooth dough
- 1 teaspoon active dry yeast
- 4½ cups flour
- ¾ cup lard or vegetable shortening
- 1 teaspoon salt, or to taste

FOR THE FILLING

- 14 cups water
- 3 cups pinto beans, soaked overnight in water to cover and drained
- ¾ cup lard or corn oil
- 1½ to 2 tablespoons salt, or to taste
- 2 to 3 cups sugar

- 6 cups vegetable oil
- 3 eggs, beaten

FIG COMPOTE
DULCE DE HIGO

Serves 8 to 10

6½ pounds figs, peeled and
quartered
2 cups water
2½ pounds sugar
10 fresh fig leaves
Whipped cream or ice cream for
garnish

The Franciscan friars established missions in the desert and the oases throughout California. They cultivated fruits and vegetables in their irrigated gardens, especially chiles, peppers, grapes, peaches, pears, and figs. This old Baja dessert from the Loreto region is traditionally made over wood fires in large copper kettles.

Place the figs in a large enamel or copper pot. Add the water, sugar, and fig leaves and cook uncovered over low heat, stirring constantly with a wooden spoon. Continue cooking until the bottom of the pot is visible and a thick syrup and paste are formed, about 3 hours. To serve, place the cooked figs in a glass bowl and cover with whipped cream.

VARIATION: This dessert can be used as a filling for pies or empanadas.

DAMIANA TEA
TÉ DE DAMIANA

Serves 8

8 cups water
2 tablespoons dried damiana
leaves

Damiana tea has enormous healing properties. It acts as a diuretic as well as a sexual stimulant. This herb grows in the desert, usually near thistle plants. In Baja, the first inhabitants used damiana leaves to heal their aches and pains.

Bring the water to a rapid boil and add the damiana leaves. Boil for 5 minutes, turn off the heat, and let stand for 5 minutes. Strain. Pour into a teapot and serve.

CHILTEPÍN CHILE SAUCE
PICKLED CHILES SONORA STYLE
PICKLED OYSTERS GUAYMAS STYLE
CHEESE SOUP
SONORA-STYLE ENCHILADAS
GUAYMAS MANTA RAY
FRIED *TOTOABA* OR HALIBUT
SONORAN FLOUR TORTILLAS
PUMPKIN IN BROWN SUGAR SYRUP
GRAPE AND MELON DRINK
BAJICOPO (WHEAT BEVERAGE)

Located in the northwestern part of Mexico, the state of Sonora is bordered by the Gulf of California to the west and the state of Chihuahua to the east, with the United States directly north. The name Sonora comes from an Indian word meaning "in the corn." The capital city, Hermosillo, was originally a Seri Indian settlement, and descendants of this tribe, as well as Opatas, Pagagos, Pimas, Yaquis and Mayos, still live in the region.

Sonora has a number of splendid beaches and important ports, like the ones at Guaymas, a fishing town, and Kino Bay, where desert cactuses grow right up to the water. The climate of the region varies dramatically with the season.

Besides the array of marine species that constitute much of the local diet, Sonora produces wheat, sesame seeds, soybeans, sugarcane, potatoes, beans, chickpeas, chiles (Anaheims, Caribs, and guajillos), sweet peppers, apples, quince, and grapes for brandy and wine. One of the most prosperous states in the republic, Sonora has a large cattle industry and is known for its fine meats and cheeses. There are also a number of turkey farms, which supply the entire country with birds for Christmas.

Various tribes, descended from the stars and from the centuries, inhabit these lands. We are known as Yaquis, Pimas, and Seris. The Seris, who came from the sea and live from the sea, are my tribe. At dusk, we Seri women listen to the sea songs that call to our souls from deep within the waters. At dawn, when the waters have receded, the beach is ablaze with shells left during the night. Each Seri woman picks up one special shell. It is called a *valma de chama* and will serve as her vessel to keep treasured celestial dust. She uses these fine powders from heaven to adorn her face, imprinting the colors and designs from this beloved earth as I have done since many moons ago. Time is reflected in the wrinkles on my face just as the implacable winds sculpt desert sands. But our lives are protected by the goddess of water and the wind god, who emerged in the beginning of all beliefs and guide all of our acts. ¶ In the last months of autumn, when the winds changed their way, my fifth granddaughter reached her fifteenth birthday and it was I who led the ceremony that transformed her into a woman. We went out into the calm waters of the sea in a small canoe made with sewn reeds. I cut her hair short, to her jaw. She left her childhood on the beach, lost in the magic dust of the sand. I wet her head with ocean water. ¶ At the same time, the men launched a boat to hunt for the turtle known as *Siete Filo,* that dark, swarthy being with an evil spirit able to possess the indomitable soul of a Seri. The traitorous animal has to be lured with soft words to attract him to the boat without awakening his evilness. When the fishermen arrived back on land, they tied the turtle in a bower and painted the shell and face with colors. Men and women also painted their bodies and adorned themselves with ornamental chains and necklaces made with shark bones as well as chains of conch shells and of *chiquiquite,* a green stone, the Seri stone. Even old men and women whose faces are marked by time and reflect the sacred wrinkles from the waters of the sea joined in the four days of celebration. Yes, we honor the old because their faces reflect the sea, that prolific womb of richness. We Seri women labored over the bounty from the sea, cooking *totoaba* and grilled shrimp over live coals, along with birds and turtles, crabs and octopus, fish broths, and the clams and oysters that we harvest when the tide goes out. ¶ According to the traditions of our race—a pure lineage—the younger women approached us, to learn from us the secrets of natural plants that help to heal aches and illnesses. To my granddaughters, I explained how to prepare a laxative from the root *chicamilla* and to make a corn porridge to calm the intestine. Also good for the stomach is *peonilla* (peony), which can be boiled or dried and made into powder. When it is put into a compress, *toloache* helps those who suffer inflammations. For fever, we use the herbs *pasmo* and anise. Hedionda is good for the worms that attack children and eat other plants. ¶ We also taught the young maidens to celebrate the ceremonies with ritual dances like the one of the wand, called *varas*. At the same time, the men performed the dance of the reed, known as *carrizos,* to calm the fury of the gods and to ask them to foretell the rain, the crops, and the harvest from the sea. ¶ With divine favor, the Seris carry their fishhooks, knives, and harpoons across the treacherous channel that separates our Isla de Tiburón (Shark Island) from the coast of Sonora, in order to trade the catch of the day. We also sell the fruits of our labor, among them marine figures made out of *palo fierro,* the tree of the desert; *coritas* (baskets) made of special *torote* wood and *ocote* (torch pine); chains of shells, snails, and seeds; and heavy, dark honey pressed from the *pitahaya.* ¶ The gods protect our race by giving each woman her own *valma de chama.* Soon my time will arrive. Soon the shell that one day so long ago I picked from the sand will be buried with me, and both of us will turn to dust. Eventually, the wind will lift up the small, shimmering particles, and we will come to rest in the soil. My dust will illuminate the land, and I will again become part of the powder with which my race paints designs on its skin.

CHILTEPÍN CHILE SAUCE
SALSA DE CHILE CHILTEPÍN

Makes about 3 cups

4 cups water
6 medium ripe tomatoes
1 medium white onion, peeled and halved
4 medium cloves garlic, peeled
½ teaspoon black peppercorns, ground
2 whole cloves, ground
½ cup dried chiltepín or other small dried red chiles, lightly toasted in a warm skillet
Salt to taste

Chiltepín chiles grow in a dry region of the Sonora Mountains, known as Baviacora, not far from the Sonora River. Cultivated in small vegetable gardens called *huertas,* this round, red chile is used to season everything from seafood broth to corn on the cob. One tiny chiltepín has the piquancy of five jalapeños and is even more potent than the legendary habanero. Serve this sauce with grilled fish. Or, bake flounder, grouper, or any other fish in it.

Bring the water to a boil in a large casserole. Add the tomatoes, onion, garlic, pepper, and cloves. Cook for 20 minutes uncovered, then cool. Drain the vegetables and reserve the water. Puree the chiles with the cooked vegetables until fairly smooth. Season with salt and add about 1½ cups of the reserved cooking liquid until the sauce has a somewhat thick consistency. Sterilize 2 medium jars and pour the sauce into the jars. Cool and then refrigerate until ready to use.

VARIATION: Puree 1½ cups tomato juice, ½ cup white wine vinegar, ½ white onion, 2 cloves garlic, ¼ cinnamon stick, 4 whole cloves, 2 fresh bay leaves, ½ teaspoon freshly ground black pepper, ½ teaspoon nutmeg, and salt to taste with ½ cup chiltepín chiles.

PICKLED CHILES SONORA STYLE
CHILES ENCURTIDOS ESTILO SONORA
Serves 6

Anaheim and poblano chiles were cultivated by the Pima Indians, the original inhabitants of the fertile Sonora River valley. This tribe was the first to establish relations with the Jesuits who settled in the area. The Spanish missionaries grew olives, grapes, and various vegetables in this rich soil. Olive oil and vinegar soon became essential ingredients in the local cooking. This recipe dates back to the seventeenth century and illustrates the culinary crossbreeding of the times. These chiles make a nice accompaniment to grilled fish and boiled crabs or shrimp.

PREPARE THE CHILES: Soak the chiles in the water, vinegar, and salt for 20 minutes. Drain and transfer them to a large jar with a tight lid.

PREPARE THE PICKLING LIQUID: Pour the vinegar into another large jar with a lid. Add the salt and cover. Shake until the salt is dissolved. Add the olive oil, garlic, peppercorns, and herbs. Cover again and shake for 2 to 3 minutes. Taste for salt and add more if needed. Pour the pickling liquid over the chiles. Shake the jar and let the chiles steep for 15 days in the lowest part of the refrigerator.

TO SERVE: Serve the pickled chiles with a salad of crisp lettuce, ripe tomatoes, and sliced onions. These chiles also can be stuffed with clams sautéed in garlic, onion, parsley, white wine, and cream. Or, try stuffing them with your favorite shrimp salad, cottage cheese, or crumbled feta cheese or any other soft cheese.

Note: In some regions in the United States poblano chiles are called fresh pasillas.

FOR THE CHILES
- 12 medium fresh poblano or Anaheim chiles, roasted, peeled, seeded, and deveined, with stems on (see page 296)
- 2 cups water
- 1/3 cup white wine vinegar
- 1/2 teaspoon salt

FOR THE PICKLING LIQUID
- 3 cups white wine vinegar
- Sea salt to taste (about 1 1/4 tablespoons)
- 1 cup extra-virgin olive oil
- 2 heads garlic, quartered but not peeled
- 1 teaspoon whole black peppercorns
- 20 fresh bay leaves
- 15 sprigs marjoram
- 1 tablespoon dried oregano leaves

PICKLED OYSTERS GUAYMAS STYLE
ESCABECHE DE OSTIÓN ESTILO GUAYMAS

Serves 16

FOR THE PICKLING MARINADE

1½	cups olive oil
20	medium cloves garlic, peeled
4	medium white onions, peeled and sliced diagonally
10	carrots, peeled, sliced, and boiled in salted water for 9 minutes
40	scallions, thinly sliced
8	fresh jalapeño chiles, halved
20	fresh bay leaves
10	sprigs thyme
10	sprigs marjoram
1	tablespoon dried oregano leaves
1½	tablespoons freshly ground black pepper
1	tablespoon allspice
1	tablespoon sugar
	Salt to taste
4	cups strong fruit vinegar, white wine vinegar, or champagne vinegar

FOR THE OYSTERS

4	cups oyster juice
240	shucked oysters

Guaymas is a picturesque port on the shore of the Sea of Cortés (Gulf of California) in the state of Sonora. When I visited this port, I learned to make this recipe, famous in Guaymas, from Dolores Torres Izabal. She recommends preparing the oysters at least a day ahead of time so they can absorb the flavor of the tangy pickling sauce. This is a perfect appetizer for a big party or a wedding, since it is easy to make in large quantities.

PREPARE THE MARINADE: Heat the oil in a large saucepan. Add the garlic cloves and brown slightly. Remove and discard half the garlic. Place the remaining garlic cloves in a blender or a food processor and puree. Brown the onions in the same saucepan. Then add the pureed garlic, the cooked carrots, and the scallions, chiles, bay leaves, thyme, marjoram, oregano, black pepper, allspice, sugar, salt, and vinegar. Boil the mixture for 15 minutes, stirring regularly with a wooden spoon.

PREPARE THE OYSTERS: Place the oyster liquor in a medium saucepan with the oysters and simmer for 8 minutes. Remove the oysters with a slotted spoon and reserve. Continue to simmer the liquid uncovered until it is reduced to 1 cup. Add the marinade and cook until the mixture comes to a boil. Add the oysters, bring to a boil, remove from the heat, and allow to cool. The sauce should not be too watery. Chill the oysters for 1 or 2 days before serving.

TO SERVE: Spoon the oysters onto a platter. Serve with plain boiled rice, crackers, or freshly made corn tortillas.

CHEESE SOUP
CALDO DE QUESO
Serves 8 to 10

The natives of Sonora learned to raise cattle from the Spaniards. Crossbreeding gave rise to superior cows able to produce top-quality milk and, of course, first-class cheeses. Well-known Anaheim chiles, or California chiles, are another pride of the region. These local chiles have a distinct, delicious flavor that works well in stuffed or pickled chile recipes, egg dishes, or seafood preparations.

Heat the butter and oil in a pot. Add the onions and sauté until lightly browned. Add the sliced chiles and cook for 8 minutes. Add the potatoes and continue cooking for another 8 minutes. Add the cheese, hot stock, and milk. Season to taste and simmer uncovered for 20 minutes.

Just before serving, add the *panela* cheese and cream. Correct the seasoning and serve hot.

Note: Oysters and fish can be added to the soup.

FOR THE SOUP

- ¹/₃ cup butter
- ¹/₃ cup vegetable oil
- 2 cups chopped white onions
- 24 fresh Anaheim chiles, roasted and peeled (see page 296), and sliced into thin strips
- 4 medium potatoes, cooked, peeled, and diced
- 3 cups diced Chihuahua, Mexican Manchego, or Monterey Jack cheese
- 8 cups hot chicken stock
- 8 cups boiling milk

Salt to taste

FOR THE GARNISH

- 1 cup *panela* or fresh mozzarella cheese
- 6 tablespoons heavy cream or yogurt

SONORA-STYLE ENCHILADAS
ENCHILADAS SONORENSES

Serves 8

FOR THE SAUCE

12 large dried colorado or ancho chiles (about 6 ounces)
4 medium ripe tomatoes
1 medium white onion, peeled and quartered
6 cloves garlic, peeled
1 teaspoon black peppercorns, ground
4 whole cloves, ground
1½ teaspoons cumin seeds, ground
Salt to taste
½ cup vegetable oil
2 onion slices
2 cups water or beef consommé

FOR THE FILLING

1½ cups finely chopped olives
1 teaspoon dried oregano
1½ cups finely chopped scallions

FOR THE ENCHILADAS

1¾ pounds fresh *masa* (corn dough)
4 ounces *cotija* or *añejo* cheese, crumbled, or cottage cheese
⅓ to ½ cup warm water
3 cups lard or vegetable oil

FOR THE GARNISH

1 cup very thinly sliced white onion
1½ cups very finely shredded cabbage
1 cup crumbled feta or *cotija* cheese

The addition of cheese to the *masa* (corn dough) gives this dish an exquisite flavor and makes these enchiladas different from similar preparations found in other parts of the country. This dish is also of note because the sauce calls for dried colorado chiles, which are known as anchos in most parts of Mexico.

PREPARE THE SAUCE: Heat a *comal* or a heavy skillet. Lightly toast the chiles, turning them on both sides. Devein the chiles, then soak them in water for 20 minutes; drain and set aside. Roast the tomatoes on all sides on the *comal* and puree with the chiles, onion, garlic, spices, and salt. Strain. Heat the oil in a frying pan and sauté the onion slices until brown. Add the chile and tomato mixture and simmer uncovered, stirring frequently, until the sauce thickens, about 25 minutes. Taste, correct the seasoning, and add the water. Simmer until the sauce thickens; keep hot.

PREPARE THE FILLING: Mix the olives, oregano, and scallions and set aside.

PREPARE THE ENCHILADAS: While the sauce is cooking, place the *masa* in a bowl and add the cheese. Add a little warm water and knead the dough until a soft but not watery consistency is obtained, about 5 minutes. Set aside for 10 minutes. Form the dough into tortillas following the directions on page 309. Stack the tortillas on a moist dishcloth and cover with a second dishcloth to keep them from drying out.

Heat the lard in a frying pan. Fry the tortillas and fold in half (into an enchilada shape). Remove from the pan, drain, and stuff with the olive mixture.

TO SERVE: Place the enchiladas on a platter, drench with the hot sauce, and garnish with the onion, cabbage, and cheese.

GUAYMAS MANTA RAY
MANTARRAYA ESTILO GUAYMAS

Serves 6 to 8

The port of Guaymas lies in a quiet bay off the Sea of Cortés (Gulf of California). Surrounded by an impressive landscape of rugged hills, the city boasts several popular bathing beaches in the nearby bays of Bocachibampo and San Carlos. In the busy harbor, ships are loaded with precious metals from nearby mines. Fishing boats also dot the harbor, often bringing back their catch of the day. Manta ray is just one of many species found in local waters; others include halibut, sole, and flounder.

PREPARE THE FISH: Bring the water to a boil in a large casserole. Add the onions, garlic, marjoram, peppercorns, and salt. Cover and let the water return to a rapid boil. Add the fish and cook until tender, 4 to 6 minutes. Drain the fish, cool, and then shred.

PREPARE THE SAUCE: Soak the chiles in the water, vinegar, and salt for 20 minutes. Drain the chiles, slice them into strips; puree with the onions, garlic, fish stock, and wine. Heat the olive oil and the butter in a medium saucepan and add the chile mixture. Season with salt and pepper and simmer uncovered until the sauce thickens, 20 to 25 minutes. Add the shredded manta ray and cook uncovered until the fish absorbs some of the sauce and the mixture becomes thick. Keep warm in a double boiler until serving time.

TO SERVE: Warm the tortillas on a preheated *comal* or griddle or in a heavy skillet. Fill each tortilla with 2 to 3 tablespoons of the fish mixture. Roll to form a *taquito* and then reheat the rolled tacos. Brush with the clarified butter and transfer to a basket lined with a napkin. Serve immediately.

FOR THE MANTA RAY

- 6 cups water
- 2 medium white onions, peeled and halved
- 1/2 head garlic, unpeeled
- 8 sprigs marjoram
- 1 teaspoon black peppercorns
- Salt to taste
- 2 pounds manta ray, skate, or baby shark

FOR THE SAUCE

- 10 medium fresh poblano or Anaheim chiles, toasted, peeled, seeded, and deveined (see page 296)
- 2 cups water
- 1/3 cup white vine vinegar
- 1/2 teaspoon salt
- 1 1/2 medium white onions, peeled and cut into pieces
- 4 medium cloves garlic, peeled
- 2 cups fish stock, reduced to 1 cup
- 1/2 cup white wine
- 1/3 cup olive oil
- 2 1/2 tablespoons butter
- Salt and freshly ground black pepper to taste
- 16 flour tortillas
- 2 to 3 tablespoons clarified butter

FRIED *TOTOABA* OR HALIBUT
TOTOABA FRITA

Serves 6

FOR THE FISH

6 *totoaba* or halibut fillets (about ¹/₂ pound each)
4 medium plus 3 large cloves garlic, peeled
8 black peppercorns
Juice of 3 medium limes
Salt to taste
³/₄ cup flour
3 cups vegetable oil

FOR THE GARNISH

1 medium head romaine lettuce, finely shredded and refrigerated
¹/₂ cup white wine vinegar or champagne vinegar
Salt and freshly ground black pepper to taste
6 tablespoons olive oil
Freshly cracked black peppercorns to taste
Lemon or lime wedges

This gold-and-blue fish is found exclusively in the Sea of Cortés (Gulf of California). The Seris, a group that has inhabited the Sonora coast for centuries, prepare the meaty fillets in this simple manner. Established along the Yaqui River in Sonora as well as on Isla de Tiburón, the Seris excel at fishing, whether using harpoons, nets, or baskets *(coritas)* made from dried branches. In the Seris' festivities, the *totoaba* rests on a bed of sticks, roasting slowly over an open fire to seal in the juices. Fishing for *totoaba* has been temporarily suspended in order to give the species time to increase its numbers. Halibut is an excellent substitute.

Place the fish in a shallow glass dish. Puree the 4 medium garlic cloves and the peppercorns; mix with the lime juice and season with salt. Spread the mixture over the fish. Marinate for 10 minutes and then refrigerate the fish until ready to use. Place the flour in a shallow bowl. Dip the fish into the flour, coating both sides well. Heat the oil in a deep casserole, a large skillet, or a wok. Add the 3 large garlic cloves and cook until brown; discard. Fry the fish in batches until crisp on both sides, about 5 minutes. Keep the fish warm in a hot oven.

TO SERVE: Cover the serving platter with the shredded lettuce and top with the fried fish. Mix the vinegar, salt, pepper, and oil. Sprinkle the vinaigrette over the fish and serve immediately. Garnish with cracked peppercorns and lemon wedges. Serve Chiltepín Chile Sauce (page 32) on the side.

SONORAN FLOUR TORTILLAS
TORTILLAS DE HARINA DE SONORA

Makes 20 to 30 tortillas

The Spanish introduced wheat to Sonora soon after the Conquest. While wooden plows once worked the fields, tractors do the job today. Traditionally, wheat was gathered by hand and then threshed with the help of a team of mules and horses. Sonoran Indians learned to plant wheat from the Spanish and soon began to make tortillas from wheat flour. The combination of flour, lard, salt, and warm water yields an especially elastic dough capable of producing tortillas called *tortillas de agua*, which are 2 feet in diameter. The following recipe makes soft tortillas, either thin or thick, of any size. This dough can be used for empanadas. Traditional Sonoran fillings include sweetened squash, fig paste, apples, and brown sugar. Or, serve hot tortillas with fish, vegetable, egg *machaca*, seafood, or cheese dishes. Large tortillas can be folded into quarters.

Beat the lard until soft. Spread the flour over a flat surface and add the salt and the yeast. Work the lard into the flour by hand, adding warm water in small amounts until the dough becomes firm but not sticky. The dough should be very elastic and shiny. Continue working the dough by pulling and stretching it, sprinkling with more flour as needed. Cover the dough with a cloth and let it rest in a warm place until doubled in volume. Work the dough with your hands again to form about 2 dozen 6-inch balls.

Preheat a thick, iron *comal* or a heavy skillet or griddle for 30 minutes over medium heat. Lightly coat the *comal* with oil. (Repeat, as needed, while cooking the tortillas.) Put the dough balls on a wooden surface and use a rolling pin to flatten the balls into very thin circles. Sprinkle the dough with flour to keep it from sticking. Reshape the tortillas by hand and then slide them onto the *comal* one at a time. Cook each tortilla for 1 minute, flip, cook for 30 seconds more, turn again, and pat with a damp cloth until it puffs slightly. Remove the tortilla and wrap it in a napkin. Repeat.

VARIATION: Whole wheat flour can be used to make the tortillas. Just add more lard and water to keep the dough elastic.

1 cup lard or vegetable shortening, at room temperature
4 cups flour
1 tablespoon salt
1 teaspoon active dry yeast
1½ to 2 cups warm water
Vegetable oil or clarified butter for greasing the *comal*

PUMPKIN IN BROWN SUGAR SYRUP
CALABAZA CON PANOCHA

Serves 16 to 20

20 pounds pumpkin, cut into
   ¼-pound slices or wedges
   and placed outside in racks
   covered with netting to dry in
   the sun for 4 or 5 days

14 *panochas,* grated, or a little
   more than 9 pounds brown
   sugar

30 fresh orange or lime leaves

About 6 cups water

1½ cups peeled pumpkin seeds

Sugarcane has been cultivated in Sonora since the first conquests of Francisco Vásquez de Coronado and Álvar Núñez Cabeza de Vaca in the 1530s. The green, swordlike leaves of the sugarcane plant adorn valleys throughout the state. Reaching a height of 8 or 9 feet, sugarcane is cut from the fields in January. Before being transported, the stalks are cut into pieces with machetes. The root of the plant is stored in a moist environment and then transplanted into the soil in March. The remainder of the plant is sent to a mill where the juice is extracted. The juice is boiled until dark to remove impurities and poured into small round or cone-shaped molds and cooled. In Sonora, the solidified, unrefined sugar is called *panocha.* This unrefined sugar, similar to what North Americans call brown sugar, goes by the name *piloncillo* in other parts of Mexico.

In a very large clay or metal pot, place a layer of pumpkin slices, with flesh facing up, and sprinkle with the *panocha.* Add some orange leaves and then cover with a layer of pumpkin slices facing down. Add more pumpkin slices facing up, sprinkle with *panocha* and leaves, and cover with pumpkin slices facing down. Repeat until all the pumpkin is used. Add enough water to cover half of the pumpkin slices. Cover the pot and cook over very low heat for 2 to 3 hours until the pumpkin becomes tender and the sugar forms a thick syrup, adding more water as necessary.

TO SERVE: Serve the pumpkin from the clay pot, if used for cooking, or on large plates. Drizzle the syrup on top and sprinkle with the pumpkin seeds.

VARIATION: This recipe can be made with individual miniature pumpkins. Cut and discard a small circle around the stem of each small pumpkin, then scrape out seeds and stringy pulp. Note that cooked pumpkin can be served with a soft cheese or over vanilla ice cream.

GRAPE AND MELON DRINK
JUGO DE UVA Y MELÓN

Serves 8

Sonora's fertile lands have benefited from many of the recent technological improvements in agriculture. The vineyards, for example, are now irrigated using a water-dripping process. As for melons, they lie in the vast Sonoran fields, adding a touch of color to the landscape.

Combine the grapes, melons, and water and puree in batches. Add sugar and pour the drink into a pitcher. Add ice cubes and serve in tall glasses.

3¼ pounds ripe green grapes
 2 ripe honeydew melons, peeled, seeded, and cut into chunks
 4 cups water
Sugar to taste
Ice cubes

BAJICOPO (WHEAT BEVERAGE)
BAJICOPO

Serves 8

The word *bajicopo* comes from the Cahita language. This beverage is prepared from wheat that is dried in the sun, then toasted and ground into a powder. The wheat powder is combined with *panocha* (also known as *piloncillo* or brown sugar) and dissolved in water. This nutritious beverage is fundamental to the diet of the Sonoran tribes.

Put 4 cups of water in a pot and bring to a rapid boil. Add the wheat and cook covered over high heat, adding more water if necessary, until the wheat is soft, about 30 minutes. Remove from the heat, strain, and spread the wheat on a baking tray. Dry the wheat in the sun or in a warm oven for several hours. Grind the dried wheat with the cloves and the cinnamon. Add 16 cups of water. Strain the mixture through a fine sieve and sweeten the liquid with *panocha*. Add ice cubes to cool the drink. Pour the drink into a pitcher and serve.

1½ cups clean wheat berries or husked wheat
 10 cloves, whole
 1 large cinnamon stick
Grated *panocha* or brown sugar to taste
Ice cubes

SINALOA

"CART" COCKTAIL
ESCUINAPA SHRIMP COCKTAIL
EL FUERTE HOT SAUCE
OYSTERS WITH CHIPOTLE SAUCE
CRISPY TACOS
CORBINA OR STRIPED BASS IN ITS OWN JUICE
MAHIMAHI WITH DATES AND MANGOES
SWORDFISH WITH CHICKPEAS AND SESAME SEEDS
PITAHAYAS WITH MANGO SAUCE
SINALOA CORN FRITTERS

South of Sonora lies the state of Sinaloa, which has the Pacific Ocean as its western border. The name Sinaloa comes from a local dialect and means "round *pitahaya*," a reference to the fruit that grows in abundance in this region. Original inhabitants of this state include the Cahitas, Tahues, Totoranes, Pacaxees, Acaxes, and Xiximes. The Jesuits arrived in 1590 and brought with them economic and agricultural developments, especially in the form of wheat and cotton.

Sinaloa has large forests and rivers as well as many natural harbors and inlets. The capital is Culiacán, which is located on the left bank of the river of the same name. Mazatlán is the most famous port in this region and one of the most beautiful along the entire Pacific coast. The diet in the flat, tropical coastal region relies on seafood as well as land crops such as tomatoes, sugarcane, corn, rice, beans, potatoes, sesame seeds, chickpeas, Carib chiles, and sweet peppers.

I was born in these lands, and I never want to leave them. When I go deep into the countryside, far from the coast, I can feel the magic powers of the inlets and bays that were formed when pieces of the sky fell to earth and shattered like crystal. Look into these waters to find the best shrimp you have ever tasted. ¶ Here in Teacapán, fishermen like myself have inherited from the ancient inhabitants of this country a very profitable technique for trapping shrimp. Look into these veins of water to see the paths that we constructed by tying the reeds together with cord to form walls along these narrow channels. Look down to the bottom of the water to see the traps we call by the name *chiqueros,* meaning "pig sty" or "shrimp pen"; they are filled with *mojarra,* sierra, *robalo,* and more. And look at the herons *(garzas)* or gray-haired pelicans poised over the reeds all day, ready to snatch any fish careless enough to jump out of the water or to venture near the surface. ¶ Throughout this zone of Escuinapa, we wait for the full moon, because the light attracts sea creatures to the surface at night. Still waters become a tapestry of fluttering prawns. Here we have good fishing from September to April; the other months are a closed season that we respect religiously. The fishing is so abundant that together a team can take in up to 40 or 50 kilos of freshwater shrimp in just one journey. The shrimp are of good size and, let me tell you, excellent flavor. Have you ever tasted tamales with shrimp barbones cooked in their shells? They are good, aren't they? What could be better than the *taquitos de Escuinapa con caldillo* (taquitos from Escuinapa stuffed with shrimp) served with a tomato and fish broth? Maybe *la machaca de marlín* (shredded marlin) or the sea scallop with small tortillas hot from the *comal* are better? Even the unusual sea *cucaracha*—a mollusk with a shell similar to that of a cockroach, but tasting like conch—served with guacamaya sauce is fantastic, isn't it? You must stay here to learn to eat these good things. You will see how we make an enormous net and tie it to a pole, in the form of a large spoon. At night we plunge it into the water, so deep it goes out of view. We retrieve the net when it is full. ¶ Of course, don't think the fishing is perfect every time. But the water is very generous and if, here or there, we cannot find much, we go toward the Isla del Bosque or Palmito Verde or nearby to the beach called La Tambora, and there, after work, we prepare for ourselves tasty fish dishes cooked slowly over a low fire. No other method produces such succulent results. We like to add the *chilito caloro*, the long chile that has a light green color, or, maybe, the *cola de rata*—"rat's tail" in your language—that in other places is called *chile de árbol*. We sometimes even use *el chile pasado*, the dried pods that North Americans know as California chiles. ¶ The fruit is good, too. We have all sorts of mangoes, but when the heat gets stronger we drink fresh *agua de ova*, and I assure you that this fruit is found only here in Sinaloa. ¶ In this place, every inhabitant has a task, because we like to work. Like the people of the Sierras, we live in permanent contact with the water. For us, of course, water means the sea, our gift from God. With many palm trees and other vegetation, this vast land has more than enough to sustain us. Besides, there are plenty of women and some men who work on handicrafts such as the pretty weavings made with palm leaves, pottery, tools (like axes), wood furniture, and nets. I bet you don't know what these things made from hollowed palm nuts in the mesh *barcinas* (palm sacks) are. That is where we keep the dried shrimp that are so famous in our country. They are used for broths, cakes, and tamales, and they are very good for you. ¶ But now you are going to have to forgive me—as you can see, the sky is trimmed with stars. It is time for me to go to work the tidelands and inlets. Afterward, if you want, we will gather for lunch and then we can continue talking.

"CART" COCKTAIL
COCTEL DE CARRETA

Serves 2

Mazatlán is known for its lively Mardi Gras, when revelers descend on the city and the streets are filled with the joy, up-roar, and clamor of people and music. Small carts selling seafood line the streets along the oceanfront called Olas Altas. Here, the breeze from the sea mixes with the spray from waves breaking forcefully over the rocks. Delicious seafood is caught during the night by fishermen who return with the rising sun. The catch is kept fresh inside the carts on piles of crushed ice. Cart owners prepare with care the garnishes—onions, fresh chiles, tomatoes, avocados, thousands of lemons, and sea salt—that will accompany the octopus, fresh oysters in their shells, clams, and sea scallops. The cart owners prove their abilities every day by combining seafood with the proper gar-nishes and, of course, ice-cold beer.

Open each sea scallop, remove the stomach and the other or-gans, and rinse the scallop briefly. Use a sharp knife to detach the scallop meat from the shell; return the scallop to the shell. (If using oysters, open each shell, slide a sharp knife under the meat to detach it, and return the oyster to the shell.) Place 2 cups of the crushed ice in each of 2 deep soup plates. Sprinkle with coarse salt. Put the scallops on the ice and squeeze lime juice over them. Drizzle the scallops with the El Fuerte Hot Sauce and olive oil. Serve with saltines.

16 baby sea scallops or oysters, in their shells
 4 cups crushed ice
Coarse salt
Fresh lime juice to taste
El Fuerte Hot Sauce (page 47), Tabasco sauce, or *guacamaya* sauce
Olive oil to taste

ESCUINAPA SHRIMP COCKTAIL
CEBICHE DE CAMARÓN DE ESCUINAPA

Serves 6 to 8

2 pounds shrimp, peeled and deveined, cooked in salted water for 2 minutes, and chilled

10 lemons, cut into wedges

2 medium red onions, peeled and thinly sliced

1 cup minced cilantro

Salt and freshly cracked black peppercorns to taste

Extra-virgin olive oil to taste

Hot sauce to taste (see Note)

Fresh or fried tortillas

The rivers of Sinaloa sing with their wealth. There are ten main aquatic arteries—the Fuerte, Presidio, Humaya, Baluarte, Sinaloa, Teacapán, Piaxtla, San Lorenzo, Tamazula, and Badiraguato rivers. The town of Escuinapa, located about 60 miles south of Mazatlán, is a fishing village where men still respect the ancient tradition of listening to the waters of the sea and the rivers. Fishing methods have not changed much over the centuries. Fishermen cut tiny pieces of bamboo and tie them together to form semicircular baskets. Wading into tidal inlets or using small rafts to go up otherwise unnavigable rivers, they move the baskets through the water in a circular or serpentine fashion to snare shrimp in the latticework. Spoonlike nets also are plunged into the water to gather the gray crustaceans. On land, the still-fluttering shrimp are spread across a table and dance in the early morning light. The robust hands of the fishermen begin to remove the heads and shells. This exquisite and exotic dish should be made with only the freshest of shrimp, like those found in the lagoons and tidal waters surrounding Escuinapa.

Divide the shrimp among 6 to 8 deep soup plates that have been chilled in the refrigerator. Garnish with the lemon wedges, onions, cilantro, and salt and cracked black peppercorns. Drizzle the plates with olive oil and hot sauce and serve with tortillas.

VARIATIONS: Drizzle with soy sauce. Cucumbers also are an appropriate garnish.

Note: There are various hot sauces that are especially good with seafood cocktails, including *guacamaya, búfalo,* Tabasco, and *huichol.*

EL FUERTE HOT SAUCE
SALSA PICANTE EL FUERTE

Makes 6 to 8 small bottles of hot sauce

Surrounded by bountiful lands, El Fuerte was founded by the Spaniards in 1563 and became the site of an important fortress in 1610. The town's name comes from the Fuerte River, which means "strong" or "robust" in English. In 1824, the town became the first capital of Sinaloa. Tomato is king in the farms of this region. The Mayo tribes first cultivated this native Mexican plant on these lands centuries ago. Today, local tomatoes are exported in vast quantities to North America. Serve this sauce with any kind of seafood cocktail, oysters, boiled or grilled shrimp, sea scallops, or grilled fish. Serve each dish with tortillas toasted on a *comal,* grilled, or deep-fried until crisp.

Bring the water to a boil in a heavy saucepan. Add the tomatoes, chiles, garlic, oregano, and 1 cup of the vinegar. Season with a small amount of salt. Cook the sauce uncovered until it becomes semithick, about 50 minutes. Add the rest of the vinegar and season to taste with salt. Puree the sauce in a blender or a food processor and strain.

Meanwhile, sterilize a funnel and 6 to 8 small bottles and their caps in boiling water for 10 minutes. Using the funnel, fill the jars immediately with the hot sauce. Seal the bottles, cool to room temperature, and refrigerate.

4 cups water
6 large ripe tomatoes, chopped
20 dried guajillo or New Mexico chiles, seeded and deveined (see page 296)
20 dried de árbol or japonés chiles
10 medium cloves garlic, peeled
1½ tablespoons dried oregano leaves
2 cups red wine vinegar or other strong vinegar
Salt to taste

OYSTERS WITH CHIPOTLE SAUCE
OSTIONES AL CHIPOTLE

Serves 8

FOR THE OYSTERS
48 regular oysters or 24 large rock oysters
2 cups water
2 pounds spinach, cleaned
Salt to taste
6 ounces canned chipotle chiles

FOR THE BÉCHAMEL SAUCE
1/2 cup butter
4 to 5 medium cloves garlic, peeled and pureed
1/4 cup flour
1 1/2 cups hot milk
4 ounces Gruyère cheese, grated
4 ounces Chihuahua or mild Cheddar cheese, grated
2 cups crème fraîche or 1 cup sour cream and 1 cup half-and-half or whipping cream
1/2 cup oyster juice
1 teaspoon powdered bouillon, or salt to taste
1 teaspoon white pepper

FOR THE GARNISH
4 cups coarse salt
3 ounces Gruyère cheese, grated
3 ounces Chihuahua or mild Cheddar cheese, grated
8 sprigs parsley
16 dried chipotle or morita chiles, rinsed

Mazatlán enjoys a number of fine beaches—Olas Altas, Playa Norte, Sábalo (with lagoons formed by the sea), Bajas, Cangrejo, Gaviota, Cerritos, and Escondida. Many boast long stretches of sand with crashing waves washing over colors and textures that range from white to dark and from powdery to rocky. The fishermen arrive on the beaches early in the morning with their little boats. Wearing snorkeling equipment and wet suits, they use nets to catch the several varieties of oysters found in these waters.

PREPARE THE OYSTERS: Shuck the oysters, reserving the shells and the juice, and refrigerate. Bring the water to a boil. Add the spinach and salt and cook for 4 minutes. Drain the spinach and soak in ice water for 3 minutes. Drain and squeeze the spinach until dry. Cut all but 2 of the canned chiles into strips and reserve separately. Mince the remaining 2 chiles and reserve for the sauce.

PREPARE THE BÉCHAMEL SAUCE: Heat the butter in a saucepan and brown the garlic. Add the flour and cook over low heat, stirring constantly, until the mixture begins to brown. Once the flour begins to bubble, gradually whisk in the milk until a thick paste is formed. Continue beating with the whisk while adding the cheeses, crème fraîche, oyster juice, and minced chiles. Season with the bouillon or salt and the white pepper. Cook for 40 minutes over low heat or until the mixture thickens.

Preheat the oven to 400°F. Line the reserved oyster shells with small beds of spinach. Place the shells on a tray spread with 2 cups of the coarse salt. Place 2 oysters in each small shell or 1 rock oyster in each large shell and garnish with a strip of chipotle. Drench with the béchamel sauce and sprinkle with the cheeses. Bake for 10 minutes or until the cheese melts. Remove from the oven.

TO SERVE: Transfer the oysters to dishes spread with the remaining coarse salt. Garnish each plate with a sprig of parsley and 2 chipotle chiles on the side.

CRISPY TACOS
TACOS TRONADORES
Serves 8

The port of Topolobampo rises high above the coast of Sinaloa, forming a small enclave for fishermen and their families. Sailors ready their tiny boats with nets and floats before looking for shrimp in the open sea. In the tranquillity of the afternoon heat, the shrimp boats silently leave town. From the bay, the verdant cliffs and mountains washed by frequent rainfall fall into the ocean to form a spectacular backdrop. Once the flotilla is out to sea, seals, walruses, and sea gulls follow the small boats as they rhythmically sail over the swells. As night falls, sparkling stars guide the sailors to the fishing grounds, where the nets are lowered to catch succulent seafood.

PREPARE THE TORTILLAS: Preheat a *comal* or a heavy skillet for 5 minutes and preheat the oven to 350°F. Heat the tortillas on the *comal,* turning them once on each side, until they are soft. Brush the tortillas with the vegetable oil and place them in narrow French bread molds so they will keep a U-shape. Place the filled molds on baking trays and bake the tortillas in the hot oven about 15 to 20 minutes until crisp.

PREPARE THE FILLING: Roast the shrimp on the hot *comal* in three batches, drizzling them with olive oil and turning them with a spatula, until they are cooked and the shells start to crisp. Remove the shrimp from the heat. When cooled, peel and devein them. On the same hot surface, cook the onions, again drizzling with olive oil, until they are evenly roasted; set aside.

PREPARE THE SAUCE: Preheat a frying pan. Add 1/3 cup of the oil and sauté the chiles for a few seconds. Sprinkle with salt and shake the skillet to make sure that the chiles are cooking on both sides. Puree the chiles, tomatoes, onions, garlic, and water. Strain the mixture through a sieve. Preheat a wok or a medium saucepan and add the remaining 1/3 cup oil. Brown onion slices and remove. Pour the strained sauce into the pan and cook over medium heat. Season with salt and continue cooking uncovered for 20 to 25 minutes or until the sauce has

FOR THE TORTILLAS
- 24 small tortillas (4 to 5 inches in diameter; cut larger tortillas with a cookie cutter to this size)
- 1 1/2 cups vegetable oil

FOR THE FILLING
- 48 medium shrimp (tiger or regular shrimp) or prawns
- Olive oil for roasting the shrimp and onions
- 1 1/2 medium white onions, peeled and sliced

FOR THE SAUCE
- 2/3 cup vegetable oil
- 12 dried de árbol or japonés chiles
- Salt to taste
- 2 1/4 pounds ripe tomatoes
- 1 1/2 medium white onions, peeled and roughly chopped
- 3 medium cloves garlic, peeled
- 3 1/2 cups water, fish stock, or chicken stock
- 2 white onion slices

FOR THE GARNISH
- 4 ripe plum tomatoes, finely chopped
- 3 cups thinly sliced romaine lettuce
- Salt to taste
- 1 1/2 cups crumbled *añejo* or dried feta cheese
- 3/4 cup crème fraîche

CONTINUED

thickened slightly. The sauce should still have a soupy consistency.

To serve: Spoon ¹/₂ cup of the hot sauce into each of 8 large, deep soup dishes. Then fill each tortilla with 2 roasted shrimp and garnish with the reserved roasted onions, the chopped plum tomatoes, and the shredded lettuce. Sprinkle with salt and the cheese and finish with a heaping teaspoon of crème fraîche. Place 3 tacos side by side in each plate. Top with more sauce. Serve immediately; otherwise the tacos will become soggy.

Note: The roasted shrimp can be chopped for the filling.

CORBINA OR STRIPED BASS IN ITS OWN JUICE
CORVINA O LOBINA EN SU JUGO

Serves 6

FOR THE VEGETABLES
- ¹/₂ cup olive oil
- 6 medium cloves garlic, peeled
- 36 tiny potatoes, unpeeled
- Salt to taste
- 2 cups fresh peas boiled in salted water until tender

FOR THE SAUCE
- 2 pounds ripe tomatoes
- 4 medium cloves garlic, peeled
- 1¹/₂ medium white onions, peeled and diced
- 6 Anaheim chiles, stemmed, seeded, and diced
- 1¹/₂ teaspoons dried oregano leaves
- 2 cups water or fish stock
- 1 tablespoon sugar

Lent is a season filled with festivities and special rituals. Each year at this time the Mayos begin their hunt for deer near the Fuerte River. They follow tracks through enchanted trails, using their melodic voices to entrance the animals with song. Grasshoppers make their cosmic fire sounds as hunters stalk their prey with caution and prudence. These Lenten hunting rituals announce the fasting of the season. Dancers are transformed into deerlike creatures and the sounds of nature are played on rattles and other percussion instruments. The sea, too, has a role in these festivities. Ceremonial chains ornamented with seashells, snails, and turquoise recall the creatures and colors of the ocean. While fasting dancers perform, cooks prepare a local fish called *corvina* (corbina). The rhythm of the dancers' steps marches on as steam billows forth from the cooking chambers that contain *corvina* or *lobina* (striped bass) culled from the waters of the Fuerte. Mixed with tiny potatoes, tomatoes, and peas grown in nearby lands, this dish relies on the juices in the fish and a simple sauce to keep the flesh moist.

PREPARE THE VEGETABLES: Heat the oil in a Dutch oven or a fish pan. Add the garlic and discard when browned. Add the potatoes, season lightly with salt, and sauté until crisp. Set the potatoes aside with the prepared peas.

PREPARE THE SAUCE: Puree the tomatoes, garlic, onions, chiles, oregano, and water. Strain the sauce into the Dutch oven and simmer gently uncovered over medium heat for 25 minutes. Add the sugar, taste, and season with salt and pepper.

PREPARE THE FISH: Wash the fish and pat dry. Sprinkle with the lemon juice and season with salt and pepper; let stand for 10 minutes, then place the fish in the sauce. Slowly simmer, covered, for 20 minutes, then turn off the heat and let stand for 10 minutes or until the fish starts to flake. Add the reserved peas and potatoes and the sprigs of fresh marjoram. Cover and cook for 6 minutes.

TO SERVE: Serve the fish directly from the pot with flour tortillas or freshly made corn tortillas.

Salt and freshly ground black
   pepper to taste

FOR THE FISH
1 whole corbina or striped bass,
    or black bass, porgy, cabrilla,
    or grouper (about
    3$^1/_2$ pounds), deboned
$^1/_3$ cup fresh lemon juice
Salt and freshly ground black
   pepper to taste
12 sprigs marjoram

MAHIMAHI WITH DATES AND MANGOES
DORADO CON DÁTILES Y MANGOS
Serves 6

At dawn, fishing boats pass Venados Island and Isla de la Piedra on their way to sea in search of *dorado,* or mahimahi. The Mazatecos fishermen are experts who know where to find this extraordinarily meaty fish in these deep ocean waters. Once they reach the special fishing grounds, they stop the boats and throw the anchors overboard. Nets are prepared while fishing rods are baited. There's no doubt when someone has hooked a *dorado.* It takes much muscle and effort to reel in this strong fish. Besides its great strength, the *dorado* is easily recognized by its bright, metallic blue and silvery or gold-hued sides. As soon as the *dorado* is on board, its coloring starts to change to gray or green. Weighing between 25 and 30 pounds, one *dorado* provides many meals. In this unusual dish, mahimahi is teamed with the exotic flavors of mangoes (first

FOR THE SAUCE
4 large ripe mangoes, peeled
    and diced, juice squeezed
    from the pit, and mixture
    pureed and strained
3$^1/_2$ cups fish stock, reduced to
    2 cups
1$^1/_2$ teaspoons cornstarch
$^1/_2$ cup butter, cut into small
    pieces
Salt and sugar to taste

CONTINUED

FOR THE MANGO GARNISH

- 3 large ripe mangoes, both sides sliced with a sharp knife, pit removed, and pulp scooped out with a spoon and sliced into 2 "fans"
- 1/3 cup clarified butter
- 3 tablespoons sugar
- 3 tablespoons kirsch or rum

FOR THE FISH

- 6 thick mahimahi, grouper, or sea bass fillets (about 1/2 pound each)
- 1 tablespoon chile powder or 1/4 cup lightly toasted and ground dried japonés or de árbol chiles
- 1 1/2 teaspoons garlic salt
- 1 tablespoon chile seeds or hot red pepper flakes

Salt and white pepper to taste

- 1/2 cup clarified butter
- 1/3 cup olive oil

FOR THE GARNISH

- 12 baby zucchini with blossoms, zucchini steamed but blossoms uncooked
- 12 large dates, pitted

brought to Mexico from the Philippines) and dates, which arrived with missionaries after the Conquest.

PREPARE THE SAUCE: Blend the pureed mangoes with the reduced fish stock and cornstarch and strain into a medium saucepan. Simmer the sauce uncovered until it starts to thicken slightly. Remove the sauce from the heat and keep warm in a double boiler. Just before serving, whisk the butter into the sauce and season with salt and sugar.

PREPARE THE MANGO GARNISH: Preheat the oven to 400°F. Place the mango "fans" in a shallow baking dish. Drizzle with the clarified butter, sugar, and kirsch. Let stand for 10 minutes, then bake until the mangoes are slightly caramelized. Keep the mangoes warm.

PREPARE THE FISH: Season the fish on both sides with the chile powder, garlic salt, chile seeds, and salt and white pepper. Heat a large, heavy ovenproof skillet for 8 minutes. Add half of the clarified butter and oil. Cook the fish in the very hot skillet for 2 to 3 minutes. Add the rest of the butter and oil, then turn the fish over and continue cooking for 3 minutes or until the surface of the fillets becomes crusty. Cover the skillet and transfer to the hot oven. Bake until the fish is cooked through, 5 to 8 minutes.

TO SERVE: Preheat 6 large, deep soup plates. Place 1 mango "fan" in each plate. Apply the finishing touches to the sauce and spoon it over the end of the "fan" and around the sides. Place a fillet over each mango "fan" and garnish each plate with the baby zucchini, zucchini blossoms, and dates. Serve immediately.

SWORDFISH WITH CHICKPEAS AND SESAME SEEDS
PEZ ESPADA CON GARBANZOS Y AJONJOLÍ

Serves 4

Mazatlán is most popular for vacations from November to May, but the fishing is good all year. Marlin are most plentiful, with sailfish and swordfish close behind. Often these fish weigh in at more than 100 pounds. Mazatlán is considered the best bill-fishing spot on the Pacific coast and there are plenty of black, blue, and striped marlin, sea bass, tuna, bonito, red snapper, and other top species to be found. This recipe combines chickpeas and sesame seeds, grown in some regions of Sinaloa, with fresh fish. It was inspired by Jean-Louis Palladin, chef at the world-famous Jean-Louis Restaurant in Washington, D.C.

PREPARE THE CHICKPEA PASTE: Heat the olive oil in a medium casserole. Add the garlic cloves and sauté, turning them with a wooden spoon, until brown. Puree the garlic with the ground sesame seeds until the mixture forms a thick paste. Add the chickpeas and reduced fish stock and process until smooth. Season with salt and refrigerate for at least 3 hours or overnight.

PREPARE THE SWORDFISH: Use a 2³/₄-inch round cookie cutter to cut the fish into 8 rounds. Combine the ground chiles, ¹/₄ cup oil, and salt and baste the fish with the mixture; marinate the fish in the refrigerator for 3 hours. Preheat the oven to 400°F. Heat the ¹/₃ cup oil and the clarified butter in a large nonstick pan for 4 minutes. Add 4 swordfish rounds to the very hot skillet and sauté for 50 seconds on each side. Remove the fish and drain on paper towels. (The fish rounds will still be quite rare.) Repeat with the remaining fish rounds. To form each swordfish cake, place 1 fish round in the center of an ovenproof dish. Use a butter knife to spread 2 tablespoons of the sesame seeds and 2 tablespoons of the chickpea paste over each round; top with a second fish round. Repeat with the remaining fish rounds, sesame seeds, and chickpea paste. (Reserve the leftover chickpea paste for the sauce.) Bake the fish cakes in the preheated oven for 8 minutes.

FOR THE CHICKPEA PASTE

- ¹/₃ cup olive oil
- 6 medium cloves garlic, peeled
- 1 cup sesame seeds, lightly toasted and ground
- 2 cups cooked chick-peas
- 2 cups fish or chicken stock, reduced to ¹/₃ cup

Salt to taste

FOR THE FISH

- 8 swordfish fillets (each weighing about 4 ounces and measuring about ¹/₂ inch thick and 3 inches in diameter)
- 6 dried de árbol or japonés chiles, lightly toasted and ground, or 3 tablespoons Chinese chile paste

¹/₃ plus ¹/₄ cup extra-virgin olive oil

Salt to taste

- ¹/₂ cup clarified butter
- ¹/₂ cup sesame seeds, lightly toasted

FOR THE SAUCE

- 3 cups fish or chicken stock, reduced to 1¹/₄ cups
- ¹/₂ cup butter, cut into pieces

CONTINUED

FOR THE GARNISH

- ½ cup sesame seeds, lightly toasted
- 12 dried chiles de árbol or japonés chiles, stir-fried in 3 tablespoons olive oil and sprinkled with salt to taste

PREPARE THE SAUCE: Heat the remaining chickpea sauce in a saucepan with the reduced fish stock and whisk in the butter to make a somewhat thin sauce. Taste and correct the seasoning.

TO SERVE: Spoon 4 tablespoons of the sauce onto each of 4 plates. Place a fish cake on top of the sauce, sprinkle with the sesame seeds, and garnish with the chiles. Serve immediately.

PITAHAYAS WITH MANGO SAUCE
PITAHAYAS CON SALSA DE MANGO

Serves 6

FOR THE MANGO SAUCE

- ½ cup sugar
- 1 cup fresh orange or tangerine juice
- 3 large ripe mangoes, peeled and diced
- ½ cup rum or kirsch
- 1 teaspoon vanilla extract

FOR THE FRUIT

- 6 medium ripe red *pitahayas* or kiwis
- ⅓ cup fresh lemon juice
- 3 large ripe mangoes
- Sugar to taste
- Fresh peppermint or spearmint leaves

The *pitahaya* fruit, which is known for its intensely flavored juice, is sweeter and more tasty when it grows in sandy desert soil. In Sinaloa, *pitahaya* plantations are covered by lush vegetation and bountiful trees, giving the state the nickname "place of the *pitahayas*." In the regions of Sinaloa where this reddish fruit grows in abundance, the *pitahaya* is often presented so as to highlight the contrast between the countless tiny black seeds and the bright pink color of the pulp.

PREPARE THE MANGO SAUCE: Heat the sugar and the orange juice uncovered in a small saucepan until the sugar is dissolved and a syrup is formed. Place the mangoes in a blender and add the orange syrup, liqueur, and vanilla extract. Blend the sauce until smooth. Strain the sauce and refrigerate for at least 3 hours or overnight.

PREPARE THE FRUIT: Peel the *pitahayas*. Refrigerate for 2 hours. Just before serving, cut the fruit into round slices, then sprinkle with the lemon juice. Peel and slice the mangoes.

TO SERVE: Chill 6 large, deep soup plates. Cover the bottoms of the plates with mango sauce. Top with alternating slices of *pitahaya* and mango. Sprinkle with sugar and garnish with mint leaves and serve.

SINALOA CORN FRITTERS
TORREJAS SINALOENSES

Makes about 25 fritters

These Sinaloan dessert fritters are made from a corn and cheese dough and served with hot brown sugar syrup. The flavors of cinnamon and anise enrich the dark sugar syrup.

PREPARE THE SYRUP: Heat the sugar and the water in a saucepan. Add the cinnamon, cloves, and anise and simmer uncovered until the liquid thickens and becomes a semithick syrup. Keep the syrup warm.

PREPARE THE FRITTERS: Place the *masa* in a bowl and add the grated cheese. Add a little warm water at a time and knead until the dough is soft and smooth. Allow to rest for 40 minutes.

Preheat the oven to 350°F. Heat the oil in a frying pan. Meanwhile, make small balls using about 1½ teaspoons of the dough for each. Line a tortilla press with plastic wrap. Place a dough ball in the tortilla press and close. Open the press, peel the plastic from the tortilla, and slide the tortilla into the hot oil. Use a spoon to baste the tortilla with the oil. Flip the tortilla so that it cooks evenly. When the tortilla becomes puffy and crisp, remove from the oil and drain on paper towels. Repeat with the remaining dough balls. Keep the fritters warm in the hot oven and serve on plates drizzled with the hot brown sugar syrup.

Note: See pages 309 to 310 for more information on making the dough and using the tortilla press.

FOR THE SYRUP

4 cups brown sugar or grated *piloncillo* (solidified brown sugar)
4 cups water
2 cinnamon sticks (each about 4 inches long)
6 whole cloves
1 teaspoon anise seeds

FOR THE FRITTERS

1 pound fresh *masa* (corn dough)
1 pound Chihuahua, Mexican Manchego, or Monterey Jack cheese, grated
About ⅓ cup warm water
3 cups vegetable oil

NAYARIT

OYSTER *SOPES*

CRAB SOUP WITH GINGER

TLAXTIHUILLI (SHRIMP STEW)

STUFFED SQUASH WITH TOMATO SAUCE

AZUFRADO OR PINTO BEANS WITH CHORIZO AND SARDINES

SLOW-GRILLED WHOLE FISH

RANCHEROS SHRIMP SAN BLAS STYLE

SPICY SAN BLAS MANGOES

BANANA-NUT CAKE

PINOLE (RED CORN BEVERAGE)

HIERBA ANÍS TEA

Farther south along the Pacific coast is the small state of Nayarit. The name comes from the Cora language and translates as "where the god of war is worshiped." Besides the Coras, the other important Indian group to settle in this region was the Huicholes.

The capital city, Tepic, is home to some impressive colonial architecture. Inland, the climate is warm in the summer and cool during the winter, but along the two hundred miles of coastline the weather is always warm. Local conditions are favorable for the cultivation of many fruits (including coconuts and some fourteen varieties of green, yellow, and red mangoes), corn, wheat, tobacco, and beans.

Nayarit is known for its beautiful beaches, especially at Rincón de Guayabitos, San Blas, and Palmar de Cuautla, as well as magnificent rivers, lagoons, waterfalls, and fertile valleys.

My Dear Agustín:

I have just returned from Nayarit and I am sure that you are not going to believe what I have to tell you. I don't know if I will be able to explain it, because the magic and mystery that surround this land are difficult to understand. I was made aware of my own spirituality and of all that I have to learn. The Huicholes and the Coras don't have to search for their spirituality; it has remained strong in them since ancient times, when legend says the eagle flew over the cactus for the very first time. ¶ Imagine, there I was, in Mexcaltitán at the legendary Aztlán, or "the house of the moon." I was surprised by how similar it was to Tenochtitlán, the city known as the "belly of the moon." On the way to my hotel, I bought a book with a map of the Aztec city and I tried to imagine the pilgrimage of this race that worshiped Quetzalcoatl, that god of goodness and beauty. This noble race traveled for 150 years, a century and a half, leaving behind people who could not go on. Those who stopped by the road founded new tribes, but all of them share the same spiritual roots. Today, those places are home to small communities of Tecos, Totorames, Aztecs, and Tepehuanes. ¶ Let me tell you that the Coras impressed and encouraged me with their fusion of beliefs. Let me also relate a bit of the local history, so you can appreciate the serene attitude of the Huicholes and their special relation to the gods. I was told by my guide that in the beginning of time a Huichol was transformed into the sun. This star spoke five languages and traveled the world for five days. After the flood waters receded he returned to the land. The water had been divided into five seas, which came to be represented by the symbol of the serpent. You can see the importance of the number five and how it relates to the five elements—wind, water, earth, sun, and the human spirit. The Huichol views the sea as a huge serpent that creates waves as it wiggles and shakes, bathing the beaches of his ancestors as it moves. He sees this image in rivers, fires, wind, rain, and clouds as well as in the form of the ribbons and headdress he wears. The deer is also revered as a symbol of fertility and sustenance. The people believe that corn plants arise from the deer—just notice the pointy "antlers" that first emerge from the earth. ¶ The people communicate with their ancestors through a peyote ceremony. Don't think this powerful hallucinogen is used daily; it is saved for special occasions. The Coras call the drug *huatari* and the Huicholes use the names *nierika* and *jículi*. Peyote will not grow in Huichol territory, so the tribe must travel to Viricota, the land of peyote, to perform the ritual at Real de Catorce. A shaman named Maracame guides them to a spot near San Luis Potosi where they can atone for sins. The pilgrimage takes many days, and on the way they walk through sacred rivers, mountains, and deserts. On the fourth or fifth night of the journey, each person ties one nut to a cactus rope to symbolize each of his transgressions. In front of the fire, each confesses his carnal sins to the gods. By the time they arrive in the desert, their souls are purified. Eventually they reach the sacred land where *jículi* lives. ¶ The Viricota ritual helps the people recover their true selves. I can't tell you how moved I was by the ceremony. The pilgrims then walk to the port of San Blas to pray to Aramara, goddess of the sea, in front of the rock known as Washiewe. This sacred rock possesses the five colors of the five seas and is covered by the crashing waves. ¶ The water also protects the serpents that communicate with the lightning living in the clouds. The serpents influence rainfall, which help *coamil* (the first seeds of various types of corn) grow into healthy crops. The water also protects the fish that donate their blood to help fertilize the soil for the proper growth of corn. A young girl, selected for her virtuous nature, is chosen for a special ritual in which she offers the blood of a fish to the sea goddess at an altar. A yellow flower, called *tuki*, is used by the Huicholes to paint their faces. When the corn is ready to be sown, the young girl cuts five *mazorcas*—"queen" ears of corn, each of a different color used in special rites—and ties them together with a ribbon. She spreads fish blood over the *mazorcas* to give them power. As she walks amid the

CUISINE OF THE WATER GODS

fields with the blood-soaked corn ears, the planting commences. The *mazorcas* are placed inside a knapsack and stored in a gourd for safekeeping. The shaman sings and dances until dawn, recalling for his Huichol brothers how all they eat is nourished by the water and by corn. ¶ The next day a man carries the knapsack filled with *mazorcas* to a fire tended by the young girl. The shaman places fish and *tejuino,* a fermented corn beverage that is quite strong, on an altar. As he prays for the *mazorcas* that will be sacrificed to feed the people, tamales are cooked over the flame. ¶ It is hard to capture this special time in words; this experience was so new and so magical for me. But I can tell you that it nourished my soul with the richness of ancient lore. ¶ Regards from your constant friend,

PATRICIA

OYSTER *SOPES*
SOPES DE OSTIONES

Serves 8

FOR THE CHILE PASTE
6 large ancho, dried cora, or guajillo chiles, seeded and deveined (see page 296)
1 cup water
2 large cloves garlic, peeled
1 teaspoon cumin
Salt to taste

FOR THE *SOPES*
2 pounds fresh *masa* (corn dough)
About ⅓ cup warm water
Olive oil for brushing the *comal*

FOR THE BEAN FILLING
¼ cup extra-virgin olive oil or lard
1½ cups cooked pinto beans, pureed (see page 102)
Salt to taste

FOR THE SAUCE
⅔ cup olive oil
¾ pound ripe tomatoes, chopped
Salt to taste
1 medium red onion, peeled and thinly sliced
2 manzano, Carib, or habanero chiles, roasted, peeled (see page 296), and thinly sliced

FOR THE GARNISH
1 cup olive oil
24 large oysters, shucked
Fresh lime juice to taste
½ pound potatoes, cooked, peeled, and diced

The splendid Nayarit coast is well suited for the cultivation of the rock oysters and the *ostión de placer,* or placer oyster (*Crassostrea corte siensis*). In the regions of Boca de Camichín and San Blas, the mixture of sweet water from inlets and salty ocean water permits the cultivation of oysters in *balsas,* wooden racks that float on the water like rafts. The rock oyster is known for its great size and is sold from small carts near the beach. These delicious oysters are often drizzled with lemon juice and very spicy *salsa huichol,* a seafood cocktail sauce. The placer oyster (also called *ostión manglar*) is more common and appears in many dishes. These oysters may be fried; seasoned with red onion and *chilacates* (Anaheim chiles) or cora or guajillo chiles; used in tacos; or garnished with lemon, *huichol* sauce, and the spicy round yellow chile known as manzano. *Sopes,* thick, round pinched tortillas, are deep-fried and then topped with a variety of ingredients and sauces.

PREPARE THE CHILE PASTE: Heat a *comal* or a heavy skillet and lightly toast the chiles. Rinse the chiles in running water and soak them in the 1 cup water for 8 minutes. Puree the chiles, soaking water, garlic, and cumin in a food processor or a blender. Season the chile paste with salt and set aside.

PREPARE THE *SOPES:* Place the *masa* in a deep bowl and start kneading until it becomes soft. Add the water a little at a time and knead until the dough is smooth and velvety. Let the dough rest for 8 minutes.

Preheat the *comal* for 10 minutes. Line a tortilla press with plastic wrap. Form 24 balls of dough, using about 1 tablespoon of the dough for each. Place a dough ball between the plastic sheets and press lightly. Open the press, flip the tortilla over, and press lightly again. Open the tortilla press and peel away the plastic wrap. Repeat with the remaining dough balls. Lightly brush the hot *comal* with the oil and slide a small tortilla onto the *comal*. Cook for 1 minute and flip with a spatula. Cook for another minute. When the tortilla starts to puff, remove from the *comal* and pinch the edges to form a small crust. Repeat with the remaining tortillas.

PREPARE THE BEAN FILLING: Preheat a medium skillet. Add the ¼ cup oil and the bean puree and cook until the mixture becomes thick. Taste, season with salt if necessary, and set aside.

PREPARE THE SAUCE: Heat a large skillet and add ⅓ cup of the oil and the tomatoes. Season with salt and cook until the sauce thickens; set aside. Heat another skillet, add the remaining ⅓ cup oil, and sauté the red onion and the chiles very briefly. Season with salt, then add the mixture to the tomato sauce and cook until the liquid is reduced. Taste and correct the seasoning.

TO SERVE: Preheat the remaining oil in a frying pan. Coat the *sopes* with the reserved chile paste and fry in the hot oil until crisp. Drain on paper towels. Preheat the *comal*. Top the *sopes* with a layer of beans and place on the hot *comal*. Then top the filled *sopes* with the oysters, lime juice, tomato sauce, diced potatoes, lettuce, red onions, and *queso fresco*. Remove with a spatula and transfer the *sopes* to a large serving platter. Garnish with the radish flowers and serve immediately.

Note: See pages 309 to 310 for more information on making the dough and using the tortilla press.

2½ cups finely shredded Bibb lettuce, refrigerated

1½ medium red onions, peeled and thinly sliced

1½ cups crumbled *queso fresco* or feta cheese

16 radishes, cut into flowers and chilled in ice water for 2 hours (see page 298)

CRAB SOUP WITH GINGER
SOPA DE JAIBA AL JENGIBRE

Serves 8

At sunrise, fishermen ready their wooden boats with nets and fishing rods. They come down by the mangrove trees, just on the side of their huts, before setting out onto the water to hunt for crabs. A touch of the Orient gives this recipe a unique flavor. Ginger was brought to Mexico by sailors running commerce between Macao and the Philippines and San Blas. Ginger works surprisingly well with traditional Mexican ingre-

FOR THE STOCK

18 cups water

2 heads garlic, halved but not peeled

20 scallions, tied together

1 knob fresh ginger (2 inches), peeled

CONTINUED

80 sprigs cilantro, tied together

Salt to taste

1½ pounds medium white, blue, or tiger shrimp, peeled and deveined (reserve the shells for the stock)

8 large crabs, cleaned (break open the undersides of the crabs and remove the organs but leave the meat) and claws cracked

FOR THE SOUP BASE

6 dried guajillo or New Mexico chiles, seeded and deveined (see page 296)

4 dried de árbol or japonés chiles, seeded and deveined

4 medium cloves garlic, peeled

1 medium white onion, peeled and cut into pieces

1 knob fresh ginger (1 inch), peeled

⅓ cup olive oil

Salt to taste

80 cilantro sprigs, tied together

½ cup fresh *masa* (corn dough)

FOR THE SHRIMP BALLS

3 eggs, beaten

3 tablespoons fresh *masa* or 2 tablespoons *masa harina* (dehydrated *masa* flour)

2 tablespoons grated fresh ginger

3 tablespoons finely chopped cilantro

Salt to taste

dients like tomatoes and chiles to create this favorite Pacific coast dish.

PREPARE THE STOCK: Bring the water to a boil in a large stockpot. Add the garlic heads, scallions, ginger, and cilantro and season with a small amount of salt. Add the shrimp shells and cook uncovered for 25 minutes. Add the crabs and the shrimp and cook for 4 minutes. Set aside to steep uncovered for 20 minutes. Remove the shrimp and the crabs and strain the remaining solids from the stock. Discard the solids. There should be about 4½ quarts of seafood stock.

PREPARE THE SOUP BASE: Preheat a *comal* or a heavy skillet for 10 minutes over medium heat. Lightly toast both kinds of chiles separately, turning them often so they don't burn. Soak the chiles in hot water until soft, about 15 minutes. Drain and puree the chiles with the garlic, onion, and ginger and 1½ cups of the seafood stock. Strain. Preheat a wok or a deep casserole. Add the oil and the chile sauce and season with a small amount of salt. Add the cilantro and simmer uncovered for 20 minutes or until the sauce thickens a bit. Dissolve the *masa* in 1 cup of the hot seafood stock. Strain and add the liquid to the chile sauce along with all but 2 tablespoons of the remaining hot seafood stock. Simmer for 20 minutes.

PREPARE THE SHRIMP BALLS: Puree the reserved cooked shrimp. Put the shrimp puree in a large bowl and mix in the eggs, the *masa,* and the reserved 2 tablespoons of seafood stock. Add the ginger and the cilantro and season with salt. Work this shrimp paste until all the ingredients are blended together. Form the dough into marble-size balls. Drop them into the stock and cook uncovered for 10 minutes. Add the reserved crabs and continue cooking for another 10 minutes.

TO SERVE: Ladle into deep bowls and serve with freshly made tortillas.

TLAXTIHUILLI (SHRIMP STEW)
TLAXTIHUILLI

Serves 6 to 8

Since pre-Hispanic times, the shrimp fishermen of the island of Mexcaltitán have readied their canoes and small boats at dawn with *chinchorros*, netlike sacks they plunge into the sea to catch shrimp. Fresh seafood is the key to this Aztec soup. The fresh shrimp are traditionally cooked in their shells and peeled at the table. However, the shrimp can be peeled before cooking if desired.

Preheat a *comal* or a heavy skillet for 20 minutes. Clean and devein the chilacate chiles. Toast them lightly, stirring very fast and pressing slightly with the back of a spoon. Do the same thing with the de árbol chiles. Rinse both kinds of chiles and cover with the 4 cups hot water. Soak for 1 hour. Puree the chiles with a small amount of hot water, the garlic, and the cumin until the mixture forms a smooth paste. Heat the oil in a deep casserole. Add the chile paste and cook uncovered over medium heat until thick. Season with salt.

Place the *masa* in a deep bowl and moisten with about 1 1/2 cups of the hot water until the mixture has a light consistency. Strain and add the liquified *masa* to the chile paste and continue cooking the paste uncovered for 10 minutes. Add the shrimp and the toasted shrimp powder and cook for 5 minutes. Add the remaining hot water and continue cooking for 15 minutes. Taste and correct the seasoning. Serve the *tlaxtihuilli* in deep bowls with limes on the side. Accompany with fresh corn tortillas.

12 dried chilacate, ancho, guajillo, or cascabel chiles
4 dried de árbol or other small red chiles
4 cups hot water
4 large cloves garlic, peeled
1 1/2 teaspoons cumin seeds
1/3 cup olive oil, lard, or vegetable oil
Salt to taste
2/3 cup fresh *masa* (corn dough)
10 to 12 cups hot water or fish stock
2 pounds shrimp or prawns, deveined, with shells on
1/2 cup dried shrimp (available at Asian markets), toasted in a warm skillet and ground
Limes for garnish

STUFFED SQUASH WITH TOMATO SAUCE
CALABAZA RELLENA CON SALSA DE JITOMATE

Serves 12

FOR THE SQUASH

8 cups water
2 medium white onions, peeled and sliced
4 medium cloves garlic, peeled
1 large round green squash (about 6 pounds)
²/₃ cup olive oil
Salt to taste
¹/₂ cup finely chopped white onion
12 eggs, beaten
¹/₄ cup crème fraîche
¹/₃ cup clarified butter

FOR THE TOMATO SAUCE

¹/₂ cup dried chiltepín, de árbol, or japonés chiles
¹/₂ cup vegetable oil plus additional for stir-frying
Salt to taste
4 small cloves garlic, peeled
8 cups water
15 large ripe plum tomatoes
4 medium white onions, peeled and quartered
2 white onion slices

Several kinds of squash are grown in Nayarit, ranging in diameter from less than an inch to 3 feet. With smooth yellow skin and soft flesh, squash is greatly appreciated by local cooks. Gourds have a thicker skin marked by small channels. They are often used by the Indians to transport water on long journeys or as household storage vessels for seeds and spices. Gourds also keep tortillas fresh and are used in many ceremonies. They may be employed as cups and dishes, depending on their size and shape, as well as instruments. When painted, carved, and finished with gold or silver, gourds are transformed into works of art called *chacuales*.

PREPARE THE SQUASH: Bring the water, onions, and garlic to a boil in a large pot. Rub the squash with ¹/₃ cup oil and salt and add it to the pot. Cover and simmer for 1¹/₂ hours. Use 2 large spoons to remove the cooked squash from the water and cool it on a rack. Cut the top open and remove the seeds. Scoop the pulp out with a spoon and chop fine; set the shell aside. Heat the remaining ¹/₃ cup oil in a casserole. Add the onion and cook uncovered until wilted. Add the squash, eggs, crème fraîche, and salt to taste and cook until the eggs are fluffy. Stuff the egg mixture back into the squash shell and baste with the clarified butter. Replace the top on the squash and reheat in a 400°F oven for 10 minutes before serving.

PREPARE THE TOMATO SAUCE: Stir-fry the chiles in a bit of oil to release their flavor. Do not overcook or they will become bitter. Blend the chiles with salt and the garlic in a mortar, spice grinder, or food processor and reserve. Bring the water to a boil in a large casserole. Add the tomatoes and the onions and cook for 20 minutes. Puree the vegetables with half of the cooking water and strain. Heat the ¹/₂ cup oil in a large casserole. Cook the onion slices until brown and then discard. Add the strained tomato sauce a little at a time. Season with salt and simmer uncovered for 15 minutes. Add the chile mixture and continue cooking over low heat for 15 minutes. If the sauce becomes too thick, add some water.

TO SERVE: Transfer the stuffed squash to a large, deep platter. Baste the inside of the squash with some of the sauce. Cover the squash with the top and serve with the remaining sauce and flour or corn tortillas.

AZUFRADO OR PINTO BEANS WITH CHORIZO AND SARDINES
FRIJOLES AZUFRADOS CON CHORIZO Y SARDINAS

Serves 10

Many types of beans are cultivated in Nayarit. One of the most popular is the *azufrado*, a special white bean streaked with yellow that is native to the region. This unusual combination of beans, sausage, chiles, and sardines makes for a particularly hearty dish. Pinto or red beans may be substituted.

PREPARE THE BEANS: Preheat a wok or a heavy skillet for 5 minutes. Add the lard and heat for 3 minutes. Add the chiles and stir-fry until crisp; set aside. Add the sausage and sauté until crisp. Add the pureed beans and simmer uncovered over low heat until semi-thick. Add the sardines and season with salt and *salsa huichol* or canned chile strips. Simmer uncovered over low heat for 10 minutes.

PREPARE THE GARNISH: Heat the oil in a frying pan. Add the garlic and sauté until brown; discard. Fry the sardines on each side for 4 minutes or until crisp. Season with salt.

TO SERVE: Scoop the beans onto a deep platter and garnish with the cheese. Place the fried sardines across the top of the beans and the fried tortillas along the sides of the platter along with the olives. Serve immediately with more *salsa huichol* or chile strips on the side.

FOR THE BEANS

- ½ cup lard or vegetable oil
- 2 ounces dried de árbol or japonés chiles
- ½ pound chorizo sausage
- 1 pound *azufrado* beans or baby white, pinto, or red beans, cooked with onion and garlic and pureed (see page 121)
- 6 canned or freshly steamed sardines, bones removed

Salt to taste

Salsa huichol or seafood cocktail sauce to taste, or canned chipotle or jalapeño chiles, cut into fine strips

FOR THE GARNISH

- ½ cup olive oil
- 4 large cloves garlic, peeled
- 12 large sardines

Salt to taste

- ½ pound *queso fresco* or feta cheese, crumbled
- 18 tortillas, fried until crisp
- 1 cup small pimiento-stuffed olives

SLOW-GRILLED WHOLE FISH
PESCADO ZARANDEADO
Serves 6

FOR THE GRILL
- 2 pounds charcoal, mesquite, or mangrove wood

FOR THE FISH
- ³/₄ cup light soy sauce
- ¹/₂ cup olive oil
- ¹/₃ cup fresh lime juice
- 4 fresh serrano chiles, finely chopped
- 1 tablespoon dried oregano leaves
- 1 teaspoon black peppercorns
- 4 pounds whole fish (red snapper, sea bass, porgy, or mullet), cut along the spine and scaled

FOR THE SAUCE
- 4 cups water
- 1¹/₂ pounds ripe tomatoes, chopped
- 8 fresh serrano chiles
- 3 large cloves garlic, peeled
- 1 medium white onion, peeled and quartered
- Salt to taste

FOR THE GARNISH
- 2 cucumbers, peeled and thinly sliced with a mandoline
- 2 medium white onions, peeled and thinly sliced with a mandoline

Zarandeado fish is a pre-Hispanic dish that comes from the island of Mexcaltitán. The fish is grilled very slowly over a gentle fire in a *zaranda*, a brick or adobe oven. Children's voices fill the local streets with offers of freshly smoked fish to passersby. Laurel leaves give the fire (and the fish) a special character, while crossing palm fronds imprint a decorative grill pattern on the fish. As for the mangrove wood fire, it lends its distinctive flavor. This coastal dish traditionally is prepared with porgy (*Lutjanus griseus*), also known as gray snapper, or striped mullet (*Mugil cephalus*). Both fish have very little fat in their skins so they will not burn during cooking. Sea bass and red snapper are other good choices. To prepare the fish, cut it open along the spine, so that the marinade can easily be absorbed by the flesh.

PREPARE THE FIRE: Place the charcoal in the grill and start the fire with paper and matches. Wait for the coals to become white and the flames to subside, about 1 hour. The fish must be cooked over a gentle fire.

PREPARE THE FISH: Combine the soy sauce, olive oil, lime juice, chiles, oregano, and black peppercorns. Place the fish in a shallow baking dish and pour the marinade over the fish and let stand for 30 minutes. Cook the fish over a low fire and baste with the marinade. Continue basting until the fish is cooked. The skin must be crisp and the flesh should be moist and flaky.

PREPARE THE SAUCE: Meanwhile, bring the water to a boil in a medium saucepan. Add the tomatoes, chiles, garlic, and onion and cook uncovered for 20 minutes. Cool and puree the sauce in a blender or a food processor. Season with salt.

TO SERVE: Transfer the fish to a large platter and cover with the tomato sauce. Garnish the edges of the platter with the cucumber and onion slices and serve with freshly made or deep-fried tortillas.

RANCHEROS SHRIMP SAN BLAS STYLE
CAMARONES RANCHEROS ESTILO PUERTO MAGICO, SAN BLAS

Serves 8

Vibrant vegetation in the form of large coconut palms adorns this tropical seaside village. San Blas is a living green canyon. Near the sea, there are estuaries and dark mangrove swamps where exposed tree roots are crusted with oysters. Coconuts, papayas, bananas, and mangoes grow everywhere. In town, the bells of San Blas call to ships that pass by the harbor on their way to Mazatlán. They play a wild melody that enchants all who can hear them ring over the blue-green waters.

Heat the oil in a deep casserole or a wok. Brown the garlic cloves and discard. Add the chopped onions and the chiles and cook uncovered over medium heat until the onions are translucent. Season with a small amount of salt while cooking. Add the chopped tomatoes and cook until the sauce thickens somewhat, about 35 minutes. Add the shrimp and cook for 3 minutes. Add the fish stock and continue cooking, covered, for 6 minutes over medium heat. Reseason with salt and cook until the sauce is thick, about 5 minutes. Do not overcook the shrimp.

TO SERVE: Serve the shrimp in a clay pot *(cazuela)* or in a deep dish with red or pinto beans, flour or corn tortillas, and pickled manzano chiles.

- 1/2 cup olive oil
- 4 large cloves garlic, peeled
- 2 medium white onions, peeled and finely chopped
- 8 fresh serrano chiles or fresh de árbol chiles

Salt to taste
- 14 ripe plum tomatoes, finely chopped
- 2 pounds large shrimp, peeled and deveined
- 1 cup fish stock

SPICY SAN BLAS MANGOES
MANGO PETACON CON CHILE

Serves 6

6 skewers or chopsticks with
   sharp ends
6 large ripe mangoes
Fresh lime juice to taste
Chile powder to taste
Salt to taste

Near San Blas, enormous mango plantations raise as many as 6 varieties of this tropical fruit. The hot coastal land (*tierra caliente*) is shaded by fronds from these beautiful trees. White blossoms cover the trees at the start of the season. After the fruit starts to grow, oval shapes in shades of yellow and red hang from the trees and a sweet aroma fills the fields. Buy mangoes several days in advance and let them soften and ripen at room temperature.

Insert a skewer into each unpeeled mango at the bottom of the pit. Peel the mango and, with a sharp knife, make vertical incisions in the flesh. Slowly separate the sections from the pit with the knife so that the flesh is attached at one end and forms a flower shape.

TO SERVE: Place the skewered mangoes in wide bowls. Sprinkle with lime juice, chile powder, and salt. The flavors will intensify with time, so set aside at room temperature for a period, if desired.

BANANA-NUT CAKE
PANQUE DE PLÁTANO Y NUEZ
Serves 8 to 10

Lush banana ranches dot the Nayarit coast. The labor-intensive farming requires the energy of the Huicholes, Coras, and Tepehuanes, who cultivate as many as 10 varieties in the region. Dried bananas, called banana *pancles,* are a local specialty. They often are served with a dark brown sugar or *panocha* syrup perfumed with anise and cinnamon.

Preheat the oven to 350°F. Butter and flour a 6-cup loaf pan. Cream the butter and the sugar with an electric mixer. Add the eggs, one at a time, beating well after each addition. Continue beating for 3 minutes. Beat in the mashed bananas. Sift the flour 3 times with the salt, baking soda, and cinnamon. Add the flour mixture along with the crème fraîche, nuts, and vanilla to the batter. Beat until smooth and thick. Pour the batter into the prepared pan. Bake for 1 hour or until golden brown. Cool completely on a rack and unmold.

TO SERVE: Place the cake on a platter and sprinkle with confectioners' sugar.

VARIATION: This cake can be kept covered in the refrigerator and sliced thin. Spread cream cheese flavored with bananas and nuts on the slices to make banana-nut sandwiches.

⅔ cup butter, softened and cut into pieces
¾ cup plus 3 tablespoons sugar
3 eggs
1⅓ cups mashed ripe bananas
2 cups flour
½ teaspoon salt
1 teaspoon baking soda
1 teaspoon cinnamon
¼ cup crème fraîche or sour cream
1 cup walnuts or pecans, finely chopped
1 tablespoon vanilla extract
Confectioners' sugar

PINOLE (RED CORN BEVERAGE)
PINOLE DE MAÍZ ROJO

Serves 10

6 cups dried red corn or white or blue corn

10 Mexican cinnamon sticks (each about 5 inches long) or regular cinnamon sticks

2 to 3 cups brown sugar or grated *piloncillo* (solidified brown sugar), or to taste

14 cups milk or water

Pinole is a corn powder used daily in Cora and Huichol ceremonies. According to the Indians' traditions, various corns—black, blue, yellow, white, and red—have different culinary uses. Dried red corn is toasted to make *esquites*, which are usually eaten with lime, salt, and ground chiles. From the toasted corn, Indians make a delicious and nutritious powder. The powder is quite fine, so it must be eaten in small quantities. In this recipe, the toasted corn is ground with cinnamon and brown sugar. The powder can be eaten as is or made into a beverage, also known as *pinole*, with the addition of water or milk.

Preheat a large *comal* or a wok for 10 minutes. Add the corn and toast until lightly colored. Add 6 of the cinnamon sticks and toast briefly. Grind the corn, cinnamon, and sugar in batches in a spice mill until powdery. In a large, heavy pan, bring the milk to a boil with the remaining 4 cinnamon sticks. Simmer uncovered for 15 minutes. Put the *pinole* in a medium bowl and start whisking in the milk until the mixture becomes a smooth paste. Add the remaining milk and whisk until the mixture is smooth and slightly thick. Return the liquid to the pan and bring to a boil. Remove the pan from the heat and serve in clay mugs or coffee cups.

HIERBA ANÍS TEA
TÉ DE HIERBA ANÍS

Serves 4

This infusion is one of the most interesting in the northern states of Mexico. In Nayarit, this herb is used by the Coras in beverages for their agricultural rituals and dances. *Hierba anís* has several health properties, including the ability to calm the stomach and to promote digestion. The plant has long, jagged, elliptical leaves and yellow flowers and gives off a very strong anise aroma. The flavor, however, has lemony undertones. Besides being used in teas, the herb may be used in savory cooking or mixed with soft cheeses.

Bring the water to a rapid boil in a deep pot. Add the *hierba anís* and boil for 4 minutes. Remove the pot from the heat and cover for 3 minutes. Strain and serve from a teapot. Add honey to taste.

4 cups water
10 sprigs *hierba anís*
Honey or sugar to taste

JALISCO

PICO DE GALLO
OCTOPUS TOSTADAS
CATFISH SOUP
HOMINY WITH SHRIMP
VALLARTA-STYLE FISH
FISH COOKED ON TWIGS
QUINCE FRUIT ROLLS
TAMARIND WATER

Jalisco lies along the mid-Pacific coast and has been inhabited since pre-Hispanic times by the Nahuas, Tarascos, Olmecas, Chichimecas, and Otomíes. The name comes from the Nahuatl language and means "sandy place." The climate is generally dry and hot. Local crops include rice, myrtle, zucchini, beans (*bayo, morado,* and *flor de mayo*), corn, carrots, potatoes, cucumbers, jicama, quince, and apricots. Tequila, which is made from agave, is from Jalisco, and the region also produces the fresh cheese known as *queso panela.*

The capital city is Guadalajara, which is surrounded by a number of artisanal centers, especially Tlaquepaque, Tonalá, and Zapotan. Guadalajara itself is considered the country's "second city" and is home to important architectural sites that date back to colonial times. The city is the birthplace of many leading artists and cultural figures and is known worldwide for its contributions to music, folklore, and crafts.

Along the coast, there are several noteworthy spots like Melaque with its soft swells, Careyes with its steep cliffs, and Puerto Vallarta, a native fishing village that has been turned into a world playground. This scenic spot is blessed with splendid beaches and surrounded by lush vegetation, making for a breathtaking setting.

Sometimes memories return all by themselves, like the stars that crowd the night sky. At other times we have to loosen the nets that hold memories tight so they may swim freely and remind us of things we have forgotten. ¶ The smooth surface of Chalapa Lake recalls the times when my papa would fish for *charales*, a tasty little white fish. I have eaten it many times, battered and fried until crisp and served with lots of chile sauce. The men wash the fried fish down with Jalisco's special tequila. ¶ My father used to take me and my brothers on overnight fishing trips in the canoe. We would fill pointed baskets called *nasas* with hard, thick tortillas as bait, to lure catfish, carp, tilapia, baby *charal*, and baby whitefish. Sometimes we sold the entire catch. At other times my mama would fry the *charales* as I do now in my tiny dining room, and I would take the fried fish to market. On weekends when out-of-towners came I sold quite a lot. My sisters and I were also taught to fillet tilapia, although we were never as able as our cousin Lupe, who could fillet thirty pounds a day. Other fish were dried and sold in faraway cities. The carp was butterflied and cured so that it would stay fresh for a long time. ¶ Of course, there are *charalitos* from other waters that are sold in my village. They come from Barra de Navidad, Melaque, and Tenacatita. For my taste, those from Tenacatita are the most satisfying. Perhaps this is because I once visited the sea there. The water stretches as far as one can see. The roar of the waves and color of the sea are unlike the calm waters of my lake. They tell me that there are coral reefs and tropical fish of all colors in these waters, and eating fish like cabrilla, sole, *dorado*, mahimahi, sea bass, red snapper, spiny lobster, grouper, manta ray, prawns, jumbo shrimp, crabs, clams, tuna, and octopus. The local women bake them in their own juices, grill them, season them with lemon or de árbol chiles—I've tried all their ways. ¶ Thanks to the secrets I have learned, people come to learn the secrets from me. My name is known, and my daily work is quite hard. But from time to time at night I can sit by the water and watch the stars gather together in the sky. I can feel how close they are to me, and I recall memories of times past.

PICO DE GALLO
Serves 6

3 medium cucumbers, peeled and sliced into sticks about ¼ inch thick and 3 inches long
1 medium ripe pineapple, peeled and sliced into sticks about ¼ inch thick and 3 inches long
1 medium jicama, peeled and sliced into sticks about ¼ inch thick and 3 inches long
18 medium limes, halved
Salt to taste
Piquín chile powder (or other hot red chili powder) to taste

For many people, the name *pico de gallo* refers to a sauce made with chopped tomatoes, chilito (small chiles), onion, lime juice, salt, and cilantro. But in Jalisco, *pico de gallo* is made with vegetables (such as cucumbers, carrots, and jicama) and fruits (such as oranges, pineapples, unripe mangoes, and quinces) and sprinkled with lots of lime juice and a good quantity of chile powder. Sometimes *pico de gallo* is sold in the streets in paper cones or in deep paper cups that hold the just-sliced fruits and vegetables. This version is a popular street cart item near the piers of Puerto Vallarta.

Prepare all the ingredients and refrigerate them until serving time. Alternate the cucumber, pineapple, and jicama sticks in 6 large wineglasses. Squeeze some lime juice into the glasses and place 2 lime halves on the sides of each glass. Sprinkle with salt and chile powder to taste. Serve immediately as a salad or as an appetizer.

OCTOPUS TOSTADAS
TOSTADAS DE PULPO

Serves 6 to 8

Tenacatita Bay on the Pacific coast has an exotic beauty. There are inlets covered with wild birds such as macaws, parrots, white herons, pelicans, sea eagles, and blue herons. There also are extensive plantations of palm trees and miles of immaculate beaches. The snorkeling is splendid in coral reefs teeming with tropical fish, octopus, lobsters, and clams. *Pez aguja* (sailfish) also is found in these waters and makes a unique local ceviche. Octopus tostadas are another specialty of the region.

PREPARE THE OCTOPUS: Heat the water in a deep casserole and add the onions, garlic, oregano, bay leaves, thyme, and marjoram. Season with salt and simmer uncovered over medium heat for 20 minutes. Add the cleaned octopus and cook covered for 1½ hours or until soft. Cool. Remove the octopus from the broth and chop. Place the chopped octopus in a deep bowl and add the garnish ingredients. Toss well and marinate for 1 to 2 hours.

PREPARE THE TOSTADAS: Heat the oil in a deep frying pan. Add the tortillas one by one and fry, turning on both sides, until crisp and light brown. Drain on paper towels and put aside.

TO SERVE: Lightly coat the tostadas with the beans. Top with the marinated octopus and onion garnish and drizzle some of the marinade over the tostadas. Serve immediately or the tostadas will become soggy.

VARIATION: Instead of octopus, the tostadas can be made with one pound of cleaned crabmeat.

FOR THE OCTOPUS
- 14 cups water
- 2 medium white onions, peeled and roughly chopped
- ½ head garlic, unpeeled
- 1½ teaspoons dried oregano leaves
- 12 fresh bay leaves
- 6 sprigs thyme
- 6 sprigs marjoram
- Salt to taste
- 4 pounds octopus, cleaned and sliced on the bias into 1-inch pieces

FOR THE GARNISH
- 1½ medium white onions, peeled and thinly sliced on the bias
- 4 to 6 dried de árbol or japonés chiles, lightly toasted in a warm skillet and crumbled
- ½ cup fresh lime juice
- 1½ teaspoons dried oregano leaves, crumbled
- Dash of freshly ground black pepper
- 1 cup light soy sauce
- ⅓ to ½ cup extra-virgin olive oil, or to taste
- Salt to taste
- *Salsa búfalo, huichol, guacamaya,* or seafood cocktail sauce to taste

FOR THE TOSTADAS
- 2 cups vegetable or olive oil
- 18 thin tortillas (5 inches in diameter; use a cookie cutter to trim larger tortillas to this size)
- 1¼ cups refried pinto beans (page 121)

CATFISH SOUP
CALDO MICHI

Serves 6

3½ quarts water

8 medium carrots, peeled and sliced

3 medium white onions, peeled and diced

4 large cloves garlic, peeled and chopped

1½ pounds ripe plum tomatoes, sliced or diced

4 catfish, carp, or black sea bass heads

3 tablespoons fresh oregano leaves

8 fresh bay leaves

80 sprigs cilantro, tied together

20 sprigs basil, tied together

8 fresh serrano chiles, halved

4 small quinces or unripe yellow plums, peeled and cut into strips

Salt to taste

3 pounds catfish fillets, cut into 6 large pieces

Lime slices

Freshly made tortillas

Caldo michi is a broth based on river or lake catfish or carp. Throughout Jalisco, this soup is nourishment for the body and the soul. Early in the morning at the San Juan de Dios market in Guadalajara, one can see broths simmering away. From boiling caldrons emanate the aromas of oregano, basil, laurel, and chiles. This dish should be eaten with freshly made tortillas to soak up the flavors of the rich broth.

Bring the water to a boil in a large stockpot. Add the carrots, onions, and garlic. Simmer uncovered for 20 minutes. Add the tomatoes, fish heads, herbs, chiles, quince, and salt to taste. Simmer uncovered for 35 minutes. Add the catfish and cook for 10 minutes or until the fish flakes. Taste and correct the seasoning.

TO SERVE: Place a piece of catfish in each of 6 deep soup bowls. Ladle the boiling broth on top and serve with lime slices and tortillas.

HOMINY WITH SHRIMP
POZOLE DE CAMARÓN

Serves 10

*P*ozole has its origins in pre-Hispanic cuisine. In this recipe, hominy is mixed with appetizing fish broth and shrimp. This dish comes from a small mountain town along the Ameca River. It has traveled downstream to Puerto Vallarta, where it is popular with fishermen and landlubbers alike.

PREPARE THE STOCK: Heat the water in a large stockpot. Add the remaining ingredients. Simmer the stock uncovered for about 1½ hours. Strain and set aside. Discard the solids.

PREPARE THE *POZOLE:* Heat all but 4 cups of the strained fish stock in a large stockpot. Add the garlic, onion, and hominy and cook covered until the corn swells and the kernels open, about 40 minutes. Heat the oil in a medium skillet. Add the shrimp and sauté until cooked through; set aside. In the same pan, sauté the shrimp heads and shells until they become crisp and red. Add the reserved 4 cups fish stock and simmer uncovered for 4 minutes. Strain the stock, discarding the solids. Add the shrimp and shrimp stock to the *pozole* and cook over low heat for 5 minutes. Grind the chiles, oregano, and black peppercorns in a spice mill. Stir the mixture and salt to taste into the *pozole*. Continue cooking for 10 minutes.

TO SERVE: Ladle the soup into 10 deep bowls and serve with the tortillas and the garnishes on the side in small dishes.

Note: Cook ¼ pound dried hominy in 2 quarts of water mixed with 1½ tablespoons of ground limestone. When the corn is tender, remove from the heat, cool, and wash the kernels to remove the skins and heads. The hominy is now ready to use in the recipe. Canned hominy can be drained and used in place of dried.

FOR THE STOCK
- 5 quarts water
- 2 medium white onions, peeled and quartered
- 2 heads garlic, halved but not peeled
- ½ rib celery, cut into pieces
- 6 carrots, peeled
- 6 dried chilacate, guajillo, or New Mexico chiles, seeded and deveined (see page 296)
- 2 pounds *mojarra*, catfish, or small red snapper, cleaned
- 1 pound fish heads
- 1 tablespoon dried oregano
- 1 teaspoon black peppercorns
- Salt to taste

FOR THE *POZOLE*
- 1 head garlic, halved but not peeled
- 1 medium white onion, peeled and halved
- 1 pound cooked hominy (see Note)
- ½ cup olive oil or lard
- 1½ pounds freshwater shrimp, rock shrimp, or prawns, peeled and deveined (shells and heads reserved)
- 8 dried chilacate, guajillo, or New Mexico chiles, seeded and deveined
- 2¼ teaspoons dried oregano
- 1 teaspoon black peppercorns
- Salt to taste

FOR THE GARNISH
- 20 tortillas (6 inches in diameter), deep-fried
- 10 limes, cut in half
- 10 radishes, finely chopped
- 2 cups shredded lettuce
- Crumbled dried oregano to taste
- Chile powder to taste

VALLARTA-STYLE FISH
PESCADO A LA VALLARTA

Serves 6

FOR THE SAUCE

- 2 cups water
- 12 medium tomatillos, husked
- 6 fresh serrano chiles
- 1 medium white onion, peeled and quartered
- 3 large cloves garlic, peeled
- 4 fresh poblano chiles, seeded and finely diced
- 4 fresh poblano chiles, roasted, peeled, seeded, and deveined (see page 296), and finely diced
- 5 medium cloves garlic, peeled and roasted
- 1/3 cup olive oil
- 2 white onion slices

Salt to taste

Freshly ground black pepper to taste

- 1 cup heavy cream
- 1 cup crème fraîche
- 2 tablespoons butter, cut into pieces

FOR THE FISH

- 6 red snapper, porgy, sole, or sea bass fillets (about 6 ounces each), slightly flattened

Juice of 3 limes

Salt to taste

Freshly ground black pepper to taste

- 1 1/2 cups grated Chihuahua, *adobera*, or Monterey Jack cheese
- 1 tablespoon minced parsley

Early in the morning as the sun's rays start to shine and bells chime, fishermen dressed in coarse white cotton pants and salmon-colored shirts carry long poles loaded with fresh catch. From hooks on the sticks hang red snapper, porgy, mackerel, sea bass, and *corvina*. Slung over the fishermen's backs, the fish sway as if they were bobbing over ocean swells.

PREPARE THE SAUCE: Heat the water in a medium saucepan. Add the tomatillos, serrano chiles, onion, and raw garlic and cook uncovered for 15 minutes. Drain and puree the cooked vegetables with 1 cup of the cooking liquid, the raw and roasted poblano chiles, and the roasted garlic. Strain. Heat the oil in a wok or a large skillet and stir-fry the onion slices. Add the sauce and cook uncovered until it thickens slightly. Season with salt and pepper. Heat the creams in a medium saucepan until thick and combine with the tomatillo sauce. Taste and correct the seasoning and whisk in the butter until the sauce has a velvety consistency.

PREPARE THE FISH: Preheat the oven to 400°F. Butter 6 oven-proof soup plates and place a fish fillet in each. Sprinkle the lime juice and salt and pepper over the fish. Cover the fish with the sauce and the cheese. Bake for 8 to 10 minutes or until the fish flakes and has a moist consistency. Garnish with the minced parsley and serve immediately.

CUISINE OF THE WATER GODS

FISH COOKED ON TWIGS
PESCADO A LA VARA

Serves 6 to 8

With their many lagoons, rivers, and streams, Mismoloya and Yelapa have immense natural beauty. Small huts and restaurants on the beach complete the rustic picture. This butterflied fish is cooked directly over a wood fire. The combination with beans and a spicy de árbol chile sauce turns a simple fish preparation into an exotic dish.

PREPARE THE FISH: Preheat a *comal* or a heavy skillet and lightly toast the chiles by turning them on all sides. Soak the chiles in hot water to cover for 3 minutes. Drain chiles and puree in a food processor or blender with the garlic until smooth. Blend in the lime juice, oil, and salt. Place the fish skin side down on a cooking tray and spread the chile paste over the uncooked fish. Marinate for 1½ hours in the lowest part of the refrigerator.

PREPARE THE BEANS: Bring the water to a boil in a large pot. Add the beans, onions, garlic, and bacon. Simmer covered over low heat for 2 hours or until beans are soft. Season with salt. Heat the oil in a medium skillet. Add the chiles and stir-fry quickly. Add the chiles to the beans while they are cooking. Add the oregano and continue cooking until the beans thicken somewhat.

PREPARE THE SAUCE: Bring the water to a boil in a large saucepan. Add the tomatoes, onion, garlic, and chiles. Cook uncovered for 20 minutes and puree in a food processor or a mortar with 1½ cups of the cooking liquid. Season with salt.

PREPARE THE FIRE: Place the wood or the charcoal on a flat surface on the ground. Use paper and matches to light the fire. When the coals are giving off even heat, drive the 2 large sticks into the ground on either side of the fire. Skewer the fish with the smaller branch and let the fish rest about 10 inches above the fire. Baste occasionally with oil and rotate gently until the fish flakes, 1 to 1½ hours, depending on the fire's intensity.

FOR THE FISH

20 dried de árbol or japonés chiles
6 medium cloves garlic, peeled
Juice of 6 limes
¾ cup olive oil
Salt to taste
5 pounds whole fish (such as sea bass, porgy, red snapper, or grouper), opened like a butterfly along the back and filleted

FOR THE BEANS

16 cups water
1 pound *bayo* or pinto beans, sorted, soaked overnight in water to cover, and drained
2 medium onions, peeled and halved
4 large cloves garlic, peeled
4 ounces bacon or ½ cup lard or olive oil
Salt to taste
⅓ cup olive oil
4 dried de árbol or japonés chiles
6 dried chilacate, guajillo, or New Mexico chiles
2¼ teaspoons dried oregano leaves

FOR THE SAUCE

3 cups water
10 ripe plum tomatoes or 14 medium tomatillos, husked
1 medium white onion, peeled and chopped

CONTINUED

3 medium cloves garlic, peeled
10 dried de árbol or japonés chiles
Salt to taste

FOR THE FIRE
4 to 5 pounds wood or charcoal (see Note)
2 large sticks plus a smaller branch

Olive oil or clarified butter for basting the fish

FOR THE GARNISH
6 to 8 limes, cut into wedges
Freshly made tortillas

TO SERVE: Place the fish on a platter with the limes. Serve with the hot beans, the tomato sauce, and freshly made tortillas.

VARIATIONS: Sauce may be drizzled on the fish. Accompany the fish with sliced cucumbers or a salad.

Note: The fish may be cooked on the grill, if desired. Set the rack to the highest position and cook the fish over low heat with the lid on until it flakes, about 25 minutes.

QUINCE FRUIT ROLLS
CUERITOS DE MEMBRILLO

Makes 6 fruit rolls

2 pounds ripe quinces
2 pounds sugar plus more for sprinkling on the fruit rolls

The *membrillo*, or quince, is cultivated in warm but temperate climates and is harvested at the end of autumn, when the fruit turns a lovely shade of yellow. The fruit is used in pastries, preserves, liqueurs, and jams. This recipe is akin to American "shoe leather" but has an unusual flavor.

Bring enough water to cover the quinces to a boil in a deep casserole. Add the quinces and simmer gently covered until they are about to lose their skins. Cool, peel, and core them. Mash the pulp and strain through a thin cheesecloth or a fine-meshed sieve. Add the sugar and cook uncovered over medium heat until the paste thickens and runs in ribbons from a spoon. Sprinkle 6 medium cookie sheets with sugar. Spread a thin layer of paste on each cookie sheet and let dry for 24 hours. With a spatula, peel off the sheets of quince. Roll up the sheets, sprinkling them with a good amount of sugar as you work. Slice the thick rolls into thin round pieces and serve on a tray lined with a doily.

TAMARIND WATER
AGUA DE TAMARINDO

Serves 8

Tamarind trees, with their halo of yellow blossoms, mark the wild and exuberant vegetation near Chamela and Carelles on the Jalisco coast. In this area, tamarind often is combined with chiles, lemon, sugar, and salt and is used to relieve digestion problems. Tamarind also makes a delicious beverage that is especially refreshing during hot weather.

Bring the water to a boil in a large pot. Add the tamarind and cook uncovered for 20 minutes. Mash the soft tamarind to extract as much flavor as possible. Strain and cool the liquid. Add the sugar and ice cubes and stir until the sugar dissolves. Refrigerate for 20 minutes. Serve the tamarind water from a pitcher and pour into glasses filled with ice cubes.

24	cups water
1½	pounds dried tamarind, barely peeled and crushed
1½ to 2	cups sugar, or to taste
30	ice cubes

COLIMA

COLIMA CEVICHE

SEAFOOD COCKTAIL

MENGUICHE

LOBSTER SOUP

SHRIMP OR LANGOUSTINES IN ADOBO WITH
CABBAGE SALAD

CRABS IN ADOBO

PLANTAIN TAMALES STUFFED WITH SEAFOOD

SWEET POTATOES IN BROWN SUGAR SYRUP

COCONUT CANDIES

CHÍA OR POPPY-SEED WATER

This tiny state—the total area is just thirty-two hundred square miles—is located along the slopes of the Sierra Madre Sur mountain chain. To the north and east is Jalisco, to the south is Michoacán. The name Colima comes from a combination of Nahuatl words that signify "place conquered by our ancestors" or "where the old god dominates."

The climate along the immediate coast is hot and humid, with milder weather in the inland valleys and mountains. Two notable topographical features are the Armería River and the Colima volcano. Better-known spots, at least to foreign visitors, include the port town of Manzanillo.

Important crops are coffee, coconuts (this area is famous for its sweets made with this staple), corn, rice, sesame seeds, sugarcane, sweet potatoes, and chiles. In the valley of Tecomán are a number of inlets for fishing that are surrounded by citrus groves. This region is one of the world's leading producers of limes.

There was a torrential rainstorm in Mexico City that night. None of us wanted to go out of the house. At last, Claire decided to rearrange the drawers in her desk. Scattered in the bottom of the last drawer on the right side were some photos. She called out, "Francisca, come here and see what I found. Do you remember?" ¶ "What is it?" ¶ "Look at what we were wearing. Thank heavens we look much better today. Remember, these are from that trip we took with Papa." ¶ "Of course. We were just little girls at the time." ¶ "More like baby doves squawking in their nest. Maybe that was why Papa so often told us to keep quiet." ¶ "Remember how surprised we were when Papa told us we were going on a trip with him? We were sitting around the table eating fish balls for lunch. I can remember when Papa said we were going, just the three of us. I was so surprised that the fish ball stuck in my throat." ¶ "For me the most incredible thing was that he was taking us to Colima." ¶ "Papa said, 'Don't look at me that way. After all, this is my homeland we are talking about.' " ¶ "How envious our brothers were!" ¶ "And Mama, too. Remember the way she yelled at us. 'Stop jumping around the table and finish eating.' " ¶ "But, inside, I couldn't stop jumping for days." ¶ "Look, Francisca. Here's a photo taken when we arrived on the coast at Manzanillo." ¶ "Remember? Papa used to call it the old port." ¶ "What did he say? Oh yes, 'the world capital of sailfish.' How proud he was of his hometown." ¶ "It was great when he acted as if he knew everything." ¶ "Remember the next day, before breakfast, when he gave us a taste of that fabulous drink they called *tuba*?" ¶ "Oh, *tuba*. What a delicacy. I never thought the sap from the coconut palm tree would be so light and sweet. How did they discover such a treat? I still remember those little tortillas filled with shredded meat or fish and the *tacos de camarón* and *alfajor de coco*. I remember the langoustine soup, the *cuachala* with chicken, pasilla chiles, and *masa* dough, and the *chilaquiles* in their delicate tomato broth. And more fantastic things to drink, of pineapple and lemon, tamarind and guava; teas made of spearmint, basil, and lemon balm; aromatic coffees from Comila plantations; frothy chocolate shakes with ground almonds; and milk laced with cinnamon. And those baskets of palm leaves that were filled with different breads—white bread from Suchitlán, hard rolls, French bread, and sesame rolls. There were eggs in a light tomato sauce and beans. And do you remember how we finished our meals with warm milk and yams, pumpkin, or large plantains cooked in brown sugar syrup, served with corn and ash tamales alongside?" ¶ "You always did love to eat. Look at this one—you can tell from my hair that Mama wasn't with us. What a mess!" ¶ "Where were we? In Majagua? What a place!" ¶ "The sun was setting on the horizon while we played in the waves." ¶ "I remember the oysters, the lobster soup, the grilled crabs, the turtle in adobo sauce, and that exquisite seafood broth cooked with the essences of epazote and chipotle chiles. I also remember refreshing concoctions made with *chía* seeds, rice, guava, limes, and oranges. Remember how I ate? My mouth waters just talking about it." ¶ "Yes, you gave quite a performance." ¶ "I can't forget Cuyutlán, either." ¶ "Remember when Papa told us how the people in Cuyutlán extracted sea salt from the lagoon?" ¶ "There were herons everywhere, and the smell and colors of the sea!" ¶ "But from this beauty came the famous *ola verde,* the great green tidal wave of May 1981. We're lucky we weren't on the beach when it struck." ¶ "I remember it was at dawn when the rumbling began, as if the sea had awakened from a long dream with tremendous fury. It came nearer and nearer, and the wave grew bigger and bigger. I wanted to run, but I was paralyzed. What a sight!" ¶ "Still, I remember best what I ate. Papa was enchanted because I tasted all the specialties from his native land—swordfish and sailfish ceviche, shrimp cakes with cactus, shrimp tacos, langoustines with garlic, hominy, *pozole,* pork in a spicy chile sauce, white and ash tamales, limes stuffed with grated coconut, and pineapple trifle. Those are pounds I will never lose."

COLIMA CEVICHE
CEBICHE ESTILO COLIMA

Serves 8 to 10 as an appetizer

The discovery of burnished red clay pots with animal figures indicates the presence of an important human settlement in this zone during early pre-Hispanic times. For centuries, the Colima coast has provided the inhabitants of the entire region with nourishment. After the Conquest, the ports were converted into strategic maritime and commercial cities. Best known is the city of Manzanillo, whose name comes from the Spanish word for the fragrant local shrub that surrounds it. For many years, residents of this port struggled against blockades imposed by pirates looking to intercept treasure-laden ships coming from the Orient. The pirates are long gone, but the air of adventure persists, as the city is now home to excellent sportfishing. This recipe, which uses species native to local waters, is based on a dish prepared by Ana María Vazquez Colmenares in her book *La Cocina de Colima*.

Place the fish in a food processor and pulse until ground fine. Transfer the ground fish to a bowl, cover with the lime juice, and let stand for 1 hour. Add the onions and marinate for another 1½ hours in the refrigerator. Strain off half of the liquid from the fish mixture. Add the carrots, tomatoes, chiles, olives, vinegar, olive oil, cilantro, oregano, pepper, and salt and stir well. Blend until the ingredients make a smooth paste.

TO SERVE: Serve the ceviche in the center of a large platter and garnish with the tortillas and the cilantro. Serve with hot sauce. The ceviche may also be spooned onto individual tortilla pieces, then garnished with the cilantro and hot sauce.

2 pounds swordfish, sailfish, marlin, or sea bass fillets
Juice of 25 limes
½ pound white onions, peeled and finely chopped
½ pound carrots, peeled and finely chopped
1 pound ripe plum or round tomatoes, finely chopped
4 fresh serrano chiles, finely chopped
1 cup finely chopped pimiento-stuffed olives
½ cup white wine vinegar
1½ cups olive oil
30 sprigs cilantro, finely chopped
1½ teaspoons dried oregano leaves, crumbled
1 teaspoon black peppercorns, ground
Salt to taste
48 tortillas, cut into 1-inch pieces and either toasted or fried
48 cilantro leaves
Hot sauce (Tabasco, *huichol*, *habanero*, or *búfalo*)

SEAFOOD COCKTAIL
COCTEL DE MARISCOS
Serves 6 to 8

1½ cups small sea scallops
1½ cups shucked oysters
30 small shrimp, steamed and peeled
1 medium white onion, finely chopped
4 fresh serrano chiles, finely chopped
3 tablespoons finely chopped cilantro
Juice of 16 limes
Olive oil to taste
Salt and coarsely ground black pepper to taste
1 large ripe avocado, peeled and diced
Hot sauce (Tabasco, *huichol*, or *búfalo*)

The hot coastal climate has given rise to numerous restaurants, both large and small, under thatched palm or bamboo roofs in places like Armería, El Paraíso, and Cuyutlán in Manzanillo Bay as well as Santiago, Miramar, Mazahua, and Playa de Oro. All kinds of fresh fish and seafood are served year-round, including *chacales* (langoustines) soup; *sopes* (small tortilla cakes) filled with beans Colima style; grilled lobster, porgy, or red snapper in adobo (chile paste sauce); and fresh swordfish or mackerel ceviche; as well as numerous dishes with freshwater shrimp, special large crabs called *moyos,* rock oysters, and clams.

Place the scallops, oysters, and shrimp in a large bowl. Stir in the onion, chiles, cilantro, lime juice, olive oil, and salt and pepper. Mix well. Spoon the cocktail into 6 to 8 tall wineglasses or small bowls and top with the avocado and hot sauce. Garnish with lime slices, if desired.

MENGUICHE

Serves 10

During the colonial epoch, inhabitants of the old haciendas combined new techniques and ingredients from Spain and Asia with Mexican staples to produce a unique gastronomic mosaic. In Colima's rural zones, women still preserve this heritage that dates back to the Conquest. This recipe, an adaptation of a dish prepared by Josefína Velázquez de León, pairs Mexican chiles and tomatoes with European dairy products for a delicious side dish that is perfect with seafood entrées.

Cut the chiles into ¼-inch strips and set aside. Heat a *comal* or a heavy skillet. Roast the tomatoes on the *comal* and transfer to a blender or a food processor. Roast the garlic with a dash of salt and puree along with the tomatoes. Strain and set aside. Heat the lard in a wok or a large casserole. Add the onion slices and discard when brown. Add the chile strips and the pureed tomatoes and simmer uncovered over high heat for 20 minutes. Reduce the heat to low, add salt to taste, the crème fraîche, and the slices of cheese. Cook for another 10 minutes.

TO SERVE: Serve the *menguiche* in a deep bowl along with freshly made tortillas.

VARIATION: Sprinkle with cilantro or parsley.

- 6 poblano chiles, roasted, peeled, seeded, and deveined (see page 296)
- 2½ pounds ripe tomatoes
- 4 large cloves garlic, peeled
- Salt to taste
- 6 tablespoons lard or vegetable oil
- 2 white onion slices
- 1½ cups crème fraîche or heavy cream or plain yogurt
- 3 small *queso fresco, panela,* or mozzarella balls (about 4 ounces each), sliced

FOR THE STOCK

18 cups hot water
2 cups white wine
2 medium white onions, peeled and halved
1 head garlic, halved but not peeled
60 sprigs parsley, tied in a bunch
60 sprigs cilantro, tied in a bunch
2 medium fish heads, cleaned
1 small whole sea bass (about 1 pound), cleaned
1 small whole *mojarra* or trout (about 1 pound), cleaned
2 langoustines, cleaned with heads and shells attached
2 crabs, cleaned
4 lobster tails, shells removed and cleaned
Salt to taste

FOR THE SOUP BASE

8 large ancho chiles or dried guajillos, seeded and deveined (see page 296), and cut in half lengthwise
8 medium ripe plum tomatoes, halved
1½ medium white onions, peeled and cut into pieces
12 large cloves garlic, peeled
1 cinnamon stick (about 3 inches long), cut into pieces
4 whole cloves
½ cup olive oil
60 sprigs parsley, tied in a bunch
60 sprigs cilantro, tied in a bunch
Salt to taste

FOR THE GARNISH

½ cup small pimiento-stuffed olives
⅓ cup small capers
8 pickled jalapeño chiles, halved
8 limes, halved

LOBSTER SOUP
CALDO DE LANGOSTA

Serves 8 to 12

This succulent soup is a specialty of Boca de Pascuales, a tiny village where fishermen preserve ancient fishing practices such as trapping lobsters by hand. With the first light of the morning, expert swimmers row their boats to the rocky shoals just off the coast. The water is clear, so they can rapidly distinguish the spiny lobsters of this zone by their brownish color and orange dots, which glisten in the bright sunshine. They pluck the tasty creatures from sparkling waters much as their ancestors did.

PREPARE THE BROTH: Pour the hot water and the wine into a large kettle or a deep stockpot. Bring to a rapid boil. Add the onions, garlic, parsley, and cilantro and simmer uncovered for 10 minutes. Add the fish heads, sea bass, *mojarra*, langoustines, and crabs and simmer over medium heat for 1 hour. Add the lobster tails and cook for 6 to 8 minutes. Remove the pot from the heat and let stand for 6 minutes. Strain. Reserve the stock, shred the fish and the seafood, and discard the other solids.

PREPARE THE SOUP BASE: Lightly toast the chiles on a preheated *comal* or in a heavy skillet. Rinse the chiles and soak in hot water for 10 minutes. Drain and puree with the tomatoes, the onions, 4 of the garlic cloves, the cinnamon, and the cloves in a blender or a food processor. Add 2 cups of the reserved fish stock and strain the sauce. Preheat a large casserole for 5 minutes. Add the oil, then brown the remaining garlic cloves and discard. Add the chile soup base and simmer uncovered over low heat until the sauce is reduced to a thick paste. Heat the remaining fish stock and stir it into the thick sauce. Simmer uncovered for 25 minutes. Add the parsley and cilantro. Season with salt.

TO SERVE: Just before serving, add the reserved fish and seafood to the boiling stock and cook for 8 minutes. Remove the bunches of herbs and ladle the soup into hot soup plates. Garnish with the olives, capers, chiles, and limes.

SHRIMP OR LANGOUSTINES IN ADOBO WITH CABBAGE SALAD
CAMARONES O CHACALES EN ADOBO

Serves 6

The rivers of Colima are divided in three principal watershed areas—the Arabesco River in the east, the Armería River in the central region, and the Naranjo River in the west. Many rivers flow into the lagoons that dot the coastal zone. These clean waters are home to numerous freshwater species, including catfish, *guavina* (*Diplectrum euryplectum*), oysters, shrimp, crayfish, and *chacales*. This last variety is similar to langoustines and ranges in size from as tiny as a shrimp to as large as a lobster. Use either shrimp, langoustines, or crayfish in this delicious dish.

PREPARE THE ADOBO: Place the chiles in a bowl, cover with the water and the vinegar, and soak for 30 minutes. Drain the chiles and puree along with one-third of their soaking liquid, 6 of the garlic cloves, and the ginger, black pepper, marjoram, bay leaves, and salt in a blender or a food processor until the mixture forms a smooth paste. Preheat a wok or a deep frying pan for 5 minutes. Add the oil and brown the remaining 4 garlic cloves. Discard the garlic and add the chile paste. Season with salt and simmer uncovered until the sauce thickens.

PREPARE THE SHRIMP: Bring the water to a boil in a medium saucepan. Add the onion, garlic, ginger, salt, peppercorns, and shrimp shells and heads. Bring the water back to a boil, add the shrimp, and cook uncovered for 1 to 2 minutes, depending on their size. (They will not be fully cooked.) Scoop out the shrimp with a slotted spoon and continue simmering the liquid uncovered until it is reduced by half. (Don't reduce too much or the stock will become too salty.) Add the shrimp to the simmering adobo and cook uncovered for 4 minutes.

TO SERVE: Alternate piles of shredded red and green cabbage on 6 deep soup plates. Drizzle with the lime juice and the olive oil. Place 4 shrimp on each dish. Strain the reduced stock, add it to the adobo sauce, and simmer uncovered for about 5 minutes. Spoon the sauce over the shrimp and serve immediately with freshly made tortillas.

FOR THE ADOBO

- 6 ounces guajillo, ancho, or chimayo chiles, seeded and deveined (see page 296)
- 3/4 cup warm water
- 1/2 cup white wine vinegar or other mild vinegar
- 10 medium cloves garlic, peeled
- 1 knob fresh ginger (about 2 inches), peeled
- 1 1/2 teaspoons black peppercorns, ground
- 1 1/2 teaspoons fresh marjoram
- 2 fresh bay leaves
- Salt to taste
- 1/2 cup vegetable or olive oil

FOR THE SHRIMP

- 4 cups water
- 1/2 medium white onion, peeled
- 4 large cloves garlic, peeled
- 1 knob fresh ginger (about 2 inches), peeled
- Salt to taste
- 20 black peppercorns
- 24 large shrimp or langoustines, peeled and deveined (shells and heads reserved)

FOR THE CABBAGE SALAD

- 1/2 head red cabbage, shredded
- 1/4 head green cabbage, shredded
- Juice of 6 limes
- 1/2 cup olive oil
- Salt to taste

CRABS IN ADOBO
MOYOS EN ADOBO

Serves 8

FOR THE ADOBO

- 10 large dried guajillo, ancho, or chimayo chiles, seeded and deveined (see page 296)
- 10 large dried ancho chiles, seeded and deveined
- 8 whole allspice
- 1 tablespoon dried oregano leaves
- 4 fresh laurel or bay leaves
- 1 teaspoon cumin seeds
- 8 medium cloves garlic, peeled
- ³/₄ cup balsamic vinegar
- 1¹/₂ teaspoons salt, or to taste
- ¹/₂ cup olive oil

FOR THE CRABS

- 8 very large crabs with abundant meat (such as Dungeness)
- ¹/₂ cup olive or corn oil
- 2 cloves elephant garlic or 8 large cloves garlic, peeled and halved

FOR THE GARNISH

- 4¹/₂ cups Morisqueta Rice (page 105)
- 1 recipe Cabbage Salad (see page 89)
- 6 plum tomatoes, sliced

*M*oyos are special large crabs from Boca de Apiza, near the Naranjo and Coahuayana rivers, which run along the border with Michoacán. *Moyos* are famous along the Colima coast because they are meatier than regular crabs and can be successfully grilled without drying out. The addition of oregano, laurel, and cumin to the standard adobo sauce gives this dish a distinctive regional flavor. The crabs must marinate for at least 12 hours, so begin the recipe well ahead of time.

PREPARE THE ADOBO: Lightly toast the guajillo chiles on a hot *comal* or in a heavy skillet, but do not let them burn. Rinse the chiles and soak in hot water for 20 minutes. Repeat the process with the ancho chiles. Drain the chiles and reserve ³/₄ cup of the soaking liquid from either of the chiles. Puree the chiles and the ³/₄ cup soaking liquid in a blender or a food processor along with the remaining ingredients until the mixture forms a smooth paste. Set the adobo aside.

PREPARE THE CRABS: Wash the crabs and make an incision on each of the legs or lightly crush each leg. Open the underside of each crab, remove the stomach, and cut in half. (Ask your fishmonger to do this if you are not sure where the stomach is located.) Place the crabs in a deep dish and daub with the chile paste. Marinate in the refrigerator for at least 12 hours or overnight. Preheat a large wok or frying pan and add the oil. Heat for 5 minutes or until very hot. Add the garlic, brown, and discard. Add 4 crabs at a time and sauté, turning once, until they are cooked through, 8 to 10 minutes. Remove the cooked crabs and repeat with the remaining crabs. Return the first batch to the skillet to heat through just before serving.

TO SERVE: Place the crabs in a deep serving dish or on a large platter and accompany with Morisqueta Rice. Toss the cabbage salad with the tomatoes and serve on the side. Use your hands or shellfish crackers to remove the meat from the shells.

VARIATION: The crabs can also be grilled and served with hot freshly made tortillas.

PLANTAIN TAMALES STUFFED WITH SEAFOOD

TAMALES DE PLÁTANO MACHO

Makes about 30 tamales

Roads and paths throughout Colima are lined by fields of sugarcane, coconut palm trees, corn, and plantains. This vast abundance has given rise to many local dishes, including tamales that combine fresh corn dough (*masa*) and plantains. Wrapped in corn or banana leaves, these excellent tamales are served with beans, rice, pork, chicken, fish (like whitebait), fresh white corn, or seafood, as in this recipe. These tamales, a specialty of Cuyutlán, combine shrimp and octopus with the plantains that are cultivated throughout Colima.

PREPARE THE FILLING: Bring the water to a boil in a large saucepan. Add the octopus, onion, garlic, and herbs and simmer gently covered for 1¹/₂ hours or until the octopus is soft. Drain, reserving 3 cups of the stock and the octopus separately. Cut the cooled octopus into small pieces. Combine the chopped octopus and the shrimp in a large glass bowl. Grind the garlic in a blender or in a spice grinder with the serrano chiles, dried chiles, and toasted cumin seeds. Stir into the glass bowl along with the tomatoes, onions, poblano chiles, cilantro, and salt to taste. Mix well and let stand for 1 hour. Refrigerate until ready to use.

PREPARE THE TAMALES: Bring the water to a boil in a medium casserole. Add the sugar, salt, plantains, and bananas and cook covered until the fruit is soft, about 30 minutes. Drain and mash the plantains and the bananas into a thick puree. Work the mashed fruit with the *masa* until a smooth dough is formed. Add the reserved octopus stock to thin the *masa*, working with your hands or a whisk to prevent lumps from forming. Add salt to taste and the lard and work the dough until it has a thin, light consistency.

Place a rack in a large pot for steaming or prepare a bamboo steamer. Pour in a generous quantity of lightly salted water and place a layer of banana leaves over the rack. Heat covered for 30 minutes. Meanwhile, spread 2 heaping tablespoons of the dough into a thin layer with a spatula over each remaining ba-

FOR THE FILLING

- 14 cups water
- 2 pounds octopus, cleaned
- 1 small white onion, peeled
- ¹/₂ head garlic, peeled
- 4 sprigs marjoram
- 4 sprigs thyme
- 2 pounds medium shrimp, peeled, deveined, and finely chopped (shells and heads reserved)
- 6 large cloves garlic, peeled
- 6 fresh serrano chiles
- 10 dried de árbol or japonés chiles, stemmed, lightly toasted in a warm skillet, soaked in hot water for 20 minutes, and drained
- 10 dried cascabel, guajillo, or New Mexico chiles, stemmed, lightly toasted in a warm skillet, soaked in hot water for 20 minutes, drained, and seeded
- 1 teaspoon cumin seeds, lightly toasted
- 12 ripe plum tomatoes, finely chopped
- 1¹/₂ medium white onions, peeled and finely chopped
- 8 fresh poblano chiles, roasted, peeled, seeded, and deveined (see page 296), and finely chopped
- 3 cups cilantro leaves, finely chopped or cut into thin strips

Salt to taste

CONTINUED

  6 cups water

  1 cup sugar, or to taste

  1 teaspoon salt

  2 pounds large ripe plantains, peeled and cut into pieces

10 ripe bananas, peeled and cut into pieces

  2 pounds fresh *masa* (corn dough)

2½ tablespoons salt, or to taste

  2 cups lard or clarified butter (simmer ½ head unpeeled garlic in fat for 10 minutes and cool for 1 hour to give dough extra flavor, optional)

  4 packages fresh banana or plantain leaves, boiled and cut into 10-inch squares

nana leaf and top with some marinated seafood. Fold one side of the leaf over the filling and fold the other side of the leaf to make a packet. Close the edges and tie the sealed package with string or thin strips of banana leaf. Place the tied bundles in the prepared steamer, leaving some space for steam to rise through the layers of tamales. Cover the tamales with more leaves and a large dishcloth. Place the lid on the steamer and cook for 1½ hours or until the tamales can be peeled from the leaves when the packages are opened.

TO SERVE: Remove the tamales from the steamer and transfer to a large platter. Or, serve the tamales directly from a bamboo steamer covered with a banana leaf cut to fit over the steamer. Accompany with ice-cold beer or a white wine with some sweetness.

SWEET POTATOES IN BROWN SUGAR SYRUP
CAMOTES ENMIELADOS

Serves 6

Steamed or grilled sweet potatoes flavored with brown sugar or *piloncillo* syrup are a familiar breakfast in Colima. This substantial treat is always accompanied by a glass of raw milk. The combination offers a vigorous start to the day.

PREPARE THE SWEET POTATOES: Preheat the oven to 400°F. Brush the peeled sweet potatoes with the melted butter and wrap each in aluminum foil. Bake until soft, about 1½ hours.

PREPARE THE BROWN SUGAR SYRUP: Bring the water to a boil in a medium saucepan. Add the brown sugar, cinnamon sticks, and cloves and simmer uncovered for about 45 minutes or until the syrup has a thick consistency. Remove the cinnamon sticks and cloves.

TO SERVE: Place the sweet potatoes on a platter and drizzle with the syrup. Serve with glasses of cold milk.

FOR THE SWEET POTATOES

- 3 medium sweet potatoes (about 10 ounces each), peeled
- 3 tablespoons melted butter

FOR THE BROWN SUGAR SYRUP

- 3 cups water
- 4 cups brown sugar or grated *piloncillo* (solidified brown sugar)
- 4 cinnamon sticks (each about 6 inches long)
- 8 whole cloves

COCONUT CANDIES
ALFAJOR

Serves 6 to 8

3 fresh coconuts or 6 cups unsweetened shredded coconut
2¼ pounds sugar
2 cinnamon sticks (each about 6 inches long)
1¾ cups water
Pink or red food coloring
40 *obleas* (thin disks similar to Communion wafers)

The first seeds from the coconut palm tree were brought to Colima in the year 1569 by Álvaro de Mendaña de Neira on his expedition from the Solomon Islands. The exploitation of the coconut gave rise to a whole new culture in the region, one devoted to securing nature's bounty from this beautiful tropical plant. One of the most important techniques is the extraction of sap that is then fermented and used in regional dishes such as *tatemado* (a combination of guajillo chiles, spices, and coconut sap), pig's feet, and fish and seafood *escabeches*. Coconut pulp is employed in the making of peerless sweets from Colima like *ante* (a triflelike dessert); *alfajor* (a candied coconut confection); limes stuffed with a mixture of coconut, eggs, milk, and sugar; and *atoles* (corn beverages). Filipinos supplied the labor that originally ran the region's coconut industry. These men, who were familiar with the ways of this magnificent plant, showed locals the methods for obtaining *tuba* (the sap) from the heart of the palm tree before it flowered and for refining this liquid into a delicious culinary ingredient.

Preheat oven to 350°F and bake the coconuts for 20 minutes or until cracks develop in the skin. When cool enough to handle, peel and grate the flesh very fine. Spread the coconut over a baking sheet or a large platter and let dry for several days. If using shredded coconut, grate in a spice grinder.

Combine the sugar, cinnamon, and water in a medium saucepan. Cook uncovered until the syrup reaches the softball stage, about 234°F on a candy thermometer. (To test, drop ½ teaspoon of the syrup into a glass of cold water. When the syrup is at the correct temperature, you should be able to gather the sugar into a soft ball with your fingers.) Remove the pan from the heat and beat in the grated coconut until the mixture forms a smooth thick paste. Remove the cinnamon sticks. Separate the coconut candy paste into 2 portions and add food coloring to 1 portion and work with a wooden spoon until the paste is bright pink. Line the bottom and the sides of an 8-by-4-inch metal mold with sides that open with the *obleas.* Spread the white coconut paste evenly into the mold and cover with the pink paste. Let the candy dry until it hardens. Unmold and cut the candy into triangles or small petits fours.

CHÍA OR POPPY-SEED WATER
AGUA DE CHÍA

Serves 8

Chía, a small sage seed used in Colima since pre-Hispanic times, comes in several varieties. One type has medicinal properties (it can cure stomachaches), while another has culinary uses. Edible *chía* seeds are called *bate,* from the Spanish word for "beat." The seeds are added to water and whisked (or beaten) continuously until a smooth, thick beverage is produced.

Place the *chía* in a pitcher or mixing bowl, add the water, and mix slowly but constantly to prevent the formation of lumps. Let stand. When the seeds have puffed slightly (after about 1 hour), stir in the lime juice and sugar to taste. (If using a mixer, pour beverage into a pitcher.) Add the ice cubes and serve in tall glasses with more ice.

1 cup *chía* or poppy seeds, toasted
16 cups water
Juice of 14 limes
Sugar or honey to taste
20 ice cubes

MICHOACÁN

CEVICHE MICHOACANO

BABY LAKE WHITEFISH TACOS

BEAN TAMALES

RICE WITH CLAMS

MORISQUETA RICE

OCTOPUS *RANCHEROS*

STEAMED FISH WITH TOMATILLO–BLACK PASILLA
CHILE SAUCE

FRIED WHITEFISH WITH PÁTZCUARO SALAD

MICHOACÁN MOLE WITH CHEESE TACOS

QUINCE FRUIT CANDY

ZAMORAN STRAWBERRY PUNCH

Michoacán is located along the central Pacific coast, due west from the state of Mexico. This land was originally inhabited by the Mazahuas, Otomíes, Nahuas, Matlazincas, and Tarascos. This last tribe has a particularly rich and significant cultural history. The name Michoacán comes either from the Nahuatl word for fish—hence, "the place of fisherman"—or from the Tarascan phrase for "near the water."

In the mountainous areas of the state, the climate is temperate. This zone is home to Zitácuaro, site of large lakes perfect for fishing, swimming, or duck hunting. The coastal climate is hot, and the region is bounded by impressive cliffs and waters both rough and placid.

The inhabitants of modern Michoacán evince their Tarascan heritage through the region's varied cuisine, which depends on rice, wheat, sugarcane, and cacao. Fruits also are quite important to the local diet, especially quince, strawberries, melons, guavas, papayas, coconuts, *chicozapotes,* and black *zapotillos.*

My life has been a curious one. I arrived in these lands thinking that I would teach. But as it happened, I was the one who learned so much. The peoples of this land—who live in the pine-covered mountains, along the shores of crystal-clear lakes, on the plains, and along the coast—have taught me about their heritage and the ancient traditions of this beautiful region. ¶ My friend, I came here as a very young man, full of desire but without much direction. I can recall my first Day of the Dead here in Pátzcuaro. Women, men, and children carried enormous bunches of marigolds to adorn their small boats. Candles were placed in the boats to illuminate the way for souls in pain, who journey at night. At dawn, the boats headed toward the largest island in the lake, Janitzio. ¶ Through my friendship with Don Macario—you must meet him someday—I was able to travel in his family's boat. I could hear impassioned voices in the distance singing in Purhé—Pirekuas telling of their history and their heritage. With the same devotion, they offered their dead relatives the foods they had enjoyed most in life, whether it was *tamales tarascos* (corn tamales with beans), *uchepos* (corn tamales made with fresh corn leaves), *corundas de Zacapú* (corn *masa* tamales wrapped in triangular corn or banana leaves), blue *atole* (a corn beverage made with milk or water), *mole Michoacano* (made with mulatos chiles, bread, garlic, tomatoes, almonds, cinnamon, ginger, coriander, and sesame seeds), *mole esperanza* (with pasillas, roasted poblanos, tomatoes, baby zucchini, and oregano), *huruchaurapti* (a tender white fish), *mojarra patzuarense* (deep-fried *mojarra*), blackberry tamales, *nacatamales* (blessed tamales), *panes de huesitos* (bone breads), or foamy Michoacán chocolate (ground and mixed by hand with sugar and *charanda* liqueur). ¶ By the water, *cayucos*—flat-bottomed boats made of pine, silver fir, or spruce—were filled with nets that the fishermen wield like extensions of their hands. The name Michoacán, as I am sure you know, means "place of the fishermen." There were small nets called *cherémecuas*, just 15 meters long, and larger nets called *warukwas,* almost 100 meters long, and even *guaromutacuas,* which look like butterflies. On the surface of the water the nets made a tapestry. Nets adorn the beaches, too, as they dry in the hot midday sun. ¶ Not too long ago, these nets were made from threads colored by natural dyes made from cochineal (a bright red insect that lives on cactus plants), indigo plants, or organo cacti. Sadly, like so many other traditions, the recipes for these natural dyes and essences have been forgotten with time. But regard for the local culture is still strong. When I came to this region, life was much as it had been centuries ago. The people maintained ancient traditions with pride. I tried to teach new generations of Tarascos about "new" ways they could adopt without abandoning the old beliefs, which have the force of centuries. Certainly their bloody struggle with the Mexicans to preserve their culture could never be forgotten. ¶ Don Macario once told me about the time when he was a young boy and the tribal elder shared with him the secrets of the water, as they had been passed down to him. The fishermen know how to interpret the blowing of the winds and the patterns of algae that form like flowers on the lake surface. They can predict when rain is approaching or when sunshine will prevail. ¶ Of course, fishing is accomplished mostly by moonlight. The rays of Nanakutsi (as the moon is called in the local language) guide the fishermen, keeping them from the shoals. Not surprisingly, the moon is a symbol of fertility for these people. Of course, when there is no moon, the boats remain on shore. ¶ My friend, I once made a journey to the ocean from here. What an extraordinary coast! The high mountains seemed to tumble right into the water. The furious waves sculpted figures in the cliffs. Yet Boca de Apiza is quiet, protected from the deafening roar of the ocean by a chain of seven small islands, where descendants of the Nahuas lead a pleasurable life amid the shade of coconut, mangrove, and banana trees. Gentle streams and still estuaries create an atmosphere that is quite different from the rough Pacific coast. Monarch butterflies find refuge in the woods here during winter. Local fishermen prepare their nets to catch porgy, sea bass, mullet, red snapper, crayfish, and baby shark. In the marshy tidelands, they look for clams, crabs, oysters, and turtles, which return in October or November to spawn on the sandy beaches. Almost extinct, this species is now protected so that it may lay its eggs undisturbed. Other unusual species inhabit the magical universe of the Tarascos. ¶ Spend some time here and you, too, will start to learn the secrets of the region. If I can help you in any way, let me know. I am always at your service. Remember, I came here as a teacher but I remain here gladly as a student.

CEVICHE MICHOACANO
CEBICHE MICHOACANO
Serves 10

The Michoacán coast is covered by palm trees that shake defiantly in the wind. Early in the morning underneath the fresh shade from the trees, the fishermen prepare simple and exquisite dishes to comfort themselves after a long night's work. In this state, they catch species like sailfish, porgy, mackerel, red snapper, sea bass, shad, and baby shark, which all can be used in appetizers like this. Men go out to sea in glass-bottomed motorboats equipped with ropes, traps, nets, and the other tools necessary for their work. Snorkelers are in charge of snaring other species like lobster, octopus, oysters, and clams.

PREPARE THE CEVICHE: Put the fish in a glass bowl. Toss with the lime juice and let stand for about 30 minutes. Season with salt, oregano, and olive oil. Set aside.

PREPARE THE GUACAMOLE: Scoop out the avocado flesh with a spoon and place it in a stone or clay mortar or in a deep bowl. Mash the avocado with a pestle or a spoon until the consistency is coarse. Stir in the onions, chiles, and lime and zucchini

FOR THE CEVICHE
2½ pounds fish fillets (such as mackerel, sea bass, red snapper, porgy, or sailfish), cleaned and cut into ¼-inch-thick pieces
Juice of 20 limes
Salt to taste
Crumbled dried oregano leaves to taste
Olive oil to taste

FOR THE GUACAMOLE
4 ripe Hass avocados, halved lengthwise and pitted
1½ medium white onions, peeled and finely chopped

CONTINUED

4 fresh serrano chiles, finely chopped
Juice of 3 limes
Juice of 1 small zucchini (use a blender or a juicer to extract the liquid)
¼ cup olive oil
Salt to taste

FOR THE TOMATO SALSA

3 large ripe tomatoes or 6 large ripe plum tomatoes, finely chopped
1 medium white onion, peeled and finely chopped
5 to 8 fresh serrano chiles, finely chopped
½ cup finely chopped cilantro
⅓ cup finely chopped parsley
Salt to taste
40 to 50 tortilla chips, toasted (or make them from scratch by cutting 10 to 15 tortillas into quarters and deep-frying them until crisp)

juices. Add the olive oil and salt and mix well until smooth and thick.

PREPARE THE TOMATO *SALSA:* Combine the tomatoes, onion, chiles, cilantro, and parsley in a bowl. Season with salt and marinate for 30 minutes in the refrigerator.

TO SERVE: Spread the guacamole on a large platter. Drain the ceviche and place on top of the guacamole. Garnish the platter with the *salsa* and serve the chips on the side. The ceviche can be served as an appetizer.

VARIATION: Top each tortilla chip with some guacamole, marinated fish, and tomato *salsa* and serve immediately.

BABY LAKE WHITEFISH TACOS
TACOS DE CHARALES

Serves 8

Pátzcuaro Lake, situated more than 2,000 meters above sea level, is fed by various streams that descend from nearby mountains. The most important of these waterways are the Chapultepec and Guaní rivers. Fishermen travel the waters of this magnificent lake at night in search of *charales*, a tiny white lake fish. Butterfly or spoon nets, called *titibuspé tacuas* or *guaromutacuas*, are used to pull these fish from the cool waters. *Charales* are cooked in many ways. Most often they are prepared in an ancho (dried red pasilla) sauce; with cactus in a tomato broth; or in a local soup with tomatoes, cilantro, *xoconoxtles* (an acidic prickly pear), and serrano chiles.

PREPARE THE SAUCE: Preheat a *comal* or a heavy skillet for about 8 minutes. Roast the chiles evenly on all sides, being careful not to burn them. Roast the tomatillos, turning often, so that they cook evenly. Roast the onion. Pour the water into a medium casserole and add the roasted chiles, tomatillos, and onion. Cook uncovered for about 10 minutes. Season with a small amount of salt, cool, and puree the mixture (including the liquid) in a food processor or a blender along with the garlic and salt to taste.

PREPARE THE FISH: Heat the oil in a wok or a deep fryer. Fry the garlic in the hot oil until brown; discard. Meanwhile, beat the eggs in a medium bowl. Beat in the heavy cream and salt to taste. Add the fish and soak for about 10 minutes. Drain the fish and place them on a baking tray spread with the flour. Shake and turn the fish in the flour to coat lightly. Fry the fish in batches until light brown and crisp. Drain well.

TO SERVE: Place the fish on a large platter and serve the sauce in a clay or stone mortar or a small bowl. Serve with guacamole and fresh tortillas made with white, blue, or red corn. Assemble tacos at the table.

VARIATION: Use 1/2 pound dried baby lake whitefish or whitebait instead of fresh. Wash the dried fish well and pat dry. Soak in the egg mixture, toss in the flour, and fry as above.

FOR THE SAUCE
- 8 dried cascabel chiles, seeded and deveined (see page 296)
- 4 dried guajillo or guajillo puya chiles, seeded and deveined
- 1/2 pound tomatillos, husked
- 1/2 medium white onion, peeled
- 2 cups water
- Salt to taste
- 4 medium cloves garlic, peeled

FOR THE FISH
- 4 cups vegetable oil
- 6 medium cloves garlic, peeled
- 3 eggs
- 1/2 cup heavy cream or crème fraîche
- Salt to taste
- 1 pound fresh baby lake whitefish or whitebait, cleaned
- 1 cup flour

FOR THE GARNISH
- Guacamole (page 99)
- 16 freshly made tortillas (page 309)

BEAN TAMALES
KURUNDAS DE FRIJOL

Makes 40 tamales

FOR THE FILLING

10	cups water
2	cups pink or other light color beans such as pinto, sorted, soaked overnight in water to cover, and drained
40	large scallions, tied in a bunch
6	dried cascabel or de árbol chiles, lightly toasted in a warm skillet

Salt to taste

FOR THE TAMALES

2¹/₄	pounds fresh *masa* (corn dough) or 4¹/₂ cups *masa harina* (dehydrated *masa* flour) mixed with 3 cups hot water and salt to taste and worked until it has the consistency of fresh *masa*
¹/₂	pound rice flour
1	tablespoon baking powder
¹/₂	pound finely grated *queso fresco* or feta cheese
2	tablespoons salt
1¹/₂ to 2	cups warm water (amount depends on the consistency of the *masa*)
1¹/₂	cups butter or lard at room temperature
20	fresh corn leaves to line the steamer, soaked in water for 30 minutes
40	fresh corn leaves for the tamales

Tamales are extremely popular in the state of Michoacán. They are stuffed with a diversity of ingredients (such as cheese, strips of fresh pasilla chiles, *salsa verde*, beans, and mushrooms) and wrapped in *totomoxtle* (dried corn leaves), banana leaves, or *papatla* (a delicious herb that infuses the corn dough with a special flavor). One tamale unique to the region is the *kurunda*, made with fresh *masa* (corn dough), lard, and salt, and wrapped in a corn leaf cooked with ash. Another is the *nacatamal*, a corn tamale with tomatoes that is used for religious ceremonies. This blessed tamale sometimes is stuffed with chiles and meat, other times with just strips of jalapeño. The *uchepo* tamale is made from freshly picked baby corn and the *chari jurinda* is made with black or blue corn and beans. There are still some small villages and towns where tamales are prepared at corner stands in large, round deep clay pots called *ollas panzonas*. More common are the big, round metal pots that maintain an even temperature and retain moisture. As in other parts of the country, tamales here are served with red or green salsa, fresh pasilla or poblano strips, and cream and accompanied with hot *atole*. The version of this beverage made with tamarind, as preferred by the Purépechas, is especially common in Michoacán.

PREPARE THE FILLING: Bring the water to a boil in a medium casserole. Add the beans, scallions, and chiles and simmer covered over medium heat for 40 minutes or until soft. (If the beans start to dry out, add some hot water.) Season with salt. Drain the beans, reserving the cooking liquid separately but discarding the scallions. Puree the beans in a food processor or a blender until smooth. If the mixture is too thick, add up to 1 cup of the reserved bean broth. Set aside.

PREPARE THE TAMALES: Place the fresh *masa*, rice flour, baking powder, cheese, and salt in a medium bowl. Add the water a little at a time and knead to form a semithick dough. In a small bowl, beat the butter until fluffy. Add the butter to the dough, beating with a whisk or an electric mixer until the dough is smooth and fluffy. To see if the dough has the right consistency, drop a small portion in a glass filled with water. The dough should be light enough to float.

Fill a large steamer with 8 to 10 cups of water. Lay 4 of the wet corn leaves on the rack in the steamer. With wet hands, roll 2 tablespoons of dough into a ball. Flatten the dough ball and fill with 1½ teaspoons of beans; roll into a croquette shape. Place the filled dough on corn leaf and fold the tamale into a triangular shape by wrapping the whole leaf around the filling. Repeat with the rest of the corn leaves and layer the tamales in the steamer. Cover the tamales with the remaining wet corn leaves, top with a wet dishcloth, and cover with the lid. Steam for about 1½ hours, adding more hot water if necessary.

PREPARE THE TOMATILLO SAUCE: Pour the water into a large casserole. Add the tomatillos, onions, garlic, and chiles and simmer uncovered over medium heat for about 30 minutes. Remove the casserole from the heat, cool, and blend the vegetables with the cooking liquid and salt to taste. Set aside.

PREPARE THE TOMATO SAUCE: See the recipe on page 106.

PREPARE THE CHILES: Cut the chiles into small strips. Preheat a skillet or a wok, then heat the oil. Sauté the onion until light brown. Add the chile strips and season with salt. Continue cooking for about 10 minutes.

TO SERVE: Place 2 tamales on each serving plate and accompany with the green tomatillo sauce and the red sauce. Garnish on top with the crème fraîche and the chile strips.

VARIATION: If fresh corn husks are not available, use dried corn leaves soaked in warm water until soft and drained.

FOR THE TOMATILLO SAUCE

6 cups water
30 tomatillos (about 2½ pounds), husked
1½ medium white onions, peeled and cut into pieces
4 to 6 large cloves garlic, peeled
10 to 16 fresh serrano chiles, stemmed
Salt to taste

FOR THE TOMATO SAUCE

1 recipe *ranchera* sauce (page 106)

FOR THE CHILES

8 fresh poblano or pasilla chiles, roasted, peeled, seeded, and deveined (see page 296)
⅓ cup olive oil or butter
1 medium white onion, peeled and sliced on the bias
Salt to taste

FOR THE GARNISH

2 cups crème fraîche or 1 cup sour cream or 1½ cups heavy cream, *jocoque* (Middle Eastern yogurt), or plain yogurt

RICE WITH CLAMS
ARROZ CON ALMEJAS

Serves 8

1½ pounds clams in the shell
2 cups long-grain rice
1 cup vegetable oil
8 medium cloves garlic, peeled
1 medium white onion, peeled and quartered
1 teaspoon saffron
2 medium ripe plum tomatoes, chopped
⅓ cup water
2⅓ to 3 cups hot water (amount depends on the type of rice)
Salt to taste
4 fresh serrano chiles
2 bunches parsley

Introduced to Mexico with the arrival of the trading vessel named *Nao de China* along the Pacific coast, rice has been a fundamental ingredient in Mexican gastronomy for centuries. Popular combinations include red rice with tomatoes, green rice with fresh pasilla or poblano chiles, rice and eggs, and saffron rice with pork ribs. Rice with clams is a specialty of the Michoacán coast.

Scrub the clam shells with a small brush to remove any dirt or sand. Refrigerate the clams until ready to use. Place the rice in a shallow dish, cover with hot water, and soak for about 15 minutes. Drain the rice and rinse under cold water until the water runs clear; drain again. Heat the oil in a large casserole, add 6 of the garlic cloves and the onion and sauté until light brown. Stir in the rice and sauté until light brown in color. Strain the rice in a sieve and transfer the garlic and onion to a blender or a food processor. Add the saffron, the tomatoes, the raw garlic cloves, and ⅓ cup of water and puree. Strain the sauce. Return the strained rice to the casserole and sauté for about 3 minutes. Add the tomato mixture to the casserole and simmer uncovered until the rice has absorbed the sauce. Add the hot water, salt to taste, chiles, parsley, and clams. Cover the casserole and simmer over low heat until the rice is fluffy, about 40 minutes.

TO SERVE: Scoop the rice and clams into 8 individual soup plates. Serve immediately.

VARIATION: Garnish the rice with 2 cups cooked string beans cut into fine strips.

MORISQUETA RICE
ARROZ MORISQUETA

Serves 8

When the first ships arrived from the Orient, they brought rice with them, which had never before been seen in the New World. Rice was at first prepared in the traditional Asian fashion. Eventually, it was adapted to local styles and ingredients. This basic preparation can be served with any main course, especially grilled fish, seafood, or red mole dishes.

5¼ cups hot water
1 tablespoon salt, or to taste
3 cups Mexican or Asian short-grain rice, washed under cold running water until the water runs clear

Put the water, salt, and rice in a steamer and cook until fluffy, 45 minutes to 1 hour.

OCTOPUS RANCHEROS
PULPOS RANCHEROS

Serves 8 to 10

The waters along the Michoacán coast crash with fury over enormous rock walls that form sheer cliffs, making for a most unforgettable sight. There are numerous shacks along the coastal road where cooks prepare succulent seafood dishes over wood-burning stoves, which impart their own distinctive flavor. Salsas made in stone mortars and small tortillas fresh from the *comal* add a delightful touch to coastal cooking. Among the many exceptional dishes of the region are fish stuffed with seafood in *ajillo* (garlic) sauce; fish in *barbacoa* (fish and chiles wrapped in banana leaves and steamed in a clay pot or underground); fish in *escabeche;* grilled sea bass; fish broth with guajillo puya chiles and epazote; red snapper in *mojo de ajo* (garlic and chile sauce); *chacales* (langoustines) in broth with guajillo chiles and epazote; shrimp tacos; and fried fish with limes.

PREPARE THE OCTOPUS: Place the octopus in a large cured clay pot or in a casserole. Add the remaining ingredients and simmer covered over medium heat for 1½ to 2 hours or until the octopus is soft. Remove the casserole from the heat and cool the octopus in the broth. Strain and reserve the octopus, dis-

FOR THE OCTOPUS

4½ pounds octopus, cleaned and cut on the bias into 2-inch pieces
2 medium onions, roasted and quartered
2 medium heads garlic, roasted and halved
2 bunches parsley, tied together
2 bunches cilantro, tied together
1 teaspoon black peppercorns
4 fresh caracolitos, manzano, or serrano chiles or banana peppers
16 cups boiling water
2 cups light beer
Salt to taste (use sparingly because the sauce is reduced)

CONTINUED

FOR THE *RANCHERA* SAUCE

- 6 cups water
- 16 medium ripe plum tomatoes
- 1½ medium white onions, peeled and sliced
- 14 medium cloves garlic, peeled
- 12 to 14 fresh serrano chiles
- ½ cup olive or corn oil or lard
- ½ cup cilantro leaves
- 1½ teaspoons salt, or to taste

card the other solids, and reserve the broth. Return the broth to the casserole and cook uncovered until reduced to 3 cups.

PREPARE THE *RANCHERA* SAUCE: Bring the water to a boil in a large saucepan. Add the plum tomatoes, onions, 6 garlic cloves, and chiles and simmer covered for about 30 minutes. Strain the contents of the saucepan and reserve the cooking liquid. Puree the solids in a food processor or a blender along with the 3 cups of reduced octopus broth and 1½ cups of the reserved cooking liquid. Heat the oil in a medium casserole, add 6 of the remaining garlic cloves, brown, and discard. Add the sauce to the hot oil and simmer uncovered over medium heat for about 30 minutes. Grind the cilantro, remaining 2 garlic cloves, and salt together in a mortar or a food processor or mince the cilantro and the 2 remaining garlic cloves very fine with a sharp knife and work in the salt. Add the cooked octopus and cilantro mixture to the sauce and continue simmering covered for about 20 minutes more. Taste for salt and reseason if necessary.

TO SERVE: Scoop the octopus into a large, deep serving dish and serve with Morisqueta Rice (page 105), fresh or toasted tortillas, black beans, and ice-cold beer.

STEAMED FISH WITH TOMATILLO–BLACK PASILLA CHILE SAUCE
PESCADO AL VAPOR CON SALSA DE TOMATILLO Y CHILE

Serves 6

From this prodigious land emerge tiny rivulets that flow into broadening streams and give life to rivers like the Tacámbaro and the Tepalcatepec. These life-sustaining arteries shelter many species of carp, black bass, catfish, and frogs. Their beauty has inspired many poets, including the composer of these lines from a local folksong:

Breezes that go whispering over the foam,
Fishermen singing of nets underneath a sky always blue . . .
Curled up in little houses between the green tulle,
They doze while enmeshed in a sea of small nets.

PREPARE THE SAUCE: Preheat a *comal* or a heavy skillet. Roast the tomatillos on all sides, turning them often to prevent burning. Transfer the roasted tomatillos to a medium casserole. Lightly toast the chiles on the *comal*, turning often and pressing them with a spatula to get an even toasting and to prevent burning. Add the chiles to the tomatillos along with the water. Cook covered until the ingredients are almost soft, 8 to 10 minutes. Add the garlic and simmer for 3 minutes more. Drain the contents of the casserole and reserve the cooking liquid. Puree the tomatillos, chiles, and garlic in a blender or a food processor along with salt to taste. If the mixture becomes too thick, add a small quantity of the cooking liquid to make a smooth sauce. Set the sauce aside.

PREPARE THE FISH: Place a rack inside a large steamer and add the water and the salt. Place a thin layer of about 10 corn leaves over the rack. Place 6 fresh corn leaves on a work surface. Place 1 fillet on each leaf, season with salt and pepper, and cover the fish with the olive oil, butter, ginger, garlic, scallions, and cilantro. Fold the corn leaf over each fish fillet to make a sealed packet, using a second leaf if necessary. Wrap the corn bundles in aluminum foil. Meanwhile, cover the steamer and heat for about 10 minutes. Place the foil packets in the hot

FOR THE SAUCE

- 1 pound baby tomatillos, husked
- 6 long dried black pasilla chiles, seeded and deveined (see page 296)
- 2½ cups water
- 2 large cloves garlic, peeled
- Salt to taste

FOR THE FISH

- 6 cups water
- 1½ teaspoons salt
- 32 fresh corn leaves
- 6 catfish, trout, carp, black bass, or sea bass fillets (about ½ pound each)
- Freshly ground black pepper to taste
- ¼ cup olive oil
- 4 tablespoons butter, diced
- 2 tablespoons finely chopped ginger
- 2 tablespoons finely chopped elephant garlic or regular garlic
- 16 scallions, thinly sliced
- 2 cups cilantro leaves

FOR THE GARNISH

- 3 cups Morisqueta Rice (page 105)
- ¾ cup cilantro leaves
- Olive oil or olive oil flavored with garlic and cascabel chiles

CONTINUED

steamer and cover with the remaining corn leaves. Cook covered for 10 to 15 minutes or until the fish is flaky but not dry.

TO SERVE: Spread a layer of rice on each serving plate. Remove the foil and open each corn package. Place the fillets on top of the rice and drizzle with some of the sauce. Garnish with the cilantro leaves and several drops of olive oil. Serve immediately.

FRIED WHITEFISH WITH PÁTZCUARO SALAD
BLANCO DE PÁTZCUARO

Serves 8

FOR THE VINAIGRETTE
- 4 teaspoons finely chopped elephant garlic or regular garlic
- 1 teaspoon coarsely ground black pepper
- 8 sprigs thyme
- 8 sprigs marjoram
- 2 sprigs spearmint
- 3 sprigs basil
- 1/3 cup fresh lime juice
- 1/3 cup white wine vinegar or other mild vinegar
- 1 tablespoon salt, or to taste
- 1 1/2 cups extra-virgin olive oil

FOR THE SALAD
- 1 medium head Bibb lettuce, cut into small wedges
- 16 scallions, cut into flowers and chilled in ice water (see page 298)
- 16 small radishes, sliced and chilled in ice water
- 4 large ripe tomatoes, cut into wedges
- 2 ripe Hass avocados, peeled and cut into 16 thick slices

Janitzio, the largest island in Pátzcuaro Lake, is inhabited mostly by fishermen and their families. At sunrise, the men go out in boats to look for lake whitefish, one of Mexico's most delicately flavored species. The men work with nets called *huarucas* or *chinchorros*. They also hunt for *mojarra*, black bass, and black perch, all of which are important sources of nourishment for the natives of Pátzcuaro and its islands. Prepare the vinaigrette 2 days ahead to allow its flavors to develop.

PREPARE THE VINAIGRETTE: Place the chopped garlic in a large bowl along with the pepper, fresh herbs, lime juice, vinegar, and salt. Mix well. Slowly whisk in the olive oil until the vinaigrette is smooth. Let the vinaigrette stand at room temperature for 2 days to heighten the flavors. Remove the herbs from the dressing just before serving.

PREPARE THE SALAD: Wash and pat the lettuce dry. Refrigerate until crisp, about 4 hours. Prepare the remaining ingredients closer to serving time.

PREPARE THE FISH: Wash and dry the fish well. Sprinkle with the lime juice, and salt and pepper. Let the fish marinate at room temperature for 45 minutes. Place the 2 cups flour in a shallow bowl and dredge the fish in the flour, shaking off the excess. Heat the oil in a deep pot or deep fryer and preheat the oven to 350°F. Meanwhile, beat the egg whites with a pinch of salt until stiff. Beat the yolks lightly and gently fold them into the whites. Gradually fold in the 2 tablespoons flour. Dip the fish in the batter and place in the hot oil. Fry as many fish as will fit comfortably in the pot, basting them frequently with the oil, until crisp and light brown. Drain on paper towels. Briefly keep the fish warm in the oven while repeating the procedure with the remaining fish.

TO SERVE: Toss the lettuce, scallions, tomatoes, avocados, chiles, cauliflower, radishes, and parsley in a large bowl with the vinaigrette. Place the fried fish on another platter and garnish with the limes. Serve immediately.

10 fresh chilaca or Anaheim chiles, roasted, peeled, seeded, and deveined (see page 296), and cut into fine strips
1 small head cauliflower, cut into florets, boiled in salted water, and refreshed in cold water
32 sprigs parsley

FOR THE FISH

8 whitefish (about 10 ounces each), boned, or 8 red snapper, sole, or flounder fillets (about 5 ounces each)
Juice of 3 limes
Salt and freshly ground black pepper to taste
2 cups plus 2 tablespoons flour
6 cups vegetable oil
10 egg whites
5 egg yolks
8 limes, halved

MICHOACÁN MOLE WITH CHEESE TACOS
MOLE DE MICHOACÁN CON TACOS DE QUESO

Serves 10

FOR THE VEGETABLE GARNISH

- 6 cups water
- 2 teaspoons salt
- 3 cups finely chopped white or yellow potatoes
- 3 cups finely chopped carrots
- 1½ cups finely chopped white onions
- 1½ cups white wine vinegar or other mild vinegar
- ¾ cup olive oil
- 1 tablespoon dried oregano leaves
- 1 teaspoon dried thyme leaves, crumbled
- 1 teaspoon black peppercorns, ground

Salt to taste

- 16 romaine lettuce leaves

FOR THE MOLE SAUCE

- 1 cup olive oil or lard
- ½ pound dried black pasilla or mulato chiles, seeded and deveined (see page 296) (prepared and allowed to dry 1 day in advance)
- ½ pound ancho chiles, seeded and deveined (prepared and allowed to dry 1 day in advance)
- 4 cups chicken stock or water
- 1 head garlic, peeled
- 4 ounces French bread, cut into pieces
- 2 medium tortillas, cut into pieces
- 1½ pounds ripe plum tomatoes, chopped

The origins of the Purépechas (also called Tarascos) are an enigma, but we do know that they settled in Michoacán and developed their own culture and cuisine. Tarascan dishes are quite distinct from other ethnic Mexican groups. At noon, the Tarascos are accustomed to eating a broth with either meat or *charales* (whitebait or baby lake whitefish) that is often flavored with prickly pears, carrots, cabbage, and ground chiles. They also enjoy *chilacayote* squash, zucchini, mushrooms, boiled eggs, thick corn *gorditas* (round tortillas stuffed with beans), *sopes* (round tortillas with pinched edges), enchiladas, *uchepos* (fresh corn tamales), fresh fish, dried *charales*, cured meat (called *cecina*), fresh and aged cheeses such as *cotija* and *queso ranchero* (*queso fresco*), and *atapakua* sauce made with different sorts of chiles. Moles are much appreciated by the Purépechas, who offer these sauces (as do residents in other parts of the country) in special festivities designed to honor the saints.

PREPARE THE VEGETABLE GARNISH: Divide the water between 2 small saucepans. Bring the water to a boil and add 1 teaspoon of salt to each pan. Add the potatoes to one pan and the carrots to the other and simmer covered over medium heat until tender but not mushy, about 10 minutes. Drain. Transfer the hot potatoes and carrots to a large bowl and mix with the onions, vinegar, olive oil, oregano, thyme, pepper, and salt. Mix well and refrigerate. Wash the lettuce leaves and pat dry. Refrigerate until serving time.

PREPARE THE MOLE SAUCE: Heat the oil in a frying pan until hot. Stir-fry both kinds of chiles until crisp. (Turn them twice to get even cooking, but do not let them burn.) Remove the chiles with a slotted spoon and soak in the chicken stock; set aside. Add the garlic to the hot oil and brown. Remove the cooked garlic with a slotted spoon and set aside in a large bowl. Add the bread to the hot oil and cook on both sides. Transfer to the bowl with the garlic. Fry the tortilla pieces on both sides and transfer to the bowl. Cook the tomatoes in the remaining oil until the sauce is smooth and thick. Scrape the sauce into the bowl with the garlic, bread, and tortillas. Puree the mixture until smooth and set aside.

Heat another skillet and toast the chile seeds, stirring often with a spoon. Set the toasted seeds aside. Toast the almonds and the sesame seeds, stirring often to get an even browning; set aside with the chile seeds. Toast the cloves, cinnamon, nutmeg, ginger, and coriander seeds and set aside with the nuts, sesame seeds, and chile seeds. Use a spice grinder to grind the seeds, nuts, and spices into a fine powder and set aside. Heat a cured clay pot for 20 minutes or a wok for about 10 minutes. Add the lard and when very hot add the onion slices. Fry the onion until brown and discard. Drain the soaking chiles, reserving the liquid. Puree with some of the soaking liquid until thick. Add the pureed chiles to the pan and simmer over low heat until the fat comes to the surface. Season with a small amount of salt. Add the reserved tomato mixture and the spice powder to the cooking mole sauce and continue simmering uncovered over very low heat, stirring occasionally, for about 2½ hours. Add enough chicken stock to thin the sauce.

PREPARE THE FILLING: While the sauce is cooking, heat the oil in a skillet, fry the tortillas, and drain. Dip the tortillas in the mole sauce and fill each with about 2 tablespoons of the grated cheese. (There should be some cheese left over.) Roll up the tortillas like soft tacos. Line up the filled tortillas on 1 large or several small platters.

TO SERVE: Pour the hot mole sauce over the filled tortillas and sprinkle with the rest of the grated cheese. Garnish the platter with the lettuce leaves filled with the reserved vegetables. Serve with ice-cold beer.

Note: Any remaining sauce can be frozen for later use.

¼ cup chile seeds or hot red pepper flakes
½ cup almonds
½ cup sesame seeds
8 whole cloves
1 cinnamon stick (about 2 inches long), cut into pieces
½ teaspoon nutmeg
1 knob fresh ginger (about 2 inches), grated
1½ teaspoons coriander seeds
1½ cups lard or extra-virgin olive oil or vegetable oil
6 white onion slices
Salt to taste

FOR THE FILLING
2 cups vegetable oil
30 tortillas
4 to 5 cups grated *cotija* or feta cheese

QUINCE FRUIT CANDY
ATE DE MEMBRLLLO

Serves 8 to 10

2½ **pounds ripe quinces, cored**
4¼ **cups sugar**

Desserts stand out on the list of Michoacán specialties, particularly such elaborate dishes as *cueritos* (fruit paste made into fine strips), *morelianas* (small sweetened milk tortillas), *borrachitos* (fruit paste with liqueur), *charamuscas* (hot *piloncillo* or brown sugar syrup splashed with ice-cold water and worked into candies), *dulces de Tuxpan* (delicious sweets from Tuxpan), *chongos zamoranos* (milk curd with sugar syrup), and *los ates* (fruit pastes from quince or guava). The incomparable *ates* from Morelia are even more tasty when served with *cotija* cheese, which is similar to feta cheese or *queso fresco*. This ancient city is the home of guava sweet rolls, flan, blackberry tamales, sweet potato pies, *buñuelos* (fritters), pumpkin in brown sugar syrup, stuffed pears, and *tamales de leche de Idaparapeo* (tamales made with a thick milk and corn porridge flavored with cinnamon).

Place the fruit in a deep casserole, add water to cover, and cook covered until soft. Puree the fruit and the cooking liquid and strain the mixture through cheesecloth. Combine the fruit pulp and the sugar in a copper or nonreactive pan. Simmer over medium heat, stirring constantly with a wooden spoon, until the mixture forms a smooth, thick paste. You should be able to pull back the paste from the pan with the spoon and have it hold its shape.

Line a 6- to 12-inch-square pan with waxed paper or parchment paper. Spread the filling into the pan, cover, and let stand at room temperature for a day or two. (The paste should harden and develop a more compact consistency.)

TO SERVE: Turn the pan onto a serving platter and remove the waxed paper. Cut the paste into thin slices and serve with a mild cheese such as *panela*, *cotija*, mild Mexican Manchego, Brie, Camembert, or Gouda.

ZAMORAN STRAWBERRY PUNCH
FRESAS DE ZAMORA

Serves 6 to 8

A wide array of flavorful fruits grow in Michoacán, including velvety cherimoyas from Ario; meaty *mameyes* from Pedernales; aromatic guavas from Jacona; figs and pears from Chilchota; sour cherries from Ajuno; melons and kumquats from Apatzingán; mangoes and bananas from Huacana; black *zapotes,* oranges, and limes from Jiquilpan; pomegranates from all central regions; and the well-known strawberries from Zamora. Refreshing homemade fruit drinks are consumed throughout Mexico, and Michoacán is no exception. This fruit punch puts Michoacán specialties to good use.

2	cups water
1 1/2	cups sugar
20 to 30	ice cubes
1	bottle Chardonnay, chilled
4	cups cider, chilled
4	cups mineral water, chilled
1 1/2	pounds watermelon, diced
1 1/2	pounds strawberries, diced
1/2	pound ripe cantaloupe, diced

Pour the water into a small saucepan. Add the sugar and bring the water to a boil, stirring occasionally to dissolve the sugar. Remove from the heat, cool, and chill in the refrigerator. Place the ice cubes in a large punch bowl and add the cold syrup, wine, cider, mineral water, watermelon, strawberries, and cantaloupe. Mix well and refrigerate for about 30 minutes.

TO SERVE: Ladle the chilled beverage and fruit into wineglasses and serve immediately.

GUERRERO

FISH ZIHUATANEJO STYLE

PAN-FRIED FISH WITH ANCHO CHILES AND LEMON
MAYONNAISE

TUNA *TAQUITOS* WITH GUACAMOLE

PLAYA LA ROPA BEANS

SHRIMP CURRY

POACHED FISH WITH CUCUMBERS, SMOKED
SALMON, AND HERB MAYONNAISE

GUINATÁN

GRILLED WHOLE FISH WITH ADOBO

FRIED *MOJARRA* WITH SQUASH, HOMINY, AND
PIPIÁN SAUCE

FRUITS OF THE GUERRERO COAST WITH
COCONUT ICE CREAM

The state of Guerrero follows the Sierra Madre del Sur from northeast to southwest and includes the plains along the Pacific Coast. The region is named for General Vicente Guerrero, a hero of the Mexican War of Independence. The Mixtecos, Tlaponecos, Nahuas, Otomangues, and Amuzgos all left their impression on this region, especially in the arena of arts and crafts.

The capital of this marvelous state is Chilpancingo, which is ringed by large green mountains. Fertile valleys and coastal plains, including such well-known beach resorts as Ixtapa-Zihuatanejo and Acapulco, are also found in this diverse state. Along the wild and remote Costa Chica and Costa Grande are extraordinary places of tropical beauty.

The town of Olinalá is known for its decorative boxes and chests made of aromatic náloe wood. Taxco boasts outstanding colonial architecture and is the center of the Mexican silver industry. Important regional crops include corn, rice, sesame seeds, cacao, bananas, peanuts, anise seeds, and annatto seeds. However, tourism is the prime economic concern in this internationally known region.

How I enjoy taking the helm of my ship. It seems to listen when I talk and speak when I am alone. Sometimes I even answer myself. My wife tells me that getting me to talk is like pulling out the words. But I would like to explain that I talk best on those lonely nights at sea. I use these great solitudes to talk to myself, the stars, and the sea. ¶ At night, while the rest of the world sleeps, we sailors head for the harbor. In our small motorboats, we make for the open sea in search of our catch. When we reach our special fishing grounds, we stop and wait. In these desolate spots, where nothing exists but the dark immensity of the ocean, where the only company is the light of a small bulb that hangs from the mast, where the continuous drumming of the sea against the boat is the only noise, we wait. During the hours a fisherman spends in this dark and impalpable universe it seems that everything is present but nothing can be reached. ¶ Perhaps this is why I talk so much with my son, even though he is not yet five years old. I sometimes feel that he is the one person in the world who listens to me. I would not say he understands, but he listens. For example, I tell him about my dawn journeys to the Costa Chica, in search of oysters to sell in the market here in Acapulco. ¶ In this work, everyone has his own specialty. Some dedicate themselves to fish, others to seafood, and with different techniques. I am thinking of Don Luis, famous snorkeler of the zone called "Costa Grande." He goes alone to snorkel these rough waters, with a rope tied to his waist and to an orange buoy—a beacon for his family in case something happens to him. One day he was working at a depth of 30 meters, gathering fish and hooking them to a line tied to his waist. The movement of the fish attracted the attention of a nearby shark and Don Luis was obliged to defend himself with his harpoon. He couldn't immediately kill the shark, so he lured the shark closer with bait, then took good aim with his harpoon. Don Luis knows that next time he may not fare so well. Similarly skilled are the divers off Punta Maldonado, who pull oysters from the rocks without allowing the waves to throw their bodies against the jagged rocks. ¶ **O**utsiders are often astonished when they see people of color here in Acapulco. They probably don't know that slaves were brought from Africa to work this land. The first slaves came aboard the *Nao de China.* I have spoken of this famous ship so many times to my son that it makes me laugh to hear of the hard time his schoolteacher has talking about this subject. Not to criticize her, but the truth is she doesn't know much about this ship that revolutionized commerce between the continents. ¶ **O**f course, I know I was born, just like my father, with a compass in hand. He was a knowledgeable man who told stories so marvelous they seemed fantastic. But as I matured, I came to understand that these tales were pure reality. I tell them to my son not to impose my will on him, but with the hope that someday he will choose to follow in my path. He will have an opportunity to form his own opinions about the things I tell him. Still, I wonder if, like me, he dreams of the Spanish boats that crossed the Pacific from Puerto de Cavite in the Philippines to Acapulco, or of pirates waiting to capture the splendid merchandise arriving from the Orient—shawls, silks, lace, linens, ivory figurines, porcelain, folding screens, medicines, ink from Canton, and the valuable spices—cloves, ginger, black and white peppercorns, curry—that changed the world. ¶ **I** have told him the legends of the Isla de la Roqueta, site of the lighthouse that guides ships into Acapulco's harbor. It is said that pirates have hidden incalculable treasures there. I cannot break the habit of talking to my son like this. When I see the astonishment and wonder in his small face, it makes me want to tell him more and more and more: about the Galeón that arrived in Acapulco once or twice a year; how the merchandise was moved to the principal plaza for a fair that lasted for a month or two; how merchants came from the interior of the country—from México City, Michoacán, Puebla, and even Veracruz—to take products from the Orient and ship them back to Spain; how soldiers, missionaries, merchants, and sailors ventured toward unknown lands, taking with them their goods and their culture. Of course, big, bright Mexican silver coins were the most precious commodity shipped across the sea. But tobacco, coffee, vanilla, chiles, allspice, hay, sugar, leather, liquor, and dyes were carried abroad as well. Imagine, my son, what enormous changes they brought to the world. ¶ I try to imagine the feasts of that era, and I think of the times I have eaten ceviche with *chilito* at the port or maybe grilled lobster, red snapper with plenty of limes, *chilaquiles* (small pieces of tortillas with ancho chile sauce and *queso fresco*), *las chilapitas* (small, deep-fried tortillas filled with beans, avocado slices, cream, and salsa), *charales* (tiny whitefish) cooked in a tomato broth and epazote, deep-fried tortillas (tostadas) served with pescadilla, iguana tamales with *salsa ranchera,* octopus in *escabeche.* Just talking with my son about those wonderful foods makes my mouth water. So, I grab his hand and we walk in silence to the market, each of us talking to ourselves about our own private fantasies and dreams.

FISH ZIHUATANEJO STYLE
TIRITAS DE PESCADO ESTILO ZIHUATANEJO
Serves 6 to 8

FOR THE FISH

- 2 pounds sea bass, tuna, swordfish, sailfish, or red snapper fillets, cut into ¼-by-2-inch strips
- Juice of 16 limes
- 8 fresh serrano or fresh de árbol chiles, thinly sliced
- 3 medium red onions, peeled and cut into thin wedges or finely sliced
- 1½ tablespoons dried oregano leaves, crumbled
- Salt to taste

FOR THE TORTILLA CHIPS

- 2 cups corn or olive oil or lard
- 24 tortillas, each cut into 6 triangular pieces
- Salt to taste

This special *cebiche* is one of the most popular at the port of Zihuatanejo. It can be eaten year-round when prepared with different fish and blended with lime juice or vinegar. The distinguished food writer Amando Farga says the word *cebiche* comes from the verb *cebar*, meaning "to penetrate" or "saturate." Like other ceviches, the seafood is "cooked" cold by the contact with the acid, which is absorbed into the fish. The sailor Vasco Nùñez de Balboa was the first Spaniard to visit this region in 1513. Indigenous fishermen greeted him with a dish similar to this preparation.

PREPARE THE FISH: Place the fish strips in a shallow dish. Toss with the lime juice and let stand for 10 minutes. Add the chiles, onions, oregano, and salt and toss well.

PREPARE THE TORTILLA CHIPS: Heat the oil in a wok or a deep fryer for 8 minutes. Add the tortilla pieces (they are called *totopos* in this state) and fry on both sides until they are crisp and light brown. Drain the chips on paper towels and sprinkle with salt.

TO SERVE: Put the fish mixture on a large platter and serve with the *totopos* to scoop up the ceviche.

PAN-FRIED FISH WITH ANCHO CHILES AND LEMON MAYONNAISE
OJOTÓN CON CHILE ANCHO Y MAYONESA AL LIMÓN

Serves 8

Not far from the picturesque town of Zihuatanejo lies world-famous Ixtapa, which means "the white place" in the native Nahuatl language. Bright sandy beaches extend more than 12 miles and offer incomparable views. The warm waters are home to a great variety of marine species and are perfect for practicing snorkeling and for sportfishing. The *ojotón* (jack mackerel) is an unusual fish named for its very large eyes. Because of its moist, tasty flesh, this fish is preferred by the inhabitants of Ixtapa. However, sea bass or sardines are particularly good alternatives.

PREPARE THE MARINADE: Lightly toast the chiles on a warm *comal* or in a warm skillet, turning them frequently to prevent burning. Rinse the toasted chiles in running water and soak for 45 minutes in the ¹/₂ cup warm water mixed with the vinegar. Drain the chiles and puree in a blender or a food processor with the garlic, peppercorns, oregano, salt, and mayonnaise mixture to make a velvety smooth sauce. Strain the sauce and season to taste.

PREPARE THE FISH: Pierce each fish with a thin metal or wooden skewer. Place the fish in a shallow dish and daub with the lime juice and sprinkle with salt and pepper. Spread the marinade on both sides of the fish and let stand for about 2 hours. Preheat the oven to 350°F. Preheat a large skillet and add the oil and the garlic. Discard the garlic when browned. Place 4 fish in the skillet and fry on one side for 3 to 4 minutes. Flip the fish and continue cooking until the flesh becomes flaky. Transfer the fish with a spatula to a large platter and keep warm in the oven while the second batch of fish is fried.

TO SERVE: Place 1 whole skewered fish on each serving plate and garnish with lime wedges and basil. Accompany with deep-fried potatoes or freshly made tortillas.

FOR THE MARINADE
- 10 dried ancho chiles, seeded and deveined (see page 296)
- ¹/₂ cup warm water
- 1 cup cider vinegar or white vinegar
- 4 medium cloves garlic, peeled
- ¹/₂ teaspoon black peppercorns
- 2¹/₄ teaspoons dried oregano leaves, crumbled
- Coarse salt to taste
- 1¹/₂ cups mayonnaise mixed with ¹/₄ cup lemon juice

FOR THE FISH
- 8 large wooden sticks or very thin skewers
- 8 whole baby mackerel, sea bass, sardines, or porgy (about ¹/₂ pound each), cleaned
- ¹/₂ cup lime juice, or to taste
- Salt and freshly ground black pepper to taste
- ¹/₂ cup olive oil or lard
- 4 large cloves garlic, peeled

FOR THE GARNISH
- 8 limes, cut in wedges
- 8 sprigs basil

TUNA *TAQUITOS* WITH GUACAMOLE
TAQUITOS DE ATÚN CON GUACAMOLE

Serves 8

FOR THE GUACAMOLE
- 1 recipe guacamole (page 141)

FOR THE SAUCE
- 6 large dried guajillo or New Mexico chiles, seeded and deveined (see page 296)
- 6 dried de árbol or japonés chiles
- 12 medium tomatillos, husked
- 3 large cloves garlic, peeled
- ½ medium white onion, peeled

Salt to taste

FOR THE TUNA
- 6 dried de árbol or japonés chiles, washed and dried
- 4 large dried guajillo or New Mexico chiles, washed and dried
- 2 dried chipotle chiles, washed and dried
- 1 teaspoon black peppercorns
- 1 cinnamon stick (about 2 inches long)
- 2 whole cloves

Pinch of saffron threads

Pinch of nutmeg

Coarse salt to taste
- 2 medium ripe plum tomatoes, chopped
- ⅓ cup cider vinegar or other mild vinegar
- 1 cup olive oil
- 1½ pounds tuna steaks

FOR THE GARNISH
- 32 small freshly made tortillas

Hot sauce to taste

The Acapulco market suddenly comes alive in the very early morning as fishermen return from their night voyages carrying small carts filled with fresh catch from the sea. In some selling spots, they weigh tiny crayfish and shrimp of all sizes from local lagoons like the ones at Coyuca and Tres Palos, and from the Sabana River. Between piles of fresh and dried chiles are mounds of fruits and vegetables—papayas, melons, watermelons, mangoes, bananas, *mameyes,* guavas, tangerines, and oranges, and carrots, radishes, zucchini, corn, *chilacayotes* (a special squash of the region), onions, garlic, lettuce, and tomatoes. The scent of basil, cilantro, epazote, avocado leaves, oregano, thyme, marjoram, and bay leaves fills the air. Fishermen offer a huge selection including sea bass, red snapper, baby shark, grouper, *pulpo* (octopus), *almejas* (clams), sierra, or mackerel, and manta ray. Seafood is sold to cooks who will make delicious coastal dishes, both simple and elaborate—everything from ceviches, cocktails, and soups to tamales, enchiladas, tostadas, and *taquitos.* Another culinary specialty from Acapulco is fish seasoned with spices, aromatic herbs, dried chiles, onion, and garlic and grilled on a bed of branches over hot coals. Tuna tacos made by local fishermen are one of the region's best dishes. Thin, hand-sized tortillas fresh from the *comal* are rolled with grilled tuna, guacamole, and a very spicy *salsa* for a delicious snack.

PREPARE THE GUACAMOLE: See the recipe on page 141.

PREPARE THE SAUCE: Lightly toast the chiles on a warm *comal* or in a warm heavy skillet. Put chiles in a large saucepan, cover with hot water, and soak for about 20 minutes. Bring the water to a boil and simmer the chiles covered for 8 minutes. Add the tomatillos and continue cooking until the tomatillos are soft. Drain the chiles and tomatillos and reserve the cooking liquid. Transfer the chiles and tomatillos to a food processor or a blender and puree along with the garlic, onion, and salt. Add about ½ cup of the reserved cooking liquid to the sauce and puree until the mixture is thinned somewhat. (The sauce should still be fairly thick.)

PREPARE THE TUNA: Lightly toast the chiles on a warm *comal* or in a warm heavy skillet. Grind the toasted chiles in a spice grinder along with the black peppercorns, cinnamon stick, cloves, saffron, nutmeg, and salt. Puree the tomatoes with the vinegar, 1/2 cup of the oil and the spice powder. Daub the tuna with these seasonings and marinate in the refrigerator for 3 hours.

Preheat a large skillet. Add the remaining 1/2 cup oil to the skillet. When the oil is hot, add the tuna and sear on each side for 3 minutes. The tuna should be pink inside and not overcooked. Cool the fish and refrigerate for 1 hour.

TO SERVE: Slice the tuna into 1/8-inch-thick pieces and place 2 or 3 slices on each tortilla. Drizzle with the guacamole and *salsa picante*, fold or roll, and serve.

PLAYA LA ROPA BEANS
FRIJOLES ESTILO PLAYA LA ROPA
Serves 8 to 10

The name Zihuatanejo comes from the Tarasco word *Cihuatlán*, which means "place ruled by women." This ancient fishing village has five main beaches: Playa El Almacén, Playa Las Gatas (named after the sharks that swim the waters off the coral reefs), Playa La Madera, and Playa La Ropa, an appellation that makes reference to a boat shipwrecked off the coast and to the fact that for some time the marine currents threw pieces of the crew's clothing (*ropa* in Spanish) on the sands. In this paradise known as Zihuatanejo, one can find many beachside restaurants offering countless local specialties, many of which are served with the preferred Mexican side dish—beans.

PREPARE THE BEANS: Bring the water to a rapid boil in a large clay pot or other deep pot. Add the beans, quartered onions, and garlic and simmer covered over low heat until the beans are tender, about 1 to 2 hours, depending on the type of bean. (Add more water if the beans start to thicken and are not yet soft.) Season with salt and continue cooking until the beans

FOR THE BEANS
- 16 cups water
- 1 pound pinto beans or other red or yellow beans, sorted, soaked overnight in water to cover, and drained
- 2 medium white or yellow onions, peeled and quartered
- 2 medium heads garlic, halved but not peeled

Coarse salt to taste
- 1/2 to 3/4 cup corn or safflower oil or lard
- 3/4 cup finely chopped white onion

CONTINUED

2 cups *queso añejo, queso fresco*, or feta cheese, finely grated

1/2 recipe tortilla chips (page 118)

are thick. Preheat a wok or a clay pot. Heat the oil for about 5 minutes, add the chopped onion, and stir constantly with a wooden spoon until the onion is caramelized. Add a small quantity of cooked beans and mash them with the spoon until thick and smooth. Add remaining beans and stir, making sure that most of the beans remain whole but that the texture is creamy. Taste and correct the seasoning. (At this point, you can cool, cover, and refrigerate the beans for up to 3 days. Reheat the beans before serving.)

TO SERVE: Spoon the beans onto a deep platter. Sprinkle with the cheese and garnish the edges of the platter with the *totopos* (chips). Serve immediately.

Note: Serve the beans as an appetizer or a side dish.

SHRIMP CURRY
CURRY DE CAMARÓN

Serves 8 to 12

2 cups finely grated fresh coconut

2 cups warm water or 1 1/2 to 2 cups coconut milk

4 tablespoons butter or clarified butter

3/4 cup olive oil

32 large shrimp, prawns, or langoustines, peeled and deveined

Coarse salt to taste

1 pound scallions, thinly sliced

3 medium carrots, peeled and grated

3 cups grated celery

2 medium apples, peeled and grated

10 medium cloves garlic, peeled and chopped

The arrival of the *Nao de China* on the Pacific coast had a profound impact on many aspects of Mexican culture. On board were items from the Orient such as fine silks, porcelain, lace, and ivory, and spices like black pepper, cinnamon, nutmeg, and ginger that soon made their way throughout the Americas. Curry was another culinary import received with pleasure by Mexico. The English word *curry* pays tribute to Tamil, a language of south India. The Tamil word *kari* refers to one type of spicy sauce, although the term *curry* is now used to describe many dishes. Serve this curry with saffron rice, raisins, deep-fried plantains, sliced scallions, chutney, grated fresh coconut, and pine nuts and/or toasted almonds. Accompany with Indian *poori* bread.

Place the coconut in a deep bowl, add the water, and let stand overnight. Strain the coconut through a piece of cheesecloth, squeezing the solids to extract as much liquid as possible. Reserve the coconut milk and discard the coconut meat. Preheat a wok or a large skillet and add the butter and the olive oil. Add the shrimp and sauté, turning once, for about 2 minutes.

Season the shrimp with salt, remove from the wok, and set aside. Add the scallions and cook slowly over medium heat until they caramelize and brown slightly. Add the carrots, celery, and apples and cook covered for 15 minutes. Meanwhile, in a mortar or a spice grinder, blend the garlic, ginger, curry powder, caraway, turmeric, cumin, cinnamon, chile powder, cloves, nutmeg, and salt to taste. Add the tomatoes, tomato puree, and ground spices to the wok and continue cooking uncovered until the oil starts to separate from the sauce. Combine the yogurt with the half-and-half and add the mixture to the wok along with the reserved coconut milk and clam juice or stock. Simmer over low heat for about 30 minutes. Just before serving time, add the shrimp and simmer for about 5 minutes. Season to taste.

TO SERVE: Place shrimp curry in a large bowl. Garnish with pickled jalapeños or chopped fresh chiles, if desired. See headnote for other serving suggestions.

VARIATION: Hollow out 2 large pineapple halves and fill with the curry or serve with a garnish of pineapple slices.

1 knob ginger (about 1 inch), peeled and chopped
6 tablespoons curry powder
1 tablespoon caraway seeds
1 tablespoon turmeric
1½ teaspoons cumin seeds
1 cinnamon stick (about 2 inches long), cut into small pieces
¼ cup chile powder or 2 dried guajillo, de árbol, or ancho chiles, seeded and deveined (see page 296), and ground
½ teaspoon cloves
¼ teaspoon nutmeg
1½ pounds ripe plum tomatoes, peeled, seeded, and finely chopped
4 ounces canned or fresh tomato puree
1½ cups plain yogurt
1 cup half-and-half
2 to 3 cups clam juice or reduced shrimp stock

POACHED FISH WITH CUCUMBERS, SMOKED SALMON, AND HERB MAYONNAISE
BOBA AL ENELDO Y SALMÓN AHUMADO
Serves 12

FOR THE CUCUMBERS
4 large cucumbers, peeled
Juice of 3 limes
1/2 cup cider vinegar or white
    vinegar
1 tablespoon dried dill
1 tablespoon sugar
Salt to taste

FOR THE MAYONNAISE
3 1/2 cups mayonnaise
1/4 cup fresh lime juice
3/4 cup chives
1/2 cup parsley leaves
2 cups watercress
1 tablespoon dried dill
Pinch of nutmeg
Salt and white pepper to taste

FOR THE FISH MARINADE
12 scallions, chopped
6 shallots, chopped
1 1/2 teaspoons dried dill
1 teaspoon black peppercorns
1 cup dry white wine
Salt to taste
2 large fish fillets such as
    halibut, red snapper, grouper,
    or sea bass (about 2 1/2 pounds
    each), bones removed

FOR THE FISH STOCK
10 cups water
1 cup dry white wine
1 1/2 medium fish heads and bones,
    washed
4 carrots, peeled and chopped
4 ribs celery, chopped
4 sprigs thyme

Traditional dances have been preserved by the inhabitants of Guerrero as a manifestation of their artistic and cultural spirit. Even today, one can appreciate special ceremonies like the "fish dance" and the "turtle dance." In the former, fishermen carry carved wooden fish over their shoulders as they parade through the village. The focal point is a large crocodile also made of wood. A man inside the crocodile makes the animal's mouth open and close. He also shakes the wire tail at the men carrying the fish. The turtle dance is performed at night as a homage to the fertility gods. Dancers give thanks to the sea for the nourishment it gives the people. One marine species celebrated is the *boba* (large gray fish), a particularly meaty fish popular along the Guerrero coast but not well known in other places. Halibut, sea bass, grouper, and red snapper may be used just as effectively. Begin this recipe 1 day ahead of serving.

PREPARE THE CUCUMBERS: Using a very sharp knife or a mandoline, slice the cucumbers paper thin. Place the cucumbers in a shallow dish and toss with the lime juice, vinegar, dill, sugar, and salt. Cover and marinate at room temperature or in the refrigerator overnight.

PREPARE THE MAYONNAISE: Puree the ingredients in a food processor or a blender until smooth. Cover and refrigerate overnight.

PREPARE THE FISH MARINADE: Combine the scallions, shallots, dill, black peppercorns, wine, and salt. Place the fish in a shallow dish and pour the marinade over the fillets. Cover and refrigerate overnight.

PREPARE THE FISH STOCK: Pour the water and the wine into a fish poacher without the rack. Add the fish heads and bones, carrots, celery, thyme, marjoram, black peppercorns, and salt. Bring the mixture to a boil and simmer covered for about 30 minutes. Place 1 or both fillets (if they will fit comfortably) on the rack and poach for about 10 minutes or until the fish flakes. Let the fish stand in the stock for about 4 minutes, remove from the poaching liquid, drain, and cool. Repeat with the remaining fillet if necessary.

To SERVE: Transfer 1 fillet to a large fish platter. Drain the liquid from the cucumbers and use half of the cucumbers to cover the top of the fillet. Spread half of the mayonnaise over the cucumbers and place the second fillet on top. Cover the second fillet with the remaining cucumbers. Spread the remaining mayonnaise on the cucumbers. Arrange the salmon slices in an overlapping pattern on top of the mayonnaise. Garnish the sides of the platter with the chilled dill and watercress. Spread the capers and chiles down the length of the fish in a thin line. Serve with lime wedges and toasted (not fried) tortillas, if desired.

4 sprigs marjoram
1 teaspoon black peppercorns
Coarse salt to taste

FOR THE GARNISH
1 pound smoked salmon, cut into paper-thin slices
1 pound fresh dill, chilled
1 pound watercress, chilled
1 tablespoon small capers
1 tablespoon fresh serrano chiles, minced

GUINATÁN

Serves 6 to 8

3 pounds salted cod, salted catfish, or any dried fish, cut into 2-inch squares and soaked in water to cover for 1 day with 2 changes of water

3 fresh coconuts, finely grated (page 297), or 8 cups unsweetened shredded coconut

4½ cups hot water

6 ounces dried guajillo or ancho chiles, seeded and deveined (see page 296), lightly toasted in a warm skillet, soaked in hot water for 20 minutes, and drained

8 black peppercorns

6 whole cloves

4 medium cloves garlic, peeled

1 tablespoon dried oregano leaves

Salt to taste

After the Conquest, the port of Acapulco was converted into one of the main sites for slave auctions. The *Galeón de Manila* was responsible for bringing the first slaves to the Americas from Asia. However, by the middle of the sixteenth century, the slave trade had shifted to Africa due to reports of the inhabitants' physical superiority. Some slaves were able to escape to remote locations like La Costa Chica or La Costa Grande, not far from Zihuatanejo. From these first Africans in Mexico, we have inherited this delicious and nutritious dish called *guinatán*. The main ingredient is salted and dried fish—usually porgy, red snapper, shark, mullet, cod, or catfish—that is cooked in coconut oil.

Drain the fish and wash under running warm water. Dry the fish and let it stand for 30 minutes. Wash again under running warm water. Dry the fish and reserve. Place the coconut in a shallow dish and add the hot water and soak for about 1 hour. Strain the coconut through a cheesecloth or a fine-meshed strainer. Transfer the liquid to a casserole or a clay pot and bring to a boil. Simmer, stirring constantly and skimming as necessary, until the oil separates from the coconut milk. Skim milk and discard.

Meanwhile, puree the drained chiles with the spices, garlic, and oregano in a food processor or a blender. Add the mixture to the simmering coconut oil and cook, uncovered, over medium heat for about 15 minutes. Add the fish, cover the casserole, and simmer for about 20 minutes or until the fish is soft. Taste for salt and add some if needed.

TO SERVE: Serve fish in a deep platter. Accompany the fish with Morisqueta Rice (page 105) or beans and freshly made tortillas.

GRILLED WHOLE FISH WITH ADOBO
PESCADO A LA TALLA

Serves 4

Costa Chica, the strip of coastal land that runs from Acapulco in Guerrero to Puerto Angel in Oaxaca, was heavily settled by Africans. During the colonization of Nueva España, the Spaniards brought several groups of African slaves from Mozambique and East Africa to take the place of natives in the fields. The African slaves worked on coffee, cotton, and sugar plantations as well as in gold and silver mines. Some of the slaves escaped to Costa Chica, then a remote part of the country far from the reach of the Spanish. The communities established here still reflect the influence of these settlers, especially the cuisine. This dish is a good example of a Guerreran recipe with African roots.

PREPARE THE FIRE: Place wood or charcoal in a grill and start the fire. Let the fire burn for 1½ to 2 hours so that the flame is even but not scorching hot (see Note).

PREPARE THE ADOBO: Preheat a *comal* or a heavy skillet and toast the chiles on all sides without burning them. Remove the chiles from the *comal*, wash, and soak them in water to cover for about 20 minutes. Roast the garlic and the onion on the hot *comal*. Drain the chiles and reserve the soaking liquid. Put the chiles in a food processor or a blender along with the roasted garlic and onion, 1 cup of the reserved soaking liquid, and the remaining ingredients. Puree into a smooth paste and set aside.

PREPARE THE FISH: Place the fish on 2 trays and sprinkle with the lime juice and salt and pepper. Daub the adobo on both sides of the fish. Let the fish marinate in the refrigerator for 30 minutes. Place the banana leaves over the hot grill. Rest a fish gently on top of each banana leaf and cover the grill with the lid so that the cooking environment remains moist. During the cooking drizzle the fish with olive oil and any adobo that remains on the trays. Season with salt and cook for about 20 minutes. (The time will vary depending on the size of the fish and the intensity of the fire.)

FOR THE ADOBO
- 12 dried large ancho chiles, seeded and deveined (see page 296)
- 2 to 4 dried moritas or chipotle chiles, seeded and deveined
- 4 medium cloves garlic, peeled
- ½ medium yellow or white onion, peeled
- 1½ teaspoons dried oregano leaves
- ½ teaspoon cumin seeds
- 2 whole cloves
- 1 cinnamon stick (about 2 inches long)
- ¼ cup white wine vinegar
- ¼ cup mayonnaise
- ½ cup olive oil
- ⅓ cup clarified butter
- Coarse salt to taste

FOR THE FISH
- 4 whole red snapper, sea bass, or sole (1½ to 2 pounds each), heads removed, butterflied, and boned
- Juice of 4 limes
- Salt and freshly ground black pepper to taste
- 4 square banana leaves (each slightly larger than the fish)
- Olive oil for cooking

FOR THE GARNISH
- ½ head Boston lettuce, washed, dried, and refrigerated for 2 hours

CONTINUED

1 head red-leaf lettuce,
  washed, dried, and
  refrigerated for 2 hours

8 medium scallions, cut into
  flowers and chilled in ice
  water for 2 hours (see page
  298)

8 radishes, thinly sliced

1 ripe avocado, peeled and
  sliced

1 teaspoon dried oregano
  leaves, or to taste

20 fresh basil leaves

1/2 cup crumbled feta cheese

Lime juice to taste

Olive oil to taste

Salt to taste

TO SERVE: Discard the banana leaves. Place each fish on a large oval dish and garnish with the lettuce, scallion flowers, radishes, avocado slices, oregano, basil, feta cheese, lime juice, and olive oil. Season with salt. Serve immediately and accompany with freshly made tortillas or beans.

Note: The fish can also be seared on top of the stove in a very hot cast-iron skillet, wrapped in banana leaves, and then placed in the oven to finish cooking.

CUISINE OF THE WATER GODS

FRIED MOJARRA WITH SQUASH, HOMINY, AND PIPIÁN SAUCE
CALABAZAS Y CHILACAYOTES EN POZOLE CON MOJARRA

Serves 6

In the state of Guerrero—land of mountains, jungles, forests, and rivers—agriculture and fishing are both important. Main rivers include the Papagayo, the San Miguel, the Ometepec, the Apitzantla, the Ixtapa, and the longest and most powerful, the Balsas, which also flows through the states of Michoacán, Oaxaca, Puebla, Tlaxcala, Mexico, and Morelos. Numerous villages along the banks of the Balsas depend on this mighty river for fishing and irrigation. Depending on the region and the time of year, fishing on the river is accomplished in different ways. When the wet season arrives, traps and nets are used to scoop fish out of waters clouded by the splashing rain. During the dry season, some men fish with *huarucas* (rope nets), or *atarrayas* (casting nets), while others even use their hands to pull fish from shallow waters. One unusual technique, known as "drying the water," involves digging a canal to divert the fish and imprison them in a narrow ditch. One man, called the *juntador*, gathers the fish from the canal. This method is a popular means for trapping *mojarra*.

PREPARE THE *PIPIÁN* SAUCE: Preheat a *comal* or a heavy skillet over low heat. Toast the pumpkin seeds evenly, but do not let them burn. Grind in a spice grinder. Roast the corn kernels, stirring often to make sure they do not burn. Grind the corn and puree with the pumpkin seed powder and the water in a blender or a food processor. Reserve some of the sauce and puree the remaining sauce with the onions, garlic, tomatillos, chiles, epazote, and *hoja santa*. Combine with the rest of the sauce and strain. Preheat a clay pot or a wok. Heat the oil and brown the onion slices. Add the sauce slowly to the pot along with the cilantro. Simmer uncovered over medium heat until the sauce starts to thicken, about 30 minutes. Season with salt and set aside.

PREPARE THE VEGETABLES AND THE HOMINY: Bring 2 cups of water to a boil in a medium saucepan. Add a pinch of salt and

FOR THE *PIPIÁN* SAUCE

- 2 cups shelled green pumpkin seeds
- 1 cup dried corn kernels or hominy
- 3 cups water or fish stock
- 1½ medium white onions, peeled
- 4 medium cloves garlic, peeled
- 10 tomatillos, husked and poached or sweated in a small quantity of water
- 6 to 12 fresh serrano chiles or fresh de árbol chiles or 4 fresh poblano chiles, seeded, deveined (see page 296), chopped
- ¾ cup chopped fresh epazote
- ¾ cup chopped fresh *hoja santa* leaves
- ½ cup olive or corn oil or lard
- 2 white onion slices
- 40 sprigs cilantro, tied in a bunch

Salt to taste

FOR THE VEGETABLES AND THE HOMINY

Salt to taste

- 1 pound zucchini, quartered or cut into rounds
- 1 pound fresh *chilacayotes* (squash) or chayotes (water pears), peeled and diced

CONTINUED

1½ cups canned cooked
hominy

FOR THE FISH

6 cups vegetable, corn, or
safflower oil
6 whole *mojarras*, trout, or
sardines (about 6 ounces
each), slit on the side,
cleaned, and marinated in
a little lime juice and salt

the zucchini. Simmer covered for 3 to 4 minutes and drain, reserving the cooking liquid. Bring 2 cups of water to a boil in
another saucepan. Add a pinch of salt and the *chilacayote* and
cook covered for about 5 minutes, depending on the texture or
softness of the vegetable. Drain and reserve the cooking liquid.
Add the zucchini, *chilacayote*, and cooked hominy to the *pipián* sauce and cook covered until thick, about 20 minutes.
Add the reserved vegetable cooking liquid to thin the sauce if
necessary.

PREPARE THE FISH: Meanwhile, heat the oil in a deep fryer or a
deep pot and fry 2 or 3 fish at a time until the exterior browns
and the flesh flakes. Repeat with the remaining fish.

TO SERVE: Spoon the sauce and the vegetables into 6 large,
deep soup plates. Top with the fried fish. Garnish with limes,
chopped radishes or onions, and cilantro, if desired.

Note: Be careful of the bones when eating *mojarra*.

Note: If dried corn is not available, toast ½ cup dried *masa harina,* which is already ground.

FRUITS OF THE GUERRERO COAST WITH COCONUT ICE CREAM
FRUTAS DE LA COSTA GUERRERENSE CON HELADO DE COCO

Serves 12

Pineapple, papaya, and mango are natural partners with coconut ice cream. This "marriage" of flavors dates back to the era of conquest and discovery. Commerce between the Philippines and the New World began in the year 1568 with the opening of a route linking Manila with Acapulco. The word *nao* ("ship") was used in combination with the ship's port of origin to refer to a ship that traveled the Pacific. Asians awaited the arrival of products from Nueva España (Mexico) carried on board the *Nao de Acapulco*. On the other hand, Mexicans were supplied with goods from the Orient by the *Nao de China.* Among the culinary treasures brought from Manila, the hub of trading activity in the East, were mangoes and coconuts, which soon became important fruits in Mexican cuisine. By the same measure, ships returned to Manila with Mexican ingredients such as pineapples, papayas, chicozapotes, avocados, corn, and chiles, which eventually made their way throughout Southeast Asia. This recipe is a good example of the culinary crossbreeding at the root of Mexican gastronomy.

PREPARE THE COCONUT ICE CREAM: Combine the milk, the vanilla beans, 1 cup of the sugar, and the grated coconut in a large saucepan. Cook over medium heat until the mixture comes to a rapid boil and the sugar has dissolved. Remove from the heat and cool for about 30 minutes to intensify the flavors. Remove and discard the vanilla beans. In a large mixing bowl, beat the egg yolks with the remaining 1 cup sugar until the mixture falls from the beaters in ribbons. Stir in the milk mixture and the cream. Pour the mixture back into the large saucepan and cook over medium heat, stirring constantly with a wooden spoon, until the custard lightly coats the spoon. Remove the pan from the heat and cool the custard to room temperature. Chill the custard in the refrigerator and process in an ice-cream machine according to the manufac-

FOR THE COCONUT ICE CREAM

- 4 generous cups milk
- 2 vanilla beans, slit lengthwise
- 2 generous cups sugar
- 3 cups finely grated coconut
- 12 egg yolks
- 2 cups heavy cream (for a tangy flavor, substitute crème fraîche for some of the cream)

FOR THE FRUIT

- 1 large ripe yellow or red papaya (about 7 pounds), peeled and cut into 12 slices (each about 2 inches thick), or 6 smaller ripe Hawaiian papayas, peeled, halved, and seeded
- 2 large or 4 small ripe pineapples, peeled, cored, and sliced into 1-inch pieces
- 6 large ripe mangoes (red or yellow), peeled and sliced
- 2 medium coconuts

CONTINUED

turer's instructions. Freeze the ice cream for about 8 hours before serving.

PREPARE THE FRUIT: Preheat the oven to 400°F. Prepare the papaya, pineapples, and mangoes. Pierce the eyes of the coconuts with a sharp instrument and pour out the liquid (reserve for other use). Bake the coconuts for 15 minutes. The coconuts should crack while baking. If not, crack the coconuts open with a hammer. When the coconuts are cool, slice the flesh away from the skin and cut each into 6 pieces.

TO SERVE: Alternate the slices of fruit on a large platter. Scoop the ice cream directly onto the center of the platter or transfer the ice cream to a large bowl and place the bowl on the platter.

VARIATIONS: Serve with passion fruit, oranges, and tangerines or grapefruit sherbet.

PUERTO ANGEL OYSTER COCKTAIL

***TOTOPOS* WITH CHILE AND SHRIMP SAUCE**

***MEMELAS* WITH ROASTED TOMATO SAUCE**

**PINOTEPA-STYLE EMPANADAS STUFFED
WITH SHRIMP**

PUERTO ESCONDIDO FISH TAMALES

SHRIMP SOUP ISTHMUS STYLE

FISH MOLE IN A POT, TEHUANTEPEC STYLE

**YELLOW SEAFOOD MOLE SAN MATEO
DEL MAR STYLE**

OAXACAN LOBSTER IN TAMARIND SAUCE

BLACK SAPODILLA WATER

Oaxaca is located along the southern Pacific coast of Mexico. Its name comes from the Nahuatl language and loosely translates as "the mountain of the gourds." The region has been inhabited by various groups who were integrated into the Zapotec culture in the east and the Mixteca tribe in the west. Several settlements of native Chatinons, Amuzgos, Mixes, and Zoques remain.

The central valleys of this large state are home to the ancestral cities of Monte Albán and Mitla. These impressive monuments stand as testaments to the strength of Mesoamerican civilizations. Because of the region's mountainous topography, towns and villages still retain much of their indigenous culture, especially as pertains to dress and craftsmanship. The coastal region, which until recently was quite isolated from the central valleys, boasts magnificent beaches at Puerto Escondido, Puerto Angel, and the Huatulco bays.

Besides the rich variety of marine life found along the coast, rice, sugarcane, corn, sweet potatoes, zucchini, *chilacayote,* cactus, cacao, agave mezcalero, and various chiles (poblanos, de aguas, Californias, jalapeños, and serranos) are all important foods in the region. Many mushrooms varieties, such as San Juans, bird's feet, and cèpes, grow in the state. Tropical fruits also are cultivated in abundance, including pineapples, *chicozapotes,* limes, pomegranates, black *zapotes,* and mangoes. Coffee is another major crop, with Oaxaca placing third in overall production in Mexico. The region of Etla is famous not only in Oaxaca but throughout the country for its cheeses, including the mozzarellalike string cheese called *quesillo.*

This is the story of a brave maiden named Xalli and her efforts to serve the gods and her people. ¶ Xalli's father, like all men from the Oaxacan coast, both Zapotecs and Huaves, was called one day to milk *púrpura caracol*—the sacred marine snail—of its special purple liquid. As part of the ritual, he abstained for a time from the pleasures of women and alcohol in order to purify his soul. And before he embarked on his mission, Xalli's father, like his ancestors, asked the heavens to guide him and help him. ¶ After walking a long trail, he spied a cluster of rocks that served as home to the sacred snail. He loosened the animal with his walking stick and by applying delicate pressure against the shell he caused the snail to expel its precious ink, catching the liquid on a skein of cotton as tradition dictated. He replaced the snail amid the rocks and sprinkled it with water to revive it. At the end of the next cycle of the moon, the snail would again be ready to expel its sacred ink. ¶ That night, Xalli started to weave a petticoat with the purple skein brought by her father. Her father had chosen a husband for her, and there was little time to prepare the garments she would need for the upcoming celebration, a marriage rite designed to protect her from sterility and assure that her family and tribal heritage carried on. ¶ One night, something made her stop weaving all of a sudden, but she could hear only silence. When she looked out to the high seas, however, she spotted a flat-bottomed canoe coming toward the shore. Inside was a strong man wearing a white shirt. When he landed on the beach, she saw that he carried beautiful flowers and fruits in his hands. With the utmost respect, he presented them to the young weaver. He stared at her for some time, and she felt the fury of the sea rising in her heart. Gently, the stranger took her hand, and she walked with him to the canoe as if in a spell. As they approached the vivid sea, she began to wake from her stupor. She realized she was leaving behind all that she loved, but she knew she could not escape. ¶ As they moved out into the rough seas, her captor grew a tail. He beat it violently to separate the waves, creating a channel through which they could travel. Mysterious sea creatures, disturbed from their deep resting spots, lined the walls of this water canyon. Then the north wind began to blow, and Xalli knew all hope was lost. Waves rose high above the boat. The south winds started to blow, too, and thunder clapped above as the wind whistled with all its force as if to blow all evil from the earth. ¶ A serpent emerged from the fury, and Xalli thought for a moment that it would challenge her abductor. She recalled the cloth she was weaving at home and the colors that it bore. She recalled the sound of the jungle that gave birth to the rivers and streams of her home. She remembered how the moon shone down on the eagle with seven heads. She gazed over at her abductor and realized that he was leading her toward her animal spirit. She knew he would help her to become one with the serpent. Her mind started to run wildly, spinning into the infinite spiral that created the snail. ¶ Again she looked at the man in the canoe, and she knew that he had been sent by the sun and fire gods to take her to meet her destiny. Her heart told her to let go of earthly existence. And, making peace with this thought, she was transformed into the *púrpura caracol*. Every twenty-eight days she gives up her magic tint to create new life among her people. Her sacrifice perpetuates the bloodline of the sons of Oaxaca.

PUERTO ANGEL OYSTER COCKTAIL
COCTEL DE OSTIONES

Serves 4

32 medium oysters, shucked
Juice of 4 limes
1 medium white onion, peeled and finely chopped
3 medium fresh serrano chiles, finely chopped
2 tablespoons finely chopped cilantro
½ cup olive oil
3 tablespoons Worcestershire sauce
Salt and freshly ground black pepper to taste
Hot sauce (*búfalo* or Tabasco) to taste

Puerto Angel is home to one of the most astonishing bays along the entire Oaxacan coastline. Beaches are bathed by intense blue waters filled with splendid natural wonders. The majority of the inhabitants of this paradisiacal place are fishermen who labor at night and during the early morning hours. Women and children go to the beach at nine o'clock in the morning to wait for the fresh catch of the day. They buy from widows and single women who sell seafood to support themselves. Of course, seafood is eaten most every day in the homes of fishermen, whether it is used in ceviches, prepared in broths, grilled, cooked on sticks over wood fires, or deep-fried. Fish is usually served with black beans, rice, potatoes, tomatoes, avocados, cabbage, onions, and freshly made tortillas. Oysters are another delicious dish from this land that the *"señoras"* on the beach prepare with plenty of seasonings. This dish has a special taste reminiscent of a warm day along the Oaxacan coast.

Gently toss all of the ingredients in a large mixing bowl. Let stand for about 20 minutes so that the flavors can blend. Serve the oyster cocktail in tall glasses with *totopos* (fried tortilla chips) or tortillas toasted on a *comal* or in a heavy skillet.

VARIATIONS: Use clams or cooked shrimp, octopus, calamari, or crab instead of oysters and add catsup, avocado, and/or chipotle chiles.

TOTOPOS WITH CHILE AND SHRIMP SAUCE
TOTOPOS CON CHINTEXTLE

Makes 24 totopos

Ana María Vazquez Colmenares, a distinguished historian who has studied the culinary traditions of Mexico, writes in her book *Tradiciones Gastronómicas Oaxaqueñas* that *totopos,* a type of tortilla common in Oaxaca, vary in size in different parts of the state. Some of the most popular *totopos* come from the Isthmus of Tehuantepec. The *masa* (corn dough) is made from coarsely ground corn and holes are cut into the tortillas so that they can easily be removed from the *comixcal.* This ovenlike cooking surface is a large clay pot that is open on either end. The pot is placed on the ground in the middle of a wood fire or in a special base that rests just above the wood. When the thick clay walls become hot, the tortillas are "glued" to the interior of the pot. Highly skilled *tortilleras* (women who make the tortillas) soak an arm in cold water and drape a tortilla over the wet limb. They then place the arm along the hot interior of the *comixcal* and stick the tortilla onto the pot. The technique used in this recipe is much simpler and a lot less dangerous.

PREPARE THE SAUCE: Preheat a *comal* or a heavy skillet and toast the chiles on all sides. Wash the chiles and soak in water to cover. Toast the dried shrimp. (If using fresh, toast with salt to taste and allow to dry for about 15 minutes before peeling.) Lightly toast the avocado leaves. Drain the chiles and grind with the toasted shrimp in a stone grinder (a *metate*), a spice grinder, or a food processor. Add the avocado leaves, garlic, and vinegar and grind into a smooth paste. Taste and correct the seasonings. (Shrimp paste will keep for a long time in the refrigerator. If desired, toasted nuts and pumpkin seeds may be added.)

PREPARE THE *TOTOPOS:* Spread the *masa* over a flat surface and add small amounts of water and the salt. Start kneading, adding more water if necessary, until the dough is smooth and has a velvety consistency. Let the dough rest for 10 minutes.

Preheat the oven to 350°F. Preheat a *comal* or a heavy skillet and brush with oil. Divide the dough into 24 balls. Line a tor-

FOR THE SAUCE

- 15 pasilla oaxaqueños chiles or 20 dried morita or mora chiles
- 10 ounces dried shrimp or 1 pound fresh shrimp

Salt to taste

- 6 fresh avocado leaves or 3 fresh *hoja santa* leaves, lightly toasted
- 1½ heads garlic, peeled
- ¾ cup cider vinegar or other strong vinegar

FOR THE *TOTOPOS*

- 2 pounds fresh regular or coarse-grained *masa*

⅓ to ½ cup warm water

- 1 teaspoon salt

Vegetable oil for lightly coating the cooking surface

CONTINUED

tilla press with plastic wrap and gently press each dough ball twice. (Do not press too hard because the tortilla should not be too thin.) With wet hands, slide the tortillas, one by one, onto the *comal*. Cook the tortilla on one side, then with the tip of a knife, make small incisions all over the top. Flip the tortilla over several times until it hardens slightly. Transfer the tortilla to the warm oven and bake for several minutes, until dry.

TO SERVE: Spread some of the sauce over each *totopo*. Sprinkle with crumbled feta cheese and pickled pasilla oaxaqueños chiles, if desired.

Note: See pages 309 to 310 for more information on making the dough and using the tortilla press.

MEMELAS WITH ROASTED TOMATO SAUCE
MEMELAS CON SALSA DE JITOMATE
Makes about 25 memelas

FOR THE LARD DRIPPINGS
2 pounds pork fat or chicken fat mixed with a small portion of meat cut into small pieces
Salt to taste

FOR THE DOUGH
2½ pounds fresh *masa*
Salt to taste
½ to ¾ cup warm water

FOR THE ROASTED TOMATO SAUCE
4 medium cloves garlic, peeled
8 fresh serrano chiles
8 large ripe plum tomatoes
Salt to taste
1½ cups hot water

The Mixtecs and Zapotecs of the *valle de Oaxaca*, or valley of Oaxaca, were gatherers and farmers. Many legends about their origins have been told over time. According to one myth, the two tribes descended from a divine couple, while another creation legend says that they both can trace their roots back to a single tree. Other versions of the story argue that they came from the earth; still others point to the sea. One theory claims that the Zapotecs were the original inhabitants of the valley. No matter what the truth is, we know that corn was—and still is—a basic source of nourishment in the local diet. This recipe for *memelas* is a good example of corn's importance. Called *memelas* or *pellizcadas* ("pinched ones") when slightly thinner and rounder (see page 230), these delicious treats are finished with lard drippings stored in enormous pails in every Oaxacan home. From early in the morning, women prepare wood fires and the *anafres* (grills) to place over them. With even clappings and rhythmic hand motions, they work the *masa* (corn dough) into ⅓-inch-thick ovals. They then prepare a water wash with limestone and brush the hot *comal* to prevent sticking. When the *comal* is ready, they slide the *masa* oval onto the hot surface. As the *memelas* cook on both sides, the women pinch the edges. Once cooked, the *memelas* are kept in a special basket, known as a *chiquichuite*, to keep them warm. The *memelas* are again placed on the *comal* and seasoned with lard drippings, which melt into the dough. The *memelas* are served with a sauce prepared in a stone *molcajete* (mortar). *Memelas* are just one of the *antojitos*, or whims, the people of Oaxaca enjoy at their famous fiestas such as Lunes del Cerro and La Guelaguetza. The latter festival loosely translates as "tortilla from the corn crops" and celebrates life in all its principal stages—birth, marriage, and death.

PREPARE THE LARD DRIPPINGS: Place the pork fat in a medium saucepan. Cover with hot water and add salt to taste. Simmer uncovered over medium heat until the lard is smooth and starts to thicken at the bottom of the pan. The lard should be slightly brownish in color. Remove the pan from the heat and let the lard cool. Strain the lard and pour into a large bowl. Store the bowl in the bottom of the refrigerator. About 3 hours before using, remove the bowl from the refrigerator and bring to room temperature.

PREPARE THE DOUGH: Spread the *masa* over a flat surface and add salt to taste. Add the water a little at a time by sprinkling it on top and knead slowly and evenly to make a smooth and soft dough that is slightly wet. Cover the dough with a damp dish towel and let rest for 20 minutes.

PREPARE THE ROASTED TOMATO SAUCE: Heat a *comal* or a heavy skillet and roast the garlic and the chiles on all sides. (If hot fireplace ashes are available, cover the chiles with the ashes and roast in the fireplace for a special flavor.) Remove the garlic and the chiles from the hot *comal* and roast the tomatoes until charred on all sides. In a mortar or a food processor, grind the garlic and the chiles with salt to taste until very smooth. Add the tomatoes and blend until smooth. Add the water and reseason. Stir in the minced onion.

PREPARE THE *MEMELAS*: Preheat the *comal* or a heavy skillet and brush with a mixture of water and powdered limestone or just plain vegetable oil to prevent sticking (see page 310). (The cooking surface has to be moist so that the dough can be pinched easily and so that the *memelas* do not become hard or

½ **medium white onion, peeled and minced**

FOR THE GARNISH
½ **pound** *queso fresco* **or feta cheese, finely crumbled**
¾ **cup finely chopped white onion**

CONTINUED

stale when reheated.) Line a tortilla press with plastic wrap. Measure between 1½ and 2½ tablespoons of dough and shape it into a thick oval. Press the dough lightly between the plastic sheets in the tortilla press, making the *memela* as thick or as thin as you like. Cook the *memela* on the hot *comal* on both sides until it starts to swell. Remove from the *comal*, cool slightly, and use your fingers to pinch a rim along the outside edges and in the middle of the *memela*. Wrap the *memela* in a cloth and repeat with the remaining dough.

TO SERVE: One by one, return the *memelas* to the *comal* and drizzle with the lard drippings. Baste the *memelas* with the roasted tomato sauce and sprinkle the cheese and the onion on top. Serve immediately.

VARIATIONS: Serve with shredded Oaxacan string cheese or mozzarella, avocados, and pickled chipotle chiles or chipotle sauce. Also, try serving *memelas* in the morning with hot coffee or the *atole* (hot corn beverage) on page 287.

Note: See pages 309 to 310 for more information on making the dough and using the tortilla press.

PINOTEPA-STYLE EMPANADAS STUFFED WITH SHRIMP
EMPANADAS DE CAMARÓN ESTILO PINOTEPA

Makes about 26 empanadas

La Costa Chica in the state of Oaxaca is distinguished from the rest of the Pacific shore by its large population of African ancestry. Chacahua and Corralero are two communities with a large black population that date back to the Conquest. In Pinotepa, where this dish hails from, there has been a blending of African and native peoples and cultures. Dried fish and dried shrimp are found in markets throughout this zone. Shrimp are especially valued by locals, who depend on nearby lagoons for this delicacy. Fresh shrimp are pulled from inlet waters and then dried in the sun and tossed with salt or smoked. After some time, the shrimp are boiled in heavily salted water until they are bright orange in color. A *sacador* is used to scoop the shrimp from the water and they are then spread out over a wooden table and salted again. Dried shrimp have many culinary uses, especially in soups, sauces, and moles. The pairing of ground fresh shrimp with the *masa* (corn dough) gives the dough for these turnovers a mild but exquisite taste of the sea.

PREPARE THE FILLING: Preheat a wok or a deep casserole, add the oil, and heat for 2 minutes. Add the garlic and sauté until light brown. Add the onions and cook until they start to caramelize. Season with a small amount of salt. Add the chiles and the tomatoes and simmer uncovered over medium heat until the sauce starts to thicken. Stir in the shrimp and cook until the sauce becomes quite thick. Reseason with salt and add the cilantro. Set aside.

PREPARE THE DOUGH: Spread the *masa* over a flat surface and start to knead in small amounts of the water until the *masa* becomes velvety and moist. Continue working the dough into a large flat rectangle. Sprinkle the surface with the chopped shrimp, lard, flour, baking powder, and a dash of salt. Work the dough again until it becomes smooth and velvety. (If the dough becomes dry, add more water in small amounts until it

FOR THE FILLING
- ½ cup olive oil
- 4 large cloves garlic, peeled and finely chopped
- 1½ medium white onions, peeled and finely chopped
  Coarse salt to taste
- 6 fresh serrano chiles or fresh de árbol chiles, minced
- 1½ pounds ripe tomatoes, finely chopped
- 1⅓ pounds freshly cooked shrimp, peeled, deveined, and finely chopped
- 1½ tablespoons finely chopped cilantro

FOR THE DOUGH
- 2 pounds fresh *masa*
- ⅓ to ½ cup warm water
- ¾ pound freshly cooked shrimp, peeled, deveined, and finely chopped
- 1 tablespoon lard or shortening
- 5 tablespoons flour
- 2 teaspoons baking powder
Salt to taste

FOR THE GUACAMOLE
- 3 ripe avocados, peeled and roughly chopped
- 4 to 8 fresh serrano chiles, roughly chopped

CONTINUED

10 tomatillos, husked and roughly chopped

2 medium cloves garlic, peeled and chopped

1/2 medium white onion, peeled and chopped

Juice of 2 limes

80 sprigs cilantro, chopped, or 1 1/2 tablespoons finely minced mint leaves

Salt to taste

FOR THE TOMATO SAUCE

1 1/2 medium white onions, peeled and finely chopped

4 large ripe tomatoes or 1 1/2 pounds ripe plum tomatoes, minced

6 to 8 fresh serrano chiles, thinly sliced

1/2 cup finely chopped cilantro

1 tablespoon dried oregano leaves, crumbled

1/3 cup fresh lime juice

1/2 cup olive oil

Salt to taste

3 cups corn or olive oil or lard

has a shiny consistency and the surface is slightly sticky to the fingers.) Let the dough rest, covered with a cloth, for 20 minutes.

PREPARE THE EMPANADAS: Shape the dough into small balls about 2 1/2 inches in diameter. Line a tortilla press with plastic wrap. Place a dough ball in the tortilla press and gently close the tortilla press. Open the press, flip the dough over, and press again to make a somewhat thin tortilla. Peel away the top sheet of plastic wrap and fill the middle of the tortilla with 1 to 1 1/2 teaspoons of the reserved filling. With the help of the plastic wrap on the bottom of the tortilla, wrap both edges around the filling. With wet hands, peel off the plastic wrap and transfer the empanada to a tray lined with plastic wrap or aluminum foil. Repeat with the remaining dough balls. (At this point, the empanadas can be covered tightly and refrigerated overnight.)

PREPARE THE GUACAMOLE: Put all of the ingredients except the salt in a food processor and pulse 4 times. Season with salt and blend until smooth.

PREPARE THE TOMATO SAUCE: Toss all of the ingredients except the salt until well mixed. Season with salt, cover, and refrigerate for 20 minutes to allow the flavors to meld.

TO SERVE: Preheat the oven to 400°F. Heat the 3 cups corn oil in a deep frying pan or a wok. Fry the empanadas in small batches, basting occasionally with the oil, until they are crisp and light brown in color. Drain on a tray lined with paper towels. Serve immediately or place the tray in the oven for 5 or 6 minutes before serving. Transfer the empanadas to the center of a large platter and serve with the guacamole and tomato sauce on either side.

Note: See pages 309 to 310 for more information on making the dough and using the tortilla press.

PUERTO ESCONDIDO FISH TAMALES
TAMAL DE PESCADO ESTILO PUERTO ESCONDIDO

Makes 40 tamales

In Oaxaca, delicious tamales are prepared with different types of corn (white, yellow, blue or black, or reddish purple or red) that are cultivated in the regions of the Zapotec, Mixe, Huave, and Chontal people. Along the Oaxacan Pacific coast, tamales are wrapped with banana leaves that have been boiled, grilled, or smoked. As for fillings, seafood, tomatoes, and tomatillos all may be used. Sauces include red, black, and yellow moles as well as ground pumpkin seeds flavored with *hoja santa*, avocado leaves, *pitiona*, *chepil*, epazote, or cilantro. Vegetables such as squash, zucchini, string beans, and tiny white beans may be paired with fresh or dried fish. *Cherna*, mullet, bonito, crab, red snapper, baby shark, and sea bass all are used in tamales. The Huaves, established in San Mateo del Mar, San Dionisio, Santa María, and San Francisco del Mar, prepare a very special type of tamale called a *guetabinguis*, which contains a whole fish (with the head and scales) and is steamed slowly to cook in its own delicious natural juices. This recipe calls for fillets, which are easier to use. Extra tamales may be frozen.

PREPARE THE FILLING: Heat the water, tomatoes, and both types of chiles in a large saucepan. Simmer covered for about 15 minutes, then add the onions and the garlic and cook covered for 30 minutes more. Puree the mixture in a food processor or a blender. Preheat a large casserole and add the oil. Sauté the onion slices until they caramelize. Add the pureed sauce and simmer uncovered over medium heat until the sauce reduces and thickens. Season with salt. Add the *masa* dissolved in water to the pan and simmer uncovered until the sauce has a velvety consistency. Set aside. Cut the fish into 1-inch cubes and set aside.

PREPARE THE TAMALES: Wash the banana leaves and boil briefly in water or wrap in a damp dishcloth and sweat in a hot oven to soften. Pat the leaves dry and cut into 40 pieces measuring 10 inches by 10 inches. Fit a steamer with a metal steaming rack or a clay tamale pot with reeds. Fill with about 12 cups of

FOR THE FILLING

- 8 cups water
- 16 medium ripe plum tomatoes
- 10 fresh serrano chiles
- 12 dried japonés or costeño chiles, lightly toasted in a warm skillet
- 2 medium white onions, peeled and cut into pieces
- 8 large cloves garlic, peeled
- 1/3 cup vegetable or corn oil
- 2 white onion slices

Salt to taste

- 1/2 cup fresh *masa* (corn dough) dissolved in 1/2 cup water
- 2 1/2 pounds fish fillets such as swordfish, sea bass, or porgy

FOR THE TAMALES

- 2 large packages fresh banana leaves
- 2 pounds fresh *masa*
- 2 to 2 1/2 cups warm water
- 1 1/2 tablespoons salt
- 1 1/2 tablespoons softened lard or melted butter

CONTINUED

water, cover the pot with a lid lined with a dishcloth, and bring the water to a medium simmer. Meanwhile, mix the *masa* with small amounts of the water and the salt until the dough is very wet. (This can be done in a standing mixer.) Beat the lard until smooth and fluffy, then start adding small amounts of water until the lard has a runny consistency like a smooth custard. Beat the lard into the dough. Spread ½ cup of the dough over the middle of each banana leaf, using the back of the spoon to get a thin, even coating on the leaf. Top the dough with 2 to 3 tablespoons of the reduced tomato sauce and place some raw fish on top. Fold one side of the leaf over the other, tucking one side into the other. Fold the ends and tie the leaves into small rectangular or square bundles. When the steam starts to come out of the pot, position the tamales on the rack, overlapping as necessary. Cover the tamales with the leftover leaves or a dishcloth and cook, covered, over medium heat for about 1½ hours or until tamales slide easily off the banana leaves.

To serve: Place the tamales on a serving plate or in a deep dish. Serve them for breakfast, lunch, or dinner. These tamales are served with different beverages such as chocolate, beer, hot coffee, or fresh fruit waters (*aguas frescas*).

Variation: Use shredded crab instead of fish.

SHRIMP SOUP ISTHMUS STYLE
CALDO DE CAMARÓN DEL ISTMO
Serves 10 to 12

At dawn, after they have been resting in their colorful hammocks, the fishermen go to the lagoons and lakes of the Isthmus of Tehuantepec to catch shrimp. They take their nets and gas lamps attached to poles with them. The lights are held near the surface of the lagoon to attract the shrimp. In September, after the rainy season, the shrimp can be found near the shore and are caught with *chinchorros,* very small nets. In February, the shrimp sink to the bottom of the lake, but the north wind carries them back to the surface. Fishermen capture shrimp of all sizes; some are quite large, while others are tiny. All are preserved by boiling them in salted water and then drying them in the sunlight. The women are charged with selling the dried shrimp, which they carry to market in baskets placed on their heads. Dressed in beautiful long skirts and blouses embroidered with silk threads, the women wear their hair pulled back to give a clear view of their outstanding facial features. The Tehuanas sit in a casual but sensual way near their baskets filled with dried shrimp. They fan away insects with an even rhythm. With calm smiles that reveal teeth adorned with gold, the women of the isthmus offer nutritious salted shrimp in various sizes that can be ground into sauces for cakes, broths, *escabeches,* rices, moles, *nopales* (cactus paddles), egg dishes, or simply eaten with lime juice. Dried shrimp can even be peeled and eaten with freshly made tortillas.

PREPARE THE STOCK: Pour the water into a large stockpot or casserole. Add the onions, scallions, garlic, fish heads, fish, shrimp shells (set the shrimp aside for the soup), epazote, black peppercorns, and salt. (Be stingy with the salt because dried shrimp are very salty.) Simmer uncovered over medium heat for 1½ to 2 hours. Remove from the heat, cool, and strain.

PREPARE THE SOUP: Preheat a *comal* or a heavy skillet. Roast the tomatoes on all sides, turning them often. Roast the onions, garlic, and chiles. Soak the roasted chiles briefly in water. Drain the chiles and puree with the tomatoes, onions, and garlic. Strain the sauce. Heat the oil in a large casserole or

FOR THE STOCK
- 18 cups water
- 4 medium white onions, peeled and halved
- 2 bunches scallions, chopped
- 2 heads garlic, halved but not peeled
- 2 medium fish heads, cut into pieces
- 4 whole *mojarras*, small red snapper, or mullet, cleaned and cut into pieces
- 1 pound dried shrimp (with shells if available), peeled and shells reserved, or 2 pounds prawns, peeled and shells reserved, deveined, and cut in half if large
- 4 large sprigs epazote
- 1 teaspoon black peppercorns
- Coarse salt to taste

FOR THE SOUP
- 10 medium ripe plum tomatoes
- 1½ medium white onions, peeled
- 10 medium cloves garlic, peeled
- 10 dried chilcosle, costeño, guajillo, or New Mexico chiles, seeded and deveined (see page 296)
- 6 dried medium ancho chiles, seeded and deveined
- 6 dried de árbol or japonés chiles
- ½ cup olive oil
- 2 white onion slices
- 6 sprigs thyme
- 6 sprigs marjoram
- 4 fresh laurel or dried bay leaves

CONTINUED

4 sprigs epazote

2 cups finely chopped carrots, blanched

3 cups finely chopped yellow potatoes, blanched

FOR THE GARNISH

1 cup finely chopped white onion

1/2 cup finely chopped epazote, cilantro, or oregano

16 medium limes, or to taste, cut into wedges

FOR THE FISH STOCK

18 cups water

4 medium fish heads, cut into pieces

2 medium onions, peeled and halved

2 heads garlic, halved but not peeled

1/2 rib celery, cut into pieces

2 bunches scallions

1 leek, cut into pieces

4 ears corn, cut into 1-inch-thick rounds

4 dried chipotle chiles, stir-fried in a little vegetable oil

Salt to taste

FOR THE MOLE

10 dried guajillo or New Mexico chiles

10 dried chilcosle chiles or any small dried chiles

saucepan and caramelize the onion slices. Add the sauce and simmer uncovered over medium heat until the sauce becomes a thick paste. Tie the herbs together and add to the sauce along with the shrimp. Simmer for 20 minutes and remove the herbs. Add the hot fish stock and the cooked carrots and potatoes. Cover and simmer for 20 more minutes.

TO SERVE: Ladle the hot shrimp soup into deep soup plates and garnish with the onion, epazote, and limes. Serve with toasted tortilla chips (*totopos*).

FISH MOLE IN A POT, TEHUANTEPEC STYLE
MOLE DE OLLA CON PESCADO ESTILO TEHUANTEPEC

Serves 8 to 10

Colorful parades and traditional dances are organized during local fiestas. The dances of Llorona and La Sandunga are especially noteworthy. San Pedro (Saint Peter), the patron of Tehuantepec, is honored with 6 days of festivities in June, during which the famous *tirada de la fruta* (dropping of the fruit) takes place under the shade of flowers. Pieces of fruit are thrown into crowds of churchgoers after services. For the parties, women dress in their best clothes and cover their heads with fine lace that shows off their splendid faces.

PREPARE THE FISH STOCK: Bring the water to a boil in a large stockpot or casserole. Add the fish heads, vegetables, and chiles and season with salt. Cover and simmer gently until the stock has a full flavor, about 1 1/2 hours. Remove the pot from the heat, cool, and strain. Reserve the strained stock and the corn slices; discard the other solids.

PREPARE THE MOLE: Preheat a skillet over medium heat. Wipe the chiles clean with a wet cloth and lightly toast. Rinse the chiles and soak in warm water for about 30 minutes. Roast the tomatoes in the skillet. Drain the chiles and puree with the roasted tomatoes, onions, and garlic in a food processor or a blender. Strain the sauce. Preheat a large casserole and add the oil. Brown the onion slices and then add the strained sauce. Simmer uncovered over medium heat until the sauce becomes thick and the oil comes to the surface. Season with salt. Add the hot stock in small quantities to combine the flavors slowly. Add the reserved corn slices and the epazote and continue cooking for about 30 minutes.

PREPARE THE DUMPLINGS: Meanwhile, spread the *masa* over a flat surface and sprinkle with the water, kneading and adding water until it has a smooth consistency. Add the lard and the salt and continue kneading until the dough is smooth. Shape $^1/_2$-inch balls of dough and make an indentation in the middle of each. Add the dumplings to the soup and cook for 10 minutes.

PREPARE THE VEGETABLES: Separately blanch the zucchini and the beans in 2 cups of salted water. Drain the vegetables when still crisp and add to the soup.

TO SERVE: When ready to serve, add the fish and cook for about 3 minutes. Serve the soup in a large clay pot or in individual soup plates.

VARIATION: Accompany with limes, chopped onions, and freshly made tortillas.

10 dried costeño or japonés chiles

6 large ripe plum tomatoes

1½ medium white onions, peeled and cut into pieces

4 medium cloves garlic, peeled

$^1/_3$ to $^1/_2$ cup olive oil or lard

2 white onion slices

Salt to taste

2 bunches epazote or cilantro

FOR THE DUMPLINGS

2 cups fresh *masa* (corn dough)

¼ cup warm water

1½ teaspoons lard or vegetable oil

Salt to taste

FOR THE VEGETABLES

8 zucchini, cut into small pieces

1 pound string beans, tips removed

FOR THE FISH

2½ pounds small sea bass, sole, halibut, or cod fillets (each about 1 inch thick)

YELLOW SEAFOOD MOLE
SAN MATEO DEL MAR STYLE
AMARILLO DE SAN MATEO DEL MAR

Serves 8 to 10

FOR THE FISH AND SHRIMP MOLE

3	large ripe plum tomatoes
1½	medium white onions, peeled
6	large cloves garlic, peeled
10	dried chilcosle chiles or 8 ancho chiles, seeded and deveined (see page 296)
6	dried guajillo or New Mexico chiles, seeded and deveined
10	ripe tomatillos, husked and boiled
14	black peppercorns
½	cinnamon stick
1	tablespoon annatto seeds, ground
4	whole cloves
½	teaspoon cumin seeds
¾	cup vegetable oil or lard

Salt to taste

½	cup fresh *masa* (corn dough)
6	cups fish stock
2½	pounds salted cod, salted striped mullet, or any dried fish, cut into 2-inch squares and soaked in water to cover for 1 day with 2 changes of water
1½	pounds shrimp, peeled and deveined
4 to 6	fresh *hoja santa* leaves or 10 fresh avocado leaves

FOR THE DUMPLINGS

1	pound fresh *masa*
1⅓	cup water

The Isthmus of Tehuantepec is inhabited by Zapotecs, Mixes, Chontales, and Huaves. This last group is distributed in four towns, the principal one being San Mateo del Mar. This beautiful town established on the sands and surrounded by water is enveloped by the sounds of the wind and the waves and the salty scent of the sea. The Ikoods are a special group of Huaves whose main activity is fishing. The exclusive domain of Ikood men, fishing is practiced in tranquil lagoons, not in the rough ocean. The waters of the open sea are so powerful, they inspire respect and fear. The Ikoods ask for the protection of the gods in special rituals, feasts, and dances dedicated to the turtle, the serpent, the storm, and the sea. The importance of fishing always stands out in these rituals. During the windy season, they eat many dishes with shrimp and fish, called *escamas. Amarillo,* an intense yellow sauce, is one of the preferred moles of the people that live near the coast.

PREPARE THE MOLE: Preheat a *comal* or a heavy skillet and roast the tomatoes on all sides, turning them often. Roast the onions, garlic, and chiles. Soak the roasted chiles briefly in water. Drain the chiles and place in a blender or a food processor with the tomatoes, onion, garlic, tomatillos, and spices and puree. Heat the oil in a large saucepan. Add the pureed chile mixture and stir-fry until the oil separates from the sauce. Season with salt. Dissolve the *masa* in a little of the fish stock and stir the mixture into the sauce. Remove the fish from the soaking liquid and pat dry. When the sauce thickens, add the fish, shrimp, and *hoja santa* leaves to the sauce. Cook uncovered for an additional 20 minutes over medium heat.

PREPARE THE DUMPLINGS: While the sauce is cooking, place the *masa* in a large bowl and add the water a little at a time and the lard, salt, and cilantro. Work the dough until smooth. Using about 1½ teaspoons of dough for each, form small balls or dumplings. Use your fingers to make an indentation on one side of each ball. Add the dumplings to the sauce along with more stock to make a light but not soupy consistency.

TO SERVE: Spoon the mole onto a serving platter and serve with the chopped onions and radishes on the side. Sprinkle with lemon juice and salt. Accompany with freshly made tortillas.

1½ tablespoons lard or bacon
drippings
Salt to taste
½ cup chopped cilantro or
epazote

FOR THE GARNISH

2 medium white onions,
peeled and finely chopped
1 cup finely chopped radishes
Fresh lemon juice to taste
Salt to taste

OAXACAN LOBSTER IN TAMARIND SAUCE
LANGOSTA EN SALSA DE TAMARINDO DE LA COSTA OAXAQUEÑA

Serves 8

The Oaxacan coast is one of outstanding beauty. Filled with abundant vegetation and exotic tropical birds, this region is home to mangoes, cherimoyas, coconuts, wild prunes, tamarinds, limes, oranges, and *zapotes* (sapodillas). Puerto Escondido is one place of spectacular beauty. Its name, which loosely translates as "hidden port," comes from fishermen who wanted to keep this bountiful location a secret. Rock oysters, mother-of-pearl oysters, manta rays that jump out of the water, and enormous lobsters with a very delicate flavor all can be found in the waters near the shore. In the markets, women carry baskets filled with fresh fruits and shrimp as well as small, freshly made tortillas. In coastal Oaxaca, tortillas are pressed by hand and are much smaller than those made in the mountains. Of course, speaking of mountains, one cannot fail to mention the mountains of plantains and bananas—there are some eleven varieties—found in the local markets.

PREPARE THE TAMARIND SAUCE: Heat a wok or a large casserole and add the butter and the oil. When the butter is melted, add the onions and cook until they are caramelized. Add the garlic and continue cooking for about 10 minutes more. Add the remaining ingredients, except the chicken stock, and cook un-

FOR THE TAMARIND SAUCE

½ cup butter
⅓ cup olive oil
2 medium onions, peeled and
chopped
6 medium cloves garlic,
peeled and chopped
2½ cups pureed fresh pineapple
1 cup fresh apricot jam
2½ cups tamarind pulp
(available in Asian or Latin
markets) or 3 pounds fresh
tamarind, soaked, cleaned,
and pureed
1 cinnamon stick (about
2 inches long)
6 whole cloves, ground
1 cup brown sugar or grated
piloncillo (solidified brown
sugar), or to taste
½ cup cider vinegar

CONTINUED

Salt to taste
1 to 2 cups chicken stock

FOR THE LOBSTER
½ cup clarified butter
½ cup olive oil
3 heads garlic, peeled
2 cups water
¾ cup cider vinegar
6 dried guajillo, ancho, or New Mexico chiles, lightly toasted in a warm skillet
12 dried japonés or costeño chiles, lightly toasted in a warm skillet
4 dried de árbol chiles, lightly toasted in a warm skillet
4 whole cloves, ground
½ teaspoon black peppercorns
½ teaspoon cumin seeds
Salt to taste
8 lobster tails, shells removed, deveined, and rinsed
⅓ cup olive oil

FOR THE GARNISH
⅓ cup olive oil
24 dried de árbol chiles
8 fresh pineapple slices (each about 1 inch thick)
8 ears corn, cooked in water with a little salt and sugar
4 cups white baby beans, cooked in water with onion and garlic
Fresh oregano leaves

covered over low heat until the sauce starts to reduce and becomes thick. Stir in small amounts of the chicken stock until the sauce has a creamy consistency. Continue cooking uncovered for about 20 more minutes. Remove the cinnamon stick, adjust the seasoning, and set aside.

PREPARE THE LOBSTER: Puree the butter, olive oil, garlic, water, and vinegar in a blender or a food processor. Add the chiles, spices, and salt and puree. Put the lobster tails in a shallow dish and pour the marinade over them. Let stand for 30 minutes to 1 hour. (The lobster tails can be covered and refrigerated overnight, if desired.) Preheat a large skillet and add the olive oil. Remove the lobster tails from the marinade and cook on each side for 3 to 4 minutes. Pour the marinade into the skillet and cook covered for 4 to 6 minutes. Do not overcook the lobster tails; they should remain moist and tender. Season with salt.

PREPARE THE GARNISH: Preheat a medium casserole. Add the oil and stir-fry the chiles. Set aside. Prepare the rest of the garnish.

TO SERVE: Preheat 8 large soup plates. Spoon the warmed tamarind sauce onto the bottom of each plate. Place a lobster tail on top and garnish the sides of the plate with the stir-fried chiles, a pineapple slice, an ear of corn, and the white beans. Sprinkle with oregano and serve immediately.

Note: Cooked lobster tails can be sliced and served on top of a small pool of tamarind sauce.

BLACK SAPODILLA WATER
AGUA DE ZAPOTE NEGRO

Serves 8

The markets in Oaxaca are a true feast of aromas and colors. There are small stands selling chocolate, *champurrado* (a corn beverage *atole*, made with sweet chocolate), plain *atole*, and all sorts of tamales. Some tamales are made with *mole colorado* (red mole), others with *mole negro* (black mole). Some are wrapped in rectangular banana leaves, others in triangular avocado leaves. Tamales may be filled with *rajas* (sliced jalapeños or chiles de agua), squash blossoms, or even *cochinillas,* insects that lend their bright red color to sweet fillings wrapped in corn husks. Many tamales are filled with chicken basted with different moles. Other special market treats include egg yolk bread, *enmoladas* (tortillas basted with mole sauce and onions), *enfrijoladas* (tortillas dipped in bean sauce and served with onions, parsley, cheese, and cream), grilled chorizo sausage, *tortillas blanditas* (soft, round versions), and *tlayudas* (light 24-inch round tortillas made by hand and cooked on a clay *comal* over a wood fire). Anything one may crave is sold here in the morning. At any time of the day one can enjoy the most popular *aguas frescas,* such as *horchata* (made with sweet rice flour, melon seeds, and cinnamon), *ciruela* (wild prune juice), and fruit drinks made with pineapple, *zapote negro* (black sapodilla), lime, melon, cherimoya and mango in season, and other exquisite tropical fruits native to the state of Oaxaca. The women have special rituals for preparing these fruit drinks and keep them fresh in large clay pots. Some fresh fruit waters are placed in *vitroleros* (large glass pitchers) that permit passersby to see the symphony of colors so particular to this region.

4 ripe black sapodillas, peeled
6 cups water
1 cup sugar, or to taste
2 cups fresh orange juice
Ice cubes

Force the peeled sapodillas through a sieve using the back of a large spoon or pass the fruit through a food mill. Place the sapodilla pulp in a large pitcher and add the water, sugar, and orange juice. Stir well and add ice before serving.

Note: Black sapodillas are in season from September through March in Oaxaca and other southern and central states in Mexico.

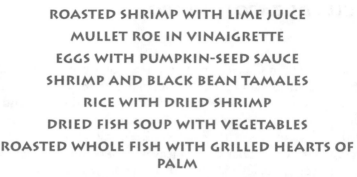

CHIAPAS

ROASTED SHRIMP WITH LIME JUICE

MULLET ROE IN VINAIGRETTE

EGGS WITH PUMPKIN-SEED SAUCE

SHRIMP AND BLACK BEAN TAMALES

RICE WITH DRIED SHRIMP

DRIED FISH SOUP WITH VEGETABLES

ROASTED WHOLE FISH WITH GRILLED HEARTS OF PALM

SQUID AND CRAYFISH WITH MUSHROOMS AND SQUASH BLOSSOMS

ZOQUE BLACK BEANS

WATERMELON IN CINNAMON SYRUP

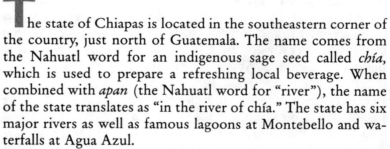

The state of Chiapas is located in the southeastern corner of the country, just north of Guatemala. The name comes from the Nahuatl word for an indigenous sage seed called *chía*, which is used to prepare a refreshing local beverage. When combined with *apan* (the Nahuatl word for "river"), the name of the state translates as "in the river of chía." The state has six major rivers as well as famous lagoons at Montebello and waterfalls at Agua Azul.

Chiapas was inhabited by the Olmecs and Mayas and is home to a number of Mexico's outstanding archaeological treasures, especially the ancient cities of Palenque, Bonampak, and Yaxhilán. The Mayan civilization was one of the most important cultures in Mesoamerica, and its descendants gave rise to the diverse groups that now live in this region.

The climate can be quite cool at higher elevations, while it is extremely hot and humid in the jungle plains. Several crops are of importance to the local economy—corn, beans, chiles, cacao, sugarcane, squash, soybeans, peanuts, papayas, melons, watermelons, guavas, tamarinds, oranges, limes, cherimoyas, soursop, and mangoes. Chiapas has vast coffee plantations and produces more beans than any other state.

Because of the diverse ethnic groups living in this region, the local gastronomy is quite varied. Fish and seafood as well as an array of local herbs are key features. Along with the states of Oaxaca and Yucatán, Chiapas has retained its cultural ties to its Indian heritage more than other regions of Mexico.

I was told to come to Chiapas to find drawings in the earth of this jungle-shaded land. I was told I would see women working clay with their hands, molding the pottery with pieces of polished stone called bash. These pieces of pottery eventually would become vessels for water or pots that could withstand fiery flames. ¶ I was told to come to Chiapas to find the light of civilization left behind by the Mayans in places like Palenque and Bonampak. I was told that on the left bank of the Usumacinta River, I would meet the Lacandóns, who are direct descendants of the Mayans and shelter ancient traditions in their jungle enclave. ¶ I was told to come to Chiapas to feel the power of the Chiapa Indians, who reside on the left bank of the Grijalva River. For a long time they resisted the advance of the Mexican Empire, and their traditions still survive today. I was told I could observe the unique clothing of the Tzeltals in Ocozingo and the Tzotzils in Zinacatán. I was told it would be an adventure to visit Comitán and to meet the Tojolabals, or to journey to Soconusco, land of the Mames and Motozintlecos. I could listen to the music of pre-Columbian instruments that accompany Zoque dances. I was told I would feel the harmonious blending of the harp and the guitar as characterized by Tzotzil music. Throughout the state, I was told I would hear joyous marimba notes. ¶ I was told to come to Chiapas to feel the attraction of powerful amber crystals. Organic remains are frozen in time in these fossils that permit the rays of the sun to be reflected in an array of tones and shades. I was told that my eyes might even change color in Chiapas as I observed the many waterfalls that cascade down rocks and cliffs throughout the land. ¶ With all these promises, I knew I had to come to Chiapas. And despite such high praise, I am still amazed and mystified by what I have found. I was captivated with the beauty of the canyon at Sumidero, the place that engendered Chiapa civilization, and the lakes of Montebello, where rare tribes like the Chuj and Jacaltecos once lived. ¶ The ubiquitous presence of water led me into conversations with fishermen throughout the state. These men maintain an almost sacred dialogue with the water and its creatures. At night, the moon over Chiapas illuminates radiant springs, streams, and rivers that rush to the coast and out to sea. A liquid curtain falls into Sumidero Canyon. The sound of rushing water is music to the ears of fishermen. They wait for the full moon, when the fishing is best. A crescent moon that points toward the mountains means that the winds will blow, and a crescent moon that points to the sea means that the rains will come. When the moon goes to sleep and the sky is dark, the sea will be tranquil, as if dreaming until the next full moon. ¶ I couldn't really imagine that there could be more to see in Chiapas than what I was told about, but there was. Each day I stumbled onto something new or totally unexpected that confirmed my belief in the magical, bewitching nature of this charming land. ¶ When I was near Paredón, I worked the "dead sea" with local men. This calm, sheltered body of water appears lifeless at times. But underneath, aquatic life teems, and from time to time the breeze pushes soft waves onto the shore. At night, fishermen rest in palm huts on the beach. They rise at four in the morning to begin a long journey in small wooden boats. Some are propelled by long oars while others have small sails. On board are plenty of *chinchorros,* small nets woven from cactus fibers, as well as other larger nets to catch an array of creatures such as catfish, porgy (which changes the color of its skin at night), robalo (with a long body and fine scales), and *besugo* (also known as *ceja de oro,* or golden eyebrow). These fish are essential to the local diet. ¶ From the time they are just eight years old, young boys venture out in boats with their fathers to learn the trade. Before I went to Chiapas, I was told I would see young men fish the *mar vivo* (open seas) of the Pacific Ocean, whose unpredictability focuses their attention

CUISINE OF THE WATER GODS

and makes the young fishermen fall in love with the fascinating maritime world. ¶ It seems as if I have always known the secrets of this hidden place. When I finally arrived, it was as if I were becoming reacquainted with an old friend.

ROASTED SHRIMP WITH LIME JUICE
CAMARÓN ASADO AL LIMÓN

Serves 8

Tapachula, situated on the left bank of the Coatán River in the Soconusco region, is surrounded by large fields of coffee, cacao, and banana trees. Although agriculture is a prime concern here, river fishing also is essential in many local dishes, including this one.

PREPARE THE SHRIMP: Preheat a wok or a deep skillet and stir-fry the shrimp in their own juices. Season with salt and cook until the shrimp are pink and the shells are crisp. Remove the shrimp from the wok, sprinkle with lime juice, and set aside. Peel shrimp when slightly cooled.

PREPARE THE GARNISH: Preheat the oven to 400°F. Preheat the oil in a wok or a deep skillet and fry the tortillas until crisp. Transfer the tortillas to paper towels with a slotted spoon. Or, brush the tortillas with water, sprinkle with salt, place on a large baking sheet, and bake until they are golden brown and crisp, about 10 minutes. Set aside. Toss the cabbage with the onion, tomatoes, and chiles in a glass bowl. Season with salt and let stand for about 1 hour before serving.

TO SERVE: Line a platter with the tortillas. Top each tortilla with 1 or 2 shrimp and some of the vegetable mixture. Serve immediately because the tortillas will become soggy.

VARIATION: Serve the tortillas on 6 to 8 individual plates that have first been dusted with chile powder.

FOR THE SHRIMP

2 pounds medium shrimp, unshelled

Sea salt to taste

Juice of 4 to 6 limes

FOR THE GARNISH

1 cup vegetable oil

32 tortilla rounds (each 1½ inches in diameter; use a cookie cutter to make even circles)

Salt to taste

2½ cups shredded white or red cabbage

½ medium white onion, peeled and finely chopped

1 pound ripe tomatoes, chopped

4 to 5 fresh serrano chiles, chopped

MULLET ROE IN VINAIGRETTE
HUEVA DE LISA EN VINAGRETA

Serves 6

FOR THE ROE

- 6 cups water
- 1 medium onion, peeled and sliced
- ½ head garlic, halved but not peeled
- 8 sprigs thyme
- 8 sprigs marjoram
- 1 teaspoon dried oregano leaves
- Salt to taste
- 4 fresh mullet roe (about 6 ounces each), rinsed and tied in cheesecloth

FOR THE VINAIGRETTE

- 1 medium white onion, peeled and thinly sliced on the bias
- ½ cup cider vinegar
- ⅓ cup balsamic vinegar
- Extra-virgin olive oil for drizzling
- Salt and coarsely ground black pepper to taste

The city of Tonalá, known as "the city of the sun," rises from the right bank of the Zanatenco River. The tremendous bounty from the lagoons, the sea, and the river are sold in this charming town with narrow streets that shield residents from the burning midday sun. The packaging and freezing of dried shrimp is one of the area's major businesses. As for the local diet, catfish, sea bass, and mullet are staples. Mullet, or *lisa* in Spanish, is eaten fresh or salted and dried. The roe is put to good use in this local recipe. Substitute other roe if you like.

PREPARE THE ROE: Bring the water to a boil in a medium casserole. Add the onion, garlic, herbs, salt, and roe and simmer covered for 20 minutes or until the roe is soft but not overcooked. (A toothpick should slide easily through the cooked roe.) Cool the roe in the liquid to room temperature and then refrigerate for 30 minutes.

PREPARE THE VINAIGRETTE: Meanwhile, place the onion slices in a glass bowl. Cover with the vinegars and drizzle with oil. Season with salt and pepper and set aside.

TO SERVE: Remove the cheesecloth from the liquid and unwrap the roe. Slice the roe into ½-inch pieces. Scatter slices of roe over a platter and drizzle with the vinaigrette and onions. Serve with slices of French bread or rolls.

EGGS WITH PUMPKIN-SEED SAUCE
HUEVOS CON PEPITA

Serves 8

This recipe for a classic Chiapas creation comes from the family of Diana Penagos. It can be served at breakfast as well as for lunch or even a simple dinner. Similar creations, all served with toasted pumpkin-seed mole, have been a part of the local cuisine since pre-Hispanic times.

PREPARE THE TOMATO SAUCE: Preheat a medium skillet, add the tomatoes and cook, turning often with tongs, until evenly roasted. Set the tomatoes aside. Roast the onion in the skillet, then roast the garlic. Puree the roasted tomatoes, onion, and garlic with the water and strain. To the same hot skillet, add the olive oil and cook the onion slices until they are caramelized. Add a small quantity of the tomato sauce to the pan and cook briefly over medium heat. Add the rest of the sauce and the chiles and season with a small amount of salt. Simmer uncovered until the sauce starts to thicken. Taste and correct the seasoning and keep warm.

PREPARE THE PUMPKIN-SEED SAUCE: Heat the water in a medium casserole along with the epazote, garlic, and 6 of the chiles. Simmer covered for about 30 minutes; strain and discard the solids. Preheat a deep skillet and toast half of the pumpkin seeds at a time. The seeds should be light brown in color; if they turn dark brown, the sauce will be bitter. Remove the seeds from the skillet and grind in a spice grinder into an oily paste. Roast the remaining 4 chiles on both sides, then roast the onion. Puree the roasted chiles, onion, and *masa* in a blender or a food processor along with the hot water; strain the sauce, discarding the solids and reserving the hot liquid. Place the ground pumpkin seeds in a bowl and start adding small quantities of the hot chile and onion liquid until the mixture becomes soft. Stir in the epazote liquid in small quantities until the sauce pours but is smooth. Gently simmer the sauce until it has a velvety consistency. Season the sauce with salt and keep warm.

FOR THE TOMATO SAUCE

- 1½ pounds ripe plum tomatoes
- 1 medium white onion, peeled
- 3 medium cloves garlic or 1 clove elephant garlic, peeled
- 1 cup water
- ¼ cup olive oil
- 2 white onion slices
- 4 fresh de árbol or serrano chiles

Salt to taste

FOR THE PUMPKIN-SEED SAUCE

- 4 to 5 cups water
- 6 sprigs epazote
- 6 medium cloves garlic, peeled
- 10 fresh serrano chiles
- 3 cups shelled pumpkin seeds
- 1 small white onion, peeled
- ⅓ cup fresh *masa* (corn dough)
- ½ cup hot water

Salt to taste

FOR THE EGGS

- 16 eggs

FOR THE GARNISH

- 16 freshly made tortillas (between 4 and 6 inches in diameter), warmed

CONTINUED

8 sprigs epazote or small fresh *hoja santa* leaves, sliced into fine julienne

PREPARE THE EGGS: Poach the eggs gently. Do not overcook them; they should not be too runny either. Or hard-boil the eggs and slice them into thin strips.

TO SERVE: Cover each of 8 serving plates with 2 warm tortillas. Top with the poached or sliced eggs and cover with the sauces. Garnish with the epazote.

SHRIMP AND BLACK BEAN TAMALES
TAMALES JUACANE

Makes 60 tamales

These tamales are typical of Jiquipilas, although they are also eaten in other regions, especially Tuxtla Gutiérrez. They can be served with *chicha* (a beverage made with the juice extracted from sugarcane) or *tepache* (a fermented drink flavored with brown sugar and pineapple rinds). These particular tamales are frequently made on holidays during Holy Week and on May 3 (Holy Cross Day) and November 1 (All Saints' Day) and 2 (Day of the Dead). Shrimp is the key ingredient, and it is pulled from shallow inlets at night with the aid of lamps or candles, which attract the shrimp. Fishermen also trap shrimp in the still waters of the Mar Muerto, or "Dead Sea."

FOR THE FILLING

12 cups water
1 pound dried black beans, sorted, soaked overnight in water to cover, and drained
1½ medium white onions, peeled and halved
3 bunches scallions, tied in a bundle
10 medium cloves garlic, peeled
10 fresh serrano, de árbol, or simojovel chiles
Sea salt to taste
½ pound tiny shrimp, peeled
3 cups shelled pumpkin seeds

FOR THE TAMALES

3½ pounds fresh *masa* (corn dough)
½ cup hot water
Salt to taste

PREPARE THE FILLING: Bring the water to a boil in a large pot. Add the beans, onions, and scallions. Cook the beans covered until soft, 1 to 1½ hours. Drain the cooked beans, discard the onions and scallions, and reserve 3½ cups of the bean cooking liquid. Puree 4 cups of the beans in a food processor or a blender with the garlic, chiles, and salt. (Reserve any remaining beans for another use.) Preheat a wok and toast the shrimp with a small amount of salt until dry. Grind the shrimp and stir into the bean mixture. Heat a medium skillet and toast the pumpkin seeds until light brown in color. Stir often with a wooden spoon to ensure even cooking and to prevent burning. Grind the seeds into a powder and stir into the bean mixture.

PREPARE THE TAMALES: Spread the *masa* over a flat surface and sprinkle with the hot water and a generous amount of salt. Knead, adding the water a little at a time, until the dough is smooth and soft, about 5 minutes. Start working in the bean cooking liquid in small amounts and continue kneading until the dough has a very soft texture. (Depending on the quality of the *masa*, you will need 2½ to 3½ cups of bean cooking liquid.) Use a spatula to coat each sweated banana leaf with 1 tablespoon of the dough. Top the dough with a *hoja santa* leaf. Place 1 tablespoon of the bean mixture in the center of the leaf and spread the mixture across the middle of the leaf. Roll each leaf into a taco shape or fold into a square packet. Close the edges and tie the bundle with banana string. Pour the 8 cups water into a large steamer fitted with a rack or a tamale pot fitted with reeds. Season the water with salt and line the rack with a layer of banana leaves. Place the wrapped tamales on top of the leaves, leaving some space for the steam to rise and to ensure even cooking of all the tamales. Cover the steamer and cook for about 1½ hours, or until the tamales can easily be peeled from the banana leaves.

TO SERVE: Place the tamales in a large bamboo steamer or on a large platter lined with a layer of *hoja santa* leaves.

VARIATION: The tamales can be served with the tomato sauce used in Eggs with Pumpkin-Seed Sauce on page 157.

Note: These tamales can be frozen.

60 fresh banana leaves (each 5 inches by 5 inches), wrapped in foil and sweated in a hot oven for 15 minutes

60 fresh *hoja santa* leaves (each 3 inches by 3 inches)

60 banana leaf strings (each 6 to 8 inches long)

8 cups water

6 fresh banana leaves for lining the steamer

10 small fresh *hoja santa* leaves for garnish

½ cup corn or safflower oil

7 medium cloves garlic, peeled

1 medium white onion, peeled and quartered

2 cups long-grain rice, washed, soaked in hot water for 10 minutes, drained, and rinsed under cold water until the water runs clear

½ pound dried shrimp, soaked in hot water for 15 minutes and drained, or 1½ pounds small fresh shrimp, peeled

½ medium white onion, peeled

⅓ cup *achiote* paste or 1½ tablespoons annatto seeds, ground

¼ pound ripe tomatoes, quartered

½ cup water

Salt to taste

1 cup finely chopped carrots, blanched in salted water for about 6 minutes

1 cup finely chopped string beans, blanched in salted water for about 6 minutes

2½ to 3 cups boiling water or chicken stock (exact amount depends on the variety of rice)

18 sprigs parsley

4 fresh serrano or jalapeño chiles

RICE WITH DRIED SHRIMP
ARROZ CON CAMARÓN SECO
Serves 8

As in the coastal regions of nearby Oaxaca, shrimp is a key ingredient for many dishes prepared along the Chiapas coast. Fresh shrimp is usually grilled or cooked in sauces, while dried shrimp appears in numerous dishes, including tamales. Dried shrimp is often seasoned with lime juice and hot sauce and served in small tortillas. In this dish, it accompanies rice, another key staple in the region.

Heat the oil in a casserole, add 4 of the garlic cloves and the onion quarters, and lightly brown. Add the rice to the casserole and stir with a wooden spoon to coat evenly with the oil. Sauté the rice until light brown in color. Drain the rice and discard the oil, garlic, and onion. Heat the casserole again, add the rice and the shrimp, and stir-fry until the shrimp turns pink. Meanwhile, puree the onion half, *achiote* paste, tomatoes, remaining 3 garlic cloves, and water in a blender or a food processor until the mixture forms a thin sauce. Strain the sauce and add it to the casserole. Simmer, stirring often with a wooden spoon, until the rice absorbs the tomato mixture. Season with salt. Add the vegetables, boiling water, 10 parsley sprigs, and chiles. Cover the casserole and cook over low heat until the rice becomes fluffy, about 40 minutes.

To serve: Serve the rice in deep soup plates with the remaining sprigs of fresh parsley.

Variation: Serve each portion of rice with 2 crayfish, either boiled or grilled.

DRIED FISH SOUP WITH VEGETABLES
PUCHERO DE PESCADO ESTILO PUERTO MADERO

Serves 8

Fishermen arrive every morning at Puerto Madero to sell freshly caught fish. At the local market, the fish are displayed on thick tables made from branches or long pieces of wood. The tables are set up under a thatched roof to shield the fish from the hot sun. Men, women, and children fillet and clean the fish with sharp blades. The women at the market have the special task of drying some of the fish. They generously coat the fish with coarse sea salt and pile the fish on top of one another in order to extract as much liquid as possible. The fish are moved into the sun and after a day or two (larger fish may take 3 days), the salted fish are transferred into sacks and stored for later use.

PREPARE THE STOCK: Place the pieces of dried fish in a large bowl with water to cover. Soak for about 4 hours, changing the water at least twice. Bring the 16 cups water to a boil in a large stockpot. Add the small cleaned fish, fish heads, roasted onions, scallions, roasted garlic, celery, turnips, peppercorns, cumin seeds, oregano, parsley, and salt. Simmer covered for about 1½ hours. Strain the stock and pour the liquid into a casserole; discard the solids. Drain the dried fish and add it to the casserole. Simmer covered for about 20 minutes or until soft. Keep the stock warm.

PREPARE THE SAUCE: Heat the oil in a casserole. Add the onion and sauté until caramelized. Puree the roasted tomatoes and add to the onion along with the green pepper. Simmer uncovered over medium heat for about 20 minutes or until the sauce has reduced and thickened. Add the vegetables along with 6 cups of the hot stock and the chile. Cover the casserole and simmer until the vegetables are cooked through, about 25 minutes. Add the rest of the stock and the fish, taste for salt, and simmer uncovered for 15 minutes.

TO SERVE: Ladle the soup into 8 deep soup plates and garnish with the parsley and the limes. Accompany with toasted tortillas.

FOR THE STOCK

- 2½ pounds salted mullet, sea bass, or cod, cut into 1-inch pieces
- 16 cups water
- 2 pounds fresh sea bass or grouper, cleaned
- 2 medium fish heads
- 1½ medium white onions, peeled and roasted
- 3 bunches scallions
- 1 head garlic, peeled and roasted
- 1 heart celery
- 6 small turnips, peeled
- 20 black peppercorns
- 12 cumin seeds
- 1½ teaspoons fresh oregano
- 40 sprigs parsley

Dash of salt

FOR THE SAUCE

- ⅓ cup olive oil
- 6 tablespoons finely chopped white onion
- 1 pound ripe tomatoes, roasted
- 1 medium green pepper, finely chopped
- 1 pound yuca, peeled and cut into 1-inch pieces
- ½ pound medium ripe plantains, peeled and cut into 1-inch pieces
- ½ pound sweet potatoes, peeled and cut into 1-inch pieces
- 2 medium chayotes (water pears) or zucchinis, peeled and quartered
- 1 fresh habanero chile

Salt to taste

FOR THE GARNISH

- 2 tablespoons minced parsley
- 8 limes, halved

FOR THE FISH

- ¼ cup *achiote* paste
- ½ teaspoon ground saffron
- 1 cinnamon stick (about 3 inches long)
- 10 dried de árbol chiles or 14 dried japonés chiles, lightly toasted in a warm skillet
- 8 medium cloves garlic, peeled
- ¾ cup cider vinegar
- ½ cup balsamic vinegar
- 1½ cups fresh orange or grapefruit juice
- 1 cup extra-virgin olive oil

Salt to taste

- 1 whole red snapper, mullet, sea bass, or baby shark (about 5 pounds)
- ½ cup clarified butter or lard

Sea salt and freshly ground black pepper to taste

- 3 large fresh banana leaves, wrapped in aluminum foil and sweated in a hot oven for 15 minutes
- 8 large sprigs epazote or thyme

Fresh bay leaves or oregano leaves to taste

FOR THE GARNISH

- 16 dried de árbol, Simojovel, or japonés chiles, stir-fried until crisp
- 32 ounces canned hearts of palm, sliced, brushed with olive oil, and lightly grilled
- 4 medium chayotes (water pears) or zucchinis, peeled, quartered, and blanched in salted water until tender
- 2 tablespoons minced epazote or cilantro

ROASTED WHOLE FISH WITH GRILLED HEARTS OF PALM
PESCADO ASADO CON PALMITO

Serves 8

The Mayan heritage endures today with majestic monuments at Bonampak, built on the banks of Lacanjá River, and Yaxchilán in the eastern section of Chiapas. The latter city was home to tremendous stone buildings, many erected along the banks of the Usumacinta River, which divides Mexico and Guatemala. Hearts of palm are a particularly important crop in this tropical climate.

Puree the *achiote* paste with the saffron, cinnamon, and chiles in a blender or a food processor. Add the garlic, vinegars, fruit juice, ½ cup olive oil, and salt and blend until the mixture forms a smooth paste. Slit the fish along the belly and debone, leaving the head and tail attached. Place the fish on a large shallow dish and baste with the marinade. Cover the fish and refrigerate for at least 3 hours or overnight.

Preheat the oven to 400°F. Pour the clarified butter and the remaining ½ cup olive oil into a large skillet set over high heat. When the fat is very hot, add the fish (reserving the marinade) and sear on both sides. Sprinkle the fish with sea salt and pepper while it cooks. Line a large roasting pan with 2 very long pieces of aluminum foil and then the sweated banana leaves. Lay the fish on top of the leaves, drizzle with the marinade and cooking juices, and top with the fresh herbs. Wrap the banana leaves over the fish and stretch the aluminum foil from the bottom of the pan over the entire package. Seal the foil tightly. Bake for 40 to 45 minutes or until the fish flakes but is not overcooked or dry.

TO SERVE: Remove and discard the aluminum foil. Transfer the fish in the banana leaves to a large platter and open the package. Top the fish with the chiles and garnish the platter with the grilled hearts of palm and the chayotes. Sprinkle the platter with the minced epazote. Serve with freshly made tortillas.

VARIATION: The fish can be stuffed with the hearts of palm and then cooked.

SQUID AND CRAYFISH WITH MUSHROOMS AND SQUASH BLOSSOMS
CALAMAR Y LANGOSTINOS CON HONGO OREJITA Y FLOR DE CALABAZA

Serves 8

Near the Guatemalan border lies the town of Puerto Madero, home to a major wharf since 1975. Numerous fishing boats return to this port laden with fresh seafood. This dish pairs two local staples, squid and langoustines, with vegetables grown in the interior regions of Chiapas. Although tree ears or chanterelles are my first choices for this dish, use any fresh wild or cultivated mushrooms that are in season. Squash blossoms should be cleaned before cooking. Simply cut them in half lengthwise and remove the tough stamens from the inside of the flowers.

PREPARE THE SQUID AND CRAYFISH: Heat the fish stock in a medium casserole. Add the onions, garlic, fresh herbs, peppercorns, cloves, and salt and simmer for 20 minutes. Add the squid and cook covered until soft, about 10 minutes. Remove the squid and set aside. Add the crayfish and simmer uncovered for 2 to 3 minutes, depending on their size. Remove and set aside with the squid and ¹/₂ cup cooking liquid.

PREPARE THE VEGETABLES: Heat the oil in a medium casserole or saucepan. Add the onions and sauté until light brown. Add the garlic, chiles, mushrooms, and squash blossoms. Season with a small amount of salt, add the cilantro and epazote sprigs, and sauté over medium heat for about 7 minutes until the liquid thrown off by the mushrooms has evaporated.

TO SERVE: Just before serving, add the reserved squid and crayfish along with ¹/₂ cup cooking liquid to the mushrooms and squash blossoms and simmer covered for about 4 minutes. Remove the tied bundles of herbs and serve on a large, deep platter. Sprinkle with the chopped cilantro and serve immediately with the tortillas.

FOR THE SQUID AND CRAYFISH

- 4 cups fish stock
- 1¹/₂ medium white onions, peeled and sliced
- 1 head garlic, halved but not peeled
- 4 fresh bay leaves
- 2 sprigs marjoram
- 2 sprigs thyme
- 8 black peppercorns
- 4 whole cloves
- Salt to taste
- 32 small squid, cleaned
- 16 medium crayfish, heads and shells removed, deveined, and cleaned

FOR THE VEGETABLES

- ¹/₃ to ¹/₂ cup extra-virgin olive oil
- 1¹/₂ medium white onions, peeled and finely chopped
- 4 medium cloves garlic, peeled and finely chopped
- 2 fresh jalapeño chiles, slit on the side
- 2 pounds mushrooms, sliced
- 1¹/₂ pounds fresh squash blossoms, cleaned
- Salt to taste
- 30 sprigs cilantro, tied
- 4 sprigs epazote, tied

FOR THE GARNISH

- 2 tablespoons finely chopped cilantro
- 32 small round tortillas (toasted or deep-fried, optional)

ZOQUE BLACK BEANS
FRIJOLES ZOQUES
Serves 8 to 10

FOR THE BEANS

- 12 cups water
- 1 pound dried black beans, sorted, soaked overnight in water to cover, and drained
- 1½ medium white onions, peeled and halved
- 3 bunches scallions, tied in a bundle
- 1 head garlic, halved but not peeled

Salt to taste

- ¾ cup corn or safflower oil or to taste
- 8 strips bacon or ¼ cup minced chorizo sausage
- 1 medium white onion, peeled and minced

FOR THE GARNISH

- 2 tablespoons olive oil
- 12 dried de árbol chiles or 20 small dried Simojovel chiles or 14 dried japonés chiles

Salt to taste

The Zoques are one of the ancient Indian communities that still exist in the state of Chiapas. The region is also home to the Lacandons, Choles, Tojolabals, Chamulas, Mames, Tzeltals, and Tzotzils. The Zoques, who live in the villages of Mezcalapa, Simojovel, and Pichucalco, speak an unusually melodic language. They cultivate coffee, cacao beans, vanilla, sugarcane, bananas, and the rare Simojovel chile, which lends its special flavor to so many of their recipes. This tiny red chile is toasted on a warm *comal* or stir-fried in oil with some salt and then ground and used in condiments. Simojovel chiles appear in numerous sauces or as garnishes for many Zoque dishes. These beans are a good accompaniment to fish, seafood, or egg dishes.

PREPARE THE BEANS: Bring the water to a boil in a large pot. Add the beans, onions, scallions, and garlic. Cook the beans covered until soft, 1 to 1½ hours. If the water evaporates before the beans soften, add small quantities of hot water. Season with salt and simmer the beans until thick. Remove the scallions and the garlic and puree the beans with ½ cup of the cooking liquid in a food processor or a blender until they form a thick puree. Preheat a medium casserole, add the oil, and fry the bacon strips until crisp. Remove the bacon and drain on paper towels. Crumble and reserve the bacon. Add the onion and cook uncovered until it has begun to caramelize. Add small portions of the bean puree, stirring constantly while cooking over medium heat. Add all of the beans and simmer uncovered until they are very thick and can be flipped like an omelet.

PREPARE THE GARNISH: Heat the oil in a medium skillet. Add the chiles and quickly stir-fry them with a pinch of salt. Do not let them burn. Remove the skillet from the heat as soon as the chiles are crisp.

TO SERVE: Scoop the beans onto a large platter and garnish with the reserved bacon and whole chiles. Or chop the chiles and sprinkle over the beans, if desired. Serve with freshly made tortillas.

VARIATIONS: Flavor the beans with a bunch of *chipilín,* an herb that grows in Chiapas and has a smoky flavor. Garnish with the chiles and crumbled feta or farmer cheese.

WATERMELON IN CINNAMON SYRUP
DULCE DE SANDÍA

Serves 8 to 10

The desserts of Chiapas are characterized by the use of fruits in heavy sugar syrups. In Mazatán, which is located on the coast near Soconusco, sweets like this one are served at the Feast of the Virgin of Concepción. According to local legend, the virgin bathed in the nearby sea and for this reason residents today still give thanks to the waters that cleansed her.

PREPARE THE WATERMELON: Cut the watermelon into thick slices. Slice away the fruit and the white part of the skin, leaving just the hard green rind. (Reserve the fruit for another use.) Place the slices of rind in a medium bowl and cover with water. Pour the limestone into ½ cup of water and stir briskly with a spoon to dissolve. Pour the limestone mixture into the bowl with the watermelon rinds and let stand for about 6 hours or overnight. Drain the rinds and rinse under running water until the water runs clear.

PREPARE THE SYRUP: Pour the water into a deep pan and add the cinnamon. Bring the water to a boil and simmer uncovered for about 20 minutes. Stir in the sugar and simmer the syrup over medium heat until it starts to thicken. Add the watermelon rinds and cook uncovered over low heat until they have absorbed some of the sugar, about 2 to 3 hours.

TO SERVE: Serve the rinds in deep bowls with the syrup drizzled on top. Garnish bowls with cinnamon sticks.

FOR THE WATERMELON
- 4 pounds unripe watermelon
- 6 tablespoons powdered limestone

FOR THE SYRUP
- 12 cups water
- 8 Mexican or regular cinnamon sticks (each about 6 inches long)
- 8 cups brown sugar or grated *piloncillo* (solidified brown sugar)

QUINTANA ROO

LOBSTER SALAD XEL-HÁ STYLE

CONCH CEVICHE WITH *HABANERO* SAUCE

ARTICHOKE HEARTS STUFFED WITH BABY SHARK

BABY SHARK *BOCADOS*

WHOLE FISH BAKED IN BANANA LEAVES

BARRACUDA WITH XCATICK CHILES, ROASTED
GARLIC, AND GREENS

BAKED SQUASH STUFFED WITH SQUID
IN MAYAN ESSENCES

YUCA AND POMPANO FRITTERS

PAPAYA IN BROWN SUGAR SYRUP

CHICOZAPOTE FROM THE SOUTHEAST

The state of Quintana Roo is located on the Yucatán Peninsula in southeastern Mexico. It is bounded by the state of Yucatán to the northwest, Campeche to the west, the Caribbean to the east, and Guatemala and Belize to the south. The state, which was the last to be admitted to the republic, is named for Andrés Quintana Roo, a leading figure in Mexico's struggle for independence. The capital is Chetumal, a city known for its extraordinary blue cenote sinkholes and lush vegetation.

The Itzaes, a Maya tribe, first settled in this area at the beginning of the fifth century. Today visitors can explore the region's past at the Mayan cities of Tulum, Cobá, and Kohuunlich. Modern pleasures draw tourists to resort islands like Cancún and Cozumel. Crystal-clear turquoise waters wash over fine sand beaches, and thousands of brilliantly colored fish and undersea vegetation dazzle divers.

This hot and humid land is rich in corn and beans, which are basic to many local dishes. Other important ingredients include squash, chayote, yuca, red onions, custard apples, mameys, and coconuts. However, the glory of Quintana Roo's cuisine is shellfish, thanks to more than five hundred miles of coastline on the Gulf of Mexico and the Caribbean. In addition, numerous freshwater ponds and creeks supply species that are central to the indigenous diet.

This is the testament of my life from the day I arrived in these new lands. ¶ My name is José Santiago de Montesinos, and I write my story on a large, pleated leaf like those the Mayans used. We set sail from Cuba and soon encountered savage seas. The wind and waves were so fierce that we had to cling to one another or grasp the main sail to stay on board. Amid the wild storms we took care to keep our schooner with the rest of the small flotilla. Finally, after many days at sea, the lookout spotted land in the distance, and my companions gazed in amazement as a magnificent stone building perched atop a cliff came into view. I now know this wondrous construction as Zamá (Tulum) or *la ciudad del amanecer,* "city of the dawn." ¶ The first thing that attracted our attention was the customs of the natives. As we disembarked we were greeted by several men, who escorted us four sailors and our captain into the presence of an old and venerable man. At once he indicated that we should scale the walls of the fortress with him. As we climbed past clay figures and huge idols carved in stone, I confess without shame that I prayed in silence to the Holy Father. ¶ When we reached the top, the old man dropped some aromatic herbs into an offering vase and lit them, releasing a strong aroma not familiar to us, but serene and soothing. The old man began to conduct some sort of ritual at one of the radiant altars, chanting a native song in a high, loud voice to invoke the spirits of his ancestors, I supposed. The beauty of the scene was unimaginable. ¶ Eventually we emerged into the surrounding jungle. To my mind, it resembled paradise. We came upon a well-constructed city whose grandeur surpassed anything in the Old World. I realized we were in the presence of a culture more advanced than our own. My eyes could not comprehend all that they saw. I literally was stunned by so much novelty. The natives were dressed in clothes that barely hid their shame, their bodies adorned with mirrorlike stones and gold jewelry that drew my gaze. We were conducted to the home of the chief leader for a meal and some refreshment. We sat underneath a grass roof and soon became intoxicated by the heavy perfume of fruits that bore no resemblance to foods we knew. I learned their names with time—jicama, *zapote,* mamey (*zapodilla*), papaya, and *anona* (cherimoya). ¶ A robust Indian ordered the women to prepare our meal. At the time I didn't know what it was that I ate, but it tasted like the food of the angels. I thought I recognized a familiar aroma, but it was only a trick of my memory. Today, I know that banquet consisted of black beans, chiles, tortillas, wild turkey, and dried fish, as well as fresh local fish that fishermen had caught early that morning. The coastal waters were home to gray mullet (*lisa*), white mullet (*Mugil curema*), sea bass, sea trout, grouper, Gulf lobster, sailfish, swordfish, porgy, barracuda, manta ray, and small turtles. I also was invited to taste honey from local hives and green water from a deep limestone well. I learned that corn is a god to the Mayans, who believe that the flesh of men is kneaded of *masa,* or corn dough. ¶ Still, I have to confess that I didn't find in this course of events the gentle life enjoyed by my compatriot Jerónimo de Aguilar y Gonzalo Guerrero, who lived with a beautiful maiden and shared his bloodline to give birth to a new lineage of men. It took me a long time to traverse these impenetrable jungles, cross through swampy marsh lands filled with mangrove trees, and walk along the long coastlines, but I must return to my native Spanish soil. As I head back to the sea, I realize this is the last time I will see these venerable waters in this corner of the world that is illuminated by another sun.

LOBSTER SALAD XEL-HÁ STYLE
ENSALADA DE LANGOSTA ESTILO XEL-HÁ

Serves 8

North of Tulum is another important site of Mayan culture, called Xel-Há. Ancient altars grace the lagoon at this seaside spot and serve as testament to the region's rich past. Today, fishermen fashion traps out of mangrove wood and palm leaves to catch the prized lobsters that inhabit local waters. In addition to the bounty from the sea, residents rely on crops grown in nearby fertile lands and ingredients like saffron that were introduced to the region by the Spanish.

PREPARE THE LOBSTER: Bring the water to a boil in a large casserole. Add the salt and the lobster tails and simmer uncovered until the lobster is almost cooked, 6 to 8 minutes. Remove the casserole from the heat, cover, and set aside for about 3 minutes. Drain and use a pair of scissors or a sharp knife to cut open the shells and remove the lobster meat. Shred the meat and set aside.

PREPARE THE SALAD: Combine the onion, mayonnaise, yogurt, juice, and roasted chile in a glass bowl. Blend together the roasted garlic and the saffron and toss with the ingredients in the glass bowl. Season with salt. Add the shredded lobster and toss well. Marinate in the refrigerator for about 2 hours.

TO SERVE: Use a 1½-inch round cookie cutter to place equal portions of the lobster salad on 8 large chilled plates. Top the salad with the thin strips of radishes and cucumbers. Garnish each plate with half of a habanero chile and sprinkle the edges with white and black pepper. Serve with toasted bread or tortillas.

VARIATION: Sprinkle the plates with finely ground pumpkin seeds.

FOR THE LOBSTER

12 cups water
Salt to taste
4 lobster tails in shells

FOR THE SALAD

1 cup finely chopped red onion
1 cup mayonnaise
1½ cups plain yogurt
½ cup fresh Seville orange juice or juice of 2 regular oranges and 2 limes
1½ tablespoons roasted and finely chopped fresh habanero or serrano chiles
2 medium cloves garlic, peeled and roasted in a hot skillet
1½ teaspoons saffron, lightly toasted in a warm skillet
Salt to taste

FOR THE GARNISH

½ long radish, sliced paper thin
2 medium cucumbers, peeled and sliced paper thin
4 fresh habanero or serrano chiles, halved
Freshly ground black pepper and white pepper to taste

CONCH CEVICHE WITH *HABANERO SAUCE*
CEBICHE DE CARACOL AKUMAL CON SALSA
DE CHILES HABANEROS

Serves 6

FOR THE CEVICHE

- 1½ medium red onions, peeled and finely chopped
- 6 medium ripe plum tomatoes, finely chopped
- 2 fresh habanero or serrano chiles, finely chopped
- 1¾ pounds fresh conch or shrimp (if using shrimp, peel and devein and simmer in boiling water for 2 minutes)
- Juice of 8 limes
- 6 tablespoons extra-virgin olive oil
- Salt to taste
- 1 medium ripe avocado, peeled and finely chopped

FOR THE *HABANERO* SAUCE

- 6 medium cloves garlic, peeled and roasted in a hot skillet
- 1 medium white onion, peeled and roughly chopped
- 12 fresh habanero or serrano chiles, chopped
- 1½ cups strong cider vinegar or white vinegar
- 1 cup boiling water
- ¼ cup extra-virgin olive oil
- Salt to taste

FOR THE GARNISH

Saltines or other crackers
Lime wedges

Wild jungle landscape meets sandy white beaches at Akumal, which is not far from the archaeological sites at Xel-Há. The village name means "nest of the turtles" in the Mayan language. In addition to the turtles that arrive each year to deposit their eggs in the sand, the nearby woods are home to numerous animals, including armadillos, deer, jaguars, wild turkeys, and rabbits. Of course, the water teems with animal life as well, including lobsters, barracuda, sailfish, crabs, shrimp, and conch. Ceviche recipes like this one date back to Mayan times and are still prepared on the beach at Akumal.

PREPARE THE CEVICHE: Combine the onions, tomatoes, and chiles in a large glass bowl. Pound the conch on a flat surface to tenderize or, if conch is not absolutely fresh, cook in boiling water until tender, about 10 minutes. Finely chop the conch (or cooked shrimp) and stir it into the mixture in the glass bowl. Add the lime juice, olive oil, salt, and avocado and toss with 2 spoons. Marinate in the refrigerator for about 20 minutes.

PREPARE THE *HABANERO* SAUCE: Puree the roasted garlic, the onion, and the chiles in a blender or a food processor. Add the vinegar, boiling water, olive oil, and salt and blend until the mixture forms a smooth sauce. Pour this fiery sauce into a bottle with a very small opening so that it may be poured one drop at a time.

TO SERVE: Transfer the ceviche to 6 small bowls. Serve with the sauce, crackers, and limes on the side.

Note: The sauce must be used in very small quantities or its intense flavor will overwhelm the delicate flavor of the conch. Use the remaining *habanero* sauce in other seafood dishes or in any recipe that calls for hot sauce.

ARTICHOKE HEARTS STUFFED WITH BABY SHARK
FONDOS DE ALCACHOFA CON CAZÓN A LA CANCÚN

Serves 8

Palm trees shading white sands and clear blue waters stand guard along Mexico's Caribbean coast. The incomparable beaches at Cancún give way to extensive coral reefs with brightly colored marine life. Snorkeling is not reserved for the professionals, as tourists and other visitors don masks to view the brilliant coral reefs. The nearby Nitchupté lagoon is ringed by dense stands of mangrove trees, which are home to more than 200 species of birds. In addition to the water and land attractions, Cancún boasts a sophisticated cuisine that is a mosaic of dishes from around the country and the world. Refined creations like this one welcome visitors to this tropical paradise.

PREPARE THE STUFFING: Preheat a large skillet, add the oil, and sauté the garlic until it is light brown. Remove garlic and puree in a blender or a food processor. Add the chopped onions to the skillet, season with salt, and cook over medium heat until they are light brown. Stir in the tomatoes and the garlic puree and simmer uncovered until the tomatoes have a very thick consistency, about 1 hour. Meanwhile, pour the water into a steamer and add the sliced onion, the garlic, and oregano. Place the fish on a rack and steam for about 10 minutes. Remove the fish, cool, and shred; strain the liquid and reserve. Stir the shredded fish, olives, capers, and parsley into the tomato sauce and simmer uncovered 25 minutes more. Add ³/₄ cup of the reserved cooking liquid from the fish along with the vinegar from the chiles and continue cooking for about 15 minutes more, or until the mixture has a thick consistency. Season with salt and set aside. (Only half of this stuffing is required for this recipe. Reserve the remaining stuffing for Baby Shark Empanadas on page 200.)

PREPARE THE ARTICHOKE HEARTS: Bring the water to a boil in a medium casserole. Add the lime juice, leek, and onion and simmer covered for 15 minutes. Add the artichoke hearts, remove

FOR THE BABY SHARK STUFFING

- 1 cup olive oil
- 4 large cloves garlic, peeled
- 2 medium white onions, peeled and finely chopped
- Salt to taste
- 2¹/₂ pounds ripe plum tomatoes, finely chopped
- 1 cup water
- ¹/₂ medium white onion, peeled and sliced
- 2 large cloves garlic, peeled and sliced
- Fresh oregano leaves to taste
- 3 pounds baby shark or cod
- 1 cup finely chopped pimiento-stuffed olives
- ¹/₂ cup baby capers
- ²/₃ cup finely chopped parsley
- ¹/₂ cup vinegar from canned chiles (reserve the pickled chiles for another use)

FOR THE ARTICHOKE HEARTS

- 3 cups water
- ¹/₂ cup fresh lime juice
- 1 leek, chopped
- 1 medium onion, peeled and chopped
- 24 large marinated artichoke hearts, drained
- Chopped parsley for garnish

CONTINUED

the casserole from the heat, cover, and let stand for about 4 minutes. Drain the artichokes, discarding the liquid and the other solids. Refrigerate the artichokes or reserve at room temperature until serving time. Stuff each artichoke with 1½ tablespoons of the shark mixture.

TO SERVE: Place 3 stuffed artichokes in each of 8 chilled soup plates. Sprinkle with chopped parsley and serve.

VARIATION: This dish can also be prepared with 8 whole artichokes. Snap off tough outer leaves, peel but do not trim away the stems, and use a small spoon to scoop out the fuzzy choke from the centers. Rub all cut surfaces with lemon juice as you work to prevent discoloration. Whole artichokes should be cooked as above until tender, about 25 minutes. Chill, stuff, and serve.

BABY SHARK *BOCADOS*
BOCADOS DE CAZÓN
Serves 8

FOR THE FILLING
½ recipe baby shark stuffing (page 171)
2 tablespoons raisins
1 teaspoon cinnamon
Dash of ground cloves

FOR THE SAUCE
1½ medium red onions, peeled and finely chopped
6 medium ripe plum tomatoes, finely chopped
1 medium cucumber, peeled and finely chopped

In northern Quintana Roo, there is a place of remarkable tranquillity called Holbox. This island paradise is surrounded by blue-green waters brimming with marine life. In fact, the region is home to a national park dedicated to snorkeling. Baby shark, in shades of gray and brown, are just one of the species that can be seen amid the black coral reefs. The water is so clear that reefs at a depth of 150 feet can be observed from the surface. Perhaps the pristine quality of the water is responsible for the impression that little has changed here since Mayan times. Shark-filled empanadas, called *bocados* in this region, are a local delicacy.

PREPARE THE FILLING: Follow the recipe for the baby shark stuffing on page 171, cutting all quantities in half. Stir in the raisins, cinnamon, and cloves when the olives and the capers are added. Cook until the stuffing is quite thick.

PREPARE THE SAUCE: Toss the onions, tomatoes, cucumber, radishes, chiles, orange juice, vinegars, and salt and pepper in a large glass bowl. Marinate in the refrigerator for about $^{1}/_{2}$ hour before serving.

PREPARE THE DOUGH: Spread the *masa* over a flat surface. Sprinkle with the flour, then add the *achiote* paste, lard, baking powder, salt, and water. Start kneading, adding the water a little at a time, until the dough is shiny and has a somewhat wet consistency. Place the dough on a plate, cover with a damp dishcloth, and let rest for about 15 minutes.

PREPARE THE *BOCADOS:* Divide the dough into 24 small balls, each about 1 inch around. Line a tortilla press with plastic wrap. Place a dough ball in the press and press lightly. Flip the tortilla over and press again very lightly. Peel away the top sheet of plastic and spread 1 teaspoon of the filling across the middle of the tortilla. With the help of the bottom sheet of plastic, fold the edges of the tortilla over the filling. With wet hands, remove the plastic and transfer the *bocado* to a tray lined with waxed or parchment paper and cover the *bocados* with plastic wrap while working. Repeat the process with the rest of the dough balls. Heat the oil and the lard in a wok or a deep frying pan. Add the *bocados* and fry until light brown, basting often with the oil to ensure even cooking. Remove the *bocados* with a slotted spoon and drain on paper towels.

TO SERVE: Place the hot *bocados* on a large warmed platter. Put the sauce in a bowl in the center of the platter and serve immediately with *Xnipec* Salsa (page 198), if desired.

Note: See pages 309 to 310 for more information on making the dough and using the tortilla press.

6 radishes, finely chopped
3 fresh habanero chiles, finely chopped
$^{1}/_{2}$ cup Seville orange or grapefruit juice combined with a dash of lime juice
$^{1}/_{3}$ cup cider vinegar or champagne vinegar
$^{1}/_{4}$ cup balsamic vinegar
Salt and freshly ground black pepper to taste

FOR THE DOUGH
$1^{1}/_{2}$ pounds fresh *masa* (corn dough)
1 tablespoon flour
1 tablespoon *achiote* paste
1 tablespoon softened lard or vegetable oil
$^{1}/_{2}$ teaspoon baking powder
1 teaspoon salt
$^{1}/_{4}$ to $^{1}/_{3}$ cup hot water
3 cups corn or safflower oil
3 tablespoons lard or extra-virgin olive oil

WHOLE FISH BAKED IN BANANA LEAVES
TIK-N-XIC

Serves 8

FOR THE FISH

1 package fresh banana leaves, wrapped in a wet dishcloth and sweated in a hot oven for 20 minutes

Juice of 8 limes

8 large cloves garlic, peeled, roasted, and ground

1 tablespoon black peppercorns, lightly roasted and ground

Sea salt to taste

1 whole grouper, pompano, porgy, sea bass, or red snapper (about 4½ pounds), deboned with head and tail attached

2 medium red onions, peeled and sliced

1 cup epazote leaves

FOR THE SAUCE

½ cup olive oil

10 cloves garlic, peeled

2 tablespoons annatto seeds

½ cup balsamic vinegar, champagne vinegar, or Seville orange juice

Salt and freshly ground black pepper to taste

FOR THE GARNISH

Pickled red onions (page 175)

Navy Beans with Habanero Chiles and Epazote (page 192)

Xnipec Salsa (page 198)

Located in the Caribbean Sea, the island of Cozumel was a sacred sanctuary where Mayan priests attended to the oracles. According to Mayan legend, the island was the house of Ixchel, goddess of the moon, who regulated the seas and the tides. Today, local fishermen still monitor the tides and the seas. *Tik-n-xic* is one of their favorite ways of preparing whole fish. The fish is butterflied, seasoned with lime, garlic, and *achiote* paste, wrapped in banana leaves, and then cooked over a wood fire. This dish is usually prepared underneath palm huts on a beach cooled by ocean breezes. It takes just as well to baking in an oven at home.

PREPARE THE FISH: Line a large baking tray with some of the banana leaves. (Save the rest for wrapping the fish.) Mix the lime juice with the ground garlic, the pepper, and salt. Brush the mixture over the inside and the outside of the fish. Let stand for about 1 hour. Stuff the fish with the red onions and the epazote.

PREPARE THE SAUCE: Preheat the oven to 400°F. Heat the oil in a medium casserole or skillet. Add the garlic and discard when browned. Add the annatto seeds and sauté over low heat until they color the oil. Remove the seeds with a strainer and discard. Remove the casserole from the heat and whisk in the vinegar and salt and pepper. Baste the fish with the prepared oil. Cover the fish with the remaining banana leaves, fold into a tightly sealed packet, and then wrap in aluminum foil. Bake the fish until the flesh flakes, 45 minutes to 1 hour.

TO SERVE: Remove the foil and the top layer of banana leaves from the fish. Place the fish and the bottom layer of banana leaves on a large platter. Garnish with red onions, navy beans, and *xnipec salsa*. Serve with freshly made small tortillas.

VARIATION: This fish can also be grilled. Butterfly the fish and baste with the marinade and the oil. Place a layer of banana leaves on the grill. Place the fish, skin side down, on top of the leaves and cover with more banana leaves to keep moist.

BARRACUDA WITH XCATICK CHILES, ROASTED GARLIC, AND GREENS
BARRACUDA CON CHILES XCATICK, AJOS ASADOS Y CHAYA

Serves 8

Isla Mujeres was founded upon rocky soil and is ringed by small cliffs and white beaches. Known today as a tourist destination, the island was uninhabited for three centuries following the Conquest. Fishermen and pirates looking to stash their loot made occasional visits, but the first post-Conquest settlers, refugees from a local war, did not arrive until the nineteenth century. Today, fishing and tourism are the main businesses. Snorkelers and fishermen alike search the brilliant waters around the island for lobsters, sea urchins, red snapper, angelfish, and barracuda, which can be quite dangerous to humans. The flesh, however, is quite delicious and takes well to this chile-based preparation.

PREPARE THE CHILES, GARLIC, AND GREENS: Slice the chiles into thin strips and set aside. Preheat the oven to 400°F. Brush the garlic with the clarified butter, sprinkle with salt, and bake until caramelized, between 30 and 45 minutes depending on the size of the garlic. Set aside. Wilt the *chaya* leaves in a covered casserole. Add the butter, season with salt, and set aside.

PREPARE THE ONIONS: Bring the water to a boil in a small saucepan, add a pinch of salt and the red onions, and simmer uncovered for about 5 seconds. Drain the onions and transfer to a small bowl. Toss with the vinegars, peppercorns, oregano leaves and salt to taste.

PREPARE THE MARINADE: In a blender or a food processor, puree the *achiote* paste, garlic, grapefruit juice, vinegar, lime juice, olive oil, oregano, peppercorns, cumin, bay leaves, marjoram, and salt. Blend until the mixture forms a smooth paste.

PREPARE THE FISH: Place the fish in a shallow dish and cover with the marinade. Let stand for about 1 hour. Heat a large skillet and roast the garlic; puree with the clarified butter and the olive oil. Add some of the roasted garlic butter to the skil-

FOR THE CHILES, GARLIC, AND GREENS
- 24 fresh xcatick (güero), jalapeño, or Anaheim chiles, roasted, peeled, seeded, and deveined (see page 296)
- 8 heads garlic, halved but not peeled
- 1/4 cup clarified butter
- Salt to taste
- 2 pounds *chaya* or spinach, washed and dried
- 3 tablespoons butter

FOR THE PICKLED ONIONS
- 2 cups water
- Salt to taste
- 2 medium red onions, peeled and thinly sliced on the bias
- 1/2 cup plus 2 tablespoons strong cider vinegar or white vinegar
- 6 tablespoons balsamic vinegar or Seville orange juice
- 1 teaspoon black peppercorns
- 1/2 teaspoon dried oregano leaves, crumbled

FOR THE MARINADE
- 1/4 cup *achiote* paste
- 6 medium cloves garlic, peeled
- 3/4 cup grapefruit juice
- 1/3 cup balsamic vinegar, white

CONTINUED

vinegar, or cider vinegar

⅓ cup lime juice or Seville
orange juice

¼ cup extra-virgin olive oil

1½ teaspoons dried oregano
leaves, crumbled

½ teaspoon black peppercorns

½ teaspoon cumin

4 fresh bay leaves

4 fresh sprigs marjoram

Salt to taste

FOR THE FISH

8 barracuda, grouper, Caribbean
red snapper, or porgy fillets
(about 6 ounces each)

10 cloves garlic, peeled

6 tablespoons clarified butter

¼ cup extra-virgin olive oil

3 cups fish stock, reduced to
1½ cups

let. Cook 4 of the fillets on one side for 2 minutes, turn over, baste with some of the marinade, and continue cooking for another 2 minutes. Set aside in a shallow dish, cover, and repeat with the other 4 fillets and the remaining roasted garlic butter. Transfer the second batch of cooked fish to the covered dish. Add the fish stock and the remaining marinade to the skillet, cover, and simmer until the sauce thickens. Season to taste with salt. Keep the sauce warm.

To SERVE: Place the fish in a hot 400°F oven and bake for 5 minutes. Rewarm the sauce if necessary. Place the fish on 8 large serving dishes and garnish one side of each plate with the chile strips and the other side with the caramelized garlic. Cover the fish with some of the *chaya*, pickled red onions, and warm sauce. Serve immediately.

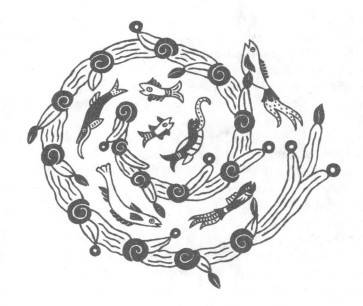

CUISINE OF THE WATER GODS

BAKED SQUASH STUFFED WITH SQUID IN MAYAN ESSENCES
CALAMAR CON ESENCIAS MAYAS ESTILO TULUM

Serves 6

The name Tulum translates as "enclosure" and perhaps refers to the many Mayan structures that once stood in this important archaeological zone. Among the buildings that still survive—all of which are among the most important monuments to ancient civilizations in the entire country—the Temple of God is particularly noteworthy. Decorated with carved symbols of the sea, the planet Venus, the stars, and serpents, this temple brings together many of the diverse elements of Mayan theology. Likewise, this dish reveals the secrets of modern Mexican cookery and its harmoninous balance of ingredients and flavors.

PREPARE THE SQUASH: Preheat the oven to 350°F. Cut a circle around the stem end of each squash. Remove the top and scoop out the stringy pulp and seeds. Drop 1 teaspoon of the butter into the cleaned squash and season with salt and pepper. Replace the top and individually wrap the squash in aluminum foil. Place the squash on a large baking tray and bake for 30 minutes or until soft but not mushy.

PREPARE THE *CHILMOLE* SAUCE: Pour the water into a medium casserole, add the tomatillos, onions, garlic, and chiles, and simmer covered over medium heat for about 20 minutes. Remove the casserole from the heat, cool, and puree the solids and cooking liquid in a blender or a food processor along with the *chilmole* paste. Heat the oil in a medium casserole and sauté the onion slices until light brown. Discard the onion, add the pureed sauce and the epazote, and simmer covered over medium heat for 30 minutes. Season with salt during the cooking and add the stock to thin the sauce. Keep the sauce warm.

PREPARE THE SQUID: Preheat a medium skillet or a wok. Heat the clarified butter and the oil, add the squid, and stir-fry the squid until just cooked. Season with the salt and pepper.

FOR THE SQUASH

- 6 small acorn squash or baby pumpkins (about ½ pound each)
- 6 teaspoons butter
- Salt and freshly ground black pepper to taste

FOR THE *CHILMOLE* SAUCE

- 3 cups water
- 1 pound tomatillos, husked
- 1½ medium white onions, peeled and cut into pieces
- 6 medium cloves garlic, peeled
- 4 fresh serrano chiles
- 3 ounces *chilmole* or *achiote* paste (see Note)
- ⅓ cup olive oil
- 2 white onion slices
- 4 sprigs epazote
- Salt to taste
- 2 cups chicken or fish stock, reduced to 1 cup

FOR THE SQUID

- ⅓ cup clarified butter
- ⅓ cup olive oil
- 36 small squid, slit open, cleaned, and surfaces scored with a sharp knife
- Sea salt and freshly ground black pepper to taste

CONTINUED

6   sprigs epazote

6   fresh xcatick (güero) or Carib chiles, halved

TO SERVE: Unwrap the squash and place in 6 large soup plates. Lift off the tops and fill with some of the *chilmole* sauce and all of the squid. Spoon more sauce into the plates and garnish with the epazote and the chiles. Serve immediately.

Note: Chilmole is a black paste made from chiles, roasted garlic, oregano, cumin, allspice, black pepper, and annatto seeds. *Chilmole* and *achiote* paste are available in Latin markets.

YUCA AND POMPANO FRITTERS
CROQUETITAS DE YUCA CON PÁMPANO
Serves 10

The Chontal people, a branch of the Mayan tribes, came from Tabasco to Quintana Roo around the year 900 B.C. They brought with them a knowledge of navigation and their excellent ability as sailors. They built ports along the coast at Cozumel, Xel-Há, and Xcaret and eventually expanded the empire south into Honduras. Mayan maritime commerce was unrivaled in Mesoamerica. One of their more unusual navigational systems was called *caracol*, after the word for "snail." At Punta Celarain in Cozumel, snail shells were positioned to capture the wind and sound a warning to incoming ships, much like a modern foghorn. Yuca and pompano are ancient ingredients that surely nourished these long-ago sailors.

FOR THE FISH

3   cups water

6   white onion slices

2   large sprigs epazote or cilantro

1   pound pompano, red snapper, barracuda, or shad fillets

PREPARE THE FISH: Bring the water to a boil in a medium saucepan along with the onion slices and the epazote. Add the fish and simmer over low heat for about 6 minutes. Turn off the heat and let stand for about 5 minutes. Drain the fish, discarding the other solids and the liquid. Finely shred the fish and set aside.

FOR THE FRITTERS

8   cups water

Salt to taste

2   pounds yuca, peeled

2   tablespoons butter

4   eggs

1   cup grated *queso cotija* or Parmesan cheese

Salt to taste

2   cups safflower or corn oil combined with 2 cups olive oil

40   thin habanero chiles

40   thin bell pepper strips

40   thin jalapeño chile strips

PREPARE THE FRITTERS: Heat the water in a medium casserole. Add the salt and the yuca and cook covered for about 30 minutes or until the yuca is soft. Drain the yuca into a fine sieve, return to the casserole, and reheat for 10 minutes to evaporate all of the liquid. Transfer the dry yuca to a large bowl. Beat in the butter until smooth. Beat in the eggs, one at a time, the cheese, and the shredded fish. Season with salt. Preheat the oil in a wok or a deep frying pan. With lightly oiled hands, nestle a strip of each chile and the bell pepper inside about 2 tablespoons of the yuca mixture. Repeat to make 40 fritters. Deep-fry the fritters, basting occasionally with the oil, until light brown. Drain on paper towels.

TO SERVE: Transfer the hot fritters to a platter lined with the shredded cabbage. Serve with lime wedges and hot sauce.

Note: Serve the fritters with the *habanero* sauce on page 170.

FOR THE GARNISH

1 medium head red cabbage, shredded
Lime wedges
Hot sauce (see Note)

PAPAYA IN BROWN SUGAR SYRUP
DULCE DE PAPAYA

Serves 8

Throughout the state of Quintana Roo, there are numerous papaya plantations, often just a few miles from the beach. This highly nutritious fruit can be eaten fresh or cooked in a sugar syrup much like pumpkin or squash is prepared in other regions.

PREPARE THE PAPAYA: Use a sharp knife to make several deep incisions down the length of the fruit. Transfer the papayas to a colander and allow the juices to drain off for 20 minutes. Wash the papayas and cut into 1-inch slices. Remove the seeds from the slices and transfer the fruit to a large bowl. Dissolve the limestone in a small amount of water and pour the mixture over the fruit. Let stand for about 3 hours. Drain and wash the papaya slices.

PREPARE THE SYRUP: Bring the water to a boil in a large saucepan. Add the sugar and spices and cook uncovered about 1 1/2 hours. Add the rinsed papaya slices and simmer uncovered until the fruit is shiny and soft, about 30 minutes.

TO SERVE: Serve the papaya slices and some of the syrup over fresh fig leaves (optional) and coconut ice cream scooped into

FOR THE PAPAYA

4 pounds unripe papayas
6 tablespoons powdered limestone

FOR THE SYRUP

16 cups water
2 1/2 pounds granulated or brown sugar or grated *piloncillo* (solidified brown sugar)
8 cinnamon sticks (each about 5 inches long)
20 whole cloves
2 whole star anise
16 fresh fig leaves (optional)
Coconut ice cream

CONTINUED

8 soup plates. Cinnamon, cloves, and star anise can be left in the syrup or removed as desired.

VARIATIONS: Serve with another tropical fruit ice cream or sorbet. Raspberry sorbet is also a nice complement to the papayas.

CHICOZAPOTE FROM THE SOUTHEAST
CHICOZAPOTE DEL SURESTE
Serves 6

6 ripe large *chicozapotes*
6 cups crushed ice

The *chicozapote* is a fruit with a sweet, delicious pulp, an oval shape, and a brownish-red or yellowish thin skin that becomes opaque as the *chicozapote* ripens. The fruit grows on long vines and may contain as many as twelve seeds, although three to six is the usual number.

Peel and quarter the *chicozapotes*. Place the crushed ice in 6 soup plates. Lay the fruit over the ice and serve immediately.

BOILED STONE CRABS WITH TWO SAUCES

SHRIMP AND AVOCADO SALAD WITH SEVILLE
ORANGE DRESSING

MAYAN SALSA

CHAYOTES WITH YUCATÁN BROTH

OCTOPUS YUCATÁN STYLE

GOUDA STUFFED WITH SEAFOOD AND *CHILMOLE*

GROUPER WITH AROMATIC SPICES

NAVY BEANS WITH HABANERO CHILES AND
EPAZOTE

MAYAN FRUIT SALAD

PASEO MONTEJO MERINGUES

The state of Yucatán occupies the northern part of the Yucatán Peninsula in southeastern Mexico. When the Spanish arrived, the natives are supposed to have said, "Uh yu uthaan," which translates as "Listen how they talk"—hence the region's name. The ancient Maya made their home here in marvelous cities like Uxmal and Chichén Itzá. They carried out advanced studies in astronomy, literature, chronology, medicine, and mathematics, to which they contributed the concept of zero.

The state is covered with lush vegetation. At one time, the natural fiber sisal was the area's main crop, but its importance has been superseded by synthetic materials. Today red onions, chaya leaves, squash, chayote, habanero chiles, annatto seeds (used to make *achiote*), canario beans, cucumbers, aloe, sapodillas, limes, watermelons, and ziricote are the major crops. Seafood, of course, plays a major role in the cuisine, as does pork. (Pigs were introduced by the Spanish, via Cuba.)

The beautiful capital city of Mérida, dubbed the "white city," is full of magic and folklore. The state is known for its fine handicrafts, exquisite cuisine, and many cenotes—natural limestone wells that open onto underground waterways. Tourists enjoy the 225 miles of beaches warmed by the strong southern sun. In addition to the attraction of marvelous water sports, visitors are drawn to a culture that still takes pride in its pre-Hispanic heritage.

When the mysterious bearded men arrived on our shores, life was forever changed. They claimed to have "discovered" our land, but they could never bring to light the secrets of the Yucatán. ¶ They came by sea, looking for wealth, and they could not understand what they could not see. They did not notice the tiny mirrors formed in the sand when waves wash over shiny grains. They could not see the arms of the land that extend like roots in jungle foliage. They did not see the bounty of Yum Chaac, the rain god, who nourishes the soil. They could not see the great Alchk'in, god of the sun, who illuminates our existence. They did not stop to see that we are human beings, too. ¶ Tepeu, Gucumatz, and Hurakán are the gods who gave life to our people and our way of life. They watched over growing crops and ripened the corn in colors of yellow, blue, purple, and white. They broke ears of corn into small kernels that could be replanted to make more life-sustaining grain. They mixed corn with water and formed the first four humans from the flesh of tree trunks. They turned red reeds into blood to give these first men and women strength and stamina. This blood also carried the secrets of Father Heaven and Mother Earth. In this manner, our people were created. So says the *Popol Vuh*, the sacred book of the Maya. ¶ Those other men, men of clay as we called them, were created by other gods. When they came here, they did not understand the power of the jaguar or the magic of the birds. These feathered birds, known by the name *quetzal*, are in contact with the thirteen heavens above, with Mother Earth, and with the great god Kukulcán, a serpent bird who guards my people. The newcomers could not understand that the gods gave us a gift in the form of the sacred waters that fill subterranean caverns. They could not see Mother Earth as she opened to show her divine liquid to us, her sons. They did not understand how the beautiful maidens and young warriors were initiated into the rites of adulthood by embracing her waters. ¶ The outsiders could not appreciate the distinct aroma of *copal* that perfumes the skies. They could not taste the special qualities of *balché*, our ritual drink prepared for festivities. They could not see the *bacabes*, the protectors, at each of the four horizons who stand guard over our people with swords of obsidian and sustain our world. ¶ Nine rivers fall under the watchful eyes of the *bacabes*. Nine mountains are guarded, as well as the red quartz of Ah Chac Mucen Cab, the sacred stone of the East. The silk trees called *ceibas* are red in the East and so are the *zapotillos* (*zapote* trees). The *chacalpucté* is their tree. The turkeys bear proud red markings, as does the corn. White quartz is the sacred stone of the North. Silk trees are white at the center. Wild turkeys are white, and so are the broad beans. Black quartz is the sacred stone of the West. The silk trees are black, as are the corn, sweet potatoes, turkeys, and beans. The black night is their house. Yellow quartz is the sacred stone of the South. Yellow sap runs in the veins of silk trees here. Yellow *pucté* trees and sweet potatoes are indigenous. Beans and turkey are yellow, of course. ¶ These four stones are the ancestors of our ancestors, according to our book *Chilam Balam*. Other gods blessed the waters, and men set out with nets, baited hooks, reed traps, and arrows to search for nourishment from the sea. They dove into the waters off coral reefs to feel the presence of Gucumatz, the feathered serpent with so much energy and vitality that it first gave birth to life. This serpent is the same one whose tail penetrates the soil and reaches to the center of Mother Earth, to the place inhabited by the nine gods of the underworld. The serpent surrounds the gods of death and draws on their energy. From this nether region, the serpent god extracts the primordial element—water. He brings it to the earth's surface in the form of rain, springs, oceans, and rivers, but, of course, all water eventually returns to the heart of the earth. ¶ The men who came to these shores on boats did not understand what was here or what we had built. We resisted destruction at their hands and fled under the green wings of Kukulcán. The feathered serpent raised us toward the heavens, toward eternity, and we were transformed into a brilliant white light. The serpent left us to rain down slowly over the earth as stardust. As celestial powder we fell deep into the sea where we live today. The Maya, who date from the beginning of all time, have returned to our origins, to the heart of all life.

BOILED STONE CRABS WITH TWO SAUCES
PLATÓN DE CANGREJOS MOROS
Serves 6 to 8

FOR THE *HABANERO* MAYONNAISE
- 2 cups mayonnaise
- ¹/₂ cup plain yogurt
- ¹/₂ cup finely chopped red onion
- Juice of 4 limes
- 1 fresh habanero or serrano chile, roasted and finely chopped
- 2 small cloves garlic, peeled, roasted, and ground
- 1 tablespoon minced cilantro
- Salt to taste

FOR THE SAFFRON MAYONNAISE
- 2 cups mayonnaise
- ¹/₂ cup plain yogurt
- Juice of 4 limes
- 2 medium cloves garlic, peeled and crushed
- ¹/₂ teaspoon ground saffron
- Salt to taste

FOR THE CRABS
- 20 cups water
- Sea salt to taste
- 4 pounds stone or other crabs
- Crushed ice
- 12 limes, halved

The beaches at Chelem and Celestún are distinguished by the sounds of the surf depositing thousands of shells in a myriad of colors on the white sands. These two paradise beaches are known for their extensive list of local culinary treats such as fish in garlic sauce or *achiote* paste, shrimp in pink mayonnaise, octopus in its own ink, and grilled lobster and conch. Large, meaty stone crabs (*cangrejos moros*) are particularly flavorful and usually served with a variety of sauces at restaurants along this magnificent shoreline.

PREPARE THE *HABANERO* MAYONNAISE: Use a spatula to combine the mayonnaise and yogurt in a medium bowl. Stir in the red onion, lime juice, chile, garlic, cilantro, and salt. Refrigerate for 2 hours.

PREPARE THE SAFFRON MAYONNAISE: Use a spatula to combine the mayonnaise and yogurt in a medium bowl. Stir in the lime juice, garlic, saffron, and salt. Refrigerate for 2 hours.

PREPARE THE CRABS: Bring the water to a boil in a large stockpot. Add sea salt to taste and the crabs. Cover and cook the crabs until bright red, about 8 minutes. Drain and cool the crabs.

TO SERVE: Place crushed ice in a deep bowl and top with the crabs. Serve with the 2 sauces and the limes.

SHRIMP AND AVOCADO SALAD WITH SEVILLE ORANGE DRESSING
ENSALADA DE CAMARÓN, AGUACATE Y NARANJA AGRIA ESTILO CHICXULUB

Serves 6

In the small port and town of Chicxulub, located along the north coast, fishing is conducted in sailboats or tiny wooden boats with motors. Fishermen capture corbina, grouper, yellowtail, red snapper, shad, sea bass, and shrimp, which are often used in ceviches, grilled, or combined with the local avocados, called *chinín*, that grow throughout the region. Like Florida avocados, the local fruit has a smooth skin and buttery flesh. This salad is given a special flavor by the Seville orange, a sour orange used since ancient Mayan times. This delicious fruit is even mentioned in early Mayan manuscripts.

Bring the water to a boil in a large pot. Add the sea salt, garlic, and herbs and simmer covered for about 10 minutes. Add the shrimp and cook uncovered for 2 minutes. Remove the pot from the heat and let stand for 1 or 2 minutes. Drain, cool, and peel the shrimp; discard the other solids and the liquid.

TO SERVE: Place the cooked shrimp on a large platter along with the sliced avocados, red onions, and tomatoes. Sprinkle the platter with the fruit juices and the vinegar and season with salt and pepper and oregano. Drizzle olive oil on top. Serve with crackers or freshly made tortillas.

VARIATION: Sprinkle the salad with 1 finely chopped habanero chile.

6 cups water
Sea salt to taste
1 head garlic, unpeeled and roasted in a hot skillet
3 sprigs marjoram
1 teaspoon dried oregano leaves
24 large brown or tiger shrimp or prawns, deveined with shells on
2 ripe smooth-skinned avocados, peeled and sliced into ¹/₂-inch wedges
1¹/₄ medium red onions, thinly sliced
4 to 6 medium ripe plum tomatoes (yellow or red), sliced
Juice of 6 Seville oranges or ³/₄ cup grapefruit juice
Juice of 3 limes
3 tablespoons white vinegar or cider vinegar
Salt and freshly ground black pepper to taste
Freshly ground oregano to taste
Extra-virgin olive oil to taste

MAYAN SALSA
SALSA MAYA

Makes 3¹/₂ to 4 cups

12 dried costeño or japonés
 chiles
Sea salt to taste
 ¹/₂ cup plus 2 tablespoons finely
 chopped cilantro
1¹/₂ pounds ripe plum tomatoes
 1 cup Seville orange juice or
 grapefruit juice
Juice of 4 limes

Most of the Mayan cenotes (natural underground reservoirs) held sacred waters that were used to sacrifice young girls and warriors. These cavities were formed when soft limestone on the surface gave way to reveal crystal-clear underground springs. The white corallike stone has been used by the inhabitants of Yucatán for centuries to make *molcajetes*, which are similar to the marble mortars that come from Europe. *Molcajetes* are cured by grinding grains, coarse salt, and Seville orange juice in the bowl and are frequently used to combine the ingredients for hot sauces like this. Serve this sauce with any kind of fish or seafood.

Preheat a *comal* or a heavy skillet and toast the chiles evenly on all sides. Place the toasted chiles in a mortar and grind with the salt and the ¹/₂ cup cilantro. Roast the tomatoes on the hot *comal* for about 5 minutes, adding a little water so that they actually sweat. Add the tomatoes to the mortar and grind until the mixture makes a smooth paste. Add the fruit juices, taste and correct the seasoning, and garnish with the 2 tablespoons cilantro.

Serve the sauce in a large *molcajete* or in a deep bowl.

VARIATION: Add 3 roasted garlic cloves and 1 finely chopped red onion to the mortar.

CHAYOTES WITH YUCATÁN BROTH
CHAYOTES EN CALDILLO YUCATECO

Serves 8

The chayote plant is a creeping vine whose fruit varies in quality depending on the care it is given. Shaped like a pear, with a watery pulp, this mild vegetable can weigh as little as 6 ounces or as much as 1¼ pounds. When mature, the chayote softens and the skin becomes almost opaque in color. Chayotes, also known as water pears or vegetable pears, are cultivated by hand and must be picked with care so as not to disturb the plant. The pulp can be prepared in various ways—boiled, battered, and deep-fried; stuffed; or cubed and used in sauces and soups. Chayote is extremely nutritious and can be taken as an antacid or to promote sound digestion. Serve this dish as an entrée or with fish.

PREPARE THE CHAYOTES: Bring the water to a boil in a large pot. Add the chayotes, sugar, salt, onion, and garlic and simmer, covered, until the chayotes are tender, about 25 minutes. Drain the chayotes, reserving some of the cooking liquid but discarding the garlic and the onion. Set the chayotes aside.

PREPARE THE BROTH: Puree the tomatoes with the water, onions, garlic, cinnamon, and saffron in a blender or a food processor. Heat the oil in a wok or a large frying pan. Brown and discard the onion slices. Strain the tomato sauce into the wok and cook uncovered over medium heat until it starts to thicken. Season with salt and add the bell pepper, almonds, raisins, olives, vinegar, spices, and chayotes. Continue cooking for about 15 minutes. (If the sauce becomes too thick, thin it with a small amount of the chayote cooking liquid.) Add the chayotes and check the seasonings. Cook for 10 minutes more.

TO SERVE: Scoop the chayotes and sauce onto a deep platter and sprinkle the parsley on top.

VARIATIONS: Boiled chayotes can be served with *jocoque* (a thick, tangy yogurt from the Middle East); stuffed with dried ricotta, hollandaise sauce, or Oaxacan string cheese; or battered with egg, deep-fried, and basted with sauce. Or brush thin slices of chayote with olive oil, sprinkle with salt, and grill.

FOR THE CHAYOTES

- 12 cups water
- 4 pounds chayotes, peeled and quartered
- 1 tablespoon sugar
- 1½ tablespoons salt
- 1 medium white onion, peeled and halved
- 4 medium cloves garlic, peeled

FOR THE BROTH

- 2½ pounds ripe plum tomatoes, chopped
- 1½ cups water
- 1½ medium white onions, peeled and roasted in a hot skillet
- 8 medium cloves garlic, peeled and roasted in a hot skillet
- 2 cinnamon sticks (each about 3 inches long)
- ½ teaspoon saffron
- ½ cup extra-virgin olive oil
- 2 white onion slices

Salt to taste
- 1 very small green bell pepper, finely chopped
- ½ cup blanched almonds
- ½ cup raisins
- ½ cup small pimiento-stuffed olives
- ¼ cup white vinegar
- ½ teaspoon black peppercorns, ground
- 6 whole allspice, ground
- 4 whole cloves, ground
- 2 tablespoons parsley

FOR THE OCTOPUS

    4   pounds octopus
   18   cups water
  1½   medium white onions,
        peeled and quartered
    8   large cloves garlic, peeled
    8   sprigs thyme
    8   sprigs marjoram
Salt to taste

FOR THE SAUCE

   ¾   cup olive oil
    6   large cloves garlic, peeled
    2   medium white onions,
        peeled and chopped
    2   medium green bell
        peppers, peeled and
        chopped
  2½   pounds ripe plum
        tomatoes, chopped
    2   ounces French bread or
        rolls, cut into small pieces
⅓ to ½ cup octopus or squid ink
    1   teaspoon black
        peppercorns, ground
    4   fresh bay leaves
   ½   teaspoon cumin seeds,
        ground
   40   sprigs parsley, tied
   ½   teaspoon freshly ground
        oregano
    6   tablespoons cider vinegar
        or other strong vinegar
Salt to taste

FOR THE GARNISH

White Rice Tamaulipas Style
        (page 245)
    3   tablespoons minced
        parsley

OCTOPUS YUCATÁN STYLE
PULPOS A LA YUCATECA
Serves 8

Bocas, a series of freshwater springs that rise up through the ocean floor and which are teeming with marine life and turtles, is located near the port of Dzilam de Bravo in the northern part of Yucatán. Crabs are particularly abundant here and are used in numerous recipes. They are also used by fishermen as bait to attract the prized octopus. Spoon-shaped nets made of natural fibers or nylon (a recent development) are filled with crabs and long wooden handles are attached to allow the fishermen to submerge the nets into deep waters. This technique is also employed to harvest shrimp, squid, and striped mullet. In these quiet bays, young boys not ready for the challenges of the open sea can learn the ways of the water in a safe, gentle environment.

PREPARE THE OCTOPUS: Clean the octopus, reserving the ink. If using large octopus, beat vigorously with a mallet to soften the flesh. Slice the octopus into ½-inch pieces. Bring the water to a boil in a pressure cooker or a casserole. Add the onions, garlic, thyme, marjoram, salt, and octopus. Cook the octopus until soft, about 35 minutes in a pressure cooker or 1 hour in a regular casserole. Set the octopus and 1½ cups of the cooking liquid aside; discard the other solids.

PREPARE THE SAUCE: Preheat a clay pot or a regular casserole. Add the oil, brown the garlic, and discard. Add the onions and sauté until light brown. Add the bell peppers and sauté for about 5 minutes. Add the tomatoes, the bread, and ⅓ cup of the reserved octopus stock and simmer covered over low heat for several minutes. Add the octopus ink, ground black pepper, bay leaves, cumin, parsley, oregano, and vinegar. Season with salt. Simmer until the sauce releases its oil and starts to thicken. Add the octopus and continue cooking for 20 minutes. When the sauce starts to thicken again, add the remaining octopus stock and continue cooking for 10 minutes longer. Taste and adjust seasonings.

TO SERVE: Mold the rice into 8 large soup plates and top with the octopus and sauce. Sprinkle with the parsley.

GOUDA STUFFED WITH SEAFOOD AND *CHILMOLE*
QUESO RELLENO DE MARISCOS AL CHILMOLE

Serves 12

During the nineteenth century, the port of Progreso, a center for the agave trade, was one of the most important points of commerce in Mexico. Fibers from the versatile plant were shipped to Europe, where they were made into sacks and garments. On their way back to Yucatán, ships transported European foodstuffs, including Gouda cheese from Holland. Locals adapted this delicious cheese in recipes like this one. Here, a whole Gouda is stuffed with seafood and *chilmole* (a black paste made from dried xcatick chiles and available in Latin markets), wrapped in cheesecloth, and steamed until soft.

PREPARE THE CHEESE: Cut off the top of the cheese and scoop out some of the insides to make a large hole. Do not let the walls become too thin. Cube the scooped-out cheese and reserve half. (Use the other half for another purpose.) Fit a deep pot with a steamer rack, add water and the herbs, and heat gently.

PREPARE THE STUFFING: Heat the oil in a large skillet or a wok. Grind the roasted garlic with the spices and the salt in a spice grinder or a food processor. Add the mixture to the hot oil and cook for 5 minutes. Dissolve the *chilmole* paste in the fish stock and add the mixture to the pan along with the seafood and the fish. Simmer covered over low heat until the oil is released from the sauce. Add the reserved cheese and stir until it is melted. Add the salt. Ladle the stuffing into the prepared cheese. Place the top back on the cheese, rub with oil, and wrap in a large piece of cheesecloth. Place the cheese on the steamer rack and cook, covered, over medium heat until almost soft, about 1 1/2 hours.

PREPARE THE *CHILMOLE* SAUCE: Meanwhile, puree the roasted onions and garlic in a food processor. Heat the oil in a large pan. Add the strained tomatillos, ground onions and garlic, and *chilmole* paste and simmer uncovered until the oil rises to

FOR THE CHEESE

- 1 whole large Gouda (about 3 pounds)
- 8 fresh bay leaves
- 8 sprigs thyme
- 8 sprigs marjoram
- 1 tablespoon fresh Yucatán or regular oregano leaves

FOR THE STUFFING

- 1/2 cup extra-virgin olive oil
- 6 medium cloves garlic, peeled and roasted in a hot skillet
- 1 teaspoon black peppercorns
- 1 teaspoon cumin seeds
- 1/2 teaspoon salt
- 4 1/2 ounces *chilmole* or *achiote* paste
- 1/2 cup fish or chicken stock
- 1 pound octopus, cooked and finely chopped
- 1 pound squid, cleaned and finely chopped
- 1 pound shrimp, peeled, deveined, and finely chopped
- 1 pound sea bass or red snapper fillets, finely chopped

Salt to taste
Olive oil for rubbing the cheese

CONTINUED

FOR THE *CHILMOLE* SAUCE

- ³/₄ cup olive oil
- 1 pound tomatillos, husked, boiled until soft, pureed, and strained
- 2 medium white onions, peeled, roasted in a hot skillet
- 1 head garlic, peeled, roasted in a hot skillet
- 6 ounces *chilmole* or *achiote* paste
- ¹/₄ cup fresh *masa* (corn dough)
- 3 cups fish or chicken stock
- 20 sprigs epazote

Salt to taste

FOR THE GARNISH

- 8 habanero chiles, roasted in a hot skillet, or canned jalapeño chiles

FOR THE *RECADO*

- 1 teaspoon black peppercorns
- 1 teaspoon coriander seeds
- 1 teaspoon saffron
- 20 fresh Yucatán oregano leaves (which are dark brown and large) or 1¹/₂ tablespoons fresh regular oregano leaves
- 4 whole cloves

the surface. Dissolve the *masa* in the fish stock and add the mixture to the pan along with the epazote and salt. Simmer uncovered until slightly thickened. Keep the sauce warm.

TO SERVE: Unwrap the cheese and place in the center of a large platter. Drench with the *chilmole* sauce and garnish with the chiles. Serve with freshly made tortillas.

VARIATION: Steam the cheese in banana leaves for a slightly different flavor.

Note: If there is extra stuffing, just reheat at serving time and use as a side dish with the cheese.

GROUPER WITH AROMATIC SPICES
MERO EN SALPIMENTADO

Serves 6 to 8

At the port of Yucalpetén, fishermen undertake trips lasting several days when searching for fresh catch. Each boat has a specialty and the vessel is designed accordingly. Both the fishermen and their boats are named for the species they hunt—*tiburoneros* (shark fishermen), *camaroneros* (shrimp fishermen), *mereros* (grouper fishermen). *Guachinangeros* (red snapper boats), for example, are made of wood and search for their catch in rocky zones near the coast. They also carry a small boat, called the *alijo* (unloading boat), that fishermen use to go on land. The *mereros* use one principal boat and various small *alijos* for fishing. When their work has been completed, the principal boat picks up fishermen in the *alijos* and brings them back to port. On land, the fishermen live in a large community, with some of the men in charge of meal preparation. This recipe uses an aromatic *recado* (ground spice mixture) to flavor the fish, a preparation common to Yucatán cuisine. The eggplant garnish reflects the influence of the Lebanese community in the region.

PREPARE THE *RECADO:* In a mortar or a spice grinder, blend the peppercorns, coriander, saffron, oregano, cloves, cinnamon, roasted onion, raw garlic, roasted garlic, parsley, vinegar, and salt into a thick paste. (This paste can be prepared in advance and refrigerated. Use for seasoning soups, meats, poultry, or seafood.)

PREPARE THE FISH: Preheat the oven to 400°F. Place the fish in a large, shallow baking dish that is flameproof and daub with the lime juice, olive oil, and salt and pepper. Let stand for about 10 minutes, then daub the insides and the skin of the fish with the *recado* and let stand for about 1 hour. Bake the fish until it flakes but is still moist, about 35 to 45 minutes. Lift the fish from the pan and set aside. Add the fish stock to the pan drippings, set the pan over a burner, and boil until the mixture makes a light sauce.

PREPARE THE GARNISH: Roast the eggplants directly over an open flame until the skin is charred. Peel and mash or blend the flesh with the garlic, lime juice, olive oil, and salt to form a thick puree.

TO SERVE: Place the fish on a large platter. Serve the eggplant puree and the fish sauce separately in bowls.

2 cinnamon sticks (each about 2 inches long)
1 medium white onion, peeled and roasted in a hot skillet
8 medium garlic cloves, peeled
8 medium garlic cloves, peeled and roasted in a hot skillet
16 sprigs Italian parsley
1/2 cup white wine vinegar or Seville orange juice
1 1/2 tablespoons salt, or to taste

FOR THE FISH
1 whole grouper (about 4 1/2 pounds), deboned with head and tail attached
1/3 cup fresh lime juice or Seville orange juice
1/2 cup extra-virgin olive oil
Salt and freshly ground black pepper to taste
4 cups fish stock, reduced to 2 cups

FOR THE GARNISH
3 to 4 large eggplants
4 small cloves garlic, peeled
Juice of 4 to 6 limes
1/2 cup extra-virgin olive oil
Salt to taste

NAVY BEANS WITH HABANERO CHILES AND EPAZOTE
FRIJOLES COLADO CON HABANERO AL EPAZOTE

Serves 6 to 8

16 cups water
1 medium white onion, peeled and quartered
1½ small heads garlic, peeled
1 pound black navy beans, sorted, soaked in water to cover for 4 hours or overnight, and drained
5 sprigs epazote
2 tablespoons corn oil or lard
Salt to taste
2 fresh habanero chiles, roasted in a hot skillet

Yucatán is a magical land full of sunshine and fields, natural underground reservoirs, fragrant trees, and exotic birds. The Indian community is nourished by corn in many forms, including hot *atole* (a sweet corn beverage) and corn on the cob cooked underground in hot coals. As always, beans are an essential element in the local diet because along with corn tortillas they provide a source of complete protein. To give better flavor to the beans, Yucatán women add epazote and fiery habanero chiles.

Bring the water to a boil in a medium casserole. Add the onion, garlic, beans, 3 epazote sprigs, and oil. Simmer covered over medium heat until the beans start to soften, about 1 hour. Season with salt and continue cooking until the beans are soft, about 30 minutes. (If the beans start to dry out before they soften, add 2 to 3 cups of boiling water.) Set the casserole aside to cool. Strain out the onion, garlic, and epazote and mash the beans. Return the beans to the casserole and continue cooking with the remaining 2 epazote sprigs and the roasted chiles. Simmer until the beans are somewhat thick. Serve hot in a deep bowl.

VARIATION: The beans can be refried in ½ to 1 cup lard or oil. First, brown onions in the fat and then cook the beans until they become very thick. Serve as a side dish.

MAYAN FRUIT SALAD
FRUTAS DE LA TIERRA MAYA
Serves 8

The houses in Yucatán are characterized by patios that overlook small orchards with plants, flowers, and aromatic fruit trees bearing papayas, mameys, *guanábanas,* mangoes, bananas, *limas* (sweet Persian limes that are particularly aromatic), oranges, *saramuyos* (the fruit from the cashew nut), guavas, and *zapotes* (sapodillas). The inheritors of Mayan tradition preserve an ancient custom when it comes to their fruit trees. When the fruit appears to be almost ripe, a *bojól* is tied to the branches to protect the harvest from the birds. A *bojól* is nothing more than a piece of wood with stones attached by strings. Another long string runs from the *bojól* into the kitchen, where women are always working. If a woman is making fresh tortillas and observes birds around the fruit tree, she forcefully pulls the *bojól* rope. The stones clap against the stick and the noise scares away the intruders.

Fruit can be divided among individual plates as you desire. I particularly like the following design: Place 1 slice of cherimoya on the left side and in the center of 8 large chilled dinner plates. Overlap the slices of *chicozapote,* mamey, and papaya on the right side and edges of the plates. Place 2 strawberries and either 1 *nanche* or 4 pineapple slices in the center of each plate. Dust the edges of the plates with cocoa powder and serve.

2 large ripe cherimoyas, each cut into 8 slices
4 ripe *chicozapotes,* each cut into 8 slices
1 ripe mamey, cut into 8 slices
2 small ripe papayas, each cut into 8 slices
16 strawberries
8 *nanches* or kumquats cooked in syrup or 1 small pineapple, peeled and sliced into $1/4$-inch triangles
Cocoa powder to taste

PASEO MONTEJO MERINGUES
MERENGUES DEL PASEO MONTEJO

Makes about 40 meringues

3 cups sugar

1¼ cups water

9 egg whites from medium eggs

Peel of 4 small limes, grated, or 1 tablespoon vanilla extract

1 cup confectioners' sugar

Mérida was always a beautiful city. Upon their arrival, the Spanish were astonished by the stone temples and palaces that graced the city, then known as *t'ho'*. The conquerors destroyed almost all of these original architectural jewels by the time the city of Mérida was founded in 1542. One of the loveliest streets, Paseo Montejo, was named after Francisco de Montejo, a founder of Mérida. The local architecture experienced another transformation toward the end of the nineteenth century with the construction of distinguished residences. These sophisticated homes were built in the French style and painted in white and soft pastel and white colors, giving the city the nickname *ciudad blanca,* or "white city." Today, along Paseo Montejo, pleasant cafés offer candies, ice cream, and these delicious meringues.

Preheat the oven to 200°F. Place the sugar and the water in a saucepan and heat. Simmer uncovered until the syrup falls in thick ribbons. Beat the egg whites until stiff peaks are formed. Add the syrup, little by little, beating constantly until the mixture is shiny. Pour into a saucepan and cook uncovered over low heat until glossy, 5 to 8 minutes. Remove from the heat. Fold in the lime peel and the confectioners' sugar.

Cut 2 pieces of paper from a brown shopping bag about the same size as a large baking sheet. Moisten. Line 2 baking sheets with the paper. Fit a pastry bag with a ½-inch- to 1-inch-wide fluted tip. Fill with the meringue mixture. Pipe the meringues in spiral mounds onto the paper-lined sheets. Bake until the meringues are light and crisp white on the outside but still soft on the inside, 1¼ to 1½ hours. Cool the meringues on a rack and serve with sherbet and blackberry or chocolate sauce.

XNIPEC SALSA

SHRIMP COCKTAIL CIUDAD DEL CARMEN STYLE

BABY SHARK EMPANADAS

ROLLED TORTILLAS IN BLACK BEAN AND
CHILTOMATE SAUCE

BLACK RICE WITH SQUID

SPAGHETTI VALENCIANA WITH SEAFOOD
AND SAUSAGES

POMPANO BAKED IN PARCHMENT PAPER,
CAMPECHE STYLE

SEA BASS IN GREEN SAUCE

YUCA FRITTERS

CAMPECHE FRUIT PLATE WITH VIRGIN HONEY

GUANÁBANA DRINK WITH LIME AND COCONUT

CAMPECHE

Campeche occupies the western end of the Yucatán Peninsula. The state is named for the pre-Hispanic town of Ah Kim Pech, or "place of serpents and ticks." Campeche has an enormously rich collection of archaeological remains left by the Maya at Edzná, Chicanná, Becán, Xpujil, Hochob, and other sites.

The fertile land produces corn, rice, sugarcane, squash, and a wide range of other vegetables. Forests contain precious woods such as mahogany and cedar, but the main economic activity in the state is fishing, with important ports at Isla del Carmen, Champotón, and Laguna de Términos, a kind of inland sea, with Ciudad del Carmen at its base.

During colonial times the capital city Campeche was much prized by European powers and raided by English, French, and Dutch pirates looking to capture some of the riches that passed through the port. Just off the coast lies a small coral island that barely rises above the surface of the water. Named Jaina, this largest necropolis (island cemetery) in America was built by the Maya. Ancient spirits live on in this bustling, modern state.

Holy Mother! My dear! Oh, this heat! And I haven't even offered you some refreshment. How about some iced myrtle tea? You know, I'm not accustomed to visitors but I am so glad you are here. So how do you like Campeche so far? Don't tell me, I can see the joy in your face. ¶ I must confess I don't really know much about the areas surrounding this blessed city. I don't get out much. You see, I am old now and spend much of the day right here. Within the city walls—the Baluarte Santa Rosa—there is an air of adventure and intrigue. Why do think the local costumes worn to market have prevailed so long here? We are quite traditional and ancient in our customs. ¶ The history of our walled city dates back centuries. During colonial times, pirates, who were mostly Englishmen, would attack frequently. Often they had been at sea for months and would capture local women when they sailed into our port. Imagine the fear and danger felt by the Indian natives. Eventually the Spanish stopped the destruction of this land and its people. They wanted to protect their own business interests, so they helped the Indians fight off the marauding pirates by building walls around the city. Underground tunnels were also constructed so residents could communicate with each other in peace. Today, many of the walls and tunnels remain. You have seen some? The doors built into the walls are the doors to the sea and to the earth and go by the names of San Román and Guadalupe. ¶ The sea is very important to my husband, Chel, who learned to fish as a young child. But now he is easily fatigued, and he ventures out only to the children. Roger, the second of our six strong boys, was strongly drawn to the sea, like his father. I could see it happening when he was just a small boy. As soon as he could walk I told Chel: "When this baby is grown, he will love the sea more than his wife." Time has proved me right. Roger says he can feel the ocean in his blood. He feels free at sea, free of everything, even good Gladys, his wife. ¶ Alas, poor Gladys. She is a good girl, a saintly girl. Just between us, my pretty one, when I am with her I

CUISINE OF THE WATER GODS

remember the good times of my youth. She has a magic tough when it comes to cooking. One of my favorites is her grilled pompano with *achiote* paste, or with green sauce made with peas or *hoja santa*. She also cooks *el pan de cazon* (tortillas layered with black beans, baby shark, and a tomato sauce), shrimp *champotón* (tiny, tiny shrimp in *escabeche*), and *tin qui poal* (baby shark pâté). I look forward to the times she serves *pargo en macum*, sliced porgy marinated in black peppercorns, Tabasco peppers, garlic, cloves, oregano, tomatoes, baby bell peppers, xcatick or banana peppers, parsley, bay leaves, and olive oil, and then wrapped in banana leaves and steamed. Other times Gladys deep-fries tortillas and tops them with black beans, pickled red onions, and crumbled cheese, or she grills manta ray and serves it Campeche style with pumpkin-seed sauce and pickled red onions. Even her most simple dishes, like fried fish served with limes, radishes, cucumbers, and *habanero* sauce, are perfect. The only thing she hasn't been able to make taste right is *dsoto-bichay,* those small tamales stuffed with pumpkin seeds and wrapped in special chaya leaves that are similar to spinach. But that dish takes a lot of patience and practice to get it just right. Even her *cochinita en pib* (pork marinated with *achiote* and cooked underground) is quite good. ¶ You know, my daughter-in-law is still very young and there is time for her to learn the more complicated stews and casseroles. In the meantime, I thank Saint Carmita that my boy is not a finicky eater. He is like his father—he loves to eat. Gladys is lucky to have such a man to cook for. He can appreciate good cooking. She also is lucky because he reserves the best of his catch for her. Although he sells most of the fish at the market, he brings home the most delicious specimens for Gladys. ¶ When Roger goes fishing he must rise at five in the morning. He travels in a small wooden boat and uses all kinds of handmade nets to trap his catch. The fishermen go in groups to special spots they know. Nets fly through the air, to catch jurel, mullet, baby shark, sea bass, grouper, blue crabs, stone crabs, squid, octopus, green turtle, tiny shrimp, and mackerel. From

October through March the fishermen ply their trade under the mountains and the lighthouse. The nervous fish come to the surface to eat and are caught in nets. Sometimes my Roger goes diving in search of conch or sea snails. He is a very good snorkeler, and luck seems to follow him wherever he goes. ¶ Oh, don't tell me that you have to leave so soon. What a pity! We were having such a nice conversation. You are such an interesting talker. Well, you know that this house is always open to you. The next time you come you must stay longer and enjoy yourself here. Come for a long visit someday soon. Well, my pretty one, farewell and may God be with you on your journey.

XNIPEC SALSA
XNIPEC (SALPICÓN)

Makes about 2 cups

40 sprigs cilantro, finely chopped

3 small white or red onions, peeled and finely chopped

2 to 4 fresh habanero (either red or yellow) or serrano chiles, finely chopped

Juice of 4 Seville oranges or ¾ cup grapefruit juice blended with a dash of lime juice

Salt to taste

The word *xnipec* comes from the Mayan language and literally translates as "dog's nose," perhaps because the flavor of the chiles, cilantro, onions, and Seville orange juice is so strong. Serve this salsa with any seafood or fish dish in need of a lively accompaniment.

Toss the cilantro, onions, chiles, and juice in a bowl. Season with salt and mix well. Serve the sauce with grilled, baked, or fried fish, vegetables, tortillas, eggs, or beans.

VARIATION: Add chopped radishes or roasted chiles.

SHRIMP COCKTAIL CIUDAD DEL CARMEN STYLE
COCTEL DE CAMARÓN ESTILO CIUDAD DEL CARMEN

Serves 4

In Campeche, the shrimp season begins in October and lasts through January. Fishermen usually wait for the winds from the north that bring the rains, which cause the shrimp to swim to the surface. The shrimp in this region are very small, with as many as half a dozen needed to cover a fingernail.

Divide the shrimp, onions, tomatoes, chiles, cilantro, and avocado among 4 tall cocktail glasses or 4 large wineglasses. Season with salt. Drizzle the lime juice, catsup, and oil over each cocktail. Serve with saltines. Allow each person to combine the ingredients at the table for a very fresh flavor.

4 cups tiny cocktail shrimp, peeled and cooked

1½ small white onions, peeled and finely chopped

4 medium ripe tomatoes, finely chopped

4 to 6 fresh serrano chiles, finely chopped

¼ cup finely chopped cilantro

1 ripe avocado, peeled and chopped

Salt to taste

Juice of 8 medium limes

1⅓ cups catsup, or to taste

⅓ cup extra-virgin olive oil

Saltines

BABY SHARK EMPANADAS
EMPANADAS DE CAZÓN

Makes about 30 empanadas

FOR THE BABY SHARK

1	cup water
1	medium white onion, peeled and sliced
15	fresh epazote leaves
1¾	pounds baby shark, grouper, shad, or cod

Salt to taste

FOR THE SAUCE

⅓ to ½	cup lard or extra-virgin olive oil
1	medium white onion, peeled and chopped
1 to 2	fresh habanero chiles, chopped
8	large ripe plum tomatoes, chopped
½	cup Seville orange juice or champagne vinegar
1	tablespoon balsamic vinegar or cider vinegar

Salt and freshly ground black pepper to taste

FOR THE DOUGH

2	pounds fresh *masa* (corn dough)
1	teaspoon baking powder
1	teaspoon salt
1	tablespoon flour
1	tablespoon lard or oil
2	tablespoons *achiote* paste
4	cups corn oil

Baby shark is a prized commodity at the Champotón market. Several species are usually on sale, with the largest often reaching 70 pounds and 7 feet in length. Other varieties, of course, are much smaller. Baby shark may be steamed, used in stuffings with chiles, or served with tortillas and beans.

PREPARE THE BABY SHARK: Pour the water into a medium fish poacher or a casserole. Add the sliced onion, epazote leaves, and fish and season with salt. Cover and poach or steam the fish for 15 minutes. Cool the fish and shred. Discard other ingredients.

PREPARE THE SAUCE: Heat the lard in a casserole. Add the onion and sauté until it starts to brown. Add the chiles and the tomatoes and simmer uncovered until the sauce starts to thicken. Add the juice and the vinegar. Season with salt and pepper and continue cooking until the sauce becomes very thick. Stir in the shredded fish and continue cooking until the mixture becomes very thick.

PREPARE THE DOUGH: Spread the *masa* over a flat work surface. Sprinkle with the baking powder, the salt, and the flour and begin to work in the lard and the *achiote* paste. Knead the dough, splashing occasionally with water, until it becomes soft and shiny. Place the dough on a plate and cover with a cloth for about 15 minutes.

PREPARE THE EMPANADAS: Line a tortilla press with plastic wrap. Divide the dough into 30 balls, each between 1 and 1½ inches in diameter. One at a time, lightly press the balls in the tortilla press. Flip each tortilla and press again. Fill the tortilla with 2 to 3 teaspoons of the fish mixture. Fold the tortilla in half and press the edges to seal. Place the empanadas on 2 baking trays lined with parchment paper, cover with plastic wrap, and refrigerate for at least 2 hours and up to 6 hours.

TO SERVE: Just before serving time, heat the oil in a deep fryer or a wok. Deep-fry the empanadas in batches, making sure to

baste all sides with the oil to ensure even cooking. Drain the empanadas on paper towels and serve hot with *Xnipec* Salsa (page 198) or any other tomato and Seville orange sauce

VARIATIONS: Add pimiento-stuffed olives, capers, raisins, or canned jalapeños to the sauce.

Note: See pages 309 to 310 for more information on making the dough and using the tortilla press.

ROLLED TORTILLAS IN BLACK BEAN AND *CHILTOMATE* SAUCE
PAPA NEGRO EN SALSA DE CHILTOMATE
Serves 8

Many Campeche specialties rely on black beans. *Joraches* are *masa* (corn dough) croquettes filled with fish or baby shark and served in a light bean broth with roasted habanero chiles. *Frijol con puerco* is a bean and pork stew garnished with radishes, onions, cilantro, and chiles. *Sopa de frijol* is a light bean soup served with pieces of tortillas, cheese, and cream. For this dish, tortillas are dipped in black beans, stuffed with hard-boiled eggs, rolled, and then drenched with *chiltomate* sauce. Pickled red onions may be used for the stuffing as well.

Heat the oil in a medium saucepan. Add the onions and sauté, stirring occasionally, until golden. Puree the tomatoes, bell pepper, and chile in a blender or a food processor. Add the pureed mixture to the saucepan and "fry" briefly. Reduce the heat and simmer uncovered until the sauce thickens and the oil rises to the top, about 45 minutes. Stir in salt to taste and keep warm.

TO SERVE: Dip the tortillas in the beans. Place about ³/₄ table-spoon chopped egg slightly off center on each tortilla. Roll tightly as for a soft taco. Place the *papas negros* on a warm platter and cover with the remaining beans. Drench with some of the hot *chiltomate* sauce and sprinkle with the cheese. Serve with the remaining *chiltomate* sauce on the side.

FOR THE *CHILTOMATE* SAUCE

¹/₃ cup corn oil, extra-virgin olive oil, or lard

1¹/₂ medium white onions, peeled and chopped

8 large ripe plum or round tomatoes, dropped in boiling water for 15 seconds, drained, cooled slightly, and peeled

1 small green bell pepper

1 fresh habanero chile

Salt to taste

FOR THE ROLLED TORTILLAS

32 small corn tortillas (about 3 inches in diameter), warmed and preferably freshly made

4 cups hot Navy Beans with Habanero Chiles and Epazote (page 192)

12 hard-boiled eggs, finely chopped

5 ounces dried feta, *cotija*, or *añejo* cheese, finely grated

FOR THE SQUID

- 1/3 cup olive oil
- 3 large cloves garlic, peeled and finely chopped
- 1 1/2 cups finely chopped white onions
- 2 pounds squid, cleaned and cut into 1-inch rings
- 4 fresh blanco, serrano, or Carib chiles, finely chopped
- 4 small green bell peppers, finely chopped
- 1/2 teaspoon ground allspice
- 1/4 to 1/3 cup squid or octopus ink

Salt to taste

FOR THE RICE

- 3/4 cup vegetable oil
- 4 large cloves garlic, peeled
- 1/2 white onion, peeled and halved
- 2 cups long-grain rice, soaked in hot water for 15 minutes, drained, and rinsed
- 3 to 3 1/4 cups hot water or fish stock (the amount depends on the variety of rice)

Salt to taste

FOR THE GARNISH

- 1 red bell pepper, cut into thin strips
- 1 yellow bell pepper, cut into thin strips
- 1 green bell pepper, cut into thin strips

BLACK RICE WITH SQUID
ARROZ NEGRO CON CALAMARES

Serves 8

By day, fishermen near Syba Playa at the north end of the city of Campeche wait ashore with their small boats. By night, they travel the dark waters of the coast looking for squid, corbina, anchovies, shad, grouper, and baby shark. Small lamps light the mist of the night and the silver moon reflects softly against the sea as the boats slide silently to work.

PREPARE THE SQUID: Heat the olive oil in a casserole. Add the garlic and the onions and cook until light brown. Add the squid and cook covered over medium heat until it starts to soften, about 5 minutes. Add the chiles, green peppers, and allspice and continue to cook covered for 10 minutes. Off the heat, add the ink and season with salt.

PREPARE THE RICE: Heat the oil in a medium casserole. Add the garlic and the onion and cook until light brown. Add the rice and cook, stirring frequently, until lightly colored. Remove the casserole from the heat and drain off the oil and discard the garlic and the onion. Add the prepared squid and cook, uncovered, over high heat until the rice absorbs the ink, about 4 minutes. Add the hot water, reseason with salt, and let boil for 3 minutes. Turn the heat to low, cover, and cook for 45 minutes or until the rice is fluffy.

TO SERVE: Place the rice in warmed soup plates and garnish with the different colored peppers.

SPAGHETTI VALENCIANA WITH SEAFOOD AND SAUSAGES
FIDEGUA VALENCIANA

Serves 12

The Spanish conquerors brought many new gastronomic traditions to Campeche. In this variation of *paella valenciana*, spaghetti substitutes for the rice to make this dish unique to the region. Use perch, grouper, sea bass, shad, or pompano fillets in this dish.

PREPARE THE SAUCE: Heat a large paella pan or skillet. Add the oil and 20 of the garlic cloves and cook until brown; discard the garlic. Add the peppers and sauté for about 5 minutes. Puree the tomatoes with the onions, the remaining 6 garlic cloves, and the saffron in a food processor or a blender. Strain the mixture into the pan and season with salt. Simmer uncovered over medium heat, stirring occasionally, until the sauce becomes very thick. Set the sauce aside.

PREPARE THE SEAFOOD AND THE FISH: Preheat a large skillet, add the oil, then cook the garlic until light brown; discard the garlic. Add the large shrimp, oysters, squid, and baby shrimp, season with salt, and sauté for 2 minutes. Remove and reserve the seafood. Add the fish, cut into bite-size squares, and sauté on both sides for a total of 2 minutes. Remove and reserve the fish.

PREPARE THE PASTA: Bring the water to a boil in a large pot. Add the onion, garlic, bay leaves, marjoram, thyme, and salt. Add the pasta and cook until almost al dente. Drain the pasta and discard the other solids.

TO SERVE: Meanwhile, reheat the sauce. Add the seafood and the fish and heat through. Add the drained pasta and toss with 2 large forks. Add thinly-sliced sausages, the peas, and the fish stock, cover, and cook for 6 minutes. Sprinkle the dish with the parsley and serve at the table from the paella pan.

FOR THE SAUCE
- 1 cup extra-virgin olive oil
- 26 medium cloves garlic, peeled
- 4 small green bell peppers, minced
- 2½ pounds ripe plum tomatoes, peeled and chopped
- 1½ medium white onions, peeled and cut into pieces
- 1½ teaspoons saffron
- Salt to taste

FOR THE SEAFOOD
- ¾ cup olive oil
- 6 medium cloves garlic, peeled
- 12 large shrimp or crayfish, peeled and deveined
- 48 small oysters, shucked
- 1 pound squid, cleaned and sliced into ½-inch rings
- 1 pound baby shrimp, peeled
- Salt to taste
- 1 pound fish fillets

FOR THE PASTA
- 18 cups water
- 1 medium white onion, peeled and halved
- ½ head garlic, unpeeled
- 2 fresh bay leaves
- 3 sprigs marjoram
- 3 sprigs thyme
- Salt to taste
- 1½ pounds spaghetti

FOR THE GARNISH
- 12 small Vienna sausages
- 1½ cups cooked peas
- 1 cup fish stock
- ½ cup minced parsley

POMPANO BAKED IN PARCHMENT PAPER, CAMPECHE STYLE
PÁMPANO EMPAPELADO ESTILO CAMPECHE

Serves 6

FOR THE *RECADO*

1 tablespoon cumin seeds

1 teaspoon cloves

1/2 teaspoon allspice

2 tablespoons chopped dried chile (such as japonés, ancho, costeño, or de árbol)

8 medium garlic cloves, peeled and roasted in a hot skillet

Salt to taste

1/2 cup Seville orange juice or grapefruit juice blended with a dash of lime juice

FOR THE FISH

1 whole pompano, sea bass, or red snapper (about 4 1/2 pounds), cleaned, slit lengthwise, and skin slashed

1/3 cup extra-virgin olive oil

FOR THE GARNISH

3 limes, halved

1 small bunch parsley

The island of Jaina in the Gulf of Mexico is an archaeological treasure. Situated in the northern reaches of Campeche, this island was central to the Mayan empire. Numerous fish inhabit the local waters, including barracuda, tuna, mackerel, red snapper, and pompano. The heady *recado* (spice paste) marries well with these delicious species.

PREPARE THE *RECADO:* In a mortar or a spice grinder, grind the cumin, cloves, allspice, chile, garlic, and salt. Add the Seville orange juice and beat into a smooth paste.

PREPARE THE FISH: Preheat the oven to 400°F. Daub the inside and the skin of the fish with the *recado*. Cut 2 pieces of parchment paper into 2 large oval shapes. Place the fish on 1 oval, drizzle with the olive oil, and cover with the second piece of parchment. Fold over both edges of the parchment paper to make a tight seal. Wrap the package in aluminum foil. Bake the fish until it flakes but is still moist, about 35 to 45 minutes.

TO SERVE: Remove the fish from the foil and paper and serve on a large platter. Garnish with limes and parsley.

SEA BASS IN GREEN SAUCE
ROBALO EN VERDE

Serves 8

This simple preparation requires an abundance of fresh greens such as cilantro, scallions, and parsley as well as tomatillos. For a quicker version, slice the fish into 1-inch-thick oval steaks and reduce the baking time to 20 minutes.

PREPARE THE FISH: Preheat the oven to 400°F. Make diagonal slashes (about 1/2 inch deep) across both sides of the fish. Place the fish in a baking dish. Sprinkle the lime juice, salt, cumin, and pepper over the fish and let stand for 1 hour.

PREPARE THE GREEN SAUCE: Meanwhile, puree the tomatillos, chiles, onions, scallions, parsley, and cilantro in a blender or a food processor. Set aside. Heat the oils in a medium saucepan and fry the garlic until brown; discard the garlic. Pour part of the blended ingredients into the oil and let sizzle for a few seconds. Add the rest of the sauce and simmer uncovered until it thickens, about 30 minutes. Add the cilantro leaves and season with salt and pepper. Pour the sauce over the fish and bake uncovered until the fish flakes easily, 45 minutes to 1 hour. Do not overcook.

TO SERVE: Transfer the fish to a platter, cover with the sauce, and garnish with the parsley and cilantro sprigs and the lime halves. Serve with white rice and freshly made tortillas or with boiled potatoes.

FOR THE FISH

- 1 whole sea bass or salmon (about 4 1/2 pounds), cleaned with head attached

Juice of 4 limes

Salt to taste

- 1 teaspoon cumin seeds, ground
- 1 1/2 teaspoons black peppercorns, coarsely ground

FOR THE GREEN SAUCE

- 3 pounds tomatillos, husked, or small green tomatoes
- 6 to 8 fresh serrano chiles or 4 jalapeño chiles
- 3 medium white onions, peeled and roughly chopped
- 20 scallions, roughly chopped
- 2 cups roughly chopped parsley
- 1 cup roughly chopped cilantro
- 1/3 cup vegetable oil
- 1/2 cup olive oil
- 14 cloves garlic, peeled
- 2 bunches cilantro leaves or Thai parsley

Salt and freshly ground black pepper to taste

FOR THE GARNISH

- 20 sprigs cilantro
- 20 sprigs parsley
- 8 limes, halved

YUCA FRITTERS
TORREJAS DE YUCA
Serves 8

1½ pounds yuca or cassava,
  peeled
Salt to taste
⅓ cup flour
1 cup sugar
2 to 3 eggs
6 tablespoons butter
4 cups corn oil
Sugar and ground cinnamon to
  taste

Yuca is a relative of the sweet potato and is used frequently in Campeche kitchens and throughout southern Mexico. This delicious dessert brings the ancient flavor of Mayan cooking into the modern age.

Bring several quarts of water to a boil in a medium saucepan. Add the yuca and salt and simmer, covered, until soft, about 30 minutes. Drain the yuca and return it to the saucepan. Cook uncovered, stirring often, until the water has evaporated, about 10 minutes. Transfer the yuca to a large bowl and beat with the flour, the sugar, eggs, and butter until the mixture is thick and smooth. Form the batter into 2-inch-round cakes. Heat the oil in a frying pan and fry, turning once, until the fritters are crisp. Remove them with a slotted spoon and drain on paper towels. Dust the fritters with sugar and cinnamon. Serve the hot fritters on a platter and accompany with either more sugar or honey.

CAMPECHE FRUIT PLATE WITH VIRGIN HONEY
MANGOS, NARANJAS Y PLÁTANOS DE CAMPECHE CON MIEL VIRGEN
Serves 4

4 ripe red or Manila mangoes,
  peeled and thinly sliced
4 oranges, peeled and sliced
4 medium ripe bananas, peeled
  and sliced on the bias
½ cup virgin honey
½ cup Grand Marnier or other
  orange liqueur
Cocoa powder or confectioners'
  sugar

Use the purest honey available for this fruit dessert. Specialty honeys with a hint of lemon, raspberry, or orange would be especially welcome.

Place the sliced mangoes on the left side of each of 4 large chilled serving plates. Place the sliced oranges along the edges of the plate and the sliced bananas on the right side. Drizzle the honey over the bottom of the plate and sprinkle with the liqueur. Dust the plate with cocoa or confectioners' sugar and serve immediately.

GUANÁBANA DRINK WITH LIME AND COCONUT
AGUAS FRESCAS DE GUANÁBANA, RODAJAS DE LIMÓN Y COCO

Makes 1 gallon

Luscious *guanábanas*, limes, and coconuts, all of which grow wild in Campeche, take on new life when combined in this thirst-quenching drink. The dark green, spine-covered rind of the *guanábana* shields a pulpy, musky flesh. Try substituting cherimoyas if *guanábanas* are unavailable.

Remove the seeds from the *guanábana* pulp and puree the pulp in a blender or a food processor along with the coconut and a little of the water. Strain the mixture into a large glass pitcher. Add the remaining water, sugar to taste, and ice cubes. Add the lime slices and mix well. Serve very cold.

2 large ripe *guanábanas*, peeled
1 cup shredded coconut, preferably fresh
4 quarts cold water
Sugar to taste
Ice cubes
6 limes, sliced

TABASCO

RADISH SALAD

CHAYOTE, CORN, AND CUCUMBER MÉLANGE

PICKLED AMASHITO CHILES

FRIED TORTILLAS STUFFED WITH GARLIC

TURTLE AND GREENS SOUP

CRAYFISH STUFFED WITH GARLIC

FRIED SEA BASS FILLETS

SEA BASS STEAMED IN GREENS

MAMEY CREAM

CHOROTE (CHOCOLATE DRINK)

Low-lying Tabasco is situated along the Gulf of Mexico. Its name comes from the Nahuatl word for "flooded land." Tabasco was the center of Olmec civilization, perhaps the most important pre-Hispanic culture. Majestic ancient carvings and sculptures reveal the region's long history as an artistic center. Tabasco is also believed to have been a corridor for several migrations of ancient peoples.

Villahermosa, the beautiful capital located along the banks of the Grijalva River, was besieged by English pirates during colonial times. Today, its streets are decorated with exotic flowers. Nearby tropical forests shelter an array of wildlife. Because of the state's great waterways, fishing is an important industry, especially in the areas of Balancán-Tenosique, Chontalpa, Emiliano Zapata, and Jonuta.

The region's fertile soils support corn, beans, sugarcane, coconuts, allspice, coffee, mameys, lemons, bananas, mangoes, tamarinds, oranges, guavas, papayas, grapefruits, and *marañón,* also known as the cashew apple. The region's most prized fruit is cacao, the berry used to make chocolate drinks since ancient times. Europeans transformed these ground berries into the chocolate confections we know today.

A good poet starts at his own house. That is why I have come back to Tabasco—to feel again in my veins the beat of the jungle, the current of the land, and the fierceness of the rivers. I have come back to sing the song of my native land. ¶ Memories came flooding back when I visited my childhood home. The scent of just-bathed women filled the house as light streamed through windows and halls. Parrots flew overhead, and brilliant flowers bloomed all around. The sight of herons carried me back to childhood mornings when the breeze was perfumed with coffee and my nanny, Julita, used to roll bean tamales in *hoja santa* leaves to make my favorite morning snack. ¶ When she was not busy pampering me, Julita prepared any number of delicious dishes. I can remember her turkey *tamalitos* seasoned with *achiote* and epazote as well as bread spread heavily with *chinín,* a plant that looks like avocado and tastes like butter. Her other specialties included turtle (cooked either in its own juices or in green sauce), octopus in its own ink, flan with milk and cinnamon, a refreshing corn and cacao bean drink, and, of course, her strong coffee. ¶ Julita was born in Villahermosa in one of the old Chontal haciendas. She used to tell me magical stories about her home and her childhood. For me, Julita had no age. As she talked about her love for the region, she peeled cacao beans and her hands became all sticky with their sap. These treasured beans would be set out in the sun to dry, toasted on the *comal,* and then blended with sugar and cinnamon to form small chocolate tablets. The beans were also made into traditional beverages once used by the Olmecs, Aztecs, and Maya in their rituals. I can recall salivating as she beat the beans and liquid rhythmically in *el molinillo,* a small wooden utensil similar to a mortar. As she rubbed the *molinillo* harder and harder between her hands, the foam would rise closer to the top of the *molinillo.* The *choc, choc, choc* grew louder while Julita repeated, as if it were some sort of prayer, the virtues of "this elixir of the gods" once so important to the Maya, Olmecs, and Aztecs. But as I licked my lips and eventually drank the sacred beverage it was with little knowledge of its significance or history. ¶ Ah, Julita, how many years have passed and how many things that seemed unimportant so long ago now come back to haunt me. There are so many images I want to revive in my mind so that I may live them once again. ¶ I remember going fishing with Uncle Toño, for example, who was the kind of uncle kids dream about. We went up along the Grijalva River, to a place where the sounds of the water and the jungle merge. We made camp in an area surrounded by vegetation of all sorts, including tall palms and banana trees. We arranged with the local fishermen to set out early on the water. With dawn's first breath, we left the camp behind in a small cedar boat. Our goal was to find *piguas,* medium to large crayfish, as well as *pejelagartos,* fish with a rough skin similar to alligator hide. We returned at noon, and Uncle Toño grilled the catch over an open fire, smoking some of it over very low heat to preserve it. I can still remember the taste of that extraordinary journey. ¶ When I was about thirteen, my aunt Chofi, Toño's wife, invited me and my cousins to Puerto Ceiba. I remember stopping on the way for Tapesco oysters, by far the most exquisite I have ever tasted. On the beach, a small rectangular frame made of branches rested about one meter above a gentle fire. The frame and poles were covered with banana and allspice leaves. The oysters were nestled inside palm fronds and placed on the leaf-covered frame. The aroma of the wood along with the strong scent of palm fronds gave the oysters a wonderful flavor. As my aunt and I watched the oysters come off the fire, I was simultaneously entranced by a glimpse of her long, slender legs. Nothing would be as before, except perhaps my love for food. ¶ Even though I was racked with guilt by my sinful thoughts, I made another trip with Uncle Toño. This time we were alone, thank God, and we took off for the port of Frontera. Once again I was witness to the generosity of the Grijalva—which all Tabascans carry in their blood—and saw how the waters give life to the dazzling city market. Launches filled with *pitahayas,* tamarinds, and *chaya* leaves carried goods to market stalls. The market itself was filled with papayas, mameys, yuca, radishes, chiles, gourds, fresh cashews, *chipilín* (an oval-shaped herb with an unusual ashy flavor), crabs, oysters, and shrimp in all sizes. In small shacks, women fanned their legs with long skirts to chase away the heat of the stoves. They prepared sea bass, freshwater shrimp wrapped in bacon, all kinds of turtles (they were abundant then and fishing for them was not prohibited as it is now) cooked in their own juices or in green sauce, plantains, and crayfish laced with garlic. I can remember small, thick tortillas stuffed with garlic and deep-fried in lard until crisp, and served with beans from the pot and with cream. ¶ I long for a universe of words to sing all that I feel about Tabasco. These first lines, however short and hastily gathered, are no less sincere. They are the start of my declaration of love.

RADISH SALAD
ENSALADA DE RÁBANOS
Serves 8

32 small radishes, finely chopped
Juice of 8 limes
Salt to taste
2 ripe avocados, peeled, sliced, and bathed in lime juice

Tabasco was the site of the first battle between Hernán Cortés and Mexican Indians and as such has a long history of cross-cultural exchanges, both friendly and hostile. As part of Cortés's victory tribute, the Indians gave him twenty slaves. Among this booty was the Indian princess Malintzin, who served Cortés as interpreter and helped make the Conquest possible. The radish, which plays a star role in this salad, made its own conquest of sorts, traveling from the Orient to Tabasco, where it was soon assimilated into the local cooking. Radishes thrive in the rich Tabascan soil, which is irrigated by the region's many rivers and streams. This salad is particularly light and refreshing, perfect for the warm Tabascan climate.

Mix the chopped radishes with the lime juice in a bowl. Season with salt and mix well. Place the radish salad on a platter and garnish with the avocado slices

VARIATION: Add chopped cilantro and red onion to taste.

CHAYOTE, CORN, AND CUCUMBER MÉLANGE
CHAYOTE, ELOTE Y PEPINO CRIOLLO

Serves 8

The market in Tabasco opens early, with the rising sun. Farmers carry deep, oval straw baskets of produce on their heads, holding on to cloths draped over the baskets to help steady them. A rainbow of colors fills the market as the fragrant fruits and vegetables are unpacked, including melons, guavas, tiny bananas, *marañón* (the fruit of the cashew tree), oranges, grapefruit, watermelons, Seville oranges, lemons, limes, cacao seeds, ears of corn, black beans, and sugarcane. Many baskets are loaded with fresh herbs such as *chipilín* (a tiny-leafed herb with an ashy flavor), *momo* (also known as *hoja santa*), regular and Tabascan parsley (which is similar to Thai parsley), *chaya* (a nutritious, heart-shaped green used like spinach), thyme, marjoram, and fresh bay leaves. In other parts of the market, fishermen bring the catch of the day, with all sorts of manta rays, baby shark, oysters, sea bass, grouper, squid, and octopus. Throughout the market, the sounds of women conversing in Chontal, Mayan, Zoque, and Spanish can be heard. As the day wears on, the aisles get more and more crowded and the heat and the humidity grow more intense. This summery dish is made with chayotes (or water pears) and fresh white corn, which have been combined in Tabascan vegetable preparations like this one since pre-Hispanic times. The conquistadors introduced cucumbers to Mexico and they now grow in abundance throughout the region.

Bring 8 cups of water to a boil in a pot. Add the chayotes and a pinch of brown sugar and salt and cook, covered, for 15 minutes or until soft. Drain and cool in ice water. Drain again and set aside. Heat the remaining 4 cups of water in a pot with a little salt. Remove the kernels from the ears of corn with a knife or a kernel remover. Add the corn kernels and the cucumbers to the pot and cook, covered, for 10 minutes. Drain and set aside. Melt the $1/2$ cup butter in a sauté pan, add the garlic and the onions and sauté for several minutes. Add the chiles, allspice, cooked vegetables, and salt to taste. Once the vegetables are heated through, swirl in the remaining 2 tablespoons butter.

FOR THE VEGETABLES

- 12 cups water
- 6 chayotes, peeled and quartered
- Brown sugar to taste
- Salt to taste
- 4 ears white corn
- 3 Creole (white cucumber) or regular cucumbers, peeled and quartered
- $1/2$ cup butter
- 4 medium cloves garlic, peeled and finely chopped
- $1 1/2$ medium white onions, peeled and finely chopped
- $1/4$ cup whole fresh amashito chiles, 2 tablespoons finely chopped habanero chiles, or $1/4$ cup finely chopped serrano chiles
- 1 teaspoon Tabascan peppercorns (allspice), ground
- 2 tablespoons butter, cut into small pieces

FOR THE GARNISH

- 2 tablespoons chopped epazote or cilantro
- $1/4$ cup finely chopped white onion

TO SERVE: Put the vegetables on a platter and sprinkle with the chopped epazote and onion. Serve this vegetable combination with chicken, fish, beef, or pork. Finish the vegetables with a touch of cream and some cheese for a luxurious dish.

PICKLED AMASHITO CHILES
CHILES AMASHITOS
Serves 8

1 pound fresh amashito, jalapeño, or serrano chiles, chopped

2 medium red onions, peeled and finely chopped

3 cups Seville orange juice or champagne vinegar

³/₄ cup fruit vinegar or balsamic vinegar

1 tablespoon black peppercorns

1 tablespoon allspice

1 tablespoon salt, or to taste

¹/₃ cup olive oil

These tiny round peppers, which are sometimes hot and sometimes mild, are a staple in Tabasco. Amashito chiles are used fresh in tomato *salsas* or pickled, as in this recipe, and served with fish and seafood dishes (especially shrimp) as well as Fried Tortillas Stuffed with Garlic (page 215). Their somewhat fruity flavor adds a distinctive touch to the cuisine of this rich land.

Place the chopped chiles in a glass container. Add the onions, orange juice, vinegar, peppercorns, allspice, and salt. Mix well, then add the oil little by little. Season again and let the chiles macerate at room temperature or in the refrigerator for 4 hours before serving.

FRIED TORTILLAS STUFFED WITH GARLIC
TORTILLAS FRITAS AL AJO

Serves 8

Fried tortillas with garlic are eaten throughout the state of Tabasco. Their heady garlic flavor makes them a delicious side dish with the fresh seafood that is so abundant in the region. They are particularly nice when served with crayfish *(piguas)*.

PREPARE THE FILLING: Heat the oil in a medium skillet. Add the garlic and cook over low heat until it begins to color. Remove the skillet from the heat and cool slightly. Add the lime juice and the water and continue cooking until the garlic is golden brown. Season with salt and set aside.

PREPARE THE TORTILLAS: Preheat a *comal* or a heavy skillet. Place the *masa* on a pastry board or a large, flat surface. Knead the *masa* with the water and salt, adding the water a little at a time, until the dough has a smooth consistency. Line a tortilla press with plastic wrap. Using a $^2/_3$-cup ball of dough for each tortilla, place the dough in the tortilla press. Press lightly to keep the tortilla somewhat thick. Remove the tortilla from the press and peel back the plastic. Moisten the palm of your right hand and place the tortilla in the center of it. With your left hand, shape the tortilla until it measures about 6 inches in diameter and $^1/_4$ inch thick. Repeat, making 8 tortillas. Cook the tortillas, one at a time, on the hot *comal*, turning twice, until slightly puffed. As soon as each tortilla comes off the *comal*, make a superficial slash mark on the side without cutting all the way through. Keep the tortillas warm by wrapping them in a dishcloth or a napkin.

Stuff $1^1/_2$ tablespoons of the reserved garlic through the slit in each tortilla. Heat the oil in a deep skillet. Fry the tortillas until golden brown. Drain on paper towels to remove the excess oil. Cut into quarters and serve immediately with boiled seafood or grilled fish.

Note: See pages 309 to 310 for more information on making the dough and using the tortilla press.

FOR THE FILLING
- 1 cup vegetable oil
- 1 cup finely chopped garlic
- Juice of 6 limes
- $^1/_2$ cup water
- Salt to taste

FOR THE TORTILLAS
- $5^1/_3$ cups fresh *masa* (corn dough)
- $^1/_3$ to $^1/_2$ cup warm water
- Salt to taste
- 8 cups sunflower or corn oil

TURTLE AND GREENS SOUP
SOPA DE TORTUGA EN VERDE
Serves 8

FOR THE TURTLE

- 5 quarts water
- 2 heads garlic, halved but not peeled
- 20 large scallions
- 2½ pounds fresh, frozen, or canned turtle meat

Salt to taste

FOR THE GREEN SAUCE

- ½ cup vegetable oil
- 2 medium white onions, peeled
- 6 medium cloves garlic, peeled
- 2 large ripe tomatoes, chopped
- 2 medium green bell peppers, chopped
- 10 scallions
- 10 fresh avocado or *hoja santa* leaves
- 2 bunches Tabascan parsley or cilantro
- 1½ teaspoons allspice
- 1 bunch *chipilín* or spinach leaves
- 20 *chaya* or Swiss chard leaves

Salt to taste

- ½ cup fresh *masa* (corn dough)
- 16 to 18 cups fish stock
- 2 fresh xcatick, serrano, or habanero chiles, chopped

The Olmecs who inhabited Tabasco revered water as a great source of power. From the Grijalva River, ancient fishermen pulled a variety of turtles. Today, their descendants must rely on other sources since turtle-fishing is prohibited in local waters. This soup dates back to pre-Hispanic times and uses the sharp flavors of greens and herbs (especially *hoja santa* and Tabascan parsley) that are native to the region. This soup was served during special ceremonies or rituals like weddings, where it most often was presented in the shell.

PREPARE THE TURTLE: In a large saucepan, bring the water to a boil along with the garlic and the scallions. Add the fresh turtle meat, if using (or frozen meat that has been defrosted), and cook, uncovered, until tender. Season with salt and allow to cool in the stock. Remove the meat and discard the liquid and the other solids. Chop the turtle meat and set aside. (Canned turtle meat may be chopped and reserved at this point.)

PREPARE THE GREEN SAUCE: Heat the oil in a large saucepan. Puree the onions and the garlic and add to the oil. Sauté briefly. Puree the tomatoes, bell peppers, scallions, avocado leaves, Tabascan parsley, allspice, *chipilín,* and *chaya* leaves in a blender or a food processor. (If necessary, do this in batches.) Add this mixture to the saucepan and simmer, uncovered, until the sauce begins to thicken. Season with salt. Keep uncovered so as not to affect the color.

Dissolve the *masa* in 2 cups of the fish stock and add the mixture to the saucepan along with the chopped chiles and the turtle meat. (Add more stock, if desired, up to a total of 18 cups.) Cover and simmer the soup. The soup is ready when it takes on a semithick consistency. Correct the seasoning. Ladle into individual soup bowls and serve hot.

VARIATION: Some of the greens may be reserved and added to the hot soup just before serving so as to retain their bright color and full flavor.

CRAYFISH STUFFED WITH GARLIC
PIGUAS AL AJO

Serves 8

The name Tabasco comes from the Nahuatl word meaning "the land that floats" or, more literally, "flooded land." The state has numerous lagoons visited by flocks of white herons as well as several major rivers, including the Grijalva, Tacotalpa, and the Usumacinta. *Piguas* (known as languostines or crayfish in the United States) are caught in special straw baskets that are thrown into the river. *Piguas* range in size from very small to the size of a lobster. Serve just two crayfish per person if using the larger variety.

Cut open each crayfish lengthwise on the stomach side. Clean the head and remove the digestive pouch from the body. Season the crayfish with salt and pepper. Stuff some crushed garlic into the slit and close with 2 toothpicks. Heat the oil in large frying pan or a wok. Fry the crayfish until the shells are crisp and deep red in color, about 2 minutes on each side. Remove and drain on paper towels. Serve the crayfish hot with the lemon halves.

32 medium crayfish

Salt and freshly ground black pepper to taste

48 cloves garlic, peeled and crushed

64 wooden toothpicks

6 cups vegetable oil

8 lemons or limes, halved

FRIED SEA BASS FILLETS
POSTA DE ROBALO

Serves 8

8 sea bass fillets with skin on (each about 1 inch thick)

4 medium cloves garlic, peeled and crushed

1 teaspoon freshly ground black pepper

1/3 cup fresh lime juice

Salt to taste

3 cups vegetable oil

4 medium garlic cloves, peeled

Flour

8 limes, halved

16 tomato slices

Parsley leaves

Pickled Amashito Chiles (page 214) or any canned or pickled chiles

One of the easiest and most delicious ways to prepare fresh sea bass is fried, accompanied by a crisp green salad or amashito chiles.

Place a layer of sea bass fillets in a glass baking dish. Daub with half of the crushed garlic, pepper, and lime juice. Sprinkle with salt. Make a second layer of fish and cover with the remaining crushed garlic, pepper, and lime juice. Sprinkle with salt and marinate in the refrigerator for 2 hours.

Heat the oil in a heavy skillet. Brown the whole garlic cloves and discard. Scoop flour onto a sheet of waxed paper. Turn the fish fillets in the flour to coat lightly. Fry 4 fillets at a time, turning once, until the fish is cooked through, 4 to 6 minutes. Remove and drain the fish on paper towels. Transfer the fish to a platter and garnish with the lime halves, tomato slices, parsley, and chiles.

SEA BASS STEAMED IN GREENS
ROBALO EN MOMO
Serves 6

The Olmecs were an advanced civilization that sculpted and shaped stones with chisels. Works were carved from large pieces of granite as well as from jade and other precious stones throughout Tabasco. In addition to their skill as artisans, the Olmecs had a highly developed understanding of herbs and their curative powers. *Hoja santa*, or *momo*, was often used as a wrapper for steamed fish, perfuming the contents of the package with its mild anise flavor. It was also added to the baths given to women after childbirth in order to ease pain.

PREPARE THE FISH: Prepare a large steamer or double boiler, then cover with a layer of 6 *hoja santa* leaves. Wash and dry the remaining leaves. Place one *hoja santa* leaf over another to make 6 separate packages. Place a fish fillet in the center of each package and sprinkle with salt and pepper. Mix the chopped onions, garlic, green peppers, and chile and spoon over the fish. Sprinkle again with salt and pepper. Drizzle lightly with olive oil and then cover the fish with the parsley, cilantro, and chopped tomatoes. Wrap the *hoja santa* leaves around the fish and use parchment paper or aluminum foil to make a sealed pouch. Place the fish pouches in the steamer in 2 layers. Cook for 10 to 15 minutes or until the fish is moist but flaky.

PREPARE THE HERB BROTH: Heat 6 cups of the fish stock in a casserole. Meanwhile, puree the herbs, chiles, onions, and garlic with the remaining 2 cups of stock until the mixture becomes a smooth paste. Strain twice to remove any large solids. Add the mixture to the stock in the casserole and boil for 8 to 10 minutes. Add the allspice and season with salt.

TO SERVE: Ladle the herb broth into 6 deep soup bowls. Remove the parchment paper or foil from the pouches and place the fish wrapped in the *hoja santa* in the bowls. Serve immediately.

FOR THE FISH
- 18 large *hoja santa*, Swiss chard, or spinach leaves
- 6 thick sea bass, salmon, pompano, or red snapper fillets (about ½ pound each)
- Salt and freshly ground black pepper to taste
- 1½ cups finely chopped white onions
- 6 medium cloves garlic, peeled and finely chopped
- 2 small green bell peppers, finely chopped
- 1 fresh xcatick chile or 2 Carib chiles, finely chopped
- Olive oil to taste
- 18 large Tabascan parsley or cilantro leaves
- 1½ cups cilantro
- 1 pound ripe plum tomatoes, finely chopped

FOR THE HERB BROTH
- 8 cups fish stock or clam juice
- 10 *hoja santa*, Swiss chard, or spinach leaves, chopped
- 1½ cups chopped cilantro
- 2 fresh jalapeño chiles, chopped
- 2 cups chopped white onions
- 4 large cloves garlic, peeled and chopped
- 6 whole allspice
- Salt to taste

MAMEY CREAM
CREMA DE ZAPOTE
Serves 8

3 large ripe mameys or 6 large ripe mangoes

1½ cups sweetened condensed milk

1 cup walnuts or pine nuts

1 cup sugar

½ cup water

⅓ cup sweet sherry

The mamey is a fruit with a rough surface but a delicate, creamy flesh. In Tabasco, the fruit is called red *zapote*, but in the rest of the country it is known by the name mamey. The Olmecs not only used the pulp for cooking but also toasted the pit to make a base for paints and a number of distinctly flavored sauces. The fruit added flavor to ritual beverages made from chocolate and *masa* (corn dough). Today, mameys are most often employed to make wonderful ice creams.

Slice open the mameys and scoop out the pulp. Add the pulp to a blender or a food processor along with the condensed milk and the nuts. Blend well and chill in individual dessert bowls for several hours. Mix the sugar and the water in a saucepan and cook, uncovered, over medium heat until the mixture forms a thick syrup. Remove from the heat and stir in the sherry. Pour the syrup over the mamey pudding. Top with whipped cream and mint, if desired.

CHOROTE (CHOCOLATE DRINK)
CHOROTE

Serves 12

This unusual beverage dates back to the time of the Olmecs, Chontals, and Maya. It combines fresh *masa* (corn dough) with cacao beans, a major crop in Tabasco, for a refreshing Indian drink often served in honor of the god Quetzalcóatl. Bitter chocolate can substitute for the cacao beans.

Bring a large quantity of water to a boil in a pot. Add the corn (but not the *masa*, if using) and the limestone and cook until very soft. Drain and cool the corn slightly. Wash the corn, rubbing vigorously to remove the skins. Rinse and drain well. Grind the corn in a meat grinder or a food processor. (If using fresh *masa*, start the recipe at this point.) Heat a *comal* or a heavy skillet. Toast the cacao beans (but not the chocolate, if using) on both sides. Chop toasted cacao beans or chocolate in a blender or a spice grinder along with a little water until the mixture forms a smooth paste. Add the cacao mixture to the *masa* and knead until the dough is light coffee in color. Put the dough in a large bowl. Gradually add the 24 cups water and beat until the mixture has the consistency of a soft drink. Sweeten with sugar and honey if desired and refrigerate. Pour the *chorote* into a pitcher or a large gourd and serve over ice in tall glasses.

$^1/_2$ pound dried white corn or 1 pound fresh *masa*

2 tablespoons powdered limestone

$^3/_4$ pound peeled cacao beans or unsweetened chocolate, broken in small pieces

24 cups water

Sugar or honey to taste

30 ice cubes

VERACRUZ

RETURN-TO-LIFE COCKTAIL

FRESHWATER SHRIMP IN PAPER CONES

CATHEDRAL-STYLE EGGS

MEXICAN FISH EMPANADAS

PELLIZCADAS CATEMACO STYLE

TACOS WITH CACTUS PADDLES, ANCHO CHILES, AND
CHIPOTLE CHILES

CHAPOPOTE RANCH ENCHILADAS

HEARTY VERACRUZ FISH SOUP

TLACOTALPEÑO RICE

POBLANO CHILES STUFFED WITH SHREDDED
LOBSTER

FRESH FRUIT PLATTER

The state of Veracruz is located in eastern Mexico along the Gulf of Mexico. The name comes from Latin words *vera* and *cruz,* which means "true cross." The northern regions of the state were settled by the Huastec tribe, while Totonacs lived in the central areas and Olmecs in the south. Each of these cultures left its mark at places like El Tajín, a splendid Totonac city near Papantla, the modern-day center for the region's vanilla industry.

The state capital is Jalapa, site of an impressive archaeological museum that houses numerous Olmec statues in an outdoor sculpture garden. The areas around Cordoba and Orizaba contain many coffee and sugarcane plantations. In fact, Veracruz produces more sugarcane than any other Mexican state. Other noteworthy products include corn, beans, rice, sorghum, wheat, tomatoes, sweet potatoes, sesame seeds, pineapples, mangoes, oranges, tangerines, grapefruit, coconuts, and the world-famous vanilla beans.

The state is crisscrossed by several large rivers and has a number of important lagoons at Tamiahua, Tampamachoco, Sontecomapan, Verdes, and Catemaco. Fishing is a major economic concern throughout the region. The lively port at Veracruz blends all this industry with local music, poetry, and folklore.

So you have come looking for Jacinto Lupercio? Well, he has not yet returned from the sea, but he will come if you have a little patience. What is that you say? Do I know him well? Well, maybe yes, maybe no. We can never completely know someone, can we? ¶ The only thing I could tell you is that he is a man of two destinies. I can't say much because I don't really have the right words, but I will explain to you as best I can. Jacinto Lupercio, "Chinto" to his friends, lived as a young boy in Catemaco, a small village some distance from the coast. At an early age, he dedicated himself quite seriously to the mastery of handicrafts. Even though he was young, his skill was noticed by the older craftsmen. ¶ But life can take some odd twists. We never know what color a fish will be before it emerges from the water. Likewise, we don't know when we are going to die or what tomorrow will bring. If we did, imagine how boring life would be. Anyway, Chinto came here to the fish markets one day and became enchanted with the movements of a young girl with dark, beautiful hair. Her rhythmic walk mimicked the movements of the sea. What man could resist altering his destiny for her? ¶ Chinto never returned to Catemaco and sent word to his family that he had become enthralled with this place. He became Lāzara's man, or, if you prefer, he made Lāzara his wife. He abandoned the artisan's life and set out with bravado to the sea. He transformed himself into a fisherman and became a good one, considering his inland roots. Everyone here liked him. In the beginning, some had doubts that he could learn the fishing trade, but Chinto demonstrated that when a man wants something badly enough he can do it. And he wanted this new life for himself because of his love for Lāzara. He learned our tricks, such as fishing with cord nets or marking limits in the sea with rope to harvest ocean fish, among them red snapper, shad, sawfish, red mullet, and *mojarra.* He learned the fishing seasons (February and March, June through August) and he went out with teams of motorboats to fish the open seas. He learned to throw nets deep in the ocean, often 165 or even 230 feet below the surface to catch prized fish like pompano. At the full moon, he learned to catch large brown shrimp in fine-meshed baskets or maybe octopus or *pargo*. He learned to distinguish all kinds of seafood delicacies. He could tell which fish were running in the water by their aroma, color, or temperament. ¶ Besides ocean fishing, Chinto learned the ways of freshwater fishing in rivers and lagoons. Sometimes, when time permits, I go to the estuaries and hunt for oysters or *lebrancha*, a fish we cure with salt. The roe from this fine fish is also salted lightly and sold fresh. When we fish rivers like the Nautla or the Actopan we use nets to trap shrimp, crab, crayfish, white bass, catfish, and tilapia. It is not easy. The river has its own ways, and we must respect them. Along the banks of the Tecolutla River run the tears of many widows and orphans who lost men in these waters. But Lāzara has never had to cry for Chinto. ¶ My friend, I remember the first time I took Chinto to the Papaloapan River for the famous feast on February 2. His eyes lit up brighter than the candles that lined the shore. Men in small rowboats and canoes had placed so many candles along the riverbanks that my memories of the light are still strong. For the festival, women cover themselves with shawls and pray for hours. The children remain silent as the procession of women moves along the river. Lāzara always marches. It seems that she is always mourning the death of someone near to her. ¶ When you meet her, you will see that she is a very strong woman who has matured much as the years age a bottle of fine wine. She still loves Chinto and takes very good care of him. He likes to say that when he married he learned to eat. He says, and it is quite true, that coastal women may bewitch men with their walk but they conquer men with their cooking. Among the many local dishes none is more famous than *vuelve a la vida* or the "return to life" cocktail made with oysters, shrimp, conch, fish, and a magical dressing that no one can resist. Whenever I have eaten at Chinto's home, Lāzara has fed me like a king. I have sampled her shredded crab cooked with tomato, parsley,

CUISINE OF THE WATER GODS

and chiles; shrimp with dried chiles or chipotle chiles; and jalapeños stuffed with tuna. At their home I have eaten many other delicacies such as roe in *escabeche*, *masa* filled with beans, octopus and squid in their own ink, *Moros y Cristianos* (black beans and white rice) served with ripe plantains, crab chile broth, and crab claws. I learned to enjoy tortillas with pumpkin seeds and fresh chile *piquín*, black sea bass with garlic and chile *guajillo*, palm flowers in tomato broth, and tamales of all kinds. Jacinto's mother showed Lāzara how to prepare *anguila*, *topote*, and *tegogol*, a mollusk similar to the snail that inhabits the waters near Catemaco. In the kitchen, there is no one more talented than Lāzara. Maybe you will be invited to taste the seafood stew she prepares with the catch of the day, epazote, jalapeños, and tomatoes. Sometimes she adds tiny eels; on other days it's red snapper, olive oil, tomatoes, capers, olives, almonds, and pickled chiles to create that famous Veracruz fish dish in the Spanish style. ¶ I won't say any more because that man coming this way—yes, that one walking with pride—is Jacinto Lupercio. You see that dark-skinned man dressed in pants and a loose shirt? He has a red kerchief tied around his neck. Well, I will leave you by yourselves to talk for a long, long time. I know not to disturb the conversation of men who have things to discuss. So, with your permission . . . Hey, Jacinto, this man is looking for you.

RETURN-TO-LIFE COCKTAIL
VUELVE A LA VIDA

Serves 8 to 10

FOR THE CRAB LEGS

20 cups water

Salt to taste

32 crab legs

FOR THE SHRIMP

20 cups water

Salt to taste

1 teaspoon *achiote* (annatto) seeds

40 large shrimp in shells

FOR THE OYSTERS

24 oysters

FOR THE CEVICHE

1 red snapper, sea bass, baby shark, bonito, or mackerel

Lime juice to cover fish

4 large ripe tomatoes (about 1½ pounds), chopped

1 medium white onion, peeled and chopped

4 fresh serrano chiles, chopped

½ cup chopped cilantro

Salt to taste

Olive oil to taste

FOR THE MAYONNAISE

1 large clove garlic, peeled

1 tablespoon water

2 tablespoons lime juice

Salt to taste

4 egg yolks

This is perhaps the most popular seafood platter in the state of Veracruz. The catch of the day and other fresh ingredients are combined to make this savory appetizer or light main course. At Mandinga and Boca del Río, two port villages, local fishermen pool their catch to assure the freshness necessary to make a perfect *vuelve a la vida*. With its distinctive seasonings, this dish shares much with Creole cooking.

PREPARE THE CRAB LEGS: Bring the water and salt to a boil in a large saucepan. Add the crab legs and cook, covered, for 10 minutes. Remove from the water and crack the shells using a pliers. Remove the crabmeat and allow to cool. Refrigerate for 1 hour.

PREPARE THE SHRIMP: Bring the water, salt, and *achiote* seeds to a boil in a large saucepan. Add the shrimp and cook, covered, until pink, 3 to 5 minutes. Remove from the water and allow to cool. Peel and refrigerate for 1 hour.

PREPARE THE OYSTERS: Shuck the oysters, using a spoon to force open the shells. Cut the tendons that attach the oysters to the shells, then return the meats to the shells and refrigerate.

PREPARE THE CEVICHE: Cut the fish into small chunks. Place in a glass bowl and cover with lime juice. Allow to marinate in the refrigerator for 3 hours. Strain off a little of the juice. Add the tomatoes, onion, chiles, cilantro, salt, and olive oil. Allow to marinate in the refrigerator for an additional 3 hours.

PREPARE THE MAYONNAISE: Place the garlic, water, lime juice, salt, and egg yolks in a blender or a food processor. Puree the ingredients well. Gradually add the oils until they are incorporated into the mixture.

TO SERVE: Place a deep bowl in the center of a serving platter. Arrange a circle of crab legs around the bowl, then arrange a row of shrimp, reserving 8 for the garnish. Place the opened oyster shells along the edge of the platter, alternating with the halved limes. Place the ceviche in a bowl on the side. Spoon the mayonnaise into the center bowl and garnish with the limes, the chopped scallions, and the reserved shrimp.

VARIATIONS: Serve with Tabasco sauce, catsup, or hot chipotle sauce, available in Latin markets.

²/₃ cup olive oil
²/₃ cup vegetable oil

FOR THE GARNISH
16 limes, halved
2 tablespoons chopped scallions

FRESHWATER SHRIMP IN PAPER CONES
CAMARONES DE RÍO EN CONOS DE PAPEL
Serves 10 to 12

Veracruz is a land where energy, color, and music dominated by the harp abound, all giving this coastal state a very special charm. Local women appear unaffected by the heat in their pristine white dresses accented with red bandannas and fans that are as pretty as they are practical. Fresh fish and seafood are plentiful. The Malecón dock is lined with makeshift stalls and nearby are special bars where merchants sell shrimp in brown paper cones directly out of wicker baskets. The vendors bring baskets with freshly cooked shrimp (still in their shells) adorned with bright green slices of lime and a dash of chile sauce. This particular recipe for freshwater shrimp in paper cones is commonly eaten as a snack or as the main course for a midday or evening meal.

15 cups water
2 to 3 tablespoons coarse salt
5½ pounds freshwater shrimp or any kind of shrimp or prawns
20 limes, halved
Tabasco sauce or any other hot sauce

Bring the water to a rapid boil in a large saucepan. Add the salt and the shrimp. Cook covered for 4 to 6 minutes and drain. Spoon the cooked shrimp into paper cones or onto a platter. Allow your guests to peel them. Serve the halved limes and hot sauce on the side.

CATHEDRAL-STYLE EGGS
HUEVOS TIRADOS CATEDRAL

Serves 8

½ cup vegetable oil or lard
16 eggs
2 cups refried beans such as
   those on page 121, seasoned
   with salt
Salt to taste
Pickled chiles or fresh salsa to taste
Freshly made corn tortillas

This is a typical breakfast dish served at the Catedral Restaurant in the port city of Veracruz. Combining eggs and beans, it offers an original alternative to the typical morning meal.

Heat the oil in a large frying pan. Place the eggs in a bowl and beat. Fold the beans into the eggs and add salt to taste. Transfer the mixture to the preheated frying pan. Cook the eggs, mixing with a fork or shaking the pan regularly, until the eggs set. Mix again or roll the eggs over with a spatula to form an omelet.

TO SERVE: Arrange the omelet on a serving platter. Garnish with the pickled chiles or fresh salsa. Serve with freshly made corn tortillas on the side.

Note: This recipe may be prepared as individual omelets, if desired.

MEXICAN FISH EMPANADAS
EMPANADAS DE PESCADO A LA MEXICANA

Serves 12

FOR THE FISH
3¼ pounds baby shark, halibut,
   red snapper, crabmeat, or cod
3 ribs celery
12 cups water
2 medium white onions, peeled
   and quartered
6 sprigs parsley
2 fresh bay leaves
2 sprigs marjoram
2 sprigs thyme
2 carrots

The state of Veracruz is blessed with wonderfully abundant waters that invite the locals to fish. These fish turnovers are an example of the imaginative regional cooking that blends the influences of Mexican and Spanish cuisines.

PREPARE THE FISH: Place all the ingredients in a large saucepan and bring to a boil. Reduce the heat and simmer covered until the fish is tender, about 10 minutes. Do not overcook. Remove from the heat and allow the stock to cool. Remove the fish and shred. The stock may be strained and served later, if desired.

PREPARE THE SAUCE: Heat the olive oil in a medium saucepan. Add the whole garlic cloves and sauté until golden brown. Remove and discard 4 of the garlic cloves; place the remaining 4 garlic cloves in a blender or a food processor and puree. Return the pureed garlic to the saucepan and add the onions, minced garlic, and tomatoes. Cook uncovered until the oil separates, then add the parsley, bay leaves, thyme, marjoram, chiles, chile juice, and white wine. Season with salt and pepper and continue cooking until the liquid is reduced by half. Add the shredded fish and continue cooking uncovered until the mixture forms a thick paste. Cool.

PREPARE THE EMPANADAS: Preheat the oven to 400°F. Place half of the puff pastry on a floured surface and extend it with a rolling pin. Cut out thirty-six 6- to 8-inch circles. Spoon 2 tablespoons of the prepared filling onto one side of each circle and fold over. Brush with the egg yolks and the butter and seal with a fork. Repeat with the remaining half of the puff pastry. Arrange the empanadas on greased baking sheets and bake for 10 minutes. Lower the oven temperature to 300°F and continue baking until golden brown, about 25 minutes more.

TO SERVE: Arrange the empanadas on a large platter. Garnish with cilantro and serve immediately.

VARIATIONS: Serve the fish stuffing with white rice, freshly made tortillas, or bean tortillas. Roll stuffing in tortillas to make soft tacos and serve with tomato sauce.

Note: This same recipe can be used to form two large turnovers, in which case you will form a 30-inch circle with each half of the puff pastry. Spoon 2 cups of the filling on one side of each dough and carefully fold over. Follow the same procedure, brushing with the egg yolks and the butter and sealing with a fork. Carefully transfer both turnovers to a greased baking sheet. Bake in a preheated 400°F oven for 15 minutes, then reduce the heat to 300°F and continue baking for 45 minutes to 1 hour or until the dough is crisp and brown. If the dough turns brown before the empanadas are well cooked, cover with aluminum foil.

6 medium cloves garlic, peeled
1 cup white wine
Salt to taste

FOR THE SAUCE
1 cup olive oil
8 large cloves garlic, peeled
1½ medium white onions, peeled and minced
6 medium cloves garlic, peeled and minced
6 large tomatoes (about 2½ pounds), roasted in a hot skillet and finely chopped
1½ cups finely chopped parsley
3 fresh bay leaves
1 sprig thyme
1 sprig marjoram
1 16-ounce can güero or jalapeño chiles, juice reserved
1 cup white wine
Salt and freshly ground black pepper to taste

FOR THE EMPANADAS
2½ pounds puff pastry or phyllo dough
Flour for rolling out the dough
3 egg yolks, beaten with 3 tablespoons milk
½ cup clarified butter

FOR THE GARNISH
Cilantro sprigs

PELLIZCADAS CATEMACO STYLE
PELLIZCADAS DE CATEMACO

Makes about 18 pellizcadas

FOR THE *PELLIZCADAS*

6 cups fresh *masa* (corn dough)

Salt to taste

¹/₃ to ¹/₂ cup warm water

1 cup melted lard or vegetable oil

FOR THE GREEN SAUCE

18 fresh small serrano chiles

6 medium cloves garlic, peeled

1¹/₂ cups chopped cilantro

¹/₃ to ¹/₂ cup water

Juice of 8 limes

Salt to taste

FOR THE GARNISH

1 cup crumbled *queso fresco* or farmer cheese

1 cup chopped white onion

This dish is typical of the area around Lake Catemaco, a lovely natural body of water surrounded by lush tropical vegetation and inhabited by dozens of species of birds. This tortilla-based snack is served with freshly caught fish that have been fried or steamed.

PREPARE THE *PELLIZCADAS:* Knead the *masa,* adding salt and the water gradually, until the dough takes on a smooth, non-sticky consistency. Line a tortilla press with plastic wrap. Using about ¹/₃ cup of dough for each *pellizcada,* form 6-inch-wide tortillas with the tortilla press. Cook the *pellizcadas* on a preheated *comal* or in a preheated heavy skillet that has been brushed with oil to be sure that the *pellizcadas* don't stick. Turn the *pellizcadas* once, then make superficial indentations with the tip of a spoon along the edges and in the center of each *pellizcada* while it is still on the *comal.* Brush with the melted lard and keep warm until serving time.

PREPARE THE GREEN SAUCE: Puree the chiles, garlic, cilantro, water, lime juice, and salt in a blender or a food processor.

TO SERVE: Heat the *pellizcadas* on a preheated *comal.* Sprinkle with the green sauce, then place a *pellizcada* on each individual serving plate or arrange on a serving platter. Garnish with the *queso fresco* and the chopped onion. Serve hot.

VARIATIONS: *Pellizcadas* may also be topped with refried beans and pork cracklings or served with a tomato sauce prepared with serrano chiles, garlic, and onion and ground in a *molcajete* (volcanic stone mortar).

Note: See pages 309 to 310 for more information on preparing the dough and using the tortilla press.

TACOS WITH CACTUS PADDLES, ANCHO CHILES, AND CHIPOTLE CHILES
TACOS DE NOPALITOS CON CHILE ANCHO Y CHILE SECO

Serves 8

Cactus paddles are eaten throughout Mexico. This common vegetable varies in size; some varieties are thin and squarish, while others are thicker and more roundish or oval. Flavors also vary, depending on the region and the species of cactus. Each part of Mexico has a favorite dish incorporating cactus paddles. In Veracruz, cactus paddles are commonly eaten in taco form, as in this recipe. This vegetable, which grows wild but is also cultivated due to demand, is high in nutritional value and is most commonly used in salads and stews.

PREPARE THE SAUCE: Heat the oil in a medium skillet and add the onion slices and brown. Meanwhile, drain the chiles and place in a blender or a food processor. Add the tomatoes, onions, and garlic. Puree the ingredients, then pour the sauce into the skillet. Season with the allspice and salt and simmer uncovered for 30 minutes.

PREPARE THE CACTUS PADDLES: Heat the water in a large saucepan. Add salt and the tomatillo husks and corn husks and bring to a boil. Add the chopped cactus paddles and cook covered for 10 to 15 minutes, or until tender. Drain in a straw basket or a colander. Remove the tomatillo and corn husks and discard. Add the cactus to the prepared sauce and simmer uncovered for about 15 minutes, or until the mixture takes on a semithick consistency. Season with salt.

TO SERVE: Heat the tortillas on a preheated *comal* or in a preheated heavy skillet until steaming hot. Spoon a small portion of the cactus paddle filling on one edge of each tortilla. Roll up the tortillas and arrange in a basket lined with a dishcloth or a cloth napkin to keep warm, or serve immediately from a platter.

FOR THE SAUCE

- ½ cup vegetable oil
- 2 white onion slices
- 6 large ancho chiles or other dried red chiles, seeded and deveined (see page 296), lightly roasted in a warm skillet, and soaked for 20 minutes
- 4 dried chipotle or morita chiles, seeded and deveined, lightly roasted in a warm skillet, and soaked for 20 minutes
- 4 large ripe tomatoes (about 2 pounds), roasted
- 1½ medium white onions, peeled and roasted
- 4 medium cloves garlic, peeled and roasted
- 1 teaspoon allspice

Salt to taste

FOR THE CACTUS PADDLES

- 8 cups water

Salt to taste

- 10 tomatillo corn husks
- 4 corn husks
- 16 medium cactus paddles, cleaned (thorns removed) and finely chopped

FOR THE TACOS

16 to 24 freshly made tortillas

CHAPOPOTE RANCH ENCHILADAS
ENCHILADAS DEL RANCHO CHAPOPOTE

Serves 8

FOR THE SAUCE

- 10 small plum tomatoes, roasted in a hot skillet
- 12 fresh serrano chiles or 6 jalapeño chiles, roasted in a hot skillet
- 2 to 3 cups water
- 1½ medium white onions, peeled and roughly chopped
- 6 medium cloves garlic, peeled and chopped
- 1¼ cups lard or vegetable oil
- 6 thin white onion slices

Salt to taste

FOR THE ENCHILADAS

- 1½ pounds fresh *masa* (corn dough)
- ½ teaspoon salt
- ¼ to ⅓ cup warm water
- 1½ to 2 cups crumbled feta cheese or *queso fresco*
- 1 medium white onion, peeled and chopped

The Huastecs, an ancient Mayan tribe that paid tribute to the Aztecs in the form of crops, first cultivated in the zone known as the Huasteca Veracruzana. They planted cotton, tomatoes, chiles, and corn, all of which are still grown in the region. These enchiladas are unique to this paradisiacal land. They are often eaten by the locals as a snack. I associate these enchiladas with the picturesque Chapopote Ranch, located on the Pantepec River, since it is a favorite dish there. The natural beauty of fertile land and flowing rivers surrounds the ranch. The lush vegetation includes abundant orange trees and crops of corn. Serve this dish with scrambled eggs, grilled langoustines, shrimp, grouper, red snapper, pompano, or pot beans.

PREPARE THE SAUCE: Place the tomatoes, chiles, water, chopped onions, and garlic in a blender or a food processor and puree until smooth (in batches if necessary). Preheat a medium skillet. Add the lard and heat. Sauté the onion slices until golden brown, then add the pureed sauce. Season with salt and simmer uncovered until the mixture thickens slightly.

PREPARE THE ENCHILADAS: Knead the *masa*, adding the salt and small amounts of the water gradually, until the dough takes on a smooth, shiny, nonsticky consistency. Shape the dough into small balls and make 6-inch-wide tortillas using a tortillas press. Cook the tortillas on a preheated *comal* or in a preheated heavy skillet, turning once with a spatula. To facilitate the puffing procedure, press the center of each tortilla with your fingertips or a cloth napkin. Remove from the *comal* after the tortilla puffs and fold in half. Wrap the tortillas in a dishcloth until serving time to keep warm.

TO SERVE: Briefly dip the folded tortillas in the warm sauce, then arrange on a serving platter. Drizzle a little more sauce over the tortillas and garnish with the cheese and the onion.

Note: See pages 309 to 310 for more information on preparing the dough and using the tortilla press. These enchiladas can be prepared with ready-made tortillas.

CUISINE OF THE WATER GODS

HEARTY VERACRUZ FISH SOUP
SOPA DE PESCADO ESTILO VERACRUZ

Serves 10

The state of Veracruz is certainly characterized by the availability of water. It is located along the Gulf of Mexico and is also blessed with abundant rivers. The Papaloapan River, which flows through the state, skirts the small village of Tlacotalpan, where fish and seafood dishes are served daily. Tlacotalpan has many small, quaint homes painted in soft pastel colors that blend with the landscape and vivid sunsets. The aroma of freshly baked bread and boiling pots of food set the scene in most kitchens, as the housewives wait for their husbands to bring home the day's catch—the essential ingredient for this hearty fish broth quite typical of the local cuisine.

PREPARE THE STOCK: Bring the water to a boil in a stockpot. Add the fish heads, onions, garlic, whole tomatoes, peppercorns, herbs, and salt and simmer uncovered for 50 minutes. Remove from the heat and strain. Reserve the stock.

PREPARE THE SOUP: Heat the olive oil in a large, heavy saucepan. Sauté the pureed garlic and the chopped onions. Place the tomatoes, raw onion, and raw garlic in a blender or a food processor and puree. If necessary, process the vegetables in batches. Add the puree to the saucepan, cooking uncovered until it thickens, about 30 minutes. Season with salt and add the oregano and the chiles. Gradually add the hot fish stock. Bring to a boil and skim any oil that rises to the surface. Add the fish. Taste and correct the seasoning and cook covered for an additional 4 minutes, or until the fish is tender.

TO SERVE: Ladle the soup into individual soup bowls. Serve with limes and fresh chiles on the side, if desired.

FOR THE STOCK

- 20 cups water
- 4 medium fish heads
- 2 1/2 medium white onions, peeled and quartered
- 2 heads garlic, halved but not peeled
- 6 large ripe plum tomatoes
- 12 black peppercorns
- 6 fresh bay leaves
- 6 sprigs thyme
- 6 sprigs marjoram
- 1 tablespoon salt, or to taste

FOR THE SOUP

- 1/2 cup olive oil
- 4 medium cloves garlic, peeled and crushed
- 3 medium white onions, peeled and finely chopped
- 2 1/2 generous pounds ripe plum tomatoes, halved
- 1 medium white onion, peeled
- 4 medium cloves garlic, peeled
- Salt to taste
- 2 teaspoons dried oregano leaves, crumbled or ground
- 4 to 6 fresh jalapeño chiles, halved
- 2 pounds grouper, sea bass, red snapper, or cod fillets, cut into chunks

FOR THE GARNISH

- 10 limes, halved

TLACOTALPEÑO RICE
ARROZ A LA TUMBADA ESTILO TLACOTALPEÑO

Serves 8 to 10

2½ cups Mexican (long-grain) rice, soaked in hot water for 15 minutes

2 cups vegetable oil

10 medium cloves garlic, peeled

1 medium white onion, peeled and halved

2 large ripe tomatoes (1 generous pound), chopped

1 medium white onion, peeled and chopped

3½ cups hot water or chicken or fish stock (or more if necessary)

Salt and freshly ground black pepper to taste

6 sprigs parsley

4 fresh jalapeño chiles

8 (6-ounce) sea bass or red snapper fillets (each about 1½ inches thick), boned

2 pounds medium shrimp, peeled and deveined, or prawns in their shells (or substitute precooked shrimp)

Chopped parsley

Considered Mexico's answer to Venice, picturesque Tlacotalpan is known for its well-seasoned cuisine. Much of the local cooking, including this substantial rice dish, shows the influence of the Spaniards as well as that of the African slaves, who first arrived in Mexico at the end of the sixteenth century. The recipe combines chiles with fish, seafood, and rice, making it a perfect side dish or main course, depending on your appetite.

Strain the soaked rice and rinse in a sieve under a stream of water until the water runs clear. Drain well. Heat the oil in a large saucepan. Add 6 of the garlic cloves and the onion halves. Brown lightly and add the rice. Fry the rice until golden brown, stirring occasionally. Strain the oil off the rice and discard the sautéed garlic cloves and onion. In a blender or a food processor, puree the tomatoes, the 4 remaining garlic cloves, and the chopped onion. Strain the mixture and add to the rice. Cook uncovered until the rice absorbs the tomato sauce and takes on a reddish color. Add the hot water and season with salt and pepper. Add the parsley, chiles, fish, and shrimp. Cover and simmer for 35 minutes. Remove from the heat and allow to rest, covered, for an additional 25 minutes.

TO SERVE: Spoon the rice into an oval casserole and garnish with chopped parsley, or serve directly from a paella pan or a large skillet.

POBLANO CHILES STUFFED WITH SHREDDED LOBSTER

CHILE POBLANO EN ESCABECHE RELLENO DE SALPICÓN DE LANGOSTA

Serves 12

This elegant dish has been prepared for centuries in Jalapa, a city near the port of Veracruz. This recipe comes from a beautiful hacienda at Lencero that has maintained the same rural but sophisticated life-style since its establishment. Enormous trees stand guard over the quiet surroundings of tropical vegetation, flowers, and plants. This dish meshes Mexican ingredients, like chiles, with elements of refined French cuisine, a combination that is quite representative of the elegant style of the hacienda itself.

Begin this recipe a day or two ahead of serving to allow the vegetables time to marinate.

PREPARE THE CHILES: Roast the chiles directly over the flame of the stove or grill, turning so that they are evenly charred. Transfer chiles to a bag, so that they will sweat for approximately 10 minutes to facilitate the skinning procedure. With gloves, remove the charred skin. Then make a small incision along the side of the chile; carefully remove the seeds and internal veins. Soak the prepared chiles in salted water with a little vinegar for about 5 minutes to reduce piquancy. Remove from the water and drain, then pat the chiles dry. Heat the oil in a medium saucepan. Brown the garlic halves and the whole garlic cloves. Once the garlic is golden brown, remove and reserve. Add the pureed garlic and the onion slices to the saucepan and cook until the onions are transparent. Add the thyme, marjoram, bay leaves, oregano, vinegar, chicken stock, allspice, black pepper, and sugar. Simmer uncovered for 20 minutes before adding salt to taste. Stir in the potatoes, carrots, zucchini, chiles, and reserved garlic and remove from the heat. Allow the vegetables to marinate for one or two days at room temperature or in the refrigerator.

PREPARE THE STUFFING: Heat the oil in a medium saucepan. Add the chopped garlic and brown slightly. Add the grated

FOR THE CHILES

- 12 large fresh poblano, de agua, or Anaheim chiles
- 1½ cups olive oil
- 1 head garlic, halved but not peeled
- 10 large cloves garlic, peeled
- 6 medium cloves garlic, peeled and pureed
- 6 medium white onions, peeled and sliced on the bias
- 10 sprigs thyme
- 10 sprigs marjoram
- 10 fresh bay leaves
- 2¼ teaspoons dried oregano leaves, crumbled
- 4 cups fruit vinegar or other mild vinegar
- 1½ cups chicken stock
- 1 tablespoon allspice
- 1 tablespoon freshly ground black pepper
- 1 tablespoon sugar, or to taste

Salt to taste

- 1 pound baby potatoes, unpeeled, boiled in salted water until just tender
- 1 pound carrots, peeled and boiled in salted water until just tender
- 1 zucchini, steamed briefly in salted water

CONTINUED

¾ cup olive oil

1½ tablespoons finely chopped
garlic

1½ medium white onions, peeled
and grated

2 generous pounds ripe
tomatoes, grated

1½ cups finely chopped
pimiento-stuffed olives

1 cup blanched and finely
chopped almonds

¾ cup finely chopped parsley

3½ pounds lobster, cleaned,
steamed briefly, and shredded
(crabmeat, baby shark, or red
snapper can be substituted)

Salt to taste

FOR THE GARNISH

Sprigs of parsley and thyme

1 (18-ounce) can güero or
jalapeño chiles

onions and cook until golden brown. Stir in the grated tomatoes and cook uncovered until the mixture thickens to form a
heavy puree. Add the olives, almonds, parsley, and shredded
lobster and simmer uncovered for 1 hour or until the excess
liquid evaporates. Add salt to taste. When the mixture is dry, it
is ready to stuff into the chiles.

TO SERVE: Bring the marinade to room temperature if necessary. Remove the chiles from the sauce and spoon the stuffing
carefully into the chiles. Arrange the chiles on a serving platter
and garnish with the pickled vegetables, fresh herbs, and güero
chiles. Serve at room temperature.

Note: If large chiles are not available, use 24 small poblanos or
even pickled canned jalapeños.

FRESH FRUIT PLATTER
PLATÓN DE FRUTAS

Serves 12

Fruit stands line the Malecón dock at the port of Veracruz. The cheerful, colorful mounds of locally grown produce are piled next to individual carts that offer rounds of freshly sliced pineapples brought in daily from nearby plantations; bright wedges of yellow papaya, also produced locally; and slices of fresh cantaloupe, jicamas, and coconut all brought to the dock from nearby farms and plantations. The array of fresh produce gives the harbor a very unique ambience, reminiscent of the paintings of the famous Mexican artist Rufino Tamayo.

Arrange the papaya slices diagonally on a large serving platter, alternating them with the pineapple and watermelon slices on one side of the platter and the mango slices on the other side. Place the plums and the guavas on the top, along with the lime halves. Refrigerate until serving time.

VARIATION: Spoon the fruit into paper cones, reminiscent of the fruit vendors at the port of Veracruz, or into dessert bowls or tall goblets. Serve chile powder and salt on the side in individual bowls. For variety, the fruit can be cut into thin strips and combined with sliced cucumber, jicama, and coconut.

1 medium ripe yellow papaya (about $2^1/_2$ pounds), peeled, sliced, and seeded

1 large ripe pineapple (about $2^1/_2$ pounds), peeled, cored, and thickly sliced

1 small ripe watermelon (about $2^1/_2$ pounds), halved, peeled, and thinly sliced

6 large ripe mangoes (preferably of different varieties), peeled and sliced

1 pound red plums, halved and pitted

1 pound yellow plums, halved and pitted

1 pound guavas, halved

8 limes, halved

Piquín chile powder (or other hot red chile powder

Salt

CRAB COCKTAIL

OYSTER COCKTAIL

BOILED CRABS WITH LIMES

SHRIMP SOUP

FRITTATA WITH CRAB, SHRIMP, AND HEARTS OF PALM

WHITE RICE TAMAULIPAS STYLE

SQUASH TAMALES

CRAYFISH IN *CHILTEPÍN* SAUCE

PICKLED SHRIMP IN ANCHO *ESCABECHE*

FISH SAUTÉED IN GARLIC-CHILE SAUCE WITH CACTUS SALAD

FISH WITH CHILE SAUCE TAMPICO STYLE

PINEAPPLE-TANGERINE JUICE

This state is located in the northeastern corner of the republic, just south of the Texas border. The name means "place of high mountains." In ancient times, the region was populated by Chichimecs and Huastecs, who were eventually subjugated by the Aztecs and became tributary nations.

In addition to numerous mountains popular with hunters and climbers, Tamaulipas has many rivers, lagoons, and lakes that are perfect for fishing or sailing. The seacoast stretches from the mouth of the Rio Grande some two hundred and fifty miles south to the Rio Pánuco. Jumbo shrimp of extraordinary quality swim in these waters, and many are processed at canneries and freezing plants in the international port at Tampico.

Near Ciudad Victoria, the state capital, are fertile valleys ideal for ranching or farming. Corn, soybeans, wheat, sugarcane, avocados, mangoes, melons, and walnuts all grow in abundance.

In this place of blessed souls, everyone who appreciates good food has eaten "at the hand" of Doña Gasparita, known throughout the city and its suburbs as a "witch in the kitchen." Through sleight of hand, she produces minor culinary miracles and thus merits the name *cebichera*. ¶ This appellation did not come without effort. As an attractive young girl she first caused a sensation with her inventive ceviches. As she matured, her repertoire expanded to include an array of dishes, each more delicious than the last. When diners would sing her praises, they often remarked that her dishes were so fine that they didn't seem real. Many argued that Gasparita added magic potions to her recipes. Many thought her food had the power to bewitch. Her beguiling appearance only added to Gasparita's reputation, which has stayed with her like the ring on her hand. ¶ Gasparita is a Creole woman full of elegance and charm. Her kin have lived in the Huasteca region for many generations. Some of her ancestors were African slaves eventually freed along with the Indians of this region. Although the legends built around Gasparita have attributed her birth to many cities, in truth she comes from Tampico. Here she grew up, attended school, and found her vocation in life. She was an orphan, without a mother, grandmother, or aunt to show her the basics of gastronomy. She taught herself by learning to distinguish between oysters from Tamiahua and Xiloxúchil. By eye, she could tell which were the freshest and most delicious. She learned to prepare oysters in many ways, simply opening them or maybe steaming or grilling them and adding a little black pepper or serving them in tamales wrapped in banana leaves. She coveted baby prawns from Tamiahua, which she used in her famous ceviches. Today, when fishermen bring shrimp from the Rivera, she cooks and salts the tiny crustaceans to preserve them. As a young woman she also learned to make *huatape*, a substantial soup with fresh corn *masa,* chile leaves, serrano chiles or piquín, and lots of green or red epazote. ¶ She occasionally uses bass that comes from the

Carrizales River. The fillets are prepared Tampiqueña style, meaning that they are grilled with a chile sauce made from dried pasillas or anchos. From the same waters fishermen pull red porgy, trout, *mojarra,* and crayfish. The crayfish (also called langoustines or *acamayas*) are cooked in a light broth that is soaked up with freshly made corn tortillas. ¶ Trout, sardines, and tilapia from the Tancoco River—waters that Gasparita says are crystal clear and produce wonderful fish—have a special place in her kitchen. From the sea, Gasparita relies on tuna, scallops, cabrilla, *cherna,* red mullet, striped mullet (both fresh and salted) with roe, Gulf lobsters, sole, pompano, swordfish, sailfish, blue marlin, shad, and red crab. With baby shark she makes numerous ceviches and tamales. Other specialties that have made Gasparita's fame grow include tamales with pumpkin, chipotles, dried red chiles, and dried shrimp; *chamiles* with fresh corn and sugar; and *tamales tampiqueños* with almonds, olives, pickled chiles, and freshwater shrimp. Diners swoon over her corn *masa* turnovers stuffed with shrimp. Sometimes she stuffs them with meat and farmer cheese instead. ¶ Of all the seafood that Gasparita uses, she regards none more highly than that from the Pánuco River. Fishermen along this river bring her their catch, and she picks only the best. As part of her payment, Gasparita gives candles to these fishermen so they can illuminate the image of Our Lady of Guadalupe that travels with them as they labor on the rough waters. This gesture adds to the supernatural myth that surrounds the cooking of Doña Gasparita. ¶ She laughs loudly when she hears some of the idle chatter and gossip associated with her name and says, lisping, that she knows it is just envy and silly superstition. The only magic, says Gasparita, is to know what preparations will bring about cures or relief from illness. Crab broth can heal fatigue, while shark-fin soup lends courage and fierceness to the men who eat it. This special soup also makes men attractive to their wives. Of course, the herbs which Gasparita uses to season her meals have their own powers. One can understand why women come to her looking for advice. They want to know what magic potions or enchanted recipes they can use to keep their husbands eating at home.

CRAB COCKTAIL
COCTEL DE CANGREJO
Serves 8

North of the city of Madero lies the village of Pueblo Viejo. Fishermen come to shore in a lagoon of the same name with fresh catch as thousands of white and brown herons circle overhead. Crab is a key ingredient in the local cooking. It is used in soups, stuffed into empanadas or soft *taquitos,* and boiled and eaten right from the shell.

PREPARE THE CRAB COCKTAIL: Toss the onions, tomatoes, olives, chiles, and crabmeat in a large bowl. Add the lime juice and the olive oil and season with salt and pepper. Toss well and refrigerate for 40 minutes.

TO SERVE: Heat a *comal* or a heavy skillet. Brush the tortillas with a small amount of water and sprinkle with salt. Toast the tortillas over medium heat until light brown on both sides. Lay each tortilla over a soup bowl or other serving dish. Spoon some crab cocktail over each tortilla and top with the pickled chiles. Drizzle the olive oil over the cocktails and sprinkle with the coarsely ground pepper and the chopped olives.

FOR THE CRAB COCKTAIL

- 1¼ cups finely chopped white onions
- 4 medium ripe tomatoes, finely chopped
- ½ cup finely chopped pimiento-stuffed olives
- 1 to 2 fresh jalapeño chiles, finely chopped
- 3 cups shredded crabmeat
- Juice of 6 limes
- 8 tablespoons olive oil
- Salt and freshly ground black pepper to taste

FOR THE GARNISH

- 8 tortillas (about 6 inches in diameter)
- Salt to taste
- 4 pickled jalapeño chiles, sliced into thin strips
- ⅓ cup olive oil
- 1 tablespoon black peppercorns, coarsely ground
- 2 tablespoons finely chopped pimiento-stuffed olives

OYSTER COCKTAIL
COCTEL DE OSTIÓN
Serves 8

6 cups shucked oysters

3 cups oyster juice

Salt to taste

2 cups catsup

Tabasco sauce to taste

1½ white onions, peeled and chopped

⅓ cup finely chopped serrano chiles

¾ cup chopped cilantro

Olive oil to taste

16 limes, halved

Crackers

A wide variety of cocktails are served along Mexico's coastline. The most popular, known as *campechanas* in Spanish, are prepared with a combination of oysters, shrimp, conch, crab, and octopus, and garnished with chopped onion, cilantro, and chiles, and olive oil. This particular recipe is typical of the Tamiahua Lagoon in the Huasteca region of the state. Freshly caught oysters are shucked and served right on the beach with a squirt of lime juice and a dash of olive oil.

Spoon the oysters into 8 large goblets and drench each serving with about ⅓ cup of the oyster juice. Season with salt. Spoon about ¼ cup of the catsup on top of the oysters in each goblet. Add a few drops of Tabasco sauce and sprinkle with the onions, chiles, cilantro, and olive oil. Garnish with the lime halves and serve crackers on the side.

BOILED CRABS WITH LIMES
JAIBAS AL NATURAL CON LIMONES
Serves 6 to 8

FOR THE CRABS

20 cups water

Sea salt to taste

18 large crabs, claws removed and reserved and bodies cracked, cleaned, and halved

FOR THE GARNISH

4 pounds crushed ice

8 limes, halved

Sportfishing in rivers, lagoons, inlets, and the open sea is popular throughout the state of Tamaulipas. Everything from catfish and sea bass to grouper and shad can be found. For the very young, trapping shrimp, crayfish, oysters, and crabs is a good way to learn the ways of the water. The freshly caught crabs are often carried in pouches fashioned from palm leaves.

Bring the water to a boil in a large pot. Add salt, then the crabs and the claws. Cook covered for about 10 minutes. Remove the pot from the heat and let stand for about 3 minutes; drain and cool the crabs.

TO SERVE: Place the crushed ice on a large platter. Place the cooked crabs and the lime halves on top of the ice and serve cold with a chile sauce such as Tabasco or *salsa búfalo*.

SHRIMP SOUP
HUATAPE DE CAMARÓN
Serves 8

Soups are a basic staple in Tamaulipas. Tortillas can be quartered and used to soak up the rich broth or added directly to the bowls to provide bulk. In addition to seafood, *huatapes* can be made with beef, pork, or chicken as well as with any number of vegetables. Fresh *masa* (corn dough), diluted in some stock, thickens this nutritious soup.

Puree the garlic, lettuce leaves, onions, chiles, tomatillos, and epazote and chile leaves in a food processor or a blender. Preheat the oil in a medium casserole. Add a small amount of the pureed mixture, let it sizzle for a few seconds, and then stir in the rest. Simmer covered until the sauce thickens, about 25 minutes. Season with salt and continue cooking for 10 minutes. Dissolve the *masa* in a small amount of the water. Stir the mixture into the sauce along with the remaining water. Simmer uncovered over low heat until the mixture starts to thicken. Add the shrimp and cook uncovered until the shrimp are bright pink, 3 to 5 minutes. Taste and correct the seasoning and serve immediately in a soup tureen or individual soup bowls.

VARIATION: Garnish each serving with fresh epazote leaves.

6 medium cloves garlic, peeled
6 leaves romaine lettuce
1¼ medium white onions, cut into pieces
4 fresh serrano chiles, cut into pieces
½ pound tomatillos, husked
20 fresh epazote leaves
20 fresh chile leaves
3 tablespoons extra-virgin olive oil or lard
Salt to taste
3½ ounces fresh *masa*
16 cups water
2 pounds fresh shrimp, peeled and deveined, or 1 pound dried shrimp, peeled

FRITTATA WITH CRAB, SHRIMP, AND HEARTS OF PALM
TORTA DE HUEVOS CON JAIBA, CAMARONES Y PALMITO

Serves 8

½ plus ⅓ cup extra-virgin olive oil

¾ cup finely chopped white onion

6 fresh serrano chiles, finely chopped

1½ cups finely chopped shrimp

1½ cups shredded crabmeat

18 ounces canned hearts of palm, finely chopped

Salt to taste

10 whole eggs

6 egg whites

¼ cup crème fraîche or heavy cream mixed with ¼ cup half-and-half or milk

Near Tampico, dense forests of precious woods shield quiet rivers and lagoons. Ebony, cedar, rubber, and lemon trees predominate in these remote areas that are home to flamingos, cranes, pheasants, and herons. The few structures in the region are made with adobe bricks and palm fronds, which also grow in abundance. Hearts of palm are used in simple dishes like this frittata with crab.

Preheat the ⅓ cup oil in a wok. Sauté the onion and the chiles until wilted. Add the shrimp and the crabmeat and stir-fry briefly. Add the hearts of palm, season with salt, remove from the heat, and cool. Whisk the eggs and the egg whites in a large bowl until thick and smooth. Whisk in the cream and stir into the contents of the wok. Heat ¼ cup of the oil in a medium nonstick skillet. Add the egg mixture, reduce the heat, and cover until the frittata starts to set. Lift the frittata into the lid of the skillet. Heat the remaining ¼ cup oil in the pan. When hot, turn the frittata back into the skillet to brown the other side.

TO SERVE: Slide the frittata onto a large platter and serve hot with a salad of tomatoes, lettuce, avocados, onions, and radishes. Serve with any kind of salsa or pickled chiles and accompany with freshly made tortillas or rolls.

WHITE RICE TAMAULIPAS STYLE
ARROZ BLANCO

Serves 8

Serve this basic rice dish with fried plantains, beans, shrimp, crayfish, or any other seafood preparation.

Soak the rice in hot water to cover for about 15 minutes. Drain the rice in a mesh sieve and rinse under running cold water until the water runs clear. Drain well. Heat the oil in a frying pan or a medium saucepan. Add the 6 garlic cloves and the halved onion and sauté until light brown. Add the rice and continue sautéing until golden brown. Stir regularly so that the rice does not stick to the bottom of the pan. Drain off the oil and remove and discard the garlic and the onion. Lower the heat and add the pureed garlic and onion. Sauté until all the moisture is absorbed. Bring the water to a boil in a separate saucepan. Add the hot water to the rice along with salt to taste. Add the parsley and the chiles without stirring. Cover the pan and simmer over low heat for about 25 minutes. Remove from the heat and allow to rest, covered, for about 30 minutes. Shake the saucepan and then remove the lid. Discard the parsley and the chiles.

TO SERVE: Place the rice on a serving platter, garnishing with the fresh parsley and chiles.

Note: This white rice can be served with any of the seafood, octopus, or squid recipes throughout the book.

FOR THE RICE

- 2 cups long-grain white rice
- 2 cups vegetable oil
- 6 medium cloves garlic, peeled
- 1 medium white onion, peeled and halved
- 3 medium cloves garlic, peeled and pureed
- 1/2 medium white onion, peeled and pureed
- 3 1/3 cups water
- Salt to taste
- 20 sprigs parsley
- 4 fresh serrano chiles or 2 jalapeño chiles

FOR THE GARNISH

- 1 small bunch parsley, stems trimmed
- 3 fresh serrano chiles or 2 jalapeño chiles

SQUASH TAMALES
TAMAL DE CALABAZA
Serves 12 to 16

FOR THE FILLING

10 dried ancho chiles, seeded and deveined (see page 296)

1½ cups dried morita chiles, dried de árbol chiles, or japonés chiles, cut into small pieces

10 medium cloves garlic, peeled

½ cup lard or vegetable oil

2 white onion slices

Salt to taste

3 pounds pumpkin or other orange squash, cut into pieces, steamed until soft, and pulp mashed

1¾ pounds dried shrimp, peeled and soaked in hot water for 10 minutes

FOR THE TAMALES

4 pounds fresh *masa* (corn dough)

3¾ cups warm water

2½ to 3 tablespoons salt or to taste

3 cups melted lard or clarified butter (see Note)

6 fresh banana leaves for lining the steamer

4 packages fresh banana leaves, wrapped in a damp dishcloth, sweated in a hot oven for

Various corn flour tamales are prepared for the Day of the Dead in the southern region of Tamaulipas. Savory fillings might include beans, pork, rabbit, dried shrimp, red snapper, baby shark, oysters, or squash. The *chilapan* is a local tamale made with seven chiles—guajillos, cascabels, anchos, moritas, pasillas, piquíns, and mulatos. Sweet tamales made with fruits and jams also are prepared for this important holiday. Fishermen of the region consume most of what they catch. The little money they earn goes for the paraffin lamps, candles, tissue paper figurines, incense, and special drinks that are used for this celebration.

PREPARE THE FILLING: Preheat a *comal* or a heavy skillet. Lightly toast both kinds of chiles, pressing them with the back of a spoon but being careful not to burn them. Soak the chiles in hot water barely to cover for 15 minutes. Blend the chiles with half the soaking liquid and the garlic into a smooth sauce; strain. Heat the lard in a medium skillet. Brown the onion slices and discard. Add the chile sauce and season with salt. Simmer uncovered until the sauce starts to thicken. Add the mashed pumpkin and the drained shrimp and cook uncovered until very thick, about 15 minutes. Set aside.

PREPARE THE TAMALES: Knead the *masa* with a small amount of the water until smooth. Place the *masa* in a bowl and start adding more water until the consistency is very soft and porridgelike. Add the salt and mix well. Add the melted lard and mix with your hands until smooth. Fill a steamer with 20 cups of water and line the rack with 3 of the banana leaves. Cover and begin heating the water. Meanwhile, spread 2 tablespoons of the dough over each banana leaf square. Cover with some of the pumpkin filling and wrap and tie the bundles. Overlap the tamales on the steamer rack so that the steam can still rise. Cover with the remaining 3 banana leaves and the lid and steam for about 1½ hours or until the tamales easily slide off the leaves when the packages are opened.

TO SERVE: Place the tamales in a steamer basket or on a large platter. Serve with strong coffee (at breakfast) or beer.

Note: The *masa* for these tamales can be prepared without fat. Use an additional 3 cups water instead and proceed with the recipe.

15 minutes, and cut into 8-inch squares

CRAYFISH IN *CHILTEPÍN* SAUCE
ACAMAYAS EN CHILTEPÍN
Serves 6

Acamayas are a special river crayfish native to this area. Between the months of April and August, fishermen set out at dawn when the tides are still low. Basketlike nets are filled with stones and lowered into the river water. When full, the nets are pulled back onto the boats. *Acamayas* usually weigh 4 or 5 ounces but may be as large as 8 ounces in some cases. On land, children also try to catch these tasty creatures by digging small ditches that fill with river water. They dangle pieces of tortillas in the water and use nets to scoop up the crayfish. In this way, even small children can help without encountering the dangers of boat fishing.

PREPARE THE MARINADE: In a mortar or a food processor, grind the garlic, piquín chiles, oil, and salt. Daub the cleaned crayfish with the paste and marinate at room temperature for about 20 minutes. Preheat a wok or a large skillet. Heat the oil, add the crayfish, and sauté on all sides. Season with salt and remove the crayfish from the wok. Set aside.

PREPARE THE SAUCE: Puree the garlic, onion, tomatoes, chiles, tortillas, and salt. Scrape the mixture into the wok and simmer uncovered over low heat for about 30 minutes. Add the crayfish and the fish stock and continue cooking uncovered for 8 minutes.

TO SERVE: Place the crayfish in 6 deep soup plates and cover with the sauce. Serve with the black beans and freshly made tortillas.

FOR THE MARINADE
- 6 medium cloves garlic, peeled
- ¼ cup dried piquín chiles or dried chipotle chiles cut into small pieces, lightly toasted in a warm skillet
- ¾ cup olive oil
- Salt to taste
- 24 crayfish (about 5 ounces each), heads cleaned and washed
- ½ cup extra-virgin olive oil

FOR THE SAUCE
- 6 medium cloves garlic, peeled
- 1 medium white onion, peeled and cut into pieces
- 2½ pounds ripe tomatoes, boiled for 25 minutes and drained
- 3 to 4 ounces dried ancho chiles, seeded and deveined (see page 296), soaked in hot water for 15 minutes, and drained
- ½ cup dried piquín chiles or dried chipotle chiles cut

CONTINUED

into small pieces, lightly
toasted in a warm skillet
2 tortillas, toasted in a warm
skillet and ground into a
fine powder
Salt to taste
¾ cup fish or chicken stock

FOR THE GARNISH
Navy Beans with Habanero Chiles
and Epazote (page 192)
Freshly made tortillas

FOR THE CHILE SAUCE
11 ounces ancho chiles, seeded
and deveined (see page 296)
3 cups white wine vinegar or
cider vinegar
2 cups water

FOR THE SHRIMP
1 bouquet garni
Salt and freshly ground black
pepper to taste
3½ pounds large shrimp,
unpeeled
1 cup olive oil
9 medium cloves garlic,
peeled
5 to 6 large white onions, peeled

VARIATION: Accompany with lentils, chickpeas, zucchini, or white rice. Sesame seeds can also be added to the sauce.

PICKLED SHRIMP IN ANCHO *ESCABECHE*
CAMARONES EN ESCABECHE ROJO
Serves 12

Shrimp is a major product in this state. Some fishermen use spoon nets, which consist of a hard wooden rim and deep, soft mesh made from plant fibers. These nets are employed in shallow or still waters. For stiffer currents, sacklike nets are filled with bait and dropped into the water. After some time, they are pulled back onto the boats and their catch is unloaded. Most shrimping is done at night by the light of the moon.

PREPARE THE CHILE SAUCE: Wash the chiles and put them in a large nonreactive bowl and cover with the vinegar and the water. Let stand overnight. Drain and grind the chiles with the soaking liquid. Pass the mixture through a sieve and set the chile sauce aside.

PREPARE THE SHRIMP: Bring several quarts of water to a boil in a large pot. Add the bouquet garni, salt and pepper, and shrimp and simmer covered for 4 minutes. Drain the shrimp, reserving some of the liquid but discarding the other solids. When the shrimp are cool, peel and devein them but leave the tails intact. Heat the oil in a large skillet. Add the garlic and sauté until brown; discard the garlic. Add the onions and the chile sauce and simmer uncovered until the oil comes to the surface. Wrap the herbs, cumin, and peppercorns in a piece of cheesecloth. Add the cheesecloth bag, sugar, salt, and garlic to the sauce. If the sauce is too thick, add a little of the reserved shrimp cooking liquid. Add the pickled chiles and their liquid along with the olives. Simmer uncovered for 1 hour and taste and correct the seasoning. Add the shrimp and simmer for 10 minutes.

TO SERVE: Serve hot or at room temperature in a bowl garnished with more olives and pickled chiles. Serve with saffron rice and pureed avocados. For special occasions, shape the saffron rice with a ring mold and serve the shrimp in the center of the unmolded circle.

and thinly sliced
- 8 fresh bay leaves
- 3 sprigs thyme
- 3 sprigs marjoram
- 8 sprigs parsley
- 1 teaspoon cumin seeds
- 12 black peppercorns
- 2 tablespoons sugar, or to taste
- 2$\frac{1}{2}$ tablespoons salt or powdered chicken bouillon
- 4 medium cloves garlic, peeled and finely chopped
- 6 ounces canned pickled jalapeño chiles with their juice
- $\frac{1}{2}$ cup whole pimiento-stuffed olives

FISH SAUTÉED IN GARLIC-CHILE SAUCE WITH CACTUS SALAD
PESCADO AL AJILLO DE CHILE DE ÁRBOL CON NOPALITOS

Serves 6

A*jillo,* a sauce made with plenty of garlic (in this case forty-eight cloves) and chiles, is used to flavor many local seafood dishes. The cactus salad provides a refreshing accompaniment.

PREPARE THE CACTUS SALAD: Heat the water in a medium pot. Add the onion, garlic, tomatillo husks, corn leaves, and cactus paddles. Season with salt and simmer covered for about 25 minutes or until the cactus paddles are soft. Drain. Reserve the cactus paddles in a large bowl and discard the other solids. Toss the hot cactus paddles with the lime juice, vinegar, oil, onions, oregano, cilantro, tomatoes, and jalapeño chiles. Season with salt and pepper. Set aside. Just before serving, stir in the cheese.

FOR THE CACTUS SALAD
- 4 cups water
- 1 medium white onion, peeled and cut into pieces
- $\frac{1}{2}$ head garlic, halved but not peeled
- 10 tomatillo husks
- 4 fresh corn leaves
- 12 medium cactus paddles, cleaned (thorns removed) and cut into $\frac{1}{8}$-inch squares

CONTINUED

Salt to taste

- ⅓ cup fresh lime juice
- ⅓ cup cider vinegar or champagne vinegar
- ¾ cup olive or vegetable oil
- 1½ cups finely chopped onions
- 1 tablespoon dried oregano leaves, crumbled
- 3 tablespoons minced cilantro
- 4 medium ripe plum tomatoes, sliced
- ½ cup finely chopped canned or fresh jalapeño chiles

Salt and freshly ground black pepper to taste

- 6 tablespoons grated feta cheese, *queso añejo*, or *queso fresco*

FOR THE FISH

- ¾ cup extra-virgin olive oil
- 6 porgy, red snapper, sea bass, or pompano fillets (about ½ pound each)

Salt and freshly ground black pepper to taste

- 48 cloves garlic, peeled
- 2 cups water
- 2 cups white wine vinegar
- 12 dried de árbol or japonés chiles, lightly toasted in a warm skillet
- 6 dried morita or chipotle chiles, lightly toasted in a warm skillet

FOR THE GARNISH

- 6 dried de árbol or japonés chiles, stir-fried in oil

PREPARE THE FISH: Heat the oil in a large skillet. Add the fish and cook for 3 minutes on each side. Season both sides with salt and pepper while the fish is cooking. Remove the fish from the skillet and set aside. Puree the garlic, water, vinegar, chiles, and salt. Add the mixture to the skillet and simmer uncovered over low heat until the garlic starts to brown. Return the fish to the skillet and continue cooking, covered, for another 4 or 5 minutes.

TO SERVE: Transfer the fish to a large platter and baste with the sauce from the skillet. Garnish the platter with the stir-fried de árbol chiles and accompany with the cactus salad. Serve with warm tortillas and black beans.

CUISINE OF THE WATER GODS

FISH WITH CHILE SAUCE TAMPICO STYLE
PESCADO ESTILO TAMPIQUEÑO

Serves 8

Tamaulipas is blessed with powerful rivers like the Bravo, San Fernando, Soto la Marina, Carrizal, Tamesí, and near the capital of Tampico, the Pánuco, which sustains life in this cosmopolitan city. After Veracruz, Tampico is Mexico's main port along the Gulf. Although diverse ethnic groups have inhabited the region for more than 3,000 years, the land and the water are still quite bountiful.

PREPARE THE FISH: Preheat the oven to 400°F. Heat the oil in a large skillet. Add the garlic and sauté until light brown. Remove the garlic with a slotted spoon and puree with the chiles and the vinegar. Pour sauce back into the pan and simmer covered, stirring occasionally, over low heat for about 25 minutes or until the oil separates. Season with the black pepper, cumin, and salt and continue cooking until the sauce has a thick consistency. Set aside to cool. Place the fish in a large baking dish and daub with some of the chile sauce and season with salt.

PREPARE THE STUFFING: Toss the ingredients together in a medium bowl. Stuff half of the mixture into the fish and sprinkle the rest over the top of the fish. Cover the fish with the remaining chile sauce and bake until the fish flakes but is still moist, 45 minutes to 1 hour, depending on the thickness of the fish.

TO SERVE: Place the fish on a large platter and garnish with the jalapeño chiles, parsley, and thyme. Serve with boiled or roasted potatoes or freshly made tortillas.

FOR THE FISH

- 1½ cups extra-virgin olive oil
- 10 medium cloves garlic, peeled
- 6 ounces ancho chiles, seeded and deveined (see page 296), soaked in hot water for 15 minutes, and drained
- ½ cup balsamic vinegar or cider vinegar
- 1 teaspoon freshly ground black pepper
- 1 teaspoon cumin seeds, ground
- Salt to taste
- 1 whole red snapper, sea bass, porgy, or trout (about 4½ pounds), cleaned, slit on the side, and deboned, with head and tail attached

FOR THE STUFFING

- 1½ medium white onions, peeled and thinly sliced on the bias
- 1¼ cups finely chopped pimiento-stuffed olives
- 6 medium cloves garlic, finely chopped
- 4 large ripe plum tomatoes, thinly sliced
- 2 tablespoons finely chopped parsley

FOR THE GARNISH

- 6 fresh or canned jalapeño chiles, sliced
- 2 tablespoons finely chopped parsley
- 2 small bunches thyme leaves, julienned

PINEAPPLE-TANGERINE JUICE
JUGO DE PIÑA A LA MANDARINA

Serves 8

1 ripe pineapple (about
   2¹/₂ pounds), peeled and sliced
2 pounds tangerines, peeled
Ice cubes

Cattle ranching and agriculture are vital industries in Tamauli-pas. In addition to tangerines, cotton, tomatoes, tomatillos, beans, corn, avocados, chiles, jicamas, and papayas are grown on local farms. Freshly squeezed juices provide refreshment for the workers laboring under the hot sun.

Put the pineapple and the tangerines through a juicer. Pour the juice into a large pitcher and add ice cubes. Serve immediately.

AVOCADO TARTS WITH SMOKED TROUT
AND TRUFFLE VINAIGRETTE

FRESHWATER CRAYFISH WITH LIMA BEANS
AND CHILE SAUCE

CHILES STUFFED WITH BEANS IN VINAIGRETTE

FARM-FRESH VEGETABLES WITH FRIED FISH

GRILLED CACTUS WITH RED AND GREEN SAUCES

MUSHROOMS WITH EPAZOTE

TLACOYOS WITH PIGEON PEAS, TEXCOCO STYLE

GUAJILLO CHILE AND GARLIC SAUCE

FAVA BEAN SOUP WITH CACTUS PADDLES

POBLANO CHILE SOUP WITH CORN AND SQUASH
BLOSSOMS, CHALCO STYLE

MUSHROOM SOUP WITH DE ÁRBOL CHILES

TEXCOCANO FISH CAKES WITH CACTUS PADDLES
AND EPAZOTE

STEAMED TROUT WITH DRUNKEN SALSA

TOLUCAN-STYLE FISH STUFFED WITH *CUITLACOCHE*

FISH IN GREEN SAUCE, CHALCHIUHTLICUE STYLE

FROGS' LEGS IN RED PUMPKIN-SEED SAUCE

HUAUZONTLES XOCHIMILCO STYLE

EGGS WITH TOMATO SAUCE AND STRING BEANS

FRIED CAULIFLOWER STUFFED WITH CHEESE

ROMPOPE MOUSSE (MEXICAN EGGNOG MOUSSE)

FIGS IN *CAPULÍN* SAUCE WITH CHOCOLATE PRALINES

TEOTIHUACÁN PRICKLY PEARS

ATOLE (HOT CORN BEVERAGE) TOLUCA STYLE

CENTRO

**MEXICO CITY AND
THE STATE OF MEXICO**

Centro, the central region of Mexico, encompasses both the state of Mexico and the Federal District, or Mexico City. In the center of the republic lies the state of Mexico, which is also the highest region in the country. The name "Mexico" comes from the Nahuatl words for "place in the navel of the moon." This area was originally populated by the Toltecs, Chichimecs,

Acolhuas, Matlazincas, Tarascans, Malinalcas, Otomíes, Ocui-tecs, and Aztecs.

Another tribe, the Teotihuacanos, left a permanent mark on this region with their majestic Pyramids of the Sun and Moon at the ceremonial center at Teotihuacán. Nahuatl-speaking tribes also founded the city of Tollocan, now know as Toluca, the capital of the state of Mexico.

In the Valley of Toluca, particularly in the Lerma area, an abundant supply of mountain water and advanced hydraulic works allow fish farming. A number of crops are raised in the fertile soil—corn, fava beans, beets, peas, apples, pears, peaches, apricots, avocados, and pecans. Animals graze on the rich land and provide local cooks with excellent cheeses and sausages that are known throughout the country.

Because of the region's proximity to the Federal District, economic activity is quite brisk. However, tranquil spas remain at sites like Ixtapan de la Sal. Water sports and hiking are quite popular at Valle de Bravo and Nevado de Toluca.

Mexico City, now the world's most populated urban area, is surrounded by the state of Mexico except at its far southern reaches, where it borders on the state of Morelos. The city was founded in 1325 by an Aztec tribe called the Mexicas, who called their great city Tenochtitlán. In 1521, the cradle of the Aztec empire fell to the Spanish, who built their own city on the ruins of the original center. Dubbed Mexico City, it be-came the capital of the Viceroyalty of New Spain.

Agriculture is still practiced within the city limits at Xochimilco, an area of quiet canals. "Chinampas"—small plots of land built on reeds and mud—are used to cultivate cactus, fava beans, carrots, tomatoes, corn, potatoes, and sweet pota-toes. These "floating gardens" are all that is left of the im-mense lake that once covered the entire region.

Ironically, this city at the heart of the country no longer has waterways of its own. Yet it is where all the seas and rivers of Mexico meet, at least figuratively, since products from each state inevitably make their way to this marvelous capital. The multiple flavors and ingredients of this enormous country fuse together in the capital region to create a world-class cuisine that reflects the city's stature not only within Mexico but in the world at large.

Many centuries ago, the Aztec tribe, guided by the light of the bountiful god Quetzalcóatl, left their homes in Aztlán, Nayarit. They ventured inland from the Pacific Coast in search of the sacred place where their god had promised they would establish a new and powerful nation. During the 150-year trek, members of the tribes split off to form small communities with their own traditions and beliefs. Many came to Tula, where the Toltecs had already established themselves, but the Aztecs knew that this place was not the one selected by their god. ¶ They continued their long journey to the south, and finally came upon the omen Quetzalcóatl had predicted. They settled at the spot where the eagle flew over the cactus, in a region dotted with lakes and ringed by mountains. ¶ When men arrived from Europe they were surprised by this magnificent tribe and the cities they had built. From the written records of these first Europeans we glean a portrait of the unequaled city of Tenochtitlán, which at the time was larger than any settlement in Europe. But there was one man who understood its value and wanted to pay respect to the many aspects of this civilization. Without scorn or evasion, he saw all, he understood all, and he told all. That singular man was Father Bernardino de Sahagún. ¶ Among the many things that Sahagún wrote about in his *General History of the Things of New Spain*, his discussion of water is unparalleled for its poetic language and deep meaning. Water is bound up with the Aztecs' universal concept of existence, art, and, of course, nourishment. In one passage, Sahagún describes the baptismal practices of the Aztecs, detailing their worship of Chalchiuhtlicue, goddess of the water, and her companion Tlaloc, the powerful and mighty queen of the sea and the rivers. ¶ "And when the midwife had arranged the baby, when she had cut his navel cord, then she bathed the baby. [As] she continued washing him, she proceeded to address him. She said to him, if male: 'Approach thy mother Chalchiuhtlicue, Chalchiuhtlatonac! May she receive thee! May she wash thee, may she cleanse thee! May she remove, may she transfer the filthiness which thou hast taken from thy mother, from thy father! May she cleanse thy heart; may she make it fine, good! May she give thee fine, good conduct!' ¶ "The midwife addressed the goddess Chalchiutlicue, the water. She said to her: 'Lady, our lady Chalchiutlicue, Chalchiuhtlatonac, the commoner hath arrived. Our mother, our father Ome tecutli, Ome ciuatl, from [above] the nine heavens, in the place of duality, hath sent him. [It is not known] how he was arrayed, the nature of that given him in the beginning, the nature of that which he came bearing, the attributes with which he came wrapped, with which he came bound. But behold, perhaps he cometh laden with the evil burdens of his mother, of his father? With what blotch, what filth, what evil of the mother, of the father doth the baby come laden? He is in thy hands. Receive him, cleanse him, wash him, for he is especially entrusted to thee, for he is delivered into thy hands. Remove the blotch, the filth, the evil of his mother, of his father! And possibly he cometh laden with the vile. May that with which he cometh laden, the evil, the bad, be washed away, be destroyed. May his heart, his life be good, may they be fine, may they be purified in order that he may live on earth peacefully, calmly. May the filth be washed away! May it be washed away, may it be destroyed in the way that hath been assigned! For he is in thy hands, lady, our lady, Chalchiuhciuatl, Chalchiutlicue, Chalchiuhtlatonac, mother of the gods, sister of the gods. For in thy hands this commoner is left. And it is thy desert, thy merit, which was given thee in the beginning, to wash, to cleanse this commoner who hath come into thy presence. Incline thy heart, our lady!' " ¶ Father Bernardino also wrote about the many species of fish and marine life that he and the other conquistadors found. He remarks that many fish are similar in appearance to those in his native Spain. He then describes hundreds of individual creatures, noting their Aztec name, appearance, and culinary uses. Here are some excerpts from his marvelous catalog of New World animal life: ¶ "*Tlacamichin* (large fish of the sea): wonderful to

CUISINE OF THE WATER GODS

eat, feeds on smaller fish. ¶ "*Coamichin* (eels): 'snake fish' with a tail, fins and scales like fish but quite oily. ¶ "*Chimalmichin* (turtles): round like a shield. ¶ "*Tecuicitli* (crabs): good-tasting, savory, somewhat like a shrimp. Only its shoulders are eaten, with black intestines. ¶ "*Tecalatl* (frogs): very large, mature female frogs. Good to eat. Countless black glistening eggs. Croakers." ¶ Water gave life to all these creatures and more. Aztec religion held that the sky was actually water. In fact, the ancient Mexicans believed that they lived in a house of water. The seas entered the land in great veins called rivers that eventually went underground and filled the mountains. As these rivers flowed from the sea they lost their bitterness or saltiness in marshes, rocks, and sands and turned sweet for drinking. Rivers also sprang from a place called Tlalocan, an earthly paradise ruled by Chalchiuhtlicue. Mountains stood guard over these springs and were themselves filled with water like glasses of water. Water flowed through all phases of life and all the elements that made up the Aztec universe. ¶ Better than all his compatriots, Sahagún wrote of the original Mexicans and recorded their beliefs for posterity. He wrote of the rivers of Mexico, the seas and Mexico, and of the life-giving water that was and still is Mexico.

AVOCADO TARTS WITH SMOKED TROUT AND TRUFFLE VINAIGRETTE
TARTAS DE AGUACATE CON TRUCHA ASALMONADA

Serves 8

FOR THE GUACAMOLE

4 or 5	large ripe avocados, peeled and finely chopped with pits reserved
1⅓	medium white onions, peeled and finely chopped
4	fresh serrano chiles, finely chopped
2	medium tomatillos, husked and finely chopped
1	baby zucchini, minced
⅔	cup chopped cilantro

Juice of 4 limes

¼ cup olive oil

Salt to taste

FOR THE VINAIGRETTE

½	cup cider vinegar, champagne vinegar, or wine vinegar
4	medium cloves garlic, peeled
2¼	teaspoons salt
1	teaspoon sugar
2	black truffles, cut into pieces
1½	cups extra-virgin olive oil

FOR THE GARNISH

4	smoked trout fillets (about ½ pound each), halved
32	chives or 32 julienned slices of *hoja santa*

The word *guacamole* comes from the ancient Nahuatl word for "sauce," *mulli.* Since guacamole is made with raw ingredients, its flavor is quite different from that of most Mexican sauces. Mexico boasts a wide variety of avocados, which come in different flavors and textures. No matter which type of avocado is used to prepare this guacamole, it is a perfect accent for *totopos* (fried tortilla wedges), shrimp tacos, *sincronizadas* (two layers of tortillas with melted cheese and ham), quesadillas (folded tortillas with melted cheese), and deep-fried fish or seafood. As for the trout, it is now farmed in mountain ponds in central Mexico along with carp and black bass. Trout is a carnivorous fish with a refined flavor and white or salmon-colored flesh. It can be grilled, steamed, sautéed in butter or olive oil with chiles, served over greens, prepared in a light chile sauce, or used in soups with epazote and chiles. This recipe makes use of the smoked form and reflects the combination of exquisite flavors that characterizes pre-Hispanic cooking.

PREPARE THE GUACAMOLE: Toss together the avocados, onions, chiles, tomatillos, zucchini, and cilantro. Add the lime juice and the olive oil and blend the ingredients until they form a thick puree. Season with salt. Place the avocado pits in the bottom of a bowl and top with the guacamole. (The pits retard discoloration of the guacamole.)

PREPARE THE VINAIGRETTE: Puree the vinegar, garlic, salt, sugar, and truffles in a blender or a food processor. Slowly add the olive oil until the ingredients make a smooth vinaigrette.

TO SERVE: Place a 3½-inch-round ring mold on a large chilled dinner plate and fill with about 2½ tablespoons of the guacamole. Carefully lift the ring mold to form the avocado "tart." Repeat the procedure on 7 more plates. Lay a piece of trout across the top of each tart and drizzle with the truffle vinaigrette. Crisscross 4 chives on top of each tart and serve cold with *totopos* (fried tortilla chips) or sesame seed bread.

FRESHWATER CRAYFISH WITH LIMA BEANS AND CHILE SAUCE
TACOS DE ACOCILES CON HABAS

Serves 8

Acociles are tiny freshwater crayfish found in the central part of Mexico. Their name comes from the Nahuatl word *cuitzilli*, meaning "one that twists in the water." The Aztecs combined marine life like *acociles*, tadpoles, frogs, snails, and whitebait with legumes and vegetables picked from their floating gardens. Many dishes were cooked in aromatic broths flavored with herbs such as epazote, *pepicha*, and *pápalo* and in moles of all sorts. Tortillas were used as utensils for soaking up broths and sauces and should be served with this dish. Note that very small shrimp may be used in place of the crayfish.

PREPARE THE CRAYFISH AND LIMA BEANS: Toss the crayfish with the lima beans, onions, chiles, cilantro, lime juice, olive oil, and salt. Mix well and set aside for 1 hour to allow the flavors to develop.

PREPARE THE CHILE SAUCE: Heat a *comal* or a heavy skillet and lightly toast the chiles without burning them. Blend the chiles with salt to taste, the garlic, and the onion in a mortar or a food processor. Roast the tomatillos on the *comal*, transfer to a medium bowl, and barely cover with water. Let stand for about 8 minutes. Add the tomatillos and the soaking liquid to the chile sauce and puree. Let stand for 1 hour for the flavors to develop.

TO SERVE: Place the crayfish and beans on a platter. Garnish with the avocado slices and chopped cilantro. Serve with the chile sauce and blue or white corn tortillas.

VARIATIONS: The seafood and lima bean mixture can be served with *sopes* (round thick tortillas with pinched edges) or tostadas and with another kind of chile sauce. This dish can also be drizzled with a small amount of olive oil if desired.

FOR THE CRAYFISH AND LIMA BEANS

- 1½ pounds baby crayfish or shrimp, peeled and boiled in salted water until cooked, about 2 minutes
- 2 cups fresh lima beans, boiled in salted water until tender
- 1½ medium white or red onions, peeled and thinly sliced
- 6 fresh serrano chiles, julienned with seeds
- 1 cup chopped cilantro

Juice of 6 limes

- ½ cup extra-virgin olive oil

Salt to taste

FOR THE CHILE SAUCE

⅓ to ½ cup dried piquín chiles or chopped de árbol chiles

Salt to taste

- 4 medium cloves garlic, peeled
- ½ small white onion, chopped
- 1 pound tomatillos, husked

FOR THE GARNISH

- 1 medium ripe avocado, peeled and thinly sliced

Chopped cilantro

FOR THE CHILES

- 16 large dried ancho chiles, seeded and deveined (see page 296) with stems on
- 2 cups water
- 3 sprigs thyme or a pinch of dried thyme
- 4 fresh bay leaves
- 3 sprigs marjoram
- 8 black peppercorns
- 6 medium cloves garlic, peeled
- ½ cup white wine vinegar
- ½ cup brown sugar or grated *piloncillo*

Salt to taste

- 8 cups refried bayo or pinto beans (see page 121)

FOR THE VINAIGRETTE

- 4 cups white wine vinegar
- 1 tablespoon black peppercorns, ground
- 1½ tablespoons salt, or to taste
- 6 medium cloves garlic, peeled and sliced
- 30 medium scallions, white parts only, sliced
- 1½ cups vegetable oil
- 1¼ cups olive oil

FOR THE GARNISH

- 16 scallions, cut into flowers and chilled in ice water for 2 hours (see page 298)
- 16 radishes, cut into flowers and chilled in ice water for 2 hours (see page 298)
- 2 ripe avocados, sliced in half lengthwise, pits removed, and pulp scooped out whole with a spoon and sliced into "fans"

CHILES STUFFED WITH BEANS IN VINAIGRETTE
CHILES RELLENOS DE FRIJOLES A LA VINAGRETA

Serves 8

In addition to the beans used in this recipe, chiles can be stuffed with cheese, seafood, or almost any food imaginable. The unusual vinaigrette is made by reducing vinegar with salt and pepper and then whisking in garlic, scallions, and oils. Use this dressing for vegetable and grain salads as well as for other room temperature preparations. Very dry chiles may be hard to work with, so seal them in a plastic bag and refrigerate overnight. The cold will make them a bit less brittle. Begin this recipe 6 to 8 hours ahead of serving to allow the chiles time to macerate in the vinaigrette.

PREPARE THE CHILES: Heat a *comal* or a heavy skillet and lightly toast the chiles on both sides. Rinse the toasted chiles under running water and set aside. Pour the 2 cups water into a medium saucepan and add the herbs, peppercorns, garlic, vinegar, brown sugar, and salt. Simmer uncovered, stirring occasionally, until the sugar has dissolved. Add the chiles and simmer uncovered for 2 minutes. Remove from the heat and let the chiles stand for another 10 minutes. Drain the chiles and discard the other solids. Fill each chile with about ½ cup of the refried beans and set aside on a large serving platter.

PREPARE THE VINAIGRETTE: Bring the vinegar, pepper, and salt to a boil in a small saucepan and reduce by half. Remove the pan from the heat and whisk in the garlic, scallions, and oils.

TO SERVE: Pour the vinaigrette over the chiles and let them macerate at room temperature or in the refrigerator for 6 to 8 hours. Garnish the platter with the scallions and radish flowers and the avocado fans and serve.

VARIATION: Use fresh roasted poblanos instead of dried anchos.

FARM-FRESH VEGETABLES WITH FRIED FISH
VERDURAS DE LA HUERTA CON CARPA O TILAPIA

Serves 8

When the conquistadors arrived in the Valley of Mexico, they found one of the most fertile and fruitful agricultural areas in the world. In addition to the great saltwater lake Texcoco, the valley is nourished in the south by two freshwater lakes at Xochimilco and Chalco, in the northeast by the springs at Xaltocan and Zumpango, and in the northwest by the Acolman River. Human settlements have lined the shores of these lakes and the banks of this river for countless centuries and each has employed the floating garden method of agricultural production. The conquistadors saw countless butterflies, migrating and indigenous birds, and flower gardens bursting with color. Chiles, onions, squash blossoms, and wild greens grew amid this biological splendor. In the distance stood vast volcanoes and forests filled with pine trees. All in all, the conquistadors had found "paradise" in the New World.

PREPARE THE VEGETABLES: Boil the potatoes in salted water until tender. Drain, slice, and reserve. Blanch the Swiss chard, spinach, and *quelites* separately in salted water for 3 minutes. Drain the greens, squeeze out the excess water with your hands, and reserve. Prepare the chiles. Heat the 7 tablespoons butter and the oil in a large saucepan. Add the onion slices and sauté until golden brown. Add the reserved vegetables, the chiles, and salt and pepper and continue to sauté over low heat. Stir in the creams and simmer uncovered until the creams thicken. Stir in the diced butter a little at a time and allow the sauce to thicken. Keep the vegetables warm.

PREPARE THE FISH: Place the fish on a large baking tray. Combine the pureed garlic, sea salt, and lime juice and pour the mixture over the fish. Let the fish marinate in the refrigerator for 30 minutes. Heat the oil in a deep pot or a wok. Add the whole garlic, cook until brown, and discard. Add the fish and deep-fry until crisp. Drain the fish on paper towels.

TO SERVE: Arrange the vegetables on a platter and sprinkle with the chopped parsley. Serve immediately with the hot fish

FOR THE VEGETABLES

- 2 pounds small red potatoes, unpeeled
- 1 pound Swiss chard, washed
- 1 pound spinach, washed
- 2 large bunches *quelites* (a wild salad green), watercress, or mâche, washed
- 6 fresh poblano chiles, roasted, peeled, seeded, and deveined (see page 296), soaked in salted water for 15 minutes, drained, and cut into thin strips
- 7 tablespoons butter
- 1/4 cup olive oil
- 2 1/2 cups diagonally sliced white onions

Salt and freshly ground black pepper to taste
- 3/4 cup crème fraîche
- 3/4 cup heavy cream
- 6 tablespoons butter, diced

FOR THE CARP

- 8 whole carp or tilapia (about 1/2 pound each), slit on the side and cleaned
- 8 medium cloves garlic, peeled and pureed
- 1 1/2 tablespoons sea salt

Juice of 16 limes

CONTINUED

4 cups corn or safflower oil
8 medium cloves garlic, peeled

FOR THE GARNISH
1/4 cup chopped parsley

on a separate platter. Or, place some of the vegetables in each of 8 large soup plates, top with the fried fish, and garnish with the chopped parsley.

VARIATIONS: The vegetables may be served separately as a main course or as a side dish with meat, poultry, or other fish entrées. Instead of deep-frying the fish, it may be covered with a garlic-chile paste (made with 12 dried guajillo or New Mexico chiles that have been stir-fried in a little oil and then pureed with the juice of 6 lemons, 6 peeled cloves of garlic, and salt) and steamed.

GRILLED CACTUS WITH RED AND GREEN SAUCES
NOPALES ASADOS
Serves 4

FOR THE RED SAUCE
3 cups water
4 large ripe plum tomatoes
4 to 6 dried catarina chiles, cascabel chiles, de árbol chiles, or japonés chiles, seeded and deveined (see page 296) and lightly toasted in a warm skillet
3 medium cloves garlic, peeled
1/2 medium white onion, peeled
Salt to taste

FOR THE GREEN SAUCE
12 tomatillos, husked and cut into pieces

Several varieties of cactus (*nopales*) have been cultivated in Mexico's semiarid desert lands since the time of the Olmecs and Toltecs. These original tribes showed others who established themselves in the central part of Mexico how to use this nutritious plant. In addition to being grilled, cactus paddles may be cooked in water with tomatillo husks and corn leaves to cut the slimy taste, used in salads, combined with scrambled eggs, simmered in soups, or even filled with cheese, dipped in batter, and fried. During the months of June, July, and August, the area around Teotihuacán is ablaze with the colors of orange, green, and red cactus flowers and is particularly beautiful. These flowers become the vibrant fruit called prickly pears that is used in dessert recipes. Although most paddles are sold cleaned, it may be necessary to remove the spines. Stand the paddles on the small end and slide a sharp knife down the surface to cut the spines at the base. Wear gloves when cleaning the paddles to protect your hands.

PREPARE THE RED SAUCE: Heat the water in a medium saucepan. Add the tomatoes, toasted chiles, garlic, and onion. Cook uncovered for 20 minutes and then puree the solids and some of the liquid in a food processor or a blender until smooth. Season with salt and set aside.

PREPARE THE GREEN SAUCE: Puree the tomatillos with the onion, garlic, chiles, cilantro, and water until smooth. Season with salt and add more water if the sauce is too thick. Set aside.

PREPARE THE CACTUS PADDLES: Heat the grill or a *comal.* Brush the cactus paddles with the olive oil and grill on one side until light brown, about 2 minutes. Season the cactus with salt. Turn and cook on the other side until light brown. Do not burn the cactus. Lightly grill the scallions and set aside with the cactus paddles.

TO SERVE: Place the sauces in 2 stone mortars *(molcajetes)* and serve with wooden spoons. Place 2 grilled cactus paddles and 4 grilled scallions on each of 4 plates and serve the garnishes on the side. Accompany with freshly made tortillas.

VARIATION: The cactus paddles can be stuffed with cheese before grilling.

$1/2$ medium white onion, peeled and cut into pieces
4   medium cloves garlic, peeled
10   fresh serrano chiles
40   sprigs cilantro, chopped with stems
$2^3/4$ cups water
Salt to taste

FOR THE CACTUS PADDLES
8   medium cactus paddles, cleaned (thorns removed) and slit at the ends
$1/4$ to $1/3$ cup olive oil
Salt to taste
16   scallions, roots trimmed

FOR THE GARNISH
$1/4$ pound pork cracklings, grated
1   ripe avocado, peeled, sliced, and sprinkled with lime juice
$1/4$ pound Oaxacan string cheese or fresh mozzarella, shredded
$1/4$ pound fresh *panela* cheese, *queso fresco,* or farmer cheese, thinly sliced into pieces

MUSHROOMS WITH EPAZOTE
HONGOS AL EPAZOTE

Serves 8

FOR THE MUSHROOMS

1/3 cup butter
1/2 cup olive oil
2 cups minced white onions
1/2 cup minced fresh serrano
chiles
1/2 cup finely chopped epazote
3 pounds white or wild
mushrooms, cleaned and sliced
Salt to taste

FOR THE GARNISH
Freshly made corn tortillas

Once situated in the great and majestic city of Tenochtitlán, the Tlatelolco market was an enormous open-air structure surrounded by arcades selling and buying everything from gold, silver, turquoise, and jade to exotic feathers, shells, snails, and woven items. Anything available in the Aztec kingdom was for sale: quails, turkey, doves, parrots, rabbits, deer. Medicinal plants, of which the Aztecs had extensive knowledge, were also on display. Some of the herbs also doubled in the kitchen, including epazote, *hoja santa*, myrtle, sorrel, *chipilín*, and *pápalo*. Vegetables such as tiny wild onions, sweet potatoes, avocados, cactus, mushrooms of diverse varieties, bouquets of squash blossoms, and fresh and dried chiles of all shapes and colors were also available. Women cooked over small grills and sold fresh tortillas stuffed with various fillings, folded, and grilled on the *comal*. This simple recipe is a fine example of the culinary delights from the imagination of these Mexican ancestors blended with more contemporary ingredients like butter and olive oil.

Heat the butter and the oil in a casserole over medium heat. Sauté the onions, chiles, and epazote until softened. Add the mushrooms and continue to sauté until they release their juices. Season with salt and cook uncovered for another 25 minutes.

TO SERVE: Transfer the hot mushrooms to a platter and serve with freshly made corn tortillas.

TLACOYOS WITH PIGEON PEAS, TEXCOCO STYLE
TLACOYOS CON ALVERJÓN ESTILO TEXCOCO
Serves 8

Netzahualcóyotl, king of Texcoco, was one of the most brilliant poets in the Nahuatl language. The kingdom was at its artistic height during his reign. Onyx-and-shell-encrusted buildings, brightly colored tapestries, magnificent gardens, and large ponds full of exotic fish could all be seen. The city itself was divided into separate quarters inhabited by different classes of laborers, including weavers, fishermen, silver workers, and jewelers. All of the local products and foods were sold at the central market *(tianguis)* along with birds and precious stones from other regions. Cooks prepared numerous dishes at the *tianguis*, including tortillas, steamed vegetables, beans, and moles in a hundred colors. With their oval shape and bean filling, *tlacoyos* were a favorite tortilla-based snack. The sound of hand clapping filled the ancient market as women prepared the *masa*. This marvelous dish still remains popular today.

PREPARE THE DOUGH: Spread the *masa* over a flat work surface. Sprinkle flour, shortening, and salt over the *masa* as well as a little water. Start kneading the *masa*, adding more water as needed, until the dough is smooth and somewhat sticky. Place the dough in a bowl, cover with a damp towel, and let rest for 30 minutes.

PREPARE THE FILLING: Puree the beans with the olive oil. Place them in a heavy skillet and cook until thick and smooth. Set aside.

PREPARE THE GREEN SAUCE: Bring the water to a rapid boil. Add the tomatillos, onions, garlic, and roasted chiles. Simmer for 20 minutes, remove from the heat, and cool for 15 minutes. Puree the solids and 2 cups of the liquid in a blender or a food processor along with the cilantro, raw onion, and salt. Set the sauce aside in a small bowl.

PREPARE THE *TLACOYOS*: Set a *comal* or a heavy skillet over medium heat and brush lightly with oil. Meanwhile, divide the dough into 20 to 24 small balls. Make an indentation in each

FOR THE DOUGH
- 2 pounds fresh blue or white corn *masa*
- 1 tablespoon flour
- 1 tablespoon vegetable shortening or lard
- 1 teaspoon salt
- 1/2 to 3/4 cup warm water

FOR THE FILLING
- 3 cups cooked pigeon peas or fava beans
- 2 tablespoons olive oil

FOR THE GREEN SAUCE
- 4 cups water
- 2 pounds tomatillos, husked
- 1 1/2 medium white onions, peeled and sliced
- 8 medium cloves garlic, peeled
- 12 fresh serrano chiles, lightly toasted in a warm skillet
- 40 sprigs cilantro
- 1/2 medium white onion, peeled and cut into pieces

Salt to taste

FOR THE GARNISH
- 1 cup finely chopped white onion

CONTINUED

2 cups finely grated fresh feta, *añejo* cheese, or *queso fresco*

ball and fill with 1 tablespoon of the filling. Roll and flatten each ball into a cigar shape. Prepare a tortilla press by lining it with plastic wrap. Lightly press a *tlacoyo* on one side. Open the press, flip the *tlacoyo*, and lightly press again until the *tlacoyo* is about 3 inches long and $\frac{1}{8}$ inch thick. Do not press the dough too hard or it will break. Also, make sure that the surface of the *tlacoyo* is smooth. Cook the *tlacoyo* on the preheated *comal*, turning it several times, until the crust starts to brown. Remove and keep warm in a basket lined with a napkin. Repeat with the other balls of dough.

TO SERVE: Place 2 or 3 *tlacoyos* on each serving plate and baste with the tomatillo sauce. Sprinkle with the chopped onion and the cheese. Serve immediately.

VARIATIONS: Serve this dish with grilled lobster, bay scallops, or shrimp or with boiled cactus.

Note: See pages 309 to 310 for more information on making the dough and using the tortilla press.

GUAJILLO CHILE AND GARLIC SAUCE
SALSA DE CHILE GUAJILLO Y AJO
Serves 8

In pre-Hispanic times, the Olmecs, Aztecs, and Otomíes prepared a similar sauce with chiles and wild onions to accompany almost any of their favorite snacks as well as to spice up any luncheon or dinner dish. They usually had a large *molcajete* (volcanic stone mortar) on hand, filled with a freshly made batch of this vibrant sauce. The *molcajete* retains a very special place in the modern-day Mexican kitchen. Because it is used daily, the porous surface seasons sauces made in this stone vessel. This sauce is particularly good with quesadillas, *pellizcadas* (freshly prepared small tortillas that are pinched around the edges and in the center to retain hot sauce), fish, seafood, vegetables, and beans.

Place the tomatillos, 4 of the garlic cloves, the onion, and the chiles in a medium saucepan. Barely cover with water and simmer uncovered for about 20 minutes. Drain and reserve the cooking liquid. In a *molcajete,* food processor, or blender, puree the cooked tomatillos, garlic, onion, and chiles along with the remaining 4 garlic cloves and salt to taste. Add about 1 cup of the cooking liquid and puree again until smooth. (Add more cooking liquid if the sauce is still thick.) Serve the sauce in a stone mortar or a small bowl.

VARIATION: Serve the sauce with *sopes,* thick tortillas pinched to form a rim or an edge after being cooked. Place the *sopes* on a grill or a *comal,* or in a heavy skillet, drizzle with oil, and brown slightly. Cover with the sauce and sprinkle with feta cheese, shredded lettuce, and crème fraîche. This sauce can also be served with the *tlacoyos* on page 265.

12 large tomatillos, husked

8 medium cloves garlic, peeled

1/2 medium white onion, peeled

6 guajillo or ancho chiles, seeded and deveined (see page 296), and toasted in a warm skillet

Salt to taste

FAVA BEAN SOUP WITH CACTUS PADDLES
SOPA DE HABAS CON NOPALES

Serves 8 to 12

FOR THE SOUP

5	quarts water
1⅓	pounds large dried fava beans or chickpeas, washed
2	medium white onions, peeled and halved
2	heads garlic, halved but not peeled
Salt to taste	
20	scallions, halved
1½	leeks
4	bunches cilantro (roughly 100 sprigs), tied together

FOR THE CACTUS PADDLES

4 to 6	cups water
Salt to taste	
½	medium white onion, peeled and chopped
½	head garlic, unpeeled
10	corn husks
10	tomatillo husks
15	cactus paddles, cleaned (thorns removed) and cut into ⅛-by-¼-inch strips

FOR THE GARNISH

4	canned jalapeño chiles, cut into strips or halved
½	cup finely chopped cilantro
12	veins from dried guajillo chiles or 6 dried de árbol chiles, stir-fried

Fava beans and cactus paddles are staples in the state of Mexico. If you visit the Santiago Tianguistengo on Tuesdays or the state capital market in Toluca on Fridays, you will see Mazahua and Otomí Indians carrying their wares for sale. Piles of fresh, unpeeled green fava beans and tall, evenly stacked piles of cactus paddles, the basic ingredients for this highly nutritious and delicious soup, have a prominent place at both locations. This recipe dates back to the colonial period, when locals began to mix native ingredients with those (such as fava beans) imported by the Spaniards, coming up with a unique cuisine.

PREPARE THE SOUP: Pour the water into a large *cazuela* (earthenware pot) or a stockpot and bring to a rapid boil. Add the fava beans, onions, and garlic. Cover and simmer the ingredients over medium heat until the beans are tender, about 2 hours. If the mixture becomes too thick, add small amounts of water to avoid scorching. Reduce the heat and add salt sparingly along with the scallions, leeks, and cilantro. Simmer the broth covered until it takes on the consistency of a semi-thick cream soup. Remove the onions, garlic, scallions, leeks, and cilantro and discard.

PREPARE THE CACTUS PADDLES: Bring the water to a rapid boil and add salt to taste. Add the onion, garlic, corn husks, and tomatillo husks and bring to a boil once again. Stir in the cactus paddles and continue cooking covered for 20 minutes or until the cactus paddles are tender. Drain the cactus and reserve. Discard the water and the other ingredients.

TO SERVE: Add the cooked cactus paddles and the jalapeño chiles to the soup. Simmer for 10 minutes. If the soup is too thick, add enough water, vegetable stock, or chicken stock to attain the desired consistency. Taste and correct the seasoning. Serve piping hot in individual soup bowls. Garnish each bowl with the chopped cilantro and the stir-fried chile veins.

POBLANO CHILE SOUP WITH CORN AND SQUASH BLOSSOMS, CHALCO STYLE
SOPA DE CHILE POBLANO AL ESTILO DE CHALCO

Serves 12

Chalco Lake is situated in the southeastern part of the state of Mexico. Covered with abundant aquatic vegetation, the lake is home to numerous birds, both local and migrating, that come to drink the nourishing waters and to feed. The lake islands of Xico, Tlapacoyan, and Mixquic are settled with small towns that come alive for the Day of the Dead celebration. The town of Chalco, located on the shore of the lake, serves as a point of commerce for these islands, linking them to the agricultural wealth of the nearby Valley of Mexico. Farmers paddle canoes around the floating gardens in order to harvest the local produce. In song, they describe their beautiful region as a place "where the water scented with flowers extends, with jade flowers and a magnificent aroma."

PREPARE THE SOUP: Heat the oil and the butter in a stockpot. Add the onions and the garlic and sauté until softened. Add the remaining vegetables and simmer covered over medium heat for 40 minutes. If necessary, add some of the chicken stock to keep the vegetables from burning. Remove the pot from the heat and transfer the contents to a food processor or a blender and puree along with some of the chicken stock. Pass the pureed vegetables through a sieve. Return the mixture to the heat along with the remaining chicken stock and the scalded milk. Simmer covered for 20 minutes or until the soup thickens. Season with salt and white pepper.

PREPARE THE MUSHROOM GARNISH: Heat the oil and the butter in a large skillet. Sauté the onion until golden brown. Add the mushrooms and the chiles, season with salt and white pepper, and cook until the liquid thrown off by the mushrooms evaporates. Add the mixture to the soup.

TO SERVE: Ladle the soup into 12 warmed soup bowls. Garnish with chopped *panela* or farmer cheese or crème fraîche and accompany with tortillas cut into pieces and fried, if desired.

FOR THE SOUP

- 1/3 cup olive oil
- 3 tablespoons butter
- 2 medium white onions, peeled and cut into pieces
- 4 medium cloves garlic, peeled
- 1/2 leek, diced
- 4 cups fresh corn kernels
- 3 carrots, peeled and diced
- 6 fresh poblano or chilaca chiles, roasted, peeled, seeded, and deveined (see page 296), soaked in salted water for 15 minutes, drained, and chopped
- 1 pound squash blossoms, cleaned
- 6 to 8 cups chicken stock
- 4 cups milk, scalded

Salt and white pepper to taste

FOR THE MUSHROOM GARNISH

- 1/4 cup olive oil
- 4 tablespoons butter
- 1 medium white onion, peeled and minced
- 1 pound chanterelle, oyster, or other fresh mushrooms, sliced
- 6 fresh poblano, chilaca, or Anaheim chiles, roasted, peeled, seeded, and deveined, soaked in salted water for 15 minutes, drained, and chopped

Salt and white pepper to taste

MUSHROOM SOUP WITH DE ÁRBOL CHILES
CALDO DE HONGOS CON CHILES DE ÁRBOL

Serves 8

1 generous pound chanterelles
  or trumpet mushrooms
1 generous pound morels or
  other wild mushrooms
½ cup olive oil
2 tablespoons butter
5 medium white onions, peeled
  and thinly sliced
3 medium cloves garlic, peeled
  and pureed
2 quarts homemade beef or
  chicken stock or 1 quart
  canned stock mixed with
  1 quart water
12 sprigs epazote or cilantro
16 dried de árbol or japonés
  chiles, lightly stir-fried
Salt and freshly ground black
  pepper to taste

Chanterelles, which are in season from April through October in Mexico, give this soup its special character. These mushrooms grow in the hills rising above the Valley of Mexico. Other notable mushrooms grown in Mexico include trumpets, *cèpes,* yellow mushrooms (known as *yemas*), *señoritas, clavitos,* and morels. Oyster or regular white mushrooms are available year-round and may be used in this soup.

Wash the mushrooms to remove the earth. Drain and slice the mushrooms very thin. Heat the oil and the butter in a large saucepan. Add the onions and the garlic and sauté until golden brown. Add the mushrooms and cook uncovered until tender, about 30 minutes. Add the stock, epazote, and 8 chiles and simmer, covered, for 20 minutes. Season with salt and pepper.

TO SERVE: Ladle the soup into individual soup bowls. Garnish each serving with 1 of the remaining stir-fried chiles and serve immediately.

TEXCOCANO FISH CAKES WITH CACTUS PADDLES AND EPAZOTE
TORTAS DE CHARALES CON NOPALITOS Y EPAZOTE TEXCOCANO

Serves 8

Since the time of King Netzahualcóyotl, the salty waters of Texcoco Lake have supported unique species not found in nearby freshwater lagoons. Fed by mineral-rich springs, the lake is home to only small fish like *charales* (whitebait) and the tiny silver fish known as *iztamichin,* both of which can be prepared when fresh or salted and dried for later use.

PREPARE THE SAUCE: Heat a *comal* or a heavy skillet. Roast the tomatoes, onions, and garlic separately. Puree the tomatoes, onions, and garlic along with the chiles, epazote, and cilantro in a food processor or a blender, in batches if necessary. Add the chicken stock and blend until smooth. Heat the oil in a large saucepan. Brown the onion slices and discard. Strain the blended sauce into the pan and simmer covered over medium heat until it thickens somewhat. Add salt and pepper to taste and set aside.

PREPARE THE FISH CAKES: Heat the *comal* and toast the fish. Put the toasted fish and the minced shrimp in a glass bowl and toss with 3 tablespoons of the flour. Use your hands to form 16 round cakes, patting them so that they are not too thick. Roll each fish cake in the remaining 3 tablespoons flour and set aside. Beat the egg whites until they form soft peaks. Gently fold in the yolks and salt. Heat the oil in a large skillet. Dip each fish cake into the egg mixture and drop gently into the hot oil, frying as many fish cakes as will fit comfortably in the pan at one time. Turn over the fish cakes and fry until light brown. Drain on paper towels.

PREPARE THE GARNISH: While the fish cakes are frying, bring the water to a boil and add salt to taste. Add the tomatillo husks, corn husks, and garlic. Allow the water to come to a boil again and add the diced cactus paddles. Cook covered over medium heat until the cactus paddles are tender, about 25 minutes. Drain the cactus in a mesh or straw strainer and rinse off

FOR THE SAUCE

- 15 large ripe plum tomatoes
- 1½ medium white onions, peeled
- 6 medium cloves garlic, peeled
- 8 dried puya, thin guajillo, or ancho chiles, stir-fried, soaked in salted water for 10 minutes, and drained
- 3 chipotle chiles, stir-fried, soaked in salted water for 10 minutes, and drained
- 2 sprigs epazote
- 10 sprigs cilantro
- 3 cups chicken stock
- ½ cup vegetable oil
- 2 white onion slices

Salt and freshly ground black pepper to taste

FOR THE FISH CAKES

- ½ pound whitebait, heads removed
- ¾ pound small shrimp, peeled, cooked, and minced
- 6 tablespoons flour
- 8 eggs, separated

Salt to taste

- 3 cups vegetable oil

FOR THE GARNISH

- 8 cups water

CONTINUED

Salt to taste
10 tomatillo husks
4 corn husks
½ head garlic, unpeeled
12 large cactus paddles, cleaned (thorns removed) and diced

the slimy liquid from the paddles. Reserve the cactus paddles and discard the other solids.

To serve: Pour the tomato sauce into a heated *cazuela* (earthenware pot) or casserole. Add the fish cakes along with the cactus paddles. Simmer uncovered over low heat for 25 minutes. Serve in the *cazuela* along with rice and beans.

Variation: A simpler garnish can be made with diced string beans that have been blanched in lightly salted water for a minute or two. In place of cooked cactus paddles, add beans to sauce along with the fish cakes.

STEAMED TROUT WITH DRUNKEN SALSA
SALSA BORRACHA CON TRUCHA AL VAPOR
Serves 8

FOR THE DRUNKEN SALSA

8 cups water
20 tomatillos, husked
6 medium cloves garlic, peeled
Salt to taste
10 dried long pasilla negro chiles or dried mulato chiles, stir-fried, seeded and deveined, cut into pieces, soaked in pulque or beer to cover for 30 minutes, and drained
1½ cups finely chopped white onions
1½ cups pulque or beer
1½ cups finely grated feta cheese or *queso fresco*
¾ cup olive oil
¾ cup chopped cilantro

The ancient inhabitants of Mexico developed various techniques to preserve fish, including salting and drying and smoking. Salting was used with almost all the fish brought from coastal zones to the central valley. However, the emperor Montezuma received fresh fish from the coast on a daily basis. Wrapped in palm leaves and covered with sea salt to protect against the elements, freshly caught Gulf species would be transported by a series of runners, who between them traversed hundreds of miles in just hours. Dried fish, which were eaten by the rest of the population, were used in soups, cakes, and tamales. Local lake fish, like the trout used in this recipe, were eaten fresh or smoked. The special drunken salsa is made with pulque, a fermented alcoholic beverage made from cactus sap. Good-quality beer may be used as a substitute.

Prepare the drunken salsa: Bring the water to a boil in a large saucepan. Add the tomatillos and simmer covered for 20 to 25 minutes. Remove the pan from the heat and allow to cool. Drain the tomatillos (reserving some of the cooking liquid) and transfer them to a *molcajete* (stone mortar), blender, or food processor. Add the garlic and salt and puree. Refrigerate the sauce until well chilled. Stir in the chiles by hand along with the onions, pulque, and cheese. Mix well, adding some of the reserved tomatillo cooking liquid to thin the sauce if needed. Pour the sauce into a *molcajete* or a medium bowl and stir in the olive oil. Garnish with the cilantro.

PREPARE THE TROUT: While the sauce is chilling, fill a large steamer with boiling water. Cut eight 10-inch squares of aluminum foil. Place a trout on each square and sprinkle with the lime juice, salt and pepper, butter, scallions, and a bit of olive oil. Seal the pouches and steam the fish until it flakes but is still moist, 15 to 20 minutes, depending on the steamer.

TO SERVE: Place 3 tablespoons of the sauce in the center of 8 large plates. Unwrap the steamed trout and place 1 fish over the sauce on each plate. Spoon another tablespoon of sauce over the fish. Serve the remaining sauce in the *molcajete* and accompany with freshly made corn tortillas.

VARIATIONS: This sauce is especially good with any grilled meat or poultry dish or with tortilla-based appetizers like *sopes* (round pinched tortillas) and *chalupas* (thin, oval-shaped pinched tortillas).

FOR THE TROUT

8 medium trout (about ¹/₂ pound each), deboned
Juice of 4 limes
Salt and freshly ground black pepper to taste
3 tablespoons butter, cut into pieces
24 scallions, thinly sliced
Olive oil to taste

TOLUCAN-STYLE FISH STUFFED WITH *CUITLACOCHE*
PESCADO A LA TOLUQUENSE RELLENO CON CUITLACOCHE

Serves 12

The tall, healthy cornfields surrounding Toluca, the state capital, are irrigated with the abundant waters of the nearby Lerma River. Besides the ears of corn yielded by these fields, a very unusual and tasty corn truffle grows on the kernels of fresh corn while the ears are still on the stalk. Produced by the excessive humidity, the fungus, known as *cuitlacoche,* is most commonly found during the rainy season. Although at first many foreigners find this vegetable unappetizing because of its grayish-black color and pungent aroma, they are pleasantly

FOR THE MARINADE

¹/₂ cup dry white wine
¹/₂ cup tequila
4 small cloves garlic, peeled and chopped
1 small white onion, peeled and pureed

CONTINUED

Freshly ground black pepper to
taste

Salt or powdered chicken bouillon
to taste

FOR THE FISH

8   fresh banana leaves
6   pounds halibut, grouper, cod,
sea bass, or salmon fillets or
1 large whole fish, deboned

FOR THE STUFFING

$^1/_2$ cup butter
$^1/_2$ cup olive oil
$^1/_2$ cup minced elephant garlic or
regular garlic
$1^1/_2$ cups sliced scallions
6   fresh serrano chiles, minced
6   (7-ounce) cans *cuitlacoche* or
$2^1/_2$ pounds frozen *cuitlacoche*
(available in Latin markets)
$^3/_4$ cup finely chopped cilantro or
epazote
Salt and freshly ground black
pepper to taste

FOR THE STOCK

6   cups water
1   cup dry white wine
$^1/_2$ cup tequila
$^1/_2$ rib celery
1   medium white onion, peeled
and halved
6   carrots, peeled
$^1/_2$ head garlic, unpeeled
1   tablespoon black peppercorns
2   medium fish heads and tails
Salt to taste

surprised by its rich, earthy flavor. This corn truffle has been used in ceremonial tamales and dark mole sauces for centuries. It is commonly mixed with corn kernels and used as a filling for the tamales. *Cuitlacoche* is said to be a remembrance of the darkness of the night, and to represent the cycle of life itself, which is accompanied by light as well as darkness. The corn truffle is often steamed and used in modern Mexican cuisine in crepe stuffings, soups, moles, tacos, and quesadillas. This ancient mushroom has also been adapted to more sophisticated dishes such as this one, which is perfect for a special occasion.

PREPARE THE MARINADE: Mix together all the ingredients in a bowl and reserve.

PREPARE THE FISH: Preheat the oven to 350°F. Wrap the banana leaves in foil and sweat until soft, about 20 minutes. Or, briefly heat the banana leaves directly over the flame of the stove to soften. Be careful not to roast or char the leaves. Once the leaves are easily pliable, remove from the oven or flame and trim off the uneven or rough edges. Set aside. Wash and clean the fish, being careful to remove any bones or scales. Transfer the fish to a large baking dish and pour the marinade over the fish. Refrigerate for at least 2 hours.

PREPARE THE STUFFING: Heat the butter and the olive oil in a medium saucepan. Add the garlic and brown. Stir in the scallions and the chiles and sauté lightly. Add the *cuitlacoche* and the cilantro and season with salt and pepper. Simmer uncovered for approximately 25 minutes.

ASSEMBLE THE FISH: Preheat the oven to 350°F. Arrange 4 of the banana leaves on a baking tray. Line half of the marinated fish fillets alongside each other over the leaves. Spoon the prepared *cuitlacoche* stuffing over each of the fillets, reserving a little bit of the stuffing for garnishing the dish before serving. Sprinkle lightly with salt and pepper and place the remaining fish fillets on top. Drizzle with any remaining marinade. Fold the banana leaves over the fish and cover with the remaining 4 leaves, being careful to totally seal the fish in leaves. Carefully double-wrap with aluminum foil if necessary, to avoid leakage and seal in the flavors. Bake for about 1 hour or until the fish flakes but is still tender and moist. Be careful not to overcook the fish.

PREPARE THE STOCK: Meanwhile, pour the water, wine, and tequila into a stockpot. Add the celery, onion, carrots, garlic, peppercorns, and fish heads and tails. Season with salt and bring to a boil. Reduce the heat and simmer uncovered until the liquid is reduced to about 1 cup, about 30 minutes to 1 hour. Strain the liquid and discard the solids.

PREPARE THE SAUCE: Heat the oil and the 4 tablespoons butter in a skillet. Sauté the chiles, onion, and garlic until the vegetables are tender. Stir in the reduced stock. Remove from the heat and place the ingredients in a blender or a food processor and puree. Return the pureed ingredients to the skillet. Add the cream and cook uncovered over medium heat until the sauce thickens. Taste and correct the seasoning. Just before serving, stir in the 1/2 cup butter, 1 tablespoon at a time. Be careful not to allow the sauce to thicken too much.

TO SERVE: Carefully unwrap the fish and serve on a platter directly from the banana leaves. Garnish the platter with the sprigs of epazote and spoon the reserved *cuitlacoche* stuffing over the fish. Serve the chile-cream sauce on the side.

VARIATION: The fish can be seared and then served with the *cuitlacoche* sauce.

Note: A side dish of sautéed corn or hominy and onion with butter and epazote or *hoja santa* goes exceptionally well with this dish.

FOR THE SAUCE

- 1/3 cup olive oil
- 1/2 cup plus 4 tablespoons butter
- 6 fresh poblano chiles, cut into strips
- 1/2 medium white onion, peeled and sliced
- 4 medium cloves garlic, peeled and minced
- 2 cups heavy cream or crème fraîche

FOR THE GARNISH

- 20 sprigs epazote or cilantro

FISH IN GREEN SAUCE, CHALCHIUHTLICUE STYLE
PESCADO EN SALSA VERDE CHALCHIUHTLICUE

Serves 8 to 10

FOR THE FISH

- 2 whole trout, red snapper, or black bass fillets (about 2¹/₂ pounds each)
- ¹/₃ cup butter, melted
- 1¹/₂ teaspoons salt
- 1 tablespoon onion salt
- 1¹/₂ teaspoons garlic salt
- 1 tablespoon freshly ground black pepper

FOR THE STUFFING

- ¹/₂ cup butter
- 1 medium white onion, peeled and grated
- 2 tablespoons flour
- ¹/₂ cup milk, warmed
- 1 cup plain yogurt
- 1 cup crème fraîche
- 2 cups grated Gruyère, Monterey Jack, Mexican Manchego, or Oaxacan string cheese

Salt to taste

FOR THE GREEN SAUCE

- 6 cups water
- 25 tomatillos, husked
- 2 medium white onions, peeled and quartered
- 4 medium cloves garlic, peeled
- 4 poblano chiles, roasted, peeled, seeded, and deveined

Chalchiuhtlicue, the goddess of water, was the subject of numerous artistic creations by the ancient tribes. Sister of the rain god Tláloc, Chalchiuhtlicue was said to have power over the seas and rivers and to have the ability to create storms. Fishermen and those who sold fresh water from their canoes in large earthenware pots honored the goddess who controlled their livelihoods. Images of the goddess were adorned with eagle feathers; chains made of precious stones such as jade, turquoise, and emeralds; and wreaths made of aromatic flowers. As the goddess who nourished all life, she was the embodiment of the link between man and the water and played an essential role in the history of these great civilizations.

PREPARE THE FISH: Place the fish fillets side by side in a large glass baking dish and drench with the melted butter. Season with the salt, onion salt, garlic salt, and pepper. Cover and marinate for 1 hour at room temperature.

PREPARE THE STUFFING: While the fish is marinating, heat the butter in a medium saucepan. Brown the onion, then add the flour and brown. Remove from the heat and stir in the warm milk, yogurt, and crème fraîche. Return the pan to the heat and simmer uncovered until the mixture begins to thicken, about 25 minutes. Add the cheese little by little. Continue to simmer until the cheese melts. Season with salt if desired. Cover and set aside until ready to bake the fish.

PREPARE THE GREEN SAUCE: Bring the water to a boil in a large saucepan. Add the tomatillos, onions, and garlic and cook for 20 to 25 minutes. Remove pan from the heat and place the cooked vegetables in a food processor or a blender, reserving the liquid. Add 2 cups of the cooking liquid and the chiles. Puree. Strain the mixture, season with salt, and set aside. Heat the olive oil in a separate saucepan. Brown the onion and then add the strained sauce. Cook uncovered over medium heat, stirring occasionally, until the mixture thickens.

Assemble the fish: Preheat the oven to 350°F. Place 1 of the fish fillets in a baking dish. Cover with the stuffing. Place the other fillet on top and cover with the tomatillo sauce. Sprinkle with the grated cheese and the cilantro. Bake the fish until it flakes easily with a fork, about 1 hour. Serve immediately.

(see page 296), soaked in water for 15 minutes, and drained

4 fresh jalapeño chiles
4 fresh serrano chiles
Salt to taste
½ cup olive oil
1 medium white onion, peeled and finely chopped

FOR THE GARNISH

2 cups grated Gruyère, Monterey Jack, Mexican Manchego, or Oaxacan string cheese
2 cups finely chopped cilantro

FROGS' LEGS IN RED PUMPKIN-SEED SAUCE
ANCAS DE RANA EN PIPIÁN ROJO

Serves 8

FOR THE *PIPIÁN ROJO*

- ³⁄₄ pound ancho chiles, seeded and deveined (see page 296), and seeds reserved (there should be about 6 tablespoons of seeds)
- ²⁄₃ cup olive oil or lard
- ¹⁄₂ pound shelled pumpkin seeds
- ¹⁄₂ cup sesame seeds
- 3 ounces cooked hominy
- 1¹⁄₂ medium white onions, peeled and cut into pieces
- 4 medium cloves garlic, peeled
- 3 to 5 cups chicken stock
- ¹⁄₃ cup olive oil
- 2 white onion slices

Salt to taste

FOR THE GARNISH

- ¹⁄₂ cup olive oil
- 2 leeks, thinly sliced
- 2¹⁄₂ pounds purslane or other wild salad green, washed and chopped
- 2 pounds Swiss chard, washed and chopped

Salt to taste

FOR THE FROGS' LEGS

- 8 whole frogs' legs, halved
- ¹⁄₃ to ¹⁄₂ cup clarified butter

Salt to taste

The meat from this river reptile has a delicate and delicious flavor. The Mazahua and Otomí people, inhabitants of the mountains in the state of Mexico, hunt for frogs amid the pine forests and freshwater springs. Early in the morning, they carry woven baskets made from palm leaves down to the banks of the Lerma River to search for this delicacy. These tribes sell their catch at the markets in Toluca and Valle de Bravo. *Pipián rojo* is a sauce made with pumpkin seeds, sesame seeds, and chiles and makes an excellent accompaniment to sautéed frogs' legs.

PREPARE THE *PIPIÁN ROJO:* Preheat a large skillet, add the chiles, and dry them for a minute or so. Add a few tablespoons of the oil and stir-fry the chiles until crisp without burning. Remove the chiles and set aside. Add the chile seeds and the pumpkin seeds to the skillet, drizzle more oil on top, and stir-fry until toasted. Remove and set aside with the chiles. Stir-fry the sesame seeds in a little more oil and set aside with the other ingredients. Add the hominy and the rest of the oil and sauté until the hominy browns lightly. Transfer the hominy to a blender or a food processor and puree along with the reserved ingredients, the onions, the garlic, and some of the chicken stock. Strain the sauce and reserve. Add the ¹⁄₃ cup oil to the saucepan and brown the onion slices. Discard the onion slices and add the sauce and salt to taste. Simmer uncovered over low heat until the oil comes to the surface. Add more chicken stock, up to 5 cups, until the sauce has a somewhat thick consistency.

PREPARE THE GARNISH: Heat the oil in a wok or a large skillet. Add the leeks, purslane, and Swiss chard and sauté until softened. Add salt to taste, cover, and cook over high heat until the greens have wilted. Set aside.

PREPARE THE FROGS' LEGS: Bring a large quantity of salted water to a boil. Add the frogs' legs and boil for 1 minute. Drain and plunge the frogs' legs immediately into ice water. Preheat a large skillet, add the clarified butter and the frogs' legs, and sauté, turning once and adding salt as desired, until the meat has a light crust. (This may have to be done in batches.) Do not overcook the meat; it should remain moist and tender.

TO SERVE: Pour the hot *pipián* sauce into a large clay serving dish or onto a large platter. Place the frogs' legs on top and garnish with the sautéed greens. Serve with blue corn tortillas.

VARIATION: Garnish the frogs' legs with black or white sesame seeds.

Note: Any remaining *pipián* sauce can be used to season enchiladas, eggs, or cactus dishes. This sauce also makes a nice accompaniment to pan-fried soft-shelled crabs.

HUAUZONTLES XOCHIMILCO STYLE
HUAUZONTLES ESTILO XOCHIMILCO

Serves 8

Countless tribes settled along the shores of Texcoco Lake. As the area became more crowded, pieces of land were constructed in the water, thus creating the *chinampas,* or artificial islands, that were so important to agricultural production in central Mexico. Crops such as wild greens, pumpkins, corn, zucchini, squash, tomatoes, red beans, chiles, and *huauzontle* (a leafy vegetable with a flavor similar to that of broccoli) were cultivated on these islands built on top of mangrove wood, hearty grasses, and mud. The crops were collected in *trajineras,* wide canoes pulled with poles that were stuck into the muddy canals that separated the islands. Eventually, the boats transported the fresh fruits and vegetables to the grandiose Tenochtitlán market. After each crop was harvested, the land of the *chinampas* was reinforced with more mud and grass. After years of such practices, the *chinampas* were no longer floating gardens but pieces of earth contiguous with the mainland. A few *chinampas* devoted to agriculture can still be seen not far from Mexico City at Xochimilco, Mixquic, and Chalco, where some inhabitants still speak Nahuatl, the ancient Aztec

FOR THE RED SAUCE

- 12 cups water
- 8 large ripe tomatoes (about 4½ pounds)
- 1 medium white onion, peeled and cut into pieces
- 4 chipotle chiles, stir-fried
- 10 cloves garlic, peeled
- 1 medium white onion, peeled
- 1 chipotle or serrano chile, stir-fried
- ⅔ cup vegetable oil
- 2 white onion slices

CONTINUED

6 fresh or canned jalapeño
chiles (make crisscross slashes
on top of each whole chile)
Salt to taste

FOR THE *HUAUZONTLES*
6 quarts water
Salt to taste
8 large branches *huauzontles*,
washed, or 3¹/₂ pounds large
spinach leaves or broccoli
with stalks
1³/₄ pounds Oaxacan string
cheese, mozzarella cheese, or
Monterey Jack cheese, cut
into 8 slices
Flour for coating the *huauzontles*
14 eggs, separated
¹/₂ teaspoon salt
1¹/₂ tablespoons flour
4 cups vegetable oil

language, and still use the same growing techniques developed
by their ancestors.

PREPARE THE RED SAUCE: Bring the water to a boil in a large
saucepan. Add the tomatoes, the cut-up onion, the chiles, and
6 of the garlic cloves. Simmer covered for 40 minutes. Remove
from the heat, cool, and drain. Blend the vegetables with the
raw onion, the remaining 4 garlic cloves, and the chipotle chile
in a food processor or a blender. Strain the mixture. Heat the
vegetable oil in a frying pan and brown the onion slices. Discard the onion slices and add the blended sauce along with the
jalapeño chiles. Simmer uncovered over low heat for 25 minutes or until the sauce thickens a bit (the consistency should
still be thin). Season with salt and set aside.

PREPARE THE *HUAUZONTLES:* Bring the water to a boil in a large
pot. Add salt and the *huauzontles* and cook covered until tender, about 12 minutes. Remove from the heat, drain, and
squeeze out the excess liquid. Allow to drain well. Fold each
branch in half and stuff with a slice of cheese to make a sand-
wich. Tie each branch together to secure the cheese in place.
Roll the branches in flour. Beat the egg whites with the salt
until stiff. Gently fold in the yolks and the 1¹/₂ tablespoons
flour. Heat the oil in a large frying pan. Dip 4 of the *huauzontles* into the egg batter and gently slide into the hot oil. Use a
spoon to baste the tops so that they brown. Continue cooking
until the batter is golden brown. Remove with a slotted spoon
and drain on paper towels. Repeat with the remaining 4 *huauzontles.*

TO SERVE: Heat the red sauce, add the fried *huauzontles,* and
gently simmer covered for about 25 minutes. Accompany with
rice, Navy Beans with Habanero Chiles and Epazote (page
192), and fresh tortillas.

VARIATIONS: Reheat the *huauzontles* in a hot oven for 15 minutes and then serve on top of the sauce. Chopped parsley or
cilantro may be added for garnish.

EGGS WITH TOMATO SAUCE AND STRING BEANS
HUEVOS HILADOS CON EJOTES

Serves 8

Eggs are commonly served for brunch. The state of Mexico is known for this particular dish, which is a combination of tomatoes, native string beans, and eggs.

PREPARE THE TOMATO SAUCE: Puree the tomatoes in a blender or a food processor along with the chiles, the quartered onion, 5 of the garlic cloves, and the water. Heat the lard in a saucepan. Add the onion slices and the remaining 2 garlic cloves, brown, and discard. Strain the tomato sauce slowly into the pan. Add the epazote and continue cooking uncovered over low heat until the sauce thickens.

PREPARE THE EGGS: Meanwhile, mix the eggs with the cream and salt. Gradually pour the mixture through a strainer and into the saucepan with the tomato sauce and cook over low heat, stirring slowly, until the eggs begin to set and form very fine threads. Add the string beans and cook uncovered for 15 minutes more.

TO SERVE: Transfer the eggs to a clay pot *(cazuela)* or a large platter and accompany with beans and freshly made corn tortillas. This dish is also good with slices of fresh cheese.

FOR THE TOMATO SAUCE

- 16 medium ripe plum tomatoes
- 8 fresh serrano chiles
- 1 medium onion, peeled and quartered
- 7 medium cloves garlic, peeled
- 2½ cups water
- ½ cup lard or corn or olive oil
- 2 white onion slices
- 6 sprigs epazote or cilantro

FOR THE EGGS

- 16 eggs, beaten
- 2 tablespoons cream
- Salt to taste
- 3 cups string beans, boiled until tender and finely diced

FOR THE GARNISH

Navy Beans with Habanero Chiles and Epazote (page 192)
Freshly made corn tortillas

FRIED CAULIFLOWER STUFFED WITH CHEESE
COLIFLOR CAPEADA
Serves 8 to 12

FOR THE SAUCE

20 medium ripe plum tomatoes
1/2 medium white onion, peeled
6 medium cloves garlic, peeled
1 1/2 medium white onions, peeled and roasted in a hot skillet
1/2 cup vegetable oil
8 scallions, sliced diagonally
8 fresh jalapeño or canned chipotle chiles, cut into strips
Salt to taste
Water or chicken stock for thinning the sauce (if needed)

FOR THE CAULIFLOWER

2 large heads cauliflower, cut into 1- to 2-inch-long florets
10 eggs, separated
Salt to taste
16 mozzarella or Monterey Jack cheese slices (2 to 3 ounces each)
Flour
Vegetable oil for frying
Chopped epazote or cilantro for garnish

Cauliflower plays a key role in the cuisine of the region. It is produced in large quantities and is among the most commonly eaten vegetables in the state of Mexico.

PREPARE THE SAUCE: Heat an adequate amount of salted water in a large pot. Add the tomatoes, the raw onion half, and 2 of the garlic cloves. Simmer uncovered for 25 minutes, remove from the heat, and cool. Drain and blend the solids with the roasted onions and the remaining 4 garlic cloves. Heat the oil in a medium casserole. Sauté the scallions and the chile strips until tender. Strain the tomato sauce into the casserole and simmer covered on low heat for 35 minutes. Season with salt. If the sauce thickens too much, add enough water or chicken stock to obtain a partially thickened sauce. Keep the sauce warm.

PREPARE THE CAULIFLOWER: While the sauce is cooking, bring an adequate amount of salted water to a boil in a large pot. Add the cauliflower and simmer covered for 8 to 10 minutes. Drain the cauliflower and refresh in ice-cold water with ice cubes for 4 minutes. Drain again. Preheat the oven to 350°F. Beat the egg whites until stiff peaks form. Lightly beat the yolks and fold into the whites with a little salt. Lay a slice of cheese over a piece of cauliflower and top with another piece of cauliflower. Secure the bundle with a toothpick and daub with flour. Heat the oil in a frying pan or a deep pot. Dip the prepared cauliflower in the eggs and fry in batches until golden brown. Drain the cauliflower on paper towels. Keep warm in the oven while frying the remaining cauliflower.

TO SERVE: Remove and discard the toothpicks from the cauliflower. Add the cauliflower to the hot sauce and sprinkle with epazote. Heat the cauliflower through but do not cook because the batter will start to crumble. Transfer the cauliflower and the sauce to a large platter and serve immediately.

VARIATION: Roasted and peeled poblano or Anaheim chiles can be used in place of the cauliflower. Stuff prepared chiles with cheese, dip in egg batter, deep-fry, and then simmer in the hot sauce. This dish can also be made with boiled chayotes (water pears), following the same technique used with the cauliflower.

ROMPOPE MOUSSE (MEXICAN EGGNOG MOUSSE)
MOUSSE DE ROMPOPE

Serves 4 to 6

Liqueurs have a special place in Mexican gastronomy. In Tenancingo, special beverages called *moscos* are made from the extract of regional fruits. Known throughout the region, these liqueurs are flavored with quince, boysenberries, and blackberries. *Rompope* is a relatively new liqueur created by nuns in the city of Puebla. It became very popular in the state of Mexico, where it is now made from a slightly different recipe and is often used for desserts. The delicate cinnamon flavor combined with the richness of egg yolks and milk and the potency of alcohol makes this liqueur a favorite in Toluca, the state capital.

Pour the *rompope* and the milk into a heavy saucepan and scald. Beat the egg yolks with $1/2$ cup of the sugar until pale. Add the salt and the cinnamon. Stir several tablespoons of the hot milk mixture into the yolks. Pour the yolk mixture into the saucepan and cook, stirring constantly, until the mixture coats a metal spoon. Soften the gelatin in the cold water and stir until dissolved. Add the gelatin to the saucepan. Strain the custard. Add the rum and the vanilla and chill until the custard begins to set slightly. Beat the egg whites until foamy. Gradually add the remaining $1/4$ cup sugar and beat until stiff. Fold the whites into the custard. Fold in the whipped cream. Chill until set.

VARIATION: Serve with almond-scented whipped cream and fresh berries in season.

$1^1/_3$ cups *rompope* (Mexican eggnog) or other eggnog
$1^1/_3$ cups milk or half-and-half
4 eggs, separated
$^3/_4$ cup sugar
Dash of salt
1 Mexican or regular cinnamon stick, broken into 1-inch pieces
$1^1/_2$ envelopes unflavored gelatin
3 tablespoons cold water
1 tablespoon rum
$1^1/_2$ teaspoons Mexican or other vanilla extract
$^3/_4$ cup heavy cream, whipped and chilled

CONTINUED

Note: The mousse may be served with either Kahlúa and Cognac sauce or fresh fruit sauce. For Kahlúa and Cognac sauce, combine ¹/₂ cup *cajeta* (canned Mexican caramel), ¹/₄ cup half-and-half, 1 tablespoon each Kahlúa and Cognac, 2 tablespoons butter, and ¹/₄ to ¹/₂ cup chopped filberts, pecans, or black walnuts in a small saucepan. Bring to a boil and simmer until the sauce thickens. Cool and serve. For fresh fruit sauce, wash 1 pint strawberries, raspberries, peach slices, or blueberries and transfer to a saucepan along with any water that clings to the fruit. Sprinkle with ¹/₄ to ¹/₂ cup sugar and stir over medium heat until the sugar melts and the fruit softens to form a sauce. If desired, add 1 tablespoon of framboise or cassis after removing the sauce from the heat.

FIGS IN *CAPULÍN* SAUCE WITH CHOCOLATE PRALINES
HIGOS CON SALSA DE CAPULÍN Y PRALINÉS DE CHOCOLATE

Serves 6

FOR THE FIGS
30 ripe figs
Corn oil for greasing the ramekins

FOR THE *CAPULÍN* SAUCE
1 pound *capulines*, cherries, or blackberries
¹/₂ cup sugar, or to taste

FOR THE CHOCOLATE PRALINES
6 tablespoons unsalted peanuts
1 cup sugar
¹/₄ cup water
1 pound couverture chocolate, semisweet and dark combined, coarsely chopped

The Spanish brought a number of fruits to the New World, including pears, apples, grapes, peaches, and figs. Natives recognized the flavor of figs (which is quite similar to that of *chicozapotes*) and quickly adopted this newcomer. In turn, the conquistadors were confused by many of the fruits they encountered. *Capulines* grew in abundance in Coyoacán, a residential suburb of the capital that was home to Cortés. He mistakenly named them after a type of European wild cherry. Although dark red or purple in color and sharing a similar sweet flavor, the two fruits are different species but may be used interchangeably in recipes like this one that marry fruits from both worlds.

PREPARE THE FIGS: Peel and cut the figs into round slices. Dampen 6 ramekins and lightly grease with corn oil. Lay the fig slices in the ramekins and press gently to compact the figs. Refrigerate for 2 hours.

PREPARE THE *CAPULÍN* SAUCE: Pit the *capulines* or the cherries or wash the berries. Place the fruit in a blender or a food processor and puree with the sugar until smooth. Strain the sauce and refrigerate for 1 hour.

PREPARE THE CHOCOLATE PRALINES: Preheat the oven to 350°F. Spread the peanuts on a baking sheet and roast for 5 minutes. Heat the sugar and the water in a small saucepan. Simmer over low heat, stirring constantly, until the syrup has a caramel color. Add the peanuts and cook for 2 minutes. Spread the candy onto a cold surface (marble is best) and cool. Grind the mixture into a coarse powder when cool. Melt the chocolate in a hot water bath and temper (work chocolate with an angled metal spatula on a cool marble surface to reduce its temperature). Add the powdered nuts and blend well. Spread the chocolate onto a large sheet of parchment paper and refrigerate until it hardens. Cut into 3-by-3-inch pieces.

TO SERVE: Unmold the figs onto 6 large white plates. Streak the plates with the *capulín* fruit sauce and garnish with the pralines. Sprinkle the edges of the plates with cocoa powder and garnish with the orange leaves. Serve immediately.

FOR THE GARNISH

Dark cocoa powder

12 fresh orange, lemon, lime, mint, or lemon basil leaves

TEOTIHUACÁN PRICKLY PEARS
TUNA DE TEOTIHUACÁN

Serves 6

18 medium ripe prickly pears
Sugar to taste
Tequila to taste
3 cups Pineapple-Tangerine Juice
   (page 252)
¹/₂ cup raspberries
Chocolate curls for garnish (see
   Note)

Teotihuacán, or "the place where men become gods," was the first true city in ancient Mexico, coming to prominence between the third and seventh centuries A.D. The ceremonial center of the city was located along both sides of the avenue known as Calzada de Los Muertos, or Avenue of the Dead. On the eastern side was the grand Pyramid of the Sun and to the north lay the Pyramid of the Moon. The Temple of Quetzalcóatl was along the southern perimeter of the sacred part of the city. The temple was adorned with feathered heads in honor of the half-eagle, half-serpent god for whom it was built. The western facade of the temple was covered with marine images. After the Conquest, the area was renamed the Ciudadela, or Citadel. Before and after the arrival of the Spanish, residents of the city depended on nearby farms for nourishment. Wild cactus, bearing fruits of various sizes and colors, have been prized for centuries. Use either red or green prickly pears for this recipe.

Peel and cut the prickly pears into ¹/₂-inch-thick round pieces. Refrigerate the fruit for 2 hours. At serving time, arrange the fruit in a circular pattern in a large, shallow bowl. Sprinkle with sugar and tequila. Pour the juice over the prickly pears and mound the raspberries in the center of the bowl. Garnish with chocolate curls.

Note: For curls, melt and temper (work chocolate with an angled metal spatula on a cool marble surface to reduce its temperature) 3 cups of high-quality chocolate. Spread the tempered chocolate over a cold surface (marble is best) and cool. Use a large metal spatula to carve out curls.

ATOLE (HOT CORN BEVERAGE) TOLUCA STYLE
ATOLE DE MAÍZ ESTILO TOLUQUEÑO

Serves 8

The Santiago Tianguistengo marketplace is among the largest in the region, second only to the market in the state capital of Toluca. Hundreds of people gather to sell their wares and produce or to shop for local fruits, vegetables, and corn. There is a special area for stalls selling freshly made chorizo—a pork sausage made from spices, chiles, onion, garlic, and sometimes, for the green version, cilantro and epazote. Most of the local snacks are accompanied with a steaming cup of hot *atole*, a corn-based beverage.

Bring the milk to a boil in a clay or heavy metal pot. Remove from the heat and allow to cool slightly. Stir in the cinnamon and the sugar. Return the pot to the heat and simmer uncovered for 40 minutes. Grind the hominy in a *metate* (stone mortar), blender, or food processor with a little milk. Gradually add the ground hominy to the hot milk. Serve immediately in clay mugs.

VARIATIONS: Pureed seasonal fruits may be added to taste. Good choices include cherimoya, passion fruit, guava, pineapple, and mango.

4 quarts milk

3 cinnamon sticks (each 6 inches long)

1½ cups sugar, or to taste

2½ cups hominy, washed

BIBLIOGRAPHY

Atlas cultural de México, Gastronomía. México: SEP, INAH, Planeta, 1988.

Barrón, Cristina, y Rafael Rodríguez-Ponga. *La presencia novohispana en el Pacífico Insular.* México: Ibero, Embajada de España, Gob. Est. de Puebla, Comisión Nacional para la cultura y las artes, 1990.

Bases para el ordenamiento costero-pesquero de Oaxaca y Chiapas (aspectos generales). México: Secretaria de Pesca, 1990.

Bretón, Yvan, y Eduardo López Estrada. *Ciencias sociales y desarrollo de las pesquerías.* México: INAH, 1989.

Catálogo de pescados y mariscos de las aguas mexicanas. México: Secretaría de Pesca, 1989.

Cecchini, Tina. *Enciclopedia de las hierbas y de las plantas medicinales.* Barcelona: Editorial De Vecchi, 1980.

Chenaut, Victoria González. *Recretario del pescador de los estados.* México: Cuadernos de la Casa Chata, Centro de Investigaciones y estudios en Antropología Social.

Comida familiar de los estados de Baja California, Campeche, Colima, Chiapas, Estado de México, Guerrero, Jalisco, Michoacán, Nayarit, Oaxaca, Quintana Roo, Sinaloa, Sonora, Tabasco, Tamaulipas, Veracruz y Yucatán. México: Banco Nacional de Crédito Rural, 1988.

Directorio Nacional de Hospedaje. México: Secretaría de Turismo.

Lenz, Hans. *México-Tenochtitlan, ciudad lacustre.* México: Edit. Miguel Angel Porrúa, 1991.

Long-Solís, Janet. *Capsicum y cultura: La historia del chilli.* México: Fondo de Cultura Económica, 1986.

Martínez, Maximinio. *Catálago de nombres vulgares y científicos de plantas mexicanas.* México: Fondo de Cultura Económica, 1987.

Morales Díaz, Armando. *La tilapia en México: Biología, cultivo y pesquerías.* México: AGT Editor, 1991.

Morley, Sylvanus. *La civilización maya.* México: Fondo de Cultura Económica, 1989.

Ochoa, Arnulfo. *Antropología de la gente del mar.* México: INAH, 1988.

Ruiz Durá, Fernanda. *Recursos pesqueros de las costas de México.* México: Noriega Editores, 1990.

Ruvalcaba, Jesús. *Vigilia y dieta básica de los huastecos: Complementos acuáticos.* México: Cuadernos de la Casa Chata.

Sada, Jorge. *Los pescadores de la laguna de Tamiahua.*

Sahagún, Fray Bernardino de. *Historia general de las cosas de la Nueva España.* México: Editorial Porrúa, 1989. Published as *General History of the Things of New Spain,* trans. Arthur Anderson et al. Logan: Utah State University Press, 1970.

Las senadores suelen guisar. México: Instituto Nacional de Protección a la Infancia, 1964.

Soustelle, Jacques. *La vida cotidiana de los aztecas en vísperas de la conquista.* México: Fondo de Cultura Económica, 1984.

Velázquez de León, Josefina. *Viajando por las cocinas de las provincias de la República Mexicana.* México.

Vilches Alcázar, Recaredo. *Pesca prehispánica: Artes, usos y costumbres.* México: Banpesca, 1980.

INGREDIENTS AND TECHNIQUES

This section covers ingredients and techniques mentioned throughout the book as well as some fishing terms of note and other items of interest. In most cases, items are listed under their English names. When appropriate, the Spanish name follows in parentheses. When no English word exists (as is the case for some fish species that only inhabit warmer waters), the name is listed in Spanish with the Latin name in parentheses.

Abalone *(abulón):* Abalone with black, red, and yellow shells inhabit the waters off the Baja coast. They attach themselves to rocks and move by muscular contractions. In Baja, abalone is often sautéed in butter and seasoned with chipotle chiles. It is also used in ceviches along with onions, avocados, and olive oil.

Acamaya (Macrobrachium roenbergii and Macrobrachium americanum): This type of crayfish or langoustine is found in freshwater lakes and rivers in Mexico. The shell is either gray, blue, or brown. It is also called *chácal, pigua, acocil,* or river shrimp.

Achiote: This brilliant red paste lends color and flavor to dishes. The paste is made from the seeds of the annatto tree, which grows throughout Yucatán. *Achiote* paste usually contains other spices and flavorings, especially black pepper, garlic, and Seville oranges.

Acocil (Cambarellus montezumae): A type of tiny langoustine that lives in the rivers of central Mexico.

Adobo: This mixture of vinegar, salt, herbs (usually oregano, laurel, thyme, and marjoram), garlic, spices (often cinnamon, cloves, and/or cumin), and chiles (usually dried anchos, mulatos, or guajillos) is used as a marinade for meats, fish, or seafood or in enchiladas. Some adobos are made with tomatoes.

Allspice: This aromatic spice is used whole to flavor broths or ground with other spices into a seasoning paste. The tree stands about 40 feet tall and grows widely in Veracruz, Oaxaca, Chiapas, and Tabasco (allspice is also known as Tabascan peppercorns). The leaves can be used as a condiment in bean dishes, soups, stocks, moles, and tamales.

Annatto seed: See *Achiote.*

Anona: This small tropical tree bears large, aromatic fruit that are similar to cherimoyas. The greenish-gray skin is tough and usually has small overlapping protrusions that resemble those of an artichoke. The creamy white flesh is studded with large, black seeds and has a rich, custardlike flavor. This fruit is sometimes called custard apple or *atemoya.*

Atarraya: This is a small round throwing net used to catch fish.

Atlapextin: This net is made from reeds sewn together into a conical shape. Fishermen usually employ this net in shallow rivers and lagoons.

Avocado: Several varieties grow in Mexico, although the Hass (with its pebbly, dark green skin) is probably the most common. The flesh of a Hass avocado is creamier than that of the larger, pear-shaped Fuerte avocado, which is easily distinguished by its pale, smooth skin. To ripen hard avocados, place them in a paper bag along with a banana or an apple for a day or two. To remove the pit, separate the avocado into two halves. Stick the blade of a large knife into the pit and twist to loosen and remove.

Avocado leaves *(hojas de aguacates):* The shiny, dark green, oval leaves from the Fuerte avocado plant are used to scent beans, broths, sauces, and moles. They may also be used to wrap tamales or to cover a lamb for roasting or grilling. Leaves from Mexican avocado plants usually have a faint anise flavor.

Ayate: This is a fine material made from the fibers of maguey cactus, cotton, or palm. It is used to make sacks and purses as well as fishing nets used in shallow rivers and lagoons.

Azufrado beans: These small white beans streaked with yellow are cultivated in Nayarit. Any small white bean may be used in their place.

Balché: This ceremonial drink of the ancient Maya is made from an infusion of the bark from the *balché* tree and water.

Banana leaves *(hojas de plátanos):* These large, flat leaves with ribs are used to wrap tamales or other foods that are steamed or baked. They lock in moisture and impart a delicious flavor that foil or paper cannot. Look for them in Mexican or Asian markets. They often come frozen in 1-pound packets. Defrost the leaves and cut them into the size needed for the recipe, discarding any ribs. To make the leaves more pliable, wrap them in a wet dishcloth and sweat them in a warm oven for 15 to 20 minutes. The leaves may also be steamed for several minutes or passed over an open flame for several seconds to acquire a subtle smoky flavor. To tie bundles, cut thin strips from the leaves and use them as strings.

Barbacoa: This is the term used for meat or fish roasted in a pit that is lined with maguey leaves or other plant material. This traditional Mexican-style barbecue can also can be prepared in the oven.

Barracuda: This predatory fish has dark green or gray skin and a silver stomach. Sometimes the skin may have a reddish tint. Young barracuda live in shallow waters along the Pacific and Gulf coasts.

Bayo beans: These light-colored beans (they are almost tan) grow in tropical zones of Chiapas. Pinto beans may be substituted.

Bream *(besugo):* This red fish has a pale stomach and faint yellow stripes on the sides. Red snapper, porgy, or grouper may be substituted.

Butter beans: These light brown beans with a buttery flavor are often refried for *enfrijoladas* or used in soups. Also known as yellow beans, they are common to central and northern regions of Mexico.

Cabrilla *(Epinephelus adscensionis, Cabrilla devoca, Palabrax maculatofasciatus):* This brown fish with red dots feeds on small fish, crabs, and shrimp near reefs in the Gulf of California. There are stripes on the sides of the body in some species. The flesh can be eaten raw, baked, steamed, or cut into pieces and used in soups. Use red snapper, sea bass, or grouper as a substitute.

Cacao: This seed from the tree of the same name is used to make chocolate. There are several varieties, all of which were ground and consumed in beverages by the Olmecs,

Aztecs, Maya, and Zapotecs at religious ceremonies. The coin-shaped seed first arrived in Spain in 1528. Soon after, Europeans fashioned the first candies using sugar from the New World. Only the species that grows in Chiapas, Tabasco, and Oaxaca is distinguished by bright orange flowers and oblong leaves. Another variety, common in Veracruz, has mauve flowers and still another, common in Tabasco, Chiapas, and Veracruz, has white flowers. Each species produces a slightly different bean.

Cactus paddles: See *Nopales.*

Caldo michi: This term is used to describe a fish soup or stew. The word *michi* comes from the Tarascan for "fish."

Capulín: See Myrtle.

Caracol púrpura: This snail inhabits the coastline of Oaxaca. When pressed, it releases a purple fluid used to dye textiles.

Cardón: This is a tall desert cactus found in Baja, Sonora, Oaxaca, and Puebla.

Carp *(carpa):* One of the first fish domesticated by man, carp was bred by the Chinese 2,500 years ago. This species was introduced in Mexico during the eighteenth century, although the existence of a red carp species dates back to pre-Hispanic times. The common Chinese carp has an olive-green back and a yellow stomach and is covered with golden scales. Carp is sold fresh, smoked, grilled with herbs, or dried with salt.

Carrizo: This bamboo plant with strong hollow stems is used to make traditional fishing baskets.

Catfish *(bagre):* This bottom-feeding fish lives in the warm waters of rivers and lagoons and is now cultivated in ponds in both Mexico and the United States. Catfish do not have scales and are generally small in size.

Cayuco: This is a canoelike vessel made from one block of *huanacaxtle* wood. It is used for fishing in calm waters because it is harder to flip than a canoe.

Cempazúchil: The yellow, golden, or orange blossoms of this marigold are placed as offerings on family altars for the Day of the Dead. Chickens are also fed these flowers to make their skin yellow.

Ceviche *(cebiche):* This is raw fish or seafood cut into small pieces and "cooked" with lemon, lime, or Seville orange juice. Many ceviches also contain minced onion, salt, cilantro, tomatoes, and/or chiles.

Charal: The *charal,* or whitebait, is a very small whitefish with silver skin that lives in lakes. Dried with or without salt, this fish can be stored for a long time. It can also be smoked and is sometimes cooked fresh with chile paste and herbs and used in tamales.

Chaya: This is the tender, heart-shaped green from the plant of the same name that grows in southeastern Mexico. Rich in nutrients, this leafy green is used like Swiss chard or spinach, the two usual substitutes. *Chaya* is a member of the spurge family, a group of shrubby plants characterized by bitter, often milky, juices.

Chayote: This mild vegetable grows on a creeping vine. It is sometimes called water pear because of its shape and somewhat watery pale green flesh and is also known as vegetable pear. The light green or yellow skin of this tropical squash is almost opaque when ripe and the vegetable weighs between 1/2 and 1 pound at maturity. Chayote is very nutritious and is traditionally eaten to promote digestion.

Cheese: A number of cheeses are used widely throughout Mexico. ADOBERA is very mild and melts well. AÑEJO and *cotija* are salty, feta-like cheeses used in enchiladas or quesadillas. AÑEJO is a fresher, creamier cheese, more like soft feta. COTIJA is usually saltier and dried feta may be used in its place. CHIHUAHUA has a nutty, mild flavor and is often used to stuff chiles. A mild white Cheddar or soft Gruyère can be used as a substitute. **Manchego,** a Spanish sheep's milk cheese, has a sharp flavor. The Mexican variety is called for in the recipes. Oaxacan string cheese, or *quesillo,* is similar to fresh mozzarella and may be braided, shaped into rounds, or pulled into long logs. It may be shredded and used in appetizers, sliced and cooked in tomato sauce with epazote, or cubed and stuffed into de agua or poblano chiles, small vegetables, or quesadillas. Tangy PANELA is made from fresh curd *(cuajada)* and can accompany boiled or broiled seafood and grilled fish like sea bass, red snapper, and grouper. QUESO PANELA sometimes appears on the table as an appetizer or is used to fill *entomatadas* (tortillas stuffed with cheese and basted with a light tomato sauce). It is also used in quesadillas or enchiladas, with cheese crumbled on top and quickly broiled. The closest American substitute is farmer cheese. QUESO FRESCO is a fresh, tangy, and somewhat salty cheese that is similar to dried farmer cheese or lightly salted feta cheese. It is also known as QUESO RANCHERO.

Chepil (Crotalaria longirostrata): The fragrant leaves of this small yellow-flowered shrub are used in Oaxaca and Chiapas, mostly to season beans, rice dishes, and tamales. Their fresh flavor is reminiscent of green beans.

Cherimoya (chirimoya): This is the name of a tropical tree that grows in Yucatán and Oaxaca as well as the large dark green fruit it bears. The outside of the fruit, with its thick, textured skin, resembles a grass-colored pinecone. Inside, the pulp is pale yellow, almost white, in color and dotted with black seeds. The very fragrant, low-acid flesh has a sweet, sometimes musky flavor with hints of vanilla and mango. Cherimoyas can be used in sorbets and other desserts or scooped right from the skin and eaten.

Cherna (Epinephelus itajara): This grayish-green fish inhabits coral reefs and underwater caverns along the Atlantic coast of Mexico. Known as jewfish in the United States, it is a member of the extended grouper and bass family.

Chilacayote: This smooth squash with watery pale green flesh measures between 2 and 8 inches in diameter. It is extremely tender and mild flavored. Chayote may be used in its place.

Chilayo (Lemai reocerus marginatus): This fleshy plant with spines has a stem that measures about 4 inches in diameter, which is used by the Mixtec Indians of Oaxaca in their diet.

Chile: There are literally hundreds if not thousands of chiles grown in Mexico. Although fresh and dried chiles are usually not interchangeable, within each category there is considerable latitude. Note that some chiles have different names depending on whether they are fresh or dried (poblanos are called anchos when dried) and depending on regional traditions (anchos have at least a half-dozen alternate names). Below are some of the most common names, with brief descriptions.

Amashito: A member of the piquín family of chiles that is shaped like a small round ball.

Very spicy and eaten when still green, it is grown in Chiapas, Tabasco, and Yucatán and commonly used in the local cuisines.

Anaheim: A long, thin chile with a conical shape that is used fresh (the color is green) or dried (the color is a deep orange or red). It has a mildly hot flavor. In northern states, it is referred to as a chile verde. When simply dried it is called a colorado chile. It is called a pasado chile when roasted, peeled, and dried.

Ancho: A dried poblano chile with a dark red color. Mildly hot, the ancho is called a pasilla chile in Michoacán, a joto chile in Aguascalientes, and a color chile in Veracruz. It is only mildly hot. In the United States it is called a pod, ancho, or pasilla chile.

Bandeño: A dried costeño chile.

Blanco: A tiny, hot chile cultivated in Chiapas and Tabasco.

Caloro: A long, thin light green chile from Chihuahua. It is also called a California chile or an Anaheim chile as well as a verde del norte.

Caracolito: A fresh chile from Nayarit.

Carib: A medium-size chile with a triangular shape. When mature it is yellow and fairly hot. If the color is pale, the chile is not fully ripe.

Cascabel: A dried reddish-brown chile with a mildly hot, nutty flavor. It is shaped like a cherry and rattles when shaken. This chile grows in Michoacán, Nayarit, and the state of Mexico.

Catarina: A dried, brownish-red chile similar in appearance to a jalapeño. It grows in central regions and is used in sauces and moles.

Chilaca: A long, thin chile ranging in length from 6 to 12 inches whose name translates as "cane." The flavor of this dark green chile is similar to that of a poblano, but it is slightly more potent and aromatic. It is called a black pasilla or pasilla negro when dried and has a sweet, spicy flavor, wrinkled surface, and intense black color. This chile is common to Michoacán, Puebla, and Querétaro.

Chilacate: A mild chile with a flavor similar to that of an Anaheim. Consumed fresh or dried, it is also called a tierra chile. This chile is grown in the north Pacific zone.

Chilcosle (or chilcoxtle): Medium dried chile, either mustard or orange in color, that is used in Oaxaca for yellow moles.

Chile de agua: A light green chile cultivated in Oaxaca. This chile has a flat, cylindrical body and is consumed when green.

Chile de árbol: A small, thin, pointed chile that is picked when dark orange or bright red in color. It is also known by the names bravo, cuauhchilli, pico de pájaro, and cola de rata. It is very hot.

Chile dulce: A sweet or bell pepper of any color. This is also known as a morrón or pimentón chile.

Chiltepín: A tiny chile that has a round shape and a bright red or orange color when mature. It comes from a small bush that grows in the mountains of Sonora. Use this uniquely spicy chile in sauces with tomatoes and tomatillos or to season seafood broths. It can also be ground and used as a rub for corn on the cob. One chiltepín has the piquancy of five jalapeños. It is consumed either fresh or dried.

Chimayo: Also known as a pod chile. It is widely grown in New Mexico, is brownish-red in color, and is about the size of a large guajillo.

Chipotle: A smoked and dried jalapeño chile with a hard brown skin. It is sometimes packed in adobo and sold canned in Latin markets.

Cola de rata: The name given to de árbol chiles in northwestern Mexico.

Color: The name given to ancho chiles in northeastern Mexico and Veracruz.

Colorado: The name given to dried Anaheim or verde del norte chiles in Baja California, Sonora, and Chihuahua.

Cora: A leathery, oval chile consumed green or dried. This very hot chile is used in *salsa huichol* and *salsa guacamaya* and in the local cuisines of Nayarit, Sinaloa, and Zacatecas.

Costeño: A medium-size fresh green chile. This is sometimes known as bandeño chile and always has a light red color when dried. It is used along the Pacific coasts of Oaxaca and Guerrero.

Guajillo: A long, wide green chile similar to an Anaheim. It is called a mirasol chile when fresh. When dried, the color changes to dark red and the name is guajillo. It is used in sauces, moles, and *pozoles.*

Guajillo puya: A small, thin dried chile that is quite pointed, deep red in color, and very hot.

Güero: A fresh pale green or yellow chile that is very hot. Known as a banana pepper, yellow wax pepper, or Hungarian wax pepper in the United States, this chile, which is grown extensively in Yucatán and sometimes called by the name xcatick, is average in size and can come in green, orange, or red shades. This chile has a thin skin and is used in stews and soups and often roasted. When pickled this chile is called a largo or carricillo.

Habanero: A small, very hot chile with several indentations and crevices. It comes in several shades of green, red, yellow, and orange. It is also called a scotch bonnet pepper.

Jalapeño: A small, conical fruit of medium to hot intensity. When fresh, the color is dark green or bright red. It also goes by the names huachinago in Puebla, jarocho and gordo in Veracruz, and cuaresmeño in central Mexico. When dried, the color is brownish red and the name is chipotle.

Japonés: A small dried serrano used in fresh salsas or cooked with tomatoes and tomatillos for various sauces. A dried de árbol chile can often be used in its place.

Largo: Another name for a pickled güero.

Manzano: A medium-size round fresh chile that is either yellow or orange and quite hot. In the mountains of Chiapas, it is called a jalapeño; in Michoacán, a perón or cera.

Mira pa'arriba: A chile that is similar to the de árbol chile. Native to Chiapas, it is deep green in color and grows on tall plants.

Mora: This chile is smaller but wider than a jalapeño. When smoked, this chile acquires a deep reddish-brown color and unique flavor welcome in soups, sauces, and moles. This chile is sometimes pickled.

Morita: A chile with a triangular shape that is reminiscent of a jalapeño or serrano, although it is smaller. It can also be smoked and dried in earthen ovens for an extraordinary taste.

Mulato: A dried mild chile similar to an ancho. When fresh it is darker than a poblano; when dried, it has a chocolate color.

Pasado: A roasted, peeled, and dried Anaheim chile.

Pasilla: A dried chilaca chile that is black in color and sometimes called a pasilla negro or a prieto chile. The same name is occasionally used to describe fresh poblanos in Michoacán and dried anchos in other regions as well as the United States.

Pasilla oaxaqueño: A smoked and dried chile with wrinkled skin and a dark brown color. This chile of average size is used widely in Oaxaca and some parts of Puebla.

Piquín: A tiny red (when mature) fruit with an oval shape. Distributed by birds, it grows on tall plants and is very hot. Consumed green or dried, this chile is cultivated along both coasts.

Poblano: A large, fresh, dark green to red chile that is among the most commonly used in Mexico. It has a long tapered shape and is often somewhat flat. Its thick skin covers an undulating surface. Mild to spicy, poblanos can be stuffed, sautéed, or pickled. The poblano is also called a pasilla in some regions.

Puya: See Guajillo puya, above.

Serrano: A small, thin fruit with thick skin and many seeds. This green chile can be mild or hot. When dried, the skin turns red and the name changes to japonés.

Simojovel: A small chile with an oval shape and an intense green color when fresh. After drying, the chile turns reddish orange or copper in color. Native to Chiapas, it is used in sauces or stir-fried and served as a garnish for various dishes.

Xcatick: The Mayan name used for the güero chile. The skin on this chile is soft and may be pale green, yellow, or red. The flavor ranges from mild to hot. It can be used in *escabeches* or roasted for use in soups and tomato sauces.

As for general preparation techniques, fresh chiles, especially jalapeños and serranos, are used whole in recipes or simply chopped. Most of a chile's heat resides in the seeds and the veins, so they can be left intact (especially serranos and jalapeños) if the chile is going to be used in a sauce. However, if the chile is going to be stuffed, make sure to remove all the seeds and veins but leave the stem.

In many cases, larger fresh chiles, like poblanos or Anaheims, are roasted and peeled before use in recipes. Begin by roasting the chiles until the skins blacken and blister. (This can be done under the broiler, directly over a gas flame, or in a warm skillet.) Sweat the roasted chiles for 5 to 8 minutes depending on the size and texture (often longer for poblanos) in a paper bag to loosen the charred skins. (The bag should be shut tight so steam can build up.) Using a small sharp knife or your fingers, peel the skins under cold running water. (It's a good idea to wear rubber gloves to protect your skin.) Then remove the stems, seeds, and fleshy veins from the inside of the chiles. To reduce the piquancy of poblanos, soak roasted and peeled whole chiles in water with 2 tablespoons each of vinegar and sugar per cup of liquid.

Dried chiles should be washed and dried before use to remove any soil. Some small dried chiles are used whole. Usually recipes will call for them to be seeded and deveined. Simply make a slit down the length of each chile and scrape out the seeds and the veins. To release their flavor, dried chiles are usually lightly toasted on a hot *comal* (a round cooking surface) or in a heavy warm skillet, stir-fried in a small quantity of oil (in both cases they should not be allowed to burn), or steeped in a hot liquid. To steep chiles, cover them with boiling water and soak for 15 minutes. Drain and reserve the liquid for sauces or stocks.

Drained chiles are often pureed in a food processor with some of the cooking liquid and other ingredients until smooth. This paste is the basis for many chile sauces.

Chile leaves: These small purple or green leaves are highly aromatic and only mildly spicy. They may be used in sauces, soups, beans, or tamales.

Chile seeds: Dried seeds from various chiles add heat to moles and *pipianes*. Crushed red pepper flakes are a less potent alternative.

Chilmole: This dark black paste is made with toasted chiles (often xcaticks or costeños), roasted onions and garlic, oregano, and Seville orange juice. It is used in Yucatán, Campeche, and Quintana Roo to season regional dishes.

Chinchorro: This small net is used for fishing in shallow lagoons and rivers.

Chinín: This small fruit is similar to an avocado. It has soft green skin and buttery flesh that is a bit watery. It is native to southeastern Mexico and Central America.

Chipilín: This herb with tiny, oval leaves lends a smoky flavor to tamale doughs, rice dishes, soups, and beans.

Chochoyón: This small *masa* (corn dough) dumpling with an indentation in the center to trap sauce is added to soups, bean dishes, and moles. The dough can be scented with fresh herbs.

Cilantro (or coriander): This green herb has serrated leaves and a distinct lemony flavor. It is very common in most regions and used widely in soups, sauces, tacos, and salsas and with avocados.

Clams *(almejas):* There are numerous varieties, including the chocolate clam (a large species found in the Sea of Cortés, or Gulf of California, and along the Chiapas and Guerrero coasts), the rooster clam (found in the northern Gulf of Mexico), and the pismo clam (found in Baja waters).

Cochinilla: This tiny insect is ground and used to give red color to sweet tamale fillings and dyes.

Coconut: Freshly grated coconut is superior to the sweetened and shredded variety sold in most supermarkets. To make it at home, pierce the eyes with a sharp instrument and pour out the liquid. Bake the coconut in a 400°F oven for 15 minutes. The coconut may crack while baking. If not, strike the coconut with a hammer. Slice out the flesh and grate by hand or in a food processor. One coconut yields about 4 cups grated. If you wish to buy grated coconut, look for the unsweetened variety sold in health food stores.

Comal: This round clay cooking surface of varying thickness has been used for centuries to make tortillas, toast spices and chiles, and roast garlic, tomatoes, tomatillos, onions, and more. A griddle or a heavy skillet, preferably cast-iron, may be used in its place.

Copal: This resin comes from the *copalcahuite* tree and is burned as incense in temples and at family altars for special occasions. There are more than forty species of this tree in Mexico.

Corbina *(corvina):* This blue-green fish with gray shading is found in Pacific waters. Use striped bass, porgy, ocean perch, or grouper as a substitute.

Corn husks: Fresh or dried husks are used to wrap tamales or to flavor stocks and soups. They are also added to the cooking water for cactus paddles to cut the sliminess of the *nopales*. They may be white, yellow, dark blue, or purple in color.

Corunda: This triangular tamale wrapped in corn leaves originated in Michoacán. It is called *kurunda* in the local Purhé language.

Crab *(cangrejo):* Green or dark blue in color, the shells of these crustaceans turn bright red when cooked. Crabs live in shallow coastal water. Of the ten appendages, only the first set of claw-bearing legs contain much meat.

Creole cucumber: Also known as Chinese cucumber, this variety has pale white skin and is very thin and long. It is often used in Yucatán and the northern states.

Cuitlacoche: This black fungus grows on ears of fresh corn and is caused by excessive humidity. Also called corn truffle, this delicacy has been used in soups, sauces, and stuffings for centuries. Unless you grow corn, fresh *cuitlacoche* is hard to find, so use canned or frozen.

Culantro (Geringium foelidum): This herb has long, jagged aromatic leaves. The small round fruit is used as a spice, often appearing in regional moles. In Tabasco, the leaves (which are called *perejil de Tabasco*) are frequently used. Similar to Thai parsley, a lemony leaf used in Asia, *culantro* leaves are wonderful in soups and stocks. It also goes by the names *cilantrón* and *cilantrillo*.

Elephant garlic: See Garlic.

Epazote *(Chenopodium ambrosioides):* This fragrant light green herb flavors bean dishes as well as tamales, sautéed mushrooms, omelets, and sauces. Also called wormwood, epazote has an anise flavor and is used in medicinal teas to treat digestive disorders.

Escabeche: This sauce or marinade is made with vinegar and often garlic, onions, whole peppercorns, laurel leaves, thyme, and marjoram. It is used to preserve or pickle meats, poultry, fish, and seafood. *Escabeche* can also be made with chiles, in which case it's called adobo.

Esmedregal (Seriola zonata): This bluish-green fish with a silver stomach travels with sharks in the Gulf and eats the scraps left behind by the large predators.

Flower garnishes (with oranges, radishes, or scallions): Halve an orange or a radish with a zigzag motion to produce flowers. Make several slits in the bottom of a scallion stalk to separate the "petals" of the flower. Chill the garnishes in ice water for 2 hours or until ready to use.

Garlic: The use of garlic differs from region to region. In the south, it is used freely; in the north, more sparingly. Small cloves are reserved for raw sauces or moles. Larger garlic and elephant garlic should be used for pickling, stews, and adobos. Elephant garlic is usually much milder than regular garlic.

Grouper *(mero):* This popular fish has a large head, reddish brown skin, and a pink abdomen. It lives in the deep waters of the Gulf and the Pacific. There are more than 400 individual species, making *mero* one of the most common fish in Mexico. It is sold fresh, frozen, or salted.

Guanábana: This fruit has a dark green rind covered with spines that shields pulpy, musky flesh. Cherimoyas make an adequate substitute.

Guavina (Diplectrum euryplectum): This fish looks like a catfish but lives in salt- or fresh-water rivers. It is dark brown with a golden stomach.

Hearts of palm *(palmito):* Palm trees grow throughout much of the country. The center of the tree is made of thin white edible layers called hearts of palm. Eaten fresh or canned, *palmito* is used in salads, soups, and tamales and may simply be steamed or roasted.

Hierba anís: This wild herb has a tarragon or anise flavor with lemony undertones. The leaves are long and jagged and the plant has small yellow flowers. It can be used to make an herbal tea that calms the stomach. It is sometimes called Mexican marigold.

Hoja santa (Piper sanctum): This aromatic plant's anise-flavored leaves are used in the regional cooking of Oaxaca, Chiapas, Tabasco, Veracruz, and Guerrero. The large green leaves are sometimes used to wrap fish or tamales and can also be chopped and used as an herbal accent in soups and sauces. It is also called *hoja de acuyo, hierba santa,* and *momo.*

Hominy: The name hominy refers to dried, large corn kernels that are soaked in water with powdered limestone until soft. The kernels are drained, skinned, and washed. These whole kernels, called hominy, are used whole to make *pozole* (a thick stew) or ground to make fresh *masa* (corn dough). Hominy can be made at home from dried flint corn or purchased in cans.

Huaruca: This weighted, pouchlike net is used to trawl deep waters for fish. Two ropes are attached to the net and usually wrapped around the arms of the fisherman. When he releases the ropes, the net plunges into the water and traps fish.

Huauzontle (Chernopodium nuttaliae): This is an ancient Aztec vegetable with a flavor similar to that of broccoli. The leafy green fronds or branches may be cooked with onion and garlic or deep-fried. It grows in Puebla and the Valley of Mexico.

Jicama: This is a root with brown stringy skin and white creamy flesh that is usually eaten raw in salads and ceviches.

Jocoque: This Middle Eastern yogurt is usually tangier than American-style yogurt. Use plain yogurt or crème fraîche as a substitute.

Jojoba: The jojoba is about three feet high and grows wild in Baja and Sonora. The sap, which has many medicinal properties, is frequently used for skin disorders, but it is also used to relieve stomachaches.

Jurel: Also known as jack crevalle, this fish has a flat body and a large head. The back is usually bluish and the stomach is either gold or silver. When young, this species lives in coastal waters, but it prefers the open sea later in life. Jurel also goes by the name bull or horse fish and is sold fresh, salted, or in the form of fish meal.

Kurunda: See *Corunda.*

Langoustine *(pigua):* Also known as crayfish, this grayish-blue or grayish-brown mollusk may be as small as a shrimp or as large as a lobster.

Laurel: This name is frequently used for bay leaves. Mexican laurel has thinner, more silvery leaves than its European cousin. Use fresh Mediterranean bay leaves as a substitute.

Limestone: The ancient Mexicans discovered that the addition of powdered limestone or lime from ground seashells could soften dried corn kernels as they cooked and helped to remove their hard-to-digest hulls. We now know that powdered limestone boosts the amount of available nutrients in corn products, especially niacin, protein, and calcium.

Along with water and dried corn, limestone is the third key ingredient for making fresh *masa* (corn dough).

Lobster *(langosta):* Gulf species have speckled reddish-brown shells, while Pacific lobsters tend to be yellowish brown. The Pacific lobster, called *langosta roja,* is among the most prized varieties in the world. It lives near the reefs that line the Baja coast and is also known as a California lobster.

Macabí (Elops saurus): This bluish-green Gulf fish is covered with fine silvery scales. A similar species, called chile fish or young ladyfish, lives in the Pacific. *Macabí* resembles a herring but is a member of the tarpon family. Fishing for *macabí* has been suspended.

Machaca: This is salted, dried, and shredded fish. It is served in the northern states with eggs or tomato sauce or used as an empanada filling. A similar egg dish can be made with minced shrimp that has been steamed or smoked.

Mackerel, Spanish: Also known as sierra, this fish has a pointed head and very sharp teeth. It usually has a bright blue body, silvery sides, and yellow spots. Spanish mackerel lives in the Gulf and is sold fresh, salted, or smoked. It is also called *caballa, serrucho, peto, carite,* and *pintado.*

Maguey: This name applies to any one of 200 species of agave that grow in semidesert conditions throughout Mexico. The fibers are used to manufacture durable goods including fishing nets, while the sap is fermented into a liquor called pulque. Since pre-Hispanic times, pulque has been used in ritual beverages and as a culinary ingredient to marinate fish, poultry, or meat or used in soups and sauces.

Mahimahi *(dorado):* This fish comes in a variety of colors but is usually black or blue. It has fine scales and can be eaten fresh or smoked. Mahimahi (sometimes called dolphin fish) usually weigh about 25 to 30 pounds and live in the open sea.

Mamey *(Calocarpum sapota):* This large oval fruit has rough brown skin and creamy red flesh. Known as red *zapote* in southern regions, the fruit may be used in sauces, beverages, or cooking. The large stone, called *pixtle,* is toasted and serves as a base for paints as well as culinary sauces and beverages. Mangoes may be used in place of mameys.

Mango: Called the king of fruits, the mango was first cultivated in Asia more than 5,000 years ago. It has an oval shape, smooth, leathery skin that can be red, pink, yellow, or green in color, and orange or yellow flesh that is very soft and highly aromatic. Several varieties of mangoes have been grown in Mexico since the Conquest and are used for desserts, sauces, and beverages. Mangoes have large, flat stones, which require some careful cutting to extract. Halve the mango like you would an avocado, remove the pit on one side, and scoop out the flesh from both sides. Or slice the mango into thirds. The middle third will contain the stone and some flesh, which can be cut away. The flesh of the other thirds can be scored, cutting to the skin but not through it. Press the skin so that the flesh "pops" like a porcupine, trim flesh, and serve.

Mangrove *(mangle):* Wood from this tropical tree grows in dense forests along the Pacific and Yucatán coasts and is frequently used in the construction of boats and wharfs. Mangrove wood can also flavor grilled foods.

Manjua (Anchoa mitchilli): This small fish with gray skin lives in salt water. It is called bay anchovy in English.

Masa (fresh): This is freshly ground corn made from hulled kernels that have been boiled and soaked in limestone-treated water. *Masa* is the basis for tortillas and for some tamales. *Masa* should be refrigerated until ready to use but will sour after several days. For longer storage, freeze fresh *masa* in a sealed plastic bag or container. See page 307 for more detailed information.

Masa harina (dried): Fresh *masa* sours quickly, so it is sold in this dried, powdered form. To reconstitute *masa harina*, add hot water and usually some salt and a small amount of all-purpose flour. Two excellent brands are made by Quaker and Maseca. The name of the latter is short for "*masa seca*," or dried *masa* in Spanish. See page 307 for more detailed information on fresh masa.

Mojarra (Diapterus olisthostomus): This small but tasty fish with very large eyes and silvery skin lives in lagoons and small rivers. White *mojarra* (sometimes called *moharra*) inhabits the Gulf as well as waters along the Pacific coast stretching southward to Peru. A striped variety is found only in the Gulf. Use trout, tilapia, sardines, or other small fish as a substitute.

Molcajete: This is a volcanic stone or a clay mortar used to grind spices and make sauces. With time, the *molcajete* becomes seasoned and imparts a delicious flavor to *salsas*. Before first use, cure the *molcajete* by grinding dried corn or rice in bowl. This process removes any powdery residue from the stone surface.

Momo: See *Hoja santa.*

Mullet *(lisa):* This large fish has a flat body and big eyes. Its back is olive green, its sides are silvery, and its stomach is white. It lives in both the Gulf and the Pacific and is sold fresh, salted, or smoked.

Mushrooms: Dozens of varieties are used throughout the country. Some of the most popular are morels, trumpets, tree ears *(hongos orejitas)*, chanterelles, and porcini.

Myrtle *(arrayán):* This small bush has tiny white flowers and dark blue, almost black, berries (called *capulínes*), which are used in desserts.

Nanche: This is a small yellow fruit that is eaten fresh or preserved in syrup. Somewhat similar to crab apples or kumquats, *nanches* are sometimes used to flavor *aguardiente* (brandy) or rum.

Nasa: This is a pointed basket used for catching fish in shallow waters. It is usually filled with bait and lowered from riverbanks or lakeshores.

Nopales: These are paddles from the prickly pear cactus, which grows throughout Mexico and the southwestern United States. Cactus is eaten as a green vegetable in most regions of Mexico. If purchased with spines, scrape them off before cooking. When boiled, *nopales* exude a slimy substance (much like that given off by okra), which must be rinsed off. *Nopales* may be used in soups, salads, or juices and can be grilled as well. They are also used medicinally in the treatment of diabetes and to aid in weight loss. There are hundreds of species, so the shapes and sizes are almost endless. The edible fruit of this plant is known as a prickly pear.

Octopus *(pulpo):* This reddish-brown or whitish-gray mollusk with eight tentacles lives under rocks or in caves at the bottom of the sea. It is found along the Gulf and Pacific coasts.

Ojotón (Trachurus symmetricus): This is a dark green or blue fish with a silver stomach that lives in deep Pacific waters. Also known as jack mackerel, *ojotón* are often caught when quite young (weighing about ½ pound) and cooked whole. Use sardines or other small fish as a substitute.

Oregano: This herbaceous plant has velvety leaves and purple flowers. There are several varieties, each with a distinct flavor. Desert oregano, which grows in Baja, Sonora, and Chihuahua, has smaller leaves and is particularly pungent. The oregano in Yucatán has very large leaves and a milder flavor.

Oyster (*ostión*): Gulf oysters live in shallow lagoons and bays, where they are now frequently cultivated. The lagoon of Tamiahua is an especially important source. Rock oysters are cultivated in Baja and other Pacific coastal areas. They have thicker shells that are dark on both the inside and the outside. These bivalves grow attached to rocks washed by crashing waves and are eaten fresh, in ceviches, or pickled.

Panocha: See *Piloncillo.*

Pápalo (Porophyllum ruderale): The name of this green herb comes from the Nahuatl word for "butterfly" and refers to the shape of the small leaves. It has a strong, sharp flavor and is highly aromatic. *Pápalo* often seasons guacamole or tacos. It is commonly used in Hidalgo, Jalisco, State of Mexico, Mexico City, and Puebla.

Papaya: This tropical fruit ranges in sizes from a mere ½ pound to more than 20 pounds. Smooth skin, either green, orange, or yellow in color, covers this pear-shaped fruit. The pale yellow flesh is smooth and has a floral, sometimes musky aroma. The center of the fruit is filled with hundreds of tiny black seeds, which have a slight peppery flavor. Papayas are very nutritious (they are rich in vitamins A and C) and can be used in desserts, sauces, or beverages.

Pepicha (*Porophyllum tagetoides*): This is a green herb with thin leaves that looks like tarragon. The flavor is reminiscent of cilantro but even stronger. *Pepicha* is often used to flavor squash or corn dishes.

Peyote: This herb has been used by Indians along the northern Pacific coast for centuries in religious celebrations. It is traditionally chewed and is capable of producing hallucinations. It is also called *jículi.*

Piloncillo: This is liquid brown sugar poured into small conical molds and cooled until hard. This sweetener is usually grated or cut into pieces before use. It is also called *panocha.* Use dark brown sugar as a substitute.

Pitahaya: This is a native American desert fruit with intense pink or red flesh and skin. The blood-red pulp holds tiny black seeds and is similar to that of the kiwi in appearance.

Pitiona: This is an aromatic herb used in Oaxaca to season moles. The flavor is reminiscent of spearmint.

Plaintain (*plátano*): Cousin to the sweet banana, this bland fruit is used primarily in savory dishes because it retains its firm shape when heated. The yellow skin turns black when ripe and the fruit is usually larger than a banana. The flesh is fairly coarse and somewhat starchy. Plantains can be grilled, fried, baked, or mashed and are often used in tamales.

Pompano (*pámpano*): This silvery fish has a dark back, a white stomach, and scales. It lives in the deep waters of the Gulf and can be used much like red snapper.

Porgy (*pargo*): A member of the snapper family, this reddish fish changes color from day to night. It lives in the deep, rocky waters of the Gulf of Mexico and the Caribbean. This scaly fish is sold fresh, frozen, or dried. A gray species lives right along the coast.

Prickly pear *(tuna):* This round or oval fruit from the cactus of the same name is covered with spines (which are usually removed during handling) and small hairs (which are not). About the size of large eggs, prickly pears come in numerous varieties with red, yellow, or green skins, although the flesh is usually magenta and studded with tiny, like-colored seeds. The pulp is soft and has a melony aroma.

Pulque: See Maguey.

Pumpkin seeds *(pepitas):* The seeds from pumpkins and other large squash have been used in numerous ways for centuries. They come in many forms, including fresh or dried, hulls on or off, and toasted or raw. The pale green seeds are often sold hulled in natural food stores. To bring out their flavor, toast pumpkin seeds in a warm skillet but do not burn them. Toasted seeds may be ground into a fine powder and used as the base for sauces, moles, or *salsas.* The toasted seeds can also be salted and served as an appetizer or used to make praline candies. Toasted pumpkin seeds are used to make *pipián rojo,* a brilliant orange-red mole used to sauce fish or poultry.

Recado: This is a spice paste that can be made with some or all of the following ingredients: annatto seeds, cumin seeds, peppercorns, coriander seeds, saffron, cinnamon, cloves, allspice, dried chiles, garlic, and Seville orange juice. The spices are usually toasted before being ground to bring out their full flavors.

Red snapper *(huachinango):* This popular Gulf fish is reddish orange in color and may be marked with dark spots that disappear with age. Some species may also have light blue stripes when alive. This fish, which is also called red porgy, is particularly popular in Campeche and Yucatán. Although a Pacific species exists, those from the Gulf have a superior flavor.

Rice: Long-grain white rice is commonly used throughout Mexico. Rice is usually soaked to rinse away some of the starchiness and to ensure a fluffy texture when cooked. While a cup of unsoaked rice is usually cooked in 2 cups of water, a cup of soaked rice requires only $1^1/_2$ to $1^2/_3$ cups of water. In Mexico, rice is often sautéed in oil and then drained once the color changes to light brown. This gives the rice a welcome nutty flavor. Always cook rice covered over a low flame for 35 to 40 minutes. Leftover rice may be refrigerated for a day and reheated in a steamer.

Sailfish *(pez vela):* The dorsal fin of this fish is shaped like a sail, hence the name. Sailfish are easily recognized by their long, needle nose (like that of a swordfish). They have bluish skin and a silvery stomach and live in the Gulf and the Pacific. Sailfish are prized sport fish.

Salsa búfalo: This hot sauce made with guajillo puya chiles is used all over Mexico for fish and seafood cocktails. Like other bottled salsas, it also contains vinegar and a variety of spices. Use with lemon or lime juice for basting grilled foods.

Salsa guacamaya: Popular in Sinaloa, this seafood cocktail sauce is made with jalapeño or de árbol chiles, vinegar, and salt.

Salsa huichol: This seafood cocktail sauce is made with cascabel chiles.

Sardines *(sardinas):* This small, long fish is dark green in color with a silver abdomen. It is found in both the Sea of Cortés (Gulf of California) and the Gulf of Mexico. Sardines are food for large carnivorous sea creatures. Humans eat sardines either fresh or canned.

Seville orange *(naranja agria):* White flowers and green leaves cover this citrus tree. The fruit is about 2 inches in diameter and has a strong acid flavor. The juice is used in pickling liquids, marinades, and tomato sauces. Seville orange juice sparks seafood dishes primarily in Veracruz, Yucatán, Campeche, and Quintana Roo. Champagne vinegar or grapefruit juice with a dash of lime juice are the standard substitutions.

Shad *(sábalo):* This fish has gray-blue skin and a silver stomach. It lives near the coast in estuaries and rivers and is sold fresh or salted. The roe is considered a delicacy and is also sold fresh or salted.

Shark, baby *(cazón):* This small gray shark has a reddish tint, rough skin, and no scales. Its back is bluish and its stomach is pale. Baby shark is often shredded and used in egg dishes or empanada stuffings.

Shrimp *(camarones):* Farmed off both the Gulf and Pacific coasts, shrimp come in white, blue, gray, and brown varieties. Brown shrimp inhabit the Gulf; gray shrimp, the Pacific. Gray Pacific shrimp are also called *kaki* or yellow-leg shrimp. All varieties can be eaten fresh, salted and dried, or smoked. To devein shrimp without shelling first, slice through the outer curve of the shrimp with a sharp knife, lift the vein with the tip of the knife, and remove.

Shrimp, dried: Look in Asian or Latin markets for this important Mexican staple. Dried shrimp are often toasted, ground, and added to soups, croquettes, or sauces. In some cases, fresh shrimp may be substituted with a slight change in flavor.

Squash blossoms: Many people are surprised to learn that there are two genders of squash blossoms. Female flowers are usually smaller than their male counterparts. Since female blossoms will bear fruit, try to pick the male blossoms if you grow zucchini during the summer. Since the blossoms are extremely perishable (they will wilt and soften within hours of picking), growing them yourself is probably the best way to ensure a steady supply. Otherwise, look for them at farmers' markets during the summer. Squash blossoms may be eaten raw, steamed, sautéed, dipped in batter and fried, or floated in soups. To clean squash blossoms, cut in half and remove the stamens.

Squid *(calamares):* This reddish-brown mollusk discharges its ink to thwart predators. It may be eaten fresh or frozen and can be used in soups, tacos, or stews.

Swordfish *(pez espada):* Known as the emperor of the sea, this fish has a powerful jaw that ends in a pointed black sword. The blackish-brown skin does not have scales. Swordfish live in the open sea on both coasts and the flesh has a strong, distinctive flavor.

Tabascan parsley: See *Culantro.*

Tabasco sauce: Also used all over Mexico, this sauce is made in Louisiana from red jalapeños. Serve it with seafood, eggs, or meats.

Tamal de ceniza: This is a pre-Hispanic tamale made with *masa* that has been prepared in ash water as opposed to limestone water, giving the dough a smoky flavor and lighter consistency. It is also called *tamal nejo* or *neco.*

Tamales: The Spanish word *tamal* derives from the Nahuatl *tamalli,* meaning "bread wrapped in corn leaves." The original inhabitants of Mexico prepared tamales from coarsely ground hominy or corn flour. Other tamales were made with finely ground corn kernels called *masa*. The corn kernels, called *nixtamal*, were ground in a stone vessel called a *metate* along with a little water. Savory tamales were made from diverse ingredients—everything from whitebait to squash blossoms, turkey in mole sauce, beans, tomatillos, chiles, and hearts of palm. Sweet dessert tamales were made with wild cactus fruits, corn, honey, wild berries, and more. With the arrival of the Spanish, the preparation of tamales changed dramatically. Lard brought by the conquistadors was added to soften and enrich tamales and new fillings like pork, cheese, and sausages were added. The production of sugar influenced sweet tamales, which were now made with marmalades and a number of new flavorings like anise, almonds, raisins, and citron.

Although the fillings may have been adapted over the centuries, the basic wrapping technique has remained the same since the days of Montezuma. White or blue corn husks, banana leaves, *hoja santa* leaves, and avocado leaves are used in different regions of the country. Size varies as well, from as thin as a finger to as large as two hands. For special occasions, the leaves are sometimes colored by natural dyes like indigo, leaving a faint tint on the tamales.

Stuffings vary from region to region. Shrimp and pumpkin are favorites in Baja, while Yoriumi beans, onions, and cilantro are common in the tamales of Sonora. Other regional favorites include *tamales barbones* (with fresh shrimp and red corn) in Sinaloa; tamales with dried shrimp in Nayarit; ash tamales in Jalisco; fresh corn tamales combined with milk curd and sugar in Colima; catfish tamales from Morelia in Michoacán; and tamales with fish and fresh *hoja santa* in Guerrero. Two specialties come from Chiapas: tamales flavored with the herb *chipilín*, cheese, tomatoes, and pumpkin seeds and tamales made with dried shrimp, beans, and *hoja santa*. *Dzoto-bichay* from Yucatán is made with *chaya* leaves, ground pumpkin, tomatoes, boiled eggs, and habanero chiles. Tamales with shredded *pejelagarto* are a favorite in Tabasco and tamales made with frogs' legs and amaranth are a specialty of Xochimilco in the center of the country.

Whatever the filling or the wrapping, tamales (along with tortillas, chiles, and beans) are an essential part of the modern mosaic that we call Mexican gastronomy. This master recipe outlines the basic technique for making tamales. In terms of fillings, use 3 to 4 cups of fish, seafood, chicken, pork, beef, and/or cheese in the sauce for savory tamales or 3 cups of sugar plus 2 cups of fruit and 1½ cups each of raisins and almonds for sweet tamales. See the recipes throughout the book for more specific ideas.

BASIC TAMALES

Makes about 60 tamales

- 2¼ pounds fresh coarsely ground *masa* for tamales or *masa* prepared with *masa harina* (see Note 1)
- 1½ to 2 cups warm water (boiling 40 tomatillo husks in the water will make the dough fluffier)
- 2 teaspoons baking powder
- ½ cup cornstarch or rice flour
- 2 to 3 tablespoons salt, or to taste (steaming will reduce the saltiness of the dough, so be generous)
- 6 ounces to 1 pound lard (homemade is usually better than commercial lard), vegetable shortening, or chicken fat (use more or less lard depending on the amount of water)

140 corn husks, washed, covered with hot water, soaked for several hours or overnight, drained, and patted dry

PREPARE THE DOUGH: Place the *masa* in a large bowl. Add the water gradually and knead the dough until it is smooth and no longer sticky. Work in the baking powder, cornstarch, and salt. In another bowl, beat the lard by hand or with an electric mixer until fluffy, about 5 minutes. Gradually incorporate the lard into the dough, working until the mixture is smooth and soft (This may be done in a food processor or a standing mixer.) Test to see if the dough is light enough by dropping a spoonful into a glass of water. If it floats, proceed with the recipe; if it sinks, continue kneading or beating.

ASSEMBLE THE TAMALES: If necessary, trim the pointed tips of the corn husks. Overlap 2 corn husks slightly on a flat work surface. Spread a spoonful of dough lengthwise down the center of the husks. Place a spoonful of filling (either sweet or savory) over the dough. Fold the sides of the corn husks inward and over the filling. Fold the narrow end of the husks toward the center. Fold the remaining end over the tamale to seal the packet. Tie the tamale with a thin strip of corn husk or kitchen string.

STEAM THE TAMALES: Fill the bottom of a steamer with water and drop in a clean coin, which will rattle if the steamer goes dry. (If the coin rattles, carefully add boiling water, making sure to avoid pouring the water directly on the tamales.) Line the steamer rack with about 10 corn husks. Place the sealed tamales upright in the steamer, making sure that they are not touching the water. Pack them firmly, but make sure to leave room for the steam to rise and the dough to swell.

Cover the tamales with more corn husks and then a clean cloth, which will absorb the condensed moisture on the lid. Cover with the lid and steam for about 1 hour. Test for doneness by removing a tamale and checking to see if the dough pulls easily away from the husk.

Note 1: If using *masa harina* instead of fresh *masa*, mix $4\frac{1}{2}$ cups *masa harina* with 3 cups hot water and salt to taste. Or, mix $2\frac{1}{2}$ cups *masa harina* with 4 cups quick grits and 3 cups hot water, milk, or chicken stock Add lard to either preparation and proceed with the recipe.

Note 2: Tamales may be reheated on a *comal* or in a heavy skillet or even in the oven. They keep well in the refrigerator for a week and can be frozen for longer periods.

PRE-HISPANIC TAMALES

Before the arrival of the Spanish, tamales were prepared without lard and moistened with just water, which sometimes had been previously used to cook vegetables or soak chiles. Inspired by the current interest in lighter cooking, this recipe re-creates the original Mexican tamale. Since there is no fat in the dough make sure to add enough water to keep the *masa* soft. Banana leaves also help seal moisture into these ancient tamales. Corn husks may also be used, but remember to soak them for 1 hour before stuffing with the *masa* and the beans. As for the filling, it is made with beans, zucchini, chayote, chiles, garlic, and cilantro and reflects the simple but healthful diet of the pre-Hispanic tribes.

Makes 32 tamales

MAKING FRESH MASA FROM DRIED CORN

Masa can also be made from 1 pound 3 ounces of dried white flint corn. Clean the corn in a colander set under running water. Wash until the water runs clear. Place the corn, 8 cups water, and 2 tablespoons powdered limestone in a clay or nonreactive pot. Stir well and bring the mixture to a boil. Cook, uncovered, until some of the corn hulls float to the surface. Skim the hulls from the pot and continue cooking covered until the corn is very soft, another 10 or 20 minutes. Remove the pot from the heat and soak the corn for at least 2 hours or overnight. Drain the corn into a colander and rub the kernels under running water to remove the hulls. Continue washing until the water runs clear. Drain the corn and grind in a food mill to a smooth or coarse texture as needed for specific recipe. Place in a bowl with ⅔ cup water and knead to make fresh *masa*.

FOR THE FILLING

- 1 pound black beans, sorted, soaked in water to cover for 4 hours or overnight, and drained
- 1 medium white onion, peeled and halved
- 1 head garlic, halved but not peeled

Salt to taste

- 1½ cups sesame seeds, toasted and ground
- 2 cups finely chopped zucchini
- 2 cups finely chopped chayote (water pear) or more zucchini
- 8 to 10 fresh serrano chiles, dried de árbol chiles, or japonés chiles, ground
- 3 cloves elephant garlic or 6 large cloves regular garlic, peeled and crushed or ground
- 2½ cups cilantro leaves with stems

FOR THE TAMALES

- 32 fresh banana leaves
- 2 generous pounds fresh *masa*
- 2½ tablespoons salt, or to taste
- ½ to ¾ cup warm water or bean cooking liquid

PREPARE THE FILLING: Place the beans in a large pot and cover with several inches of water. Add the onion and the garlic and simmer covered until the beans are almost tender. (If necessary, add more hot water during the cooking, but the beans should not be soupy when done.) Discard the onion and garlic. Season with salt. Stir in the sesame seeds, zucchini, chayote, chiles, and elephant garlic and continue cooking uncovered until thick, about 30 minutes more. Stir in the cilantro and set aside.

PREPARE THE TAMALES: Cut the banana leaves into 14-inch squares (saving the scraps) and boil or steam the leaves for 20 minutes to make them pliable. The leaves may also be wrapped in a damp cloth and sweated in a 350°F oven for 20 minutes. Set the softened leaves aside. Put the *masa* and the salt in a large bowl. Add a little of the water and begin kneading. Continue adding water and kneading until the dough is smooth and not sticky but still quite moist. The dough should have a very damp consistency. Shape the dough into small balls about 2½ inches in diameter. Line a tortilla press with a sheet of plastic wrap. Center a dough ball on the press and cover with a second sheet of plastic. Close the press. Open the press and carefully peel away the top piece of plastic. Flip the dough into a moistened hand and use the other to hand peel away the second sheet of plastic. (The dough can also be flipped directly onto the banana leaf. Peel top piece of plastic and proceed.) Center the dough on a prepared banana leaf and repeat with the remaining dough balls. Spoon about 1½ tablespoons of the bean filling into each tamale. Fold the banana leaves into small packets, folding each side of the leaf toward the center of the tamale. Tie the overlapping pieces of banana leaf tightly with kitchen string or a thin strip of banana leaf cut from scraps. Place a rack in a steamer and fill with about 12 cups of water. (Make sure that the water does not touch the rack.) Cover the rack with some of the cut banana leaves and arrange the tamales in the steamer, positioning them vertically, one next to the other. Cover with more leaves and a dishcloth to trap the steam. Place the lid on the steamer and cook until the tamales can be peeled easily off the leaves, 1 to 1½ hours.

TO SERVE: Arrange the tamales on a serving platter and serve with any red or green sauce. Leftover tamales may be reheated on a warm *comal* or in a heavy skillet. They also can be chopped and added to tomato sauce.

Tamarind *(tamarindo):* This tree has its origins in Asia but has been cultivated in America for several centuries. Brown pods about 4 inches long hang from the branches and are similar in appearance (although they are somewhat larger) to vanilla beans. The brownish-orange inside of the pod is very acidic and used to make candies, beverages, and sauces. Tamarind also has laxative properties.

Tatemar: This is a quick-grilling technique used with meats, vegetables, and fruits often covered with aromatic leaves to seal in the juices.

Tejocote: This acidic yellow fruit is similar to a crab apple and is used in syrups and punches. It is also called *hazarole.*

Tejuino: This is an alcoholic beverage made from fermented dried corn. It is also called *tesguin* or *tescuin.* Originally from Tarahumara, *tejuino* is now consumed all over the country.

Tendal: This large net is similar to a *chinchorro.* It is used primarily in the Papaloapan River in the state of Veracruz.

Tilapia: This bottom-feeder has a compressed gray body with five vertical lines and a spotted tail. It lives in fresh water and is cultivated in ponds like catfish.

Tismichi: This small, eellike species inhabits the Tlacotalpan River in Veracruz. It is fished only in September and is sold fresh, dried, or salted.

Toloache: This plant is reported to have narcotic effects. The name comes from the Nahuatl word *toloa,* meaning "to bend the head." Although known to cause heart irregularities, it was frequently used in ancient rituals.

Tomatillos: This mildly acid fruit looks like a small green tomato and is a staple in Mexican cooking. Its tart lemony flavor works well raw in fresh *salsas.* Tomatillos may also be roasted or boiled for 20 minutes or so and then pureed for use in cooked sauces. The fruit is sheathed in a papery husk, which must be removed before cooking. The husks may be added to broths for flavor or to the cooking water for *nopales,* where they have a yeasty effect that cuts the sliminess of the cactus paddles. Water boiled with tomatillo husks is also added to fresh *masa* to make it lighter and fluffier.

Tortillas: Corn, which according to ancient mythology was born as a god, is perhaps the quintessential ingredient that ties together the diverse cooking of Mexico's far-flung regions. Corn most often appears on the table in the form of tortillas, the illustrious queen of Mexican cuisine. The round shape reminiscent of the sun or maybe an angel's halo is known from Baja to Yucatán and even beyond the borders of Mexico. Used in countless regional preparations, tortillas may be large (for *tlayudas*), tiny (for *salbutes*), medium (for *sopes*), oval (for *chalupas*), folded and swollen (for *peneques*), elongated (for *huaraches*), oval and stuffed (for *tlacoyos*), thick and round (for *gorditas*), deepfried (for tostadas), dipped in sauces (for enchiladas), cut into chips and fried (for *totopos*), or sliced into thin strips (for soups).

Tortillas begin with dried corn kernels. Because the hulls are difficult to digest, the kernels are simmered and soaked in water treated with several tablespoons of powdered limestone. Most of the skin is rubbed off under running water (some skin gives the *masa* texture) and the hearts of the corn kernels are then ground into a fresh dough called *masa*. Warm dough emerges from the mill and is spread across a flat surface to cool. Water and sometimes a dash of salt are added and the dough is kneaded until the lumps have been worked out. Small portions of the dough are pinched off and rolled into balls. Each ball is then stretched into a circular form. The clapping and patting of hands continues to stretch the dough even thinner. Banana leaves or plastic wrap may be used to flatten the dough and prevent it from sticking to the hands, which otherwise must be moistened. Wooden or metal presses make the process easier, but some patting is still involved as the tortilla is transferred to a hot *comal* or a heavy skillet. Water (with limestone for a clay comal) and/or oil is lightly brushed on the cooking surface to prevent sticking. When the tortilla starts to change color, it is flipped with wet fingers or a thin spatula. Another turn and a simple press of the fingers makes the tortilla inflate and allows it to finish cooking. The tortilla is taken off the *comal*, flattened with both hands if puffed, sprinkled with salt, and eaten immediately. It can be filled and rolled to form a taco. Tortillas can be made from yellow, white, blue, black, or red corn. Below are two methods for preparing fresh tortillas.

BASIC TORTILLAS

Makes about 12 tortillas

FROM *MASA HARINA* (DEHYDRATED MASA FLOUR)

2	cups *masa harina* (the Quaker and Maseca brands are excellent and available in the baking aisle of many supermarkets)
¼ to ⅓	cup flour
Dash of salt	
1½ to 1¾	cups warm water

FROM *FRESH MASA*

2	cups fresh *masa* (sold in Latin markets)
½	teaspoon salt
⅓ to ½	cup warm water

PREPARE THE DOUGH: Select either *masa harina* or fresh *masa* and place the dry ingredients in a large bowl. Gradually add the water and turn the dough out onto a flat work surface. Knead with dampened hands for 5 to 8 minutes or until the dough is smooth and silky but not sticky. The dough should be soft enough to pinch some easily between two fingers. Allow the dough to rest as an ungreased *comal* or a heavy skillet is heated. When the *comal* is hot, line a tortilla press with two squares of plastic wrap. Pinch off enough dough to make a ball about 1 to 1½ inches in diameter. Place the dough between the plastic and close the tortilla press. Press lightly, then flip the tortilla in plastic, press gently again, open the press, remove the tortilla, and peel away the plastic. Toss the tortilla back and forth between your wet hands several times to aerate it slightly. (If the tortilla edges are cracked, the dough needs more moisture.) Repeat with the remaining dough.

PREPARE THE TAMALES: Slide the tortillas, one at a time, onto the hot *comal* and cook for about 30 seconds. Flip the tortilla and cook for about 30 to 60 seconds more. Turn again, press with your fingertips to puff the tortilla, and finish cooking for 30 seconds. (If the tortilla colors unevenly, the *comal* may be too hot. Also, if the tortilla sticks, lightly grease the cooking surface with a light coating of oil.) Wrap the cooked tortillas in a clean dishcloth to keep them warm and pliable while the remaining tortillas are cooked. Use the tortillas immediately or cool, wrap tightly, and refrigerate for up to 1 week. Reheat on a *comal* before using.

Totoaba (Cynoscion macdonaldi): This is a large meaty fish with gold and blue colors. When dead, the skin becomes blue and gray. Found in the Sea of Cortés (Gulf of California), it is also called *machorro* or *corvina* (corbina). Since fishing for *totoaba* has been suspended, halibut is a good substitute.

Totopos: This is the term used to describe deep-fried tortillas, either round or in the shape of chips. These crunchy tortillas are served with refried beans. They also form the base for *chilaquiles* (scrambled eggs with tortillas) and can be covered with various chile sauces.

Tuba: This is the name for liquor obtained from coconut palm trees. Popular along the coasts of Colima, Michoacán, and Guerrero, it is usually mixed with strawberries, limes, lemons, cinnamon, and/or celery to make various beverages.

Tuna *(atún):* Yellowfin is the most prized variety and very hard to find. Bluefin is also of exceptional quality. This large sport fish is found in deep waters off the Pacific coast.

Yuca: This tropical plant has large, thick leaves, white flowers, and an edible root that is used much like potatoes in Tabasco, Campeche, Yucatán, Chiapas, and Quintana Roo. Yuca root, also known as cassava, has thick, stringy brown skin and hard, creamy flesh. It can be used to thicken soups or fried to make fritters and chips. Most often, it is boiled and seasoned.

Zapote: This is the generic name for a family of plants bearing fruit of various colors. Black *zapotes* and *chicozapotes* come from the sapodilla plant. *Chicozapotes* have an oval shape and brownish-red or yellow smooth skin. Black *zapotes* have very smooth skin and chocolate-brown flesh. Each fruit contains about three to six seeds and grows on long vines in tropical climates. The soft pulp is used to make candies, sorbets, and puddings. It can also be eaten fresh. Red *zapotes* are better known as mameys or *mamey zapotes.*

INDEX